Splash
of Colors

Splash of Colors

THE SELF-DESTRUCTION OF BRANIFF INTERNATIONAL

John J. Nance

William Morrow and Company, Inc.   New York   1984

Library of Congress Cataloging in Publication Data

Nance, John J.
  Splash of colors.

  Includes index.
  1. Braniff Airways.   I. Title.
HE9803.B73N36   1984   387.7'065'73   83-25072
ISBN 0-688-03586-8

Printed in the United States of America

First Edition

2 3 4 5 6 7 8 9 10

To Bunny

My Love, My Partner, My Wife

AUTHOR'S NOTE

This is a true story in every respect. Every event and every conversation actually occurred, and every person referred to is real. I have fabricated nothing.

At the back of the book there are two appendices that may be useful to you while reading the story. Appendix 1 provides selected financial information on Braniff's performance and profitability in the years 1965 through 1981. Appendix 2 contains information on the scope of the research for this work and my methodology, along with a more detailed listing of specific source material. In addition, in the center of the book there is a collection of photographs, the majority of which were previously unpublished.

J.J.N.

Contents

AUTHOR'S NOTE   7

INTRODUCTION   11

  1. Seizing the Opportunity   13

  2. The Rules Were Always Changing   18

  3. Of Old Dogs and New Tricks   27

  4. The Driving Force   35

  5. The Image of a Legend   44

  6. The More Conservative Risk   51

  7. A Pretty Expensive Game   63

  8. Little Room for Error   71

  9. Strategic Decisions   81

10. Biting the Hand   89

11. To Err Is Human—Except in the Airline Business   98

12. Gaudily Colored Aircraft from the Colonies   105

13. Today London, Tomorrow the World   118

14. The Best and the Biggest   135

15. The First General Alarm   147

16. The Honorable Way Out   157

17. The Demon Is All Too Real   170

18. A Different Brand of Anger   178

19. Crass, Inept, Nasty, Rude, and Lazy   183

20. Casey at the Bat   195

21. A Chill of Apprehension   206

22. A Loose Cannon on a Rolling Deck   229

23. A New Round of Fear   236

24. Search for the Master Plan   245

25. Too Late to Mend Fences   258

26. Dr. Putnam to the Rescue   267

27. A Double-edged Sword   280

28. The Path of Despair and Disgust   290

29. The Monkey on American's Back   300

30. Self-inflicted Wounds   311

31. A Ghost of a Chance   326

32. An Emotional Roller Coaster   341

33. All Hell Was Breaking Loose   355

34. The Last Pumpkin   371

35. The True Assets of Braniff   376

36. The Fight of a Phoenix   390

Appendix 1   399

Appendix 2   404

Acknowledgments   413

Index   417

INTRODUCTION

Large airlines in the United States simply do not go out of business. That was an axiom in American commercial aviation—until the evening of May 12, 1982. On that date, the nation's eighth-largest carrier—Dallas-based Braniff International—suddenly halted all flight operations over three continents. At 12:01 A.M. of the same dark night, the company filed for protection under Chapter 11 of the United States Bankruptcy Code.

How could a vibrant and pace-setting company such as Braniff have come to such an end? How could nearly nine thousand employees suddenly find themselves unemployed after fighting so hard to save their company?

In the swirling aftermath of confusion and tawdry financial greed—in the maze of paperwork and proposals, charges and countercharges that raged like a Texas tornado around the plight of Braniff and the human pain of its people—the resulting debris of words and anger and grounded airplanes obscured the true story. The press and the public clamored in a frenzy of recrimination for quick and easy answers to what was in truth an incredibly complex and Byzantine trail of twists and turns, intrigue and miscalculations. It was a trail leading from the distant past of a small Oklahoma airline through an unprecedented odyssey of flamboyant expansion and profitable, stylistic accomplishment under the iron-fisted leadership of one of the giants in American aviation—all the way to the dusty despair and destruction of the summer of 1982. It was an all too familiar human tale of paradise lost and lessons ignored, played out with "flying colors" against the background of the dangerous new world of unfettered competition unleashed by the Airline Deregulation Act of 1978.

What follows is a business tragedy—a corporate collapse—in human terms.

Splash
of Colors

Seizing the Opportunity

CHAPTER **1** Tom McGrew had caught the news item in *Aviation Daily* the previous Wednesday morning, October 18, 1978. Congress had just passed the Airline Deregulation Act of 1978, and as soon as Jimmy Carter got around to signing the controversial legislation, his Civil Aeronautics Board—dominated by Carter appointees—was to begin the opening round, giving away approximately thirteen hundred unused domestic airline routes. According to *Aviation Daily*, they were going to do it in pure democratic fashion—whoever was physically first to file route requests at the CAB docket section after the President signed the bill would get first choice. Unfortunately, no one knew exactly when that was going to happen. McGrew, one of the senior attorneys from the prestigious Washington law firm of Arnold and Porter, knew as he scanned the item that every other Washington lawyer who had an airline for a client would be reading the same thing. McGrew's client was Braniff International in Dallas, and they would definitely want in on this.

Tom McGrew placed a hasty call to Braniff's Dallas headquarters, getting Vice President for Regulatory Proceedings Tom Robertson and his assistant Bob Culp on the line for a quick conference.

"By God, fellows," McGrew said, "a line's going to be forming at the CAB, and we'd better be in there!"

Robertson, Culp, and Russ Thayer, who was titular president of Braniff under Chairman Harding Lawrence, agreed. McGrew tore out for the CAB's nearby building on Connecticut Avenue with an associate in tow.

United Airlines had been the only major carrier to support airline deregulation openly. When McGrew dashed up to the front of the CAB's building to claim the seventh spot and join the other airline representatives in the beginning of an untidy vigil that was to last for a week, it was United's legal people who had taken the first place in the newly formed line. Allegedly they had been tipped off in gratitude.

Exactly one week later, on Wednesday morning, October 25, 1978, Tom McGrew and an associate once again climbed out of a car in front of the CAB's building, this time in a bitterly cold wind at 6:35 A.M. Properly attired in three-piece suits and expensive overcoats, they proceeded to replace one of the young messengers who had been holding Braniff's place in relays in the ragtag line for the previous seven days. It had been quite a circus for the usually ordered and conservative proceedings of the CAB, but since Carter had finally signed the bill the previous evening, the sidewalk vigil was about to end with a platoon of lawyers advancing on the CAB's docket clerk. It had taken the better part of the week to ready the huge stack of paperwork required for Braniff's application. Unlike the other lawyers representing other airlines and carrying their CAB filings in small briefcases or packages, Tom McGrew was shepherding two hand trucks loaded with five heavy cardboard boxes containing Braniff's requests. Within hours the scope of those requests would astound the industry.

The initial shock wave of the bitterly opposed Airline Deregulation Act, which shortly would wreak havoc throughout the once-stable airline industry, had not caught Braniff International napping. The flamboyant and profitable airline, renowned for splashy advertising and high-fashion tastes, had been expanding and growing for the previous thirteen years under the leadership of one of the second-generation pioneers of American commercial aviation, Harding Luther Lawrence, and as usual, Lawrence had a battle plan. Executing a corporate pirouette after three years of attempting to quell the deregulatory fever infecting Congress, Lawrence had decided to use the anticipated route freedom resulting from the bill as a springboard to expansion. Indeed, in Lawrence's strategic vision, Braniff had no choice. In the coming airline civil war he foresaw, Braniff had to grow or die.

McGrew's hurried phone call had simply accelerated the process. Harding Lawrence had directed his people to prepare the time bomb that Tom McGrew and his associate finally began wheeling toward the seventh-floor docket section a little after 8:30 A.M.: a filing for 626 of the approximately 1,300 routes!

The industry was stunned when the word spread. The news burst in the faces of the more conservative members of the airline community, thrusting Braniff once more into the crucible of controversy and reinforcing the myth that Lawrence was the ranking wild-eyed gambler of the industry.

As the reams of paper were being received by the docket clerk at the CAB, Tom Robertson sat in his office in the Braniff Building in Dallas's Exchange Park watching the beginning of the workday from his seventh-floor window and trying to get a sense of what was ahead. Robertson, a trim, cultured native Texan with a pleasant face and thinning silver hair, was nearing retirement. He had been the airline's chief liaison with the CAB since long before Harding Lawrence had arrived from Continental Airlines as Braniff's new president in 1965. The changes to his airline that had followed had been seismic and exciting, transforming Braniff from a stagnating regional carrier with a largely ignored South American route system into a highly profitable and highly visible carrier that virtually hungered for new routes. That was Tom's job: applying for and plowing through the mind-numbing bureaucratic requirements to win new routes for Braniff. By 1978 he was one of the most respected and successful practitioners of the art, but the new deregulation bill was taking away his canvas. By 1985 there was to be no CAB and no governmental control over the domestic air routes. Airlines would be able to fly any route they wanted to fly in the United States, and much of the expertise and technical knowledge Tom Robertson had spent decades refining would become useless.

The previous week around the Braniff headquarters had been a frenzy of activity as Robertson had tried in vain to convince Lawrence not to ask for so many of the unused routes—tried to persuade him with carefully documented arguments that it was a mistake, and possibly a pivotal one. Lawrence had listened carefully but overruled a cautious approach. Even though he had no intention of operating anything but a carefully selected fraction of the routes, he was convinced the large filing was the best course. The airline already had route applications pending for a dizzying array of national and international routes and had started flying nonstop from Dallas to London earlier in the year. This new opportunity was a partial shortcut to his goals. The possibility that the CAB, the industry, and the press would react negatively to Braniff's massive route request wasn't that important to him.

Lawrence was convinced that the window of deregulation would only be open a few years. If, in that time, he could construct a sufficiently large route system (and thus a large revenue base) while the routes were there for the asking, his airline could survive in a deregulated world dominated by airlines the size of United and American. Harding Lawrence, who had guided Braniff to great heights of profitability through his brilliant strategic planning and long-range foresight, believed that after several years of chaos, frantic mergers, and ruinous competition in the industry, Congress would admit their mistake and slam that deregulatory window shut once again. When that happened, Braniff would already have grandfather rights and would be able to keep whatever routes it had acquired.

Tom Robertson's voice was not the only one raised in opposition to the chairman's plans for massive expansion, but in the almost monarchical atmosphere of Braniff's senior management in 1978, those who possessed sufficient self-confidence to present a case against the chairman's ideas to the chairman himself were a rather small cadre. It wasn't that Lawrence wouldn't listen to his people—he would always listen to arguments and ideas backed by sound thought and preparation—but he had no tolerance whatsoever for unpreparedness or unsupported opinions. As Braniff had grown from revenues of $100 million per year to revenues of $1 billion per year under Lawrence's dynamic leadership, his tight control of the company and his free expression of dissatisfaction—his almost legendary temper—in the face of any substandard performance twisted his image in the eyes of Braniff people at all levels. The lower ranks erroneously saw him as uncaring. At the same time, the weaker members of his senior management grew to fear his displeasure and developed elaborate techniques for never telling him things they were afraid he didn't want to hear. It was the outbreak of a progressive corporate disease that had the effect of choking off much of the vital communication from within the company—communication the chairman should have received. Lawrence wanted advice, ideas, and information from all levels and especially from his senior people. Unfortunately, many of them were too afraid of the chairman really to communicate with him.

Even his Board of Directors, comfortable with his increasingly profitable record and the voluminous amount of information Lawrence gave them, had little advice for him. Old Harding had successfully zigged too many times when the rest of the industry had zagged to be questioned seriously, even if his new master plan might seem risky. As Lawrence had pointed out, to be too conservative in the face of deregulation would eventually put an end to Braniff's record of high profits (if not Braniff itself) as other carriers large and small jumped into Braniff's bread-and-butter markets. The only way to survive and compete was to do what Lawrence had been doing so well since he came aboard in 1965—expand.

Unfortunately, not even Lawrence could see a major danger that further expansion held for Braniff in particular—a danger having little to do with whether he could afford to buy more planes and hire more crews. Lawrence's stylish airline had outgrown its senior management team. Its burgeoning national and international route system simply had grown too complex for his people to handle with the precision and quality of service he demanded. Nor did Lawrence realize how desperately the company that he had been busily expanding year by year needed a similar expansion in the size and sophistication of its middle- and lower-level management group. The oversight was one of a number of startling and fundamental flaws in the company's managerial philosophy—flaws that by 1978 were beginning to show up in the form of seriously inconsistent service.

Just when Braniff desperately needed a few years of stability and an intensive overhaul of all levels of its management, just when it needed to hire some of the best and the brightest young managers from similar positions in other airlines to revitalize Braniff's inbred senior ranks, its hardworking but all too self-defensive managers were being confronted with the opening round of what was to be an aggregate 54 percent expansion in a twenty-four-month period. There was no way even Braniff's dedicated people could handle it.

Lawrence was launching his cherished airline on a course that would either catapult it into the ranks of the largest carriers on the planet, or destroy it. It was supposed to be a safe bet. Harding Lawrence never rolled dice without assured odds, but the factors that would in hindsight reveal the expansion program as a gamble (and ultimately determine the company's fate) could hardly be foreseen by anyone in 1978.

Tom Robertson, standing at his office window in Dallas waiting for word from McGrew that the filing was complete, wasn't visualizing failure as a possibility for Braniff. Certainly no dark thoughts of corporate holocaust flickered across his mind's eye, but he was apprehensive. He thought back to a time thirteen years before when he had suddenly been confronted with Harding Lawrence's master plan for Braniff Airways—a time when Lawrence was still executive vice president of Continental Airlines. Tom Robertson had been asked to fly out to Los Angeles to meet with Lawrence for unknown reasons, only to discover that Lawrence's accession to the presidency of Braniff was only a few months away and that his new boss-to-be wanted an intensive all-day briefing on all facets of the operation. During that same meeting Lawrence told Robertson of the plans he was formulating for Braniff—plans that were global in scope and very exciting (especially to a man like Tom Robertson, who had struggled unsuccessfully for ten years to get new routes for Braniff).

There would be many in the industry, rank-and-file employees and senior management alike, who would think that Lawrence's plan for building Braniff into a carrier to rival United and Eastern in size was a contemporary idea. Robertson knew better. Lawrence had come on board from Continental in 1965 with a blueprint in his brilliant, visionary mind for expansion that spanned at least the next two decades.

The Rules
Were Always Changing

CHAPTER 2 On Wednesday, January 20, 1965, Lyndon Baines Johnson was about to be sworn into office as a fully elected occupant of the White House, having crushed Republican Senator Barry Goldwater in the general election of the previous November.

Having a Texan in control of the White House bestowed a sort of legitimacy on being both a Texan and a businessman. Even in the mid-1960s, too many businesspeople in the power centers of the

Eastern Seaboard nurtured stereotypes of Texans as men who could be successful in business only if they drilled a successful oil well, despite the fact that Texas cities such as Dallas and Houston had evolved into important power and financial centers (in banking, insurance, aerospace, and investment). Men such as Troy Post (riding that morning in the plush rear seat of a long, black limousine from Dulles International Airport toward the center of Washington to attend the inauguration) had become millionaires without ever once bringing in a wildcat gusher.

Post, born in the dust of little Haskell, Texas, had schooled himself in nearly everything a man could learn about the insurance business from an investor's point of view and had parlayed his expertise into first one, then several major insurance companies, and then into a holding company he had created to manage all his creations and acquisitions. Post was chairman and principal stockholder of Greatamerica Corporation, headquartered on the top floor of Jimmy Ling's new LTV (Ling-Temco-Vought, Inc.) Tower in downtown Dallas, and Greatamerica had just purchased an airline— thirty-seven-year-old Braniff Airways, headquartered near Dallas's Love Field.[1]

Accompanying Post in the Cadillac's backseat was Executive Vice President Harding L. Lawrence of Continental Airlines. Lawrence was a native of Gladewater, Texas (though he was born in Oklahoma). Lawrence had flown in from Los Angeles eager to discuss the possibility of leading the planned transformation of Braniff (under Greatamerica's direction) into a far larger and far more dynamic airline than it was that first month of 1965.

As the sleek limo negotiated the heavy traffic inbound to the heart of the national capital, Post and Lawrence concluded a deal that would quickly bring Lawrence back to Texas as president of Braniff Airways, stripping Continental's Bob Six of his right-hand man. Thus began an astoundingly innovative and profitable transformation of the quiet and traditionally conservative Braniff into a

[1] James J. Ling, president of LTV, was also a Texan. In the spring of 1965 he was busily writing a new chapter in American corporate history with his complicated and highly successful transformation of what had started as a small electronics firm (Ling Altec) into a major, multibillion-dollar conglomerate. Ling's pioneering of the high-wire art of conglomerate-building and such Byzantine concepts as "redeployment" of subdivisions of public corporations was making Dallas a very exciting place for a businessman to live.

pacesetting leader in commercial aviation. The deal would also forge a close working relationship between Lawrence and still another Texan who had initiated the whole thing, a brilliant young financier named C. Edward Acker, who was destined to become one of the most respected airline executives in the nation.

Ed Acker, six-feet-four with a slightly owlish look and the perpetual trace of a sardonic smile on his face, was a graduate of Southern Methodist University in Dallas. Acker, whose business acumen and ability with corporate finance matters were very advanced, had joined Post's Greatamerica Corporation as senior vice president for finance in the early 1960s.[2] Shortly after arriving at Greatamerica, Acker had dusted off and updated a study he had done several years before of what he considered one of the most poorly managed companies with one of the greatest untapped potentials in the area: Braniff Airways. After a few months of consideration, Post and Fitts agreed, and Greatamerica acquired controlling interest in the airline in the spring of 1964.

While they were considering Braniff as an acquisition, Acker had flown out to Los Angeles and discussed the possibility of an eventual merger between Continental Airlines and a revitalized Braniff under Greatamerica's ownership. It was during those meetings with Continental's founder and chairman, the legendary Bob Six, that Acker got to know Six's dynamic executive vice president, Harding Lawrence.

Lawrence was actually running Continental in every way except title, but Bob Six just wouldn't completely relinquish the controls. As the mid-1960s approached and Harding Lawrence realized Six's plans for complete retirement from active management were still over the horizon, he began to consider other options. The possibility of taking over as president of Braniff was one of them.

On a Christmas visit back to his wife's home in Greenville, Texas, in December 1964, Lawrence stopped by Acker's office in the LTV Tower in Dallas to outline an impressive list of ideas he thought could be implemented at Braniff. He also clearly indicated that he would consider being the one to carry them out.

Troy Post and Grant Fitts had originally asked Ed Acker to take over as head of Braniff, but Acker had never run a company that

[2] Greatamerica was essentially a three-man holding company with Post as the investor, Grant Fitts as the chief executive, and Ed Acker as the one who analyzed and directed the investments. The corporation controlled an impressive list of insurance companies worth hundreds of millions of dollars.

size before—let alone an airline—and didn't feel capable of doing the job justice. In fact, the aviation terminology alone had been foreign enough. Ed Acker asked Braniff to send over a tutor, and for an entire week in November 1964, Braniff Vice President Tom Robertson spent his working hours with Acker, bringing him up to speed on the intricacies of running an airline and interpreting the jargon.

"Where do you want to start, Ed?"

"Well, I guess we'd better begin with the basics. For instance, what's an RPM?"

Robertson sat across from Acker's desk on the top floor of the LTV Tower and stared in disbelief. "You're kidding? You're *not* kidding!"

"No, I'm not," Acker replied, laughing.

"Okay Ed, an RPM is the most basic measure of airline performance we have: revenue passenger mile. It provides a measurement of how many miles have been flown during a given segment of time with one passenger. In other words, if we fly a hundred-mile flight with two revenue-paying passengers, we have flown two hundred revenue passenger miles, or RPMs."

After a quick graduation from Robertson's course, Acker looked once again at the prospect of taking over Braniff, measured what he knew of the airline business against what he should know, and decided to recommend Harding Lawrence for the airline presidency instead.

Of course, Braniff already had a president: Charles E. Beard, a man who had started as general traffic manager for the airline in 1935 and who by the early 1950s was essentially running the company as executive vice president for founder Tom Braniff. When Tom Braniff died in a private-plane crash in 1954, Beard took over as president, keeping Braniff compact and profitable through most of the lethargic fifties. Beard's conservative, gentlemanly style, however, was no match for the dynamic changes that the sixties had thrust upon the airline industry with the advent of jet airliners and rising union militancy. Braniff lagged behind in jet purchases and route expansion as Beard's conservatism frustrated the desires of many of the airline's upper management to keep pace with such carriers as Six's highly innovative Continental. Braniff's management simply wasn't keeping up with the company's potential, and from his office in downtown Dallas, Ed Acker had noticed.

Beard, approaching his sixty-fifth birthday with no real desire to retire, ostensibly had been grooming one of his senior vice presidents and pioneer pilots, R. V. Carlton, to take over when he stepped down. Suddenly in early 1965 the new owners stepped in and forcibly retired Chuck Beard, announcing Lawrence for the top spot instead.

Beard would be profoundly shocked to discover in future years that his perception of pre-Lawrence Braniff wasn't shared by Lawrence, Greatamerica, nor many of the new people who came in under Lawrence. Constant references by Braniff itself to its pre-1965 status as a "dusty little Texas airline," or alternately as a "modest regional carrier" were fighting words to the old guard and even to many of those who stayed on.[3] Even native Dallasites were led to believe that Braniff had been a diminutive regional carrier on the brink of extinction when Greatamerica and Lawrence had come riding to the rescue.

As is so often the case, the truth lay somewhere in between. In the spring of 1965, Braniff International Airways was not a sure bet for long-term competitive survival in the dawn of the commercial jet age, but neither was it on the brink of corporate extinction. It certainly was not a dynamic carrier—not possessed of the internal enthusiasm and determination it sorely needed to keep pace with the industry—but neither was it fair to call Braniff a "modest regional carrier" (as Lawrence and Acker and so many others regarded it).

Braniff had an operating international airline system extending from Denver to the west and Minneapolis-St. Paul and Chicago to the north, to New York and Washington on the East Coast and as far south as Buenos Aires, Argentina. In fact, its international system dated back to 1946, when the CAB and President Truman had awarded Braniff the biggest challenge of its young corporate existence: a long, thin, but substantial route system into the Caribbean, South America, and Central America—which Braniff could fly provided it set up the necessary arrangements. The system included Cuba, Panama, Colombia, Ecuador, Peru, Bolivia, Paraguay, Brazil, and Argentina, but to put it into operation, Braniff's people literally had to build the support facilities and many of the radio aids and negotiate through complicated legal, social, and political entangle-

[3] As Beard wrote in an angry letter to the editor of the *Dallas Morning News* in the last few years of his life, "If Braniff in 1965 was a 'modest regional carrier,' it was undoubtedly the world's largest." Characteristically, the paper never printed the letter—Beard by that time belonged to a forgotten era.

ments with constant diplomacy. It was a pioneering and prodigious undertaking, and Braniff accomplished it in just two years.

Flying passengers for hire as part of the fledgling airline industry of the late 1920s was a risky business without parallel in today's transportation industry. Companies were formed and sold, divided, subscribed, bankrupted, and reincorporated with blinding speed. Capitalization often was insufficient to even buy gasoline, and fatal crashes were all too common. But the business did have one unlimited commodity: vast quantities of enthusiasm and entrepreneurial spirit trembling on the threshold of a promising, uncharted, and seemingly unlimited new business frontier unfettered by governmental regulation. It was a vastly different environment from the world of heavy-handed governmental control that later shaped, guided, and decreed nearly every move of the airline industry, but protected it as well—from the demands and responsibilities of competition and from its own errors. Those lusty days of fabric-covered wings and unstable, unreliable air machines flying in the dawn of a new industry were an irresistible siren song to American entrepreneurs.

Such was the atmosphere in 1928 when Tom Braniff, then a successful forty-five-year-old insurance pioneer from Oklahoma City, acquired an interest in a single-engine Stinson airplane. His younger brother Paul had been a flyer in World War I, and in 1928, finding brother Tom in possession of a part interest in a private airplane, Paul convinced him of the wisdom of starting an airline between Oklahoma City and Tulsa (then joined only by the whistle-stopping slowness of the St. Louis and San Francisco Railroad and by a tortuous and periodically impassable road). When the deal was struck, Paul Braniff became the first pilot, and before twelve months had passed, the little airline was operating five single-engine Stinsons on a route system that extended as far south as North Texas.

In 1929, however, Tom Braniff sold the company to another fledgling entity called Universal Airlines System, which in turn was itself sold to another organization called simply the Aviation Corporation. One year after acquiring Universal and its Braniff Division, the Aviation Corporation (for unknown reasons) decided to shut down the Braniff operation, thus paving the way for the second birth of an airline entity called Braniff.[4]

---

[4] Ironically, the Aviation Corporation (which terminated the corporate life of the original Paul R. Braniff, Incorporated) was one of the forerunner companies of the

The corporate entity that was to dominate Dallas-Fort Worth air-line operations for many years was the re-created Braniff, Braniff Airways, Incorporated, brought into corporate existence on November 3, 1930, with Tom Braniff as President and Paul Braniff as Secretary-Treasurer—and still chief pilot.

The new Braniff began with a new aircraft: the Lockheed Vega, a powerful single-engine, high-wing metal monoplane that was capable of the blinding speed of 150 miles per hour with six passengers. The airline resumed service to the Texas destinations, but it added Chicago and St. Louis to the northeast as well in 1931. Expansion was limited for an airline with no airmail contracts, but in 1934 Braniff finally grabbed one, taking airmail route AM-9 from Chicago to Dallas via Kansas City and a multitude of intermediate stops. By January 1, 1936, Braniff had grown to a fleet of seven new twin-engine Lockheed Electras, two Ford Tri-Motors, four Lockheed Vegas, and one Stinson kept for flight training.

In addition, the company had two airmail route contracts extending from Chicago to Brownsville, Texas; a maintenance base in Dallas; and over fifty employees, among whom was Charles E. Beard, who had come on board in 1935 as general traffic manager based in the airline's Oklahoma City headquarters. (Braniff also had gobbled up its first competitor, acquiring Fort Worth-based Bowen Airlines in late 1935.)

Tom Braniff was in charge in those days as World War II approached. His style of management was clearly paternalistic—he was, after all, considerably older at age fifty than the majority of his employees, and his demonstrable concern for them was the progenitor of the phrase and the concept that there existed a "Braniff family" that included all the employees of the company.

It was still a shaky business that Tom and Paul Braniff were pursuing—the public was a long way from accepting commercial air travel as a viable or sane alternative to the safety of America's extensive passenger rail system—but if nothing else it was exciting as a business as well as an operation. Survival was never really assured: The rules were always changing, the number of passengers varied as much as the midwestern weather, and the competition was too keen for complacency. Even the act of paying the employees could

---

airline that would be widely accused of contributing to the demise of the second Braniff—Braniff International—some fifty-three years later: American Airlines.

be exciting, since there wasn't always enough money around to accomplish the task. Pilots and their families would sometimes be authorized to keep any passenger fares collected to apply to their overdue wages. As the decade drew to a close, however, little Braniff acquired a sparkling new type of airliner from Paul Douglas's aircraft factory in California: the DC-2 and later the DC-3. The increased safety factor and appeal of the "giant" new airliners seemed to be a harbinger of succes and permanency.

Braniff began coming of age as a service organization. Hostesses were added, and the emphasis on building a reputation for first-class, kid-glove care of its passengers began to build a loyal following of business passengers.[5]

In 1938 Congress decided to create order in the chaotic airline industry through the passage of a momentous piece of legislation known as the Civil Aeronautics Act of 1938. The act granted route certificates to any carrier then in existence for any route they were then operating (a process known as "grandfathering") and provided for the development and iron-fisted control of the airline industry through the creation of the Civil Aeronautics Board—the CAB. The new system provided the operational latticework for the next forty years and provided the legal and geographical structure—the operating rules and philosophies—under which two entire generations of airline managers and presidents would learn their craft.

In the first generation were the former entrepreneurs, the wildcatters of aviation who had taken the risks of trying to make money in the brave new world of airline flying and mail transportation: men such as Bob Six of Continental, World War I ace Eddie Rickenbacker of Eastern, Juan Trippe of Pan Am, C. E. Woolman of Delta, and the Braniff brothers, Tom and Paul.

In the second generation were the airline leaders who would join after 1938 and whose entrepreneurial tendencies would be tightly governed by the structured world of the Civil Aeronautics

[5] That reputation would continue to grow. In fact, Braniff would even pick up its passengers in limousines at their homes for no extra charge—a service that became too costly to continue by the early 1950s. In the late fifties, however, a progressive sloppiness and lethargy began to encroach on the operation, eroding Braniff's public respect and leading to the joke that it was the world's largest unscheduled airline. Apparently Braniff wasn't the only airline to suffer under the yoke of this flip moniker. Eddie Rickenbacker's Eastern Air Lines, itself deserving at the time of a poor reputation for service and on-time operation, was also called the world's largest unscheduled carrier.

Board. It would be the ripping away of this intricate structure with the Airline Deregulation Act of 1978 that would put so many of those same second-generation airline managers adrift in another brave new world that many were ill suited to comprehend or handle. Deregulation, after all, demanded born-again entrepreneurs, but the old breed who were still vital and active in 1938 would be gone from the executive suites forty years later, and the managers they had nurtured and reared in the business would know nothing of true, free-market airline management in the United States of the 1980s.

When World War II exploded, the War Department pressed the newly certificated Braniff Airways (and its counterparts throughout the country) into operating a separate airline division just to provide military transport. In the process, the war planners requisitioned some of Braniff's new Douglas DC-3's and DC-2's for immediate military use. The new military division (Braniff's Cargo Air Contract Division) had the beneficial effect, however, of giving Braniff's executives and pilots valuable international experience flying outside the confines of the continental United States to Panama and other locations. Meanwhile, Braniff continued to add a few domestic routes as the company matured operationally. After the war the company repatriated most of its drafted airplanes and dipped into war surplus for several DC-4's, as well as ordering the new DC-6 (both four-engine airliners), while the workhorse DC-3 remained the backbone of the fleet. Headquarters had moved south from Oklahoma City to Dallas's Love Field in 1942, and as the postwar economy of Dallas and Fort Worth began to accelerate, Braniff's traffic—and income—were among the beneficiaries.

Braniff Airways stood on the brink of genuine success in the late 1940s, and by 1950 the company had cranked up most of its new South American operation after a dazzling display of energy and skill in overcoming the difficulties of opening up the new system. Such achievements as well as its growing payroll gained Braniff Airways acceptance as a substantial and mature member of the Dallas community as well as the airline community.

Whatever its failures in the late 1950s and early 1960s (and there were to be many), Braniff had been an aviation pioneer of major import, a fact of which too many recent employees and the American public would remain largely unaware.

Of Old Dogs and New Tricks

The control yoke in pilot Buddy Huddleston's hands was shuddering as his twin-engine Grumman Mallard amphibian strained and bucked under an increasing burden of ice that was slowly, inexorably destroying his capability to stay airborne. Behind him in the cabin was a load of ten prominent Texas and Louisiana businessmen returning on this Sunday, January 10, 1954, from a duck-hunting trip staged by Huddleston's employer, United Gas Company, at Grand Chenier, Louisiana. As Huddleston and his copilot battled the stricken aircraft—forcing the throttles to the firewall and clawing for every inch of altitude—such passengers as World War I flying ace Edgar Tobin and Tom E. Braniff, the president of Braniff Airways, gripped their armrests and tried to spot something through the cabin windows besides the grayness of the icy overcast.

The Mallard was down to fifteen hundred feet now, descending steadily, the controls becoming slower and slower to respond to Huddleston's frantic attempts to hold altitude. The shuddering of the aircraft as it hovered on the edge of a stall made reading the instruments almost impossible, but Huddleston could see the airspeed dancing wildly in the vicinity of ninety miles per hour.

Shreveport was just ahead, invisible in the darkening overcast just after sundown, but the fast-moving cold front that had pushed under a mass of warm, moist gulf air had created an area of airborne icing conditions much farther south than the pilots had expected, and they were flying the one aircraft in the company's fleet that had no deicing equipment on the wings.

"Tell Shreveport tower we're going to put her onto Wallace Lake if we can get there," Huddleston told his copilot, "and tell them we've iced up . . . losing altitude . . . visibility almost zero." Huddleston could barely make out occasional ground features through the murk as his craft continued down, the engines screaming at full power.

It was 5:50 P.M. when Huddleston—trying to stay airborne until he could locate the lake—saw instead the foggy outlines of what appeared to be trees and cabins through his ice-covered windshield. Instinctively he yanked the control column, knowing the instant he did so that it wouldn't do any good—the aircraft was too iced up and too heavy to gain an inch of altitude. The soul-wrenching sound of screeching metal ripping away as the left wing contacted a tree was followed by the slow-motion impact of the cockpit with the wooden buildings of a fishing camp on the north shore of Wallace Lake. Huddleston, his copilot, and their ten passengers tumbled in instantaneous deadly confusion through a mass of tearing metal as the disintegrating aircraft and its human occupants died in a ball of twisted wreckage and flames.

The loss of Tom Braniff hit Dallas hard. He had become a deeply respected member of the Dallas business and social community and a man of great generosity with his time and money. Aside from the obvious grief of loyal employees and friends and the formal change of the presidency to Chuck Beard, the impact on Tom Braniff's airline was far more subtle.

The "Braniff family" was real—similar to the cohesive organizational camaraderie that Delta Air Lines' founder, C. E. Woolman, had created in his airline. Stories abound of employees old and new, of high rank and the lowest, being asked out to Bess and Tom Braniff's house for dinner. His annual appearance at the company Christmas party as Santa Claus was something he seemed to enjoy deeply, and his genuine though paternalistic interest in his employees' welfare was sincere. "We'd do anything for Mr. Braniff!" was a phrase that friends of Braniff employees were used to hearing. His interest in his employees, especially in later years, may have stemmed in part from the loss of his own two children: a son, Thurman, killed in a private-plane crash in the mid-1930s, and a daughter, Jeanne, who had died in 1948.

Tom Braniff was a businessman of the old school in which hard work and frugality were to be expected of one's employees, but he had always displayed a respect for his people regardless of their position or his. Such respect was to disappear slowly from the company's managerial style as the years after 1954 progressed without his leadership.

Tom Braniff was not universally thought of as a warm and caring employer. To his pilots especially he seemed to be the slightly aloof owner who was civil and friendly but who wouldn't think to express his appreciation for an extra act of courtesy such as loading or unloading the boss's bags. His people had also begun to form unions, a move Braniff did nothing to impede. The inevitability of a conflict finally erupted on April 13, 1953, when the air carrier mechanics' union went on strike to shut down the airline.

They didn't succeed. The airline kept flying, and when the strike was over forty-four days later, not all of their number were invited back to work, and not all who were invited came back. But during the strike, with managers and vice presidents down on the ramp fueling airplanes and sweeping out the hangars, Tom Braniff watched a picket line of his mechanics nearly drowning in the downpour of a Texas springtime thunderstorm, and he ordered one of his managers to gather up some rainsuits, coffee, and donuts and take them to them. The manager on the other end of the office telephone line was astounded.

"But Mr. Braniff, those guys out there are on strike, sir. They're trying to shut us down!"

"I understand that, Buford, but they're still my boys, and I don't want them to get sick. Look at them out there! You go get those things and go treat them like human beings out there and be nice to them."

Buford Minter, general superintendent of maintenance, did as he was told, only to have difficulty getting the men on the picket line to accept the coffee and donuts: They were as suspicious of his intentions as he had been incredulous of Tom Braniff's request.

Paternalistic management, a form that has blended so well with the cultural influences of the Japanese in their management, had been a tolerated form of control in many American companies. The independence of the individual worker—whether mechanic, pilot, or vice president—was growing in the 1950s, influenced by the catharsis and the homogenizing effects of World War II as well as by the country's cultural maturation and loss of innocence. It was no longer enough for a man just to have a job. It was becoming important to him as well that his company accord him respectful treatment, giving him credit for having at least some intelligence and individual worth. That changed the protocol for employers who had operated as a form of corporate "father": It was no longer possible for such an employer to do such things as hand out grocery items at a company Christmas party without insulting his employees—a practice that had been an annual tradition with Tom Braniff until the early 1950s, when a large number of his people sent the groceries back one Christmas with a note: "If this is the best you can do, you need it more than we do!"

The strains of employee independence against Tom Braniff's form of traditional management were beginning to show on the morning of January 11, 1954, when Dallas citizenry opened their *Dallas Morning News* and discovered that he was gone. His passing marked more than the loss of a seventy-year-old corporate patriarch. It also marked the end of an era.

Charles E. Beard took over as president of Braniff, running things with a firm, conservative hand. He was perceived as being a bit cold personally, but he was not aloof. He was a formal, correct, and polished man, tall and rather thin, given to wearing a pencil-thin moustache and rimless spectacles. He tended to blend into the crowd, and in fact one of his favorite forms of contact with the people was to pop up anonymously in a line at a Braniff ticket counter or some other work station and introduce himself with: "Hi, I'm Chuck Beard. I work for Braniff, too."

The combination of Tom Braniff's personal and paternal touch and Chuck Beard's pragmatic, correct management had worked well. Without Mr. Braniff, however, shades of alienation began to creep into the employees' perception of just how much of a "family" their airline still was. Throughout the late 1950s and early 1960s an "us against them" attitude began to develop in various areas of the employee group as something very valuable slipped from the grasp of the Braniff people—a sense of common enterprise. The loss was, perhaps, an inevitable legacy of growth and time, but by the 1960s it had begun to show in the operation and on-time record of the airline.

What was more disturbing was the apparent confusion of Beard and his people over how to correct things. Complex personnel relations challenges of the kind facing Braniff were beyond Beard's training and expertise as a corporate manager, leading to some rather basic mistakes. Beard and many of his senior people failed to recognize how unprepared Braniff's middle and lower managers were in too many cases. They were good people, often with limited formal management education and little company training, thrust into jobs for which many weren't really qualified, and often paid little more than the people they were managing. The result was increasing employee dissatisfaction and alienation, much of which had focused on Chuck Beard personally by 1960, as represented by a favorite union retort of that period to any company pronouncement: "The company is simply muttering through its Beard!"

On-the-job experience, native intelligence, and years of practice had made the system work to that point, but the challenges of the 1960s and the massive growth Braniff would undergo in the late 1970s would leave too many managers in the dust, scrambling to hide their inadequacies.

It was this imperfect structure, then, that awaited Harding Luther Lawrence on April 1, 1965 when he moved into the president's office in the Braniff Building in Dallas. The weak and shifting sands of unstable lower management constituted the foundation on which Lawrence would unknowingly try to build his modern organization.

The tension of anticipation in the Braniff Board room was visible on the faces of many of the senior staff assembled there on the late April morning in 1965 reserved for the first formal meeting under Harding Lawrence. Meticulously groomed and wearing a dark suit, his jet black hair combed straight back from his forehead, Lawrence arrived at eight-thirty on the dot and began shaking hands as he moved around the long table. Lawrence had actually been in and out of Dallas over the previous month in preparation for the takeover learning the details of the operation and meeting the men who would be his vice presidents—his senior staff. He had also spent a considerable amount of time consulting with Ed Acker and Grant Fitts at Greatamerica over the first moves in their carefully laid master plan to transform Braniff into a pacesetting airline whose stock, presumably, could be made to soar in value with the dynamic changes ahead.

This was also the kickoff of a routine that would become a company institution at Braniff over the next fifteen years: the weekly staff meeting.[1]

[1] The staff meetings began as a forum for lively exchanges of ideas and information, as Lawrence always intended them to be. By the 1970s, however, the propensity of normal individuals to want to avoid confrontation, and Lawrence's tendency to vent his feelings and frustrations instantly and with little delicacy to the bearer of bad news, had changed the nature of the weekly meetings. They became "sunshine

On this April morning in 1965, Lawrence took his place at the head of the table and began talking about what was to come, his resonant voice and polished delivery holding the group's rapt attention as he described the immense challenge and the equally immense opportunities that lay ahead for all the people of Braniff.[2]

"There are no limits to what we can achieve, no limits to the greatness we can instill in this airline, but it depends on a dedication to hard work, long hours, and a complete rebirth of the company."

Braniff, he said, had to double its size in the next five years and achieve a completely new image.

As the new president spoke, gesturing in enthusiastic emphasis as he outlined the exciting new changes, a hard edge crept into his voice, and he paused momentarily before saying that he wasn't asking their cooperation, he was insisting on it. It would be a team effort, he said, and if there was anyone who didn't feel capable of, or willing to, uphold his portion of the load on Lawrence's terms, he should "step aside and let those who want to join this program do so."

Those who met his gaze had no reason to doubt the man's sincerity, but few realized how demanding a taskmaster he would turn out to be.

Harding Lawrence took control of Braniff with the urgency of a rescue missionary. Route applications had to be filed with a vengeance and given companywide support, and above all, Braniff's dowdy image had to be changed. To Lawrence, Braniff—as Acker had warned him—was as much as ten years behind the industry in

---

meetings," so called because the smart executive showed up only to "pump sunshine" —tell the boss only good news—since any problem often invited cross-examination and sometimes the verbal wrath of the chairman. No one wanted to be on the receiving end of such lectures in front of his fellow officers, junior and senior. By the late seventies the meetings were largely worthless as sources of useful information for Lawrence, and by the spring of 1980 he dropped them altogether, canceling them week by week.

[2] Lawrence felt he would be "in enemy territory over there" at Braniff and expected determined resistance from the old guard to the sweeping changes he was planning. Consequently, as a precondition to leaving Continental, he insisted that Ed Acker join Braniff at the same time as one of his senior vice presidents. Acker would handle the areas of Braniff's finance and administration and be a strong friend in camp in addition to the board members, who were mostly Greatamerica loyalists. Acker agreed to join, but he also retained his job at Greatamerica, spending 40 percent of his time there and 60 percent at Braniff—until LTV bought Greatamerica and Braniff in 1967.

some areas, especially in computerization and financial reporting systems and controls. In addition, the fleet of aircraft had become a hodgepodge with a large order for the British-built BAC-111 twin jet about to be delivered, a fleet of Lockheed Electras, and four Boeing 707-227 jetliners, a model built specifically for Braniff with a special, higher-powered Pratt & Whitney engine. The specially ordered jetliner was obtained specifically to one-up American Airlines' 707 model, the dash 123 version. Pre-Lawrence Braniff had been able to crow about having "the world's fastest jetliner" between Dallas and New York, but the problems created by having just four of a single type of aircraft cost time and money. Braniff couldn't trade or exchange engines for that particular 707 with any other airline. Consequently, when one of these planes needed a spare engine or engine parts somewhere other than in Dallas, it usually was out of service for at least a day.

To correct such fleet problems, new aircraft orders had to be placed and some existing orders canceled. During Lawrence's first week, he executed a previously decided-upon order for eighteen new jets, including twelve of the new trijet Boeing 727's.

In 1961 at Continental, Lawrence had been one of the driving forces behind an overhaul of Continental's image with the initiation of the "Proud Bird with the Golden Tail" campaign and the advent of gold uniforms. That had successfully garnered nationwide attention. Now in 1965 he turned to the same think-tank advertising group that had helped him in the latest (1964) revision of that Continental Airlines campaign, Jack Tinker and partners. (Tinker and his people were associated with the McCann-Erickson agency of New York and all were members of the Interpublic Group of Companies, Inc.)

Tinker's team leader on the Braniff account was the same captivating young thirty-six-year-old blonde who had impressed Lawrence so much the year before at Continental—Mary Wells. It was she who shouldered the task of changing Braniff's image and formulating the razzle-dazzle campaign Lawrence would need to thrust Braniff International—as it was now to be called—into the national spotlight. The choice of Mary Wells would prove to be brilliant and historic, in both the worlds of commercial aviation and advertising.

Lawrence also brought in a high-quality interior designer from Santa Fe, New Mexico, named Alexander Girard, to transform

Braniff's waiting rooms, ticket counters, aircraft interiors, and even the food service equipment into something stylish in place of the traditional items most carriers used. For the Braniff uniforms, Italian couturier Emilio Pucci was retained.

Those in Dallas who were familiar with the worlds of high fashion or progressive artistic interior design were puzzled. What could the likes of Pucci and Girard do for an airline? Airlines of the mid-1960s, as everyone knew, were mostly conservative, with military-style uniforms and dull-gray fabric interiors, augmented by nothing more exciting in most aircraft than the name of the line stenciled on the back of each headrest.

Girard, Pucci, and Mary Wells, however, were planning a minor revolution. In coordination with Mary Wells and her people, the team began to focus on a splashy theme involving a multitude of colors to enliven the airline's image. Girard had looked long and hard at Braniff's traditional three-color paint job on the airplanes and decided that it was all wrong, and with that conclusion, Mary Wells began turning the top of the Braniff maintenance hangar into a paint shop as she laboriously tested color after color on pieces of sheet metal placed on the roof in the sunlight. Pucci, meanwhile, was having similar thoughts about doing away with the traditional military uniforms, especially since a host of new synthetic fabrics in bright colors were available for travel wardrobes.

Suddenly, in late September, the new campaign began to surface, the biggest jolt being the first full-scale test of the "Easter egg" solid-color scheme for the aircraft. After two other prop aircraft had been used as test cases, a brand-new BAC-111 twin jet was pulled into the hangar and the fuselage was painted orange, with the wings white. The Braniff executives who saw its debut within the privacy of the closed and guarded hangar were shocked, especially when they tried to fathom what the other color schemes, ranging from ochre to emerald green, would look like in the light of day.

The campaign incorporated Pucci's heart-stopping uniform designs in wild colors—an incredible wardrobe for the flight attendants, and a happy, swirling kaleidoscope of color centered around the "jelly bean" fleet of airliners that were to be introduced with the catchphrase "Braniff presents the end of the plain plane!"

Lawrence and the management team were nervous. The departure from tradition was almost total, and though the quality and the reputation of the well-known Pucci and Girard would protect

34

against total public rejection, no one knew what the public's reaction would be. Lawrence knew the campaign wasn't much of a financial risk. Changes of some sort in paint for the aircraft and changes in uniform would have had to be made in any event, and even if these changes failed to generate traffic and had to be abandoned, it would be only a setback, not a disaster. Nevertheless, nervousness and uncertainty made the subsequent decision to go ahead and implement the campaign a bit frightening.

Finally, in the first week of November the campaign broke and the newly painted aircraft were taxied out of the hangar with the appropriate fanfare of bands, crowds, and press. Dallas and the Southwest were being treated to the emergence of a new and startling butterfly of an airline bursting forth where a rather familiar old moth of a carrier had been.

The Driving Force

CHAPTER 4 The impact of the "end of the plain plane" campaign on the consciousness of the nation was immediate. Mary Wells had said at the outset that if the campaign was to succeed, it would have to be sufficiently newsworthy to be featured in *Life* magazine. Within the next six months that benchmark was reached as *Life, Time, Newsweek, Business Week, Aviation Week,* and an untold number of smaller publications picked up the story: "Wild Hue Yonder: Pucci designs uniform suited to the jet age" (*Life*), "Braniff Refuels on Razzle-Dazzle" (*Business Week*), "Color it Braniff" (*Newsweek*). Suddenly Braniff was getting nationwide attention (helped by a supporting, multimillion-dollar advertising blitz). Braniff, Americans suddenly realized, was a pacesetting airline and not a resort in the Canadian Rockies (people had consistently confused the name Braniff with Banff). The public perception grew that not only was it an airline, it was also a modern, chic company with the *chutzpah* and the bravado to buck the dowdy traditions of military uniforms and dull paint jobs—a company that was trying to make flying fun! That was precisely the attitude Mary Wells and her team (who formed their own agency in mid-1966 called Wells Rich Greene, Inc.) had set out to create.

What's more, it was beginning to show up on the bottom line with thumping success. As mid-1966 approached, Braniff's stock had done precisely what Harding Lawrence had been hired to make it do. From less than $24 per share in early 1965, it had passed $125 per share on its way to $200 by April 1966, with earnings up 58 percent and the passenger count up 18 percent. When the first year under Lawrence's presidency was summarized in the annual report for 1965, the results included a 17.84 percent increase in revenues and a 58.25 percent rise in profits!

The report also included information of the company's 50 percent increase in utilization of the jet fleet, a new round-the-clock maintenance program, and the refinancing of Braniff's long-term debt on an unsecured basis to provide the money for new aircraft.

What wasn't included was the information that Harding Lawrence was driving himself with a crushing work schedule. Pre-Lawrence executive-suite hours at Braniff had been 9:00 A.M. to 4:00 P.M. (a country-club atmosphere, in Acker's estimation), but the new president's style, as well as that of the Greatamerica organization, was a myopically dedicated 8:00 A.M. to 10:00 P.M. daily. The other key people at the airline were expected to follow at a similar clip.

For many of the old guard the pace from 1965 into 1967 was exciting, but his senior team was having trouble keeping up.[1]

Quite a few Braniff officers recall seeing little of their families during those first two years. Lawrence himself would remain on the job sometimes twenty hours per day, having lunch at his desk and working straight through weekends. When he and other top executives set out on familiarization trips to the various Braniff outstations, the schedule of those visits was equally exhausting. Lawrence,

---

[1] In a Kansas City hotel room at 7:30 A.M. one morning in late 1965 Harding Lawrence looked at a couple of his sleepy executives who were late reporting to his morning "briefing" (after six hours of sleep) and said, "I don't understand you guys . . . here we have this tremendous opportunity to accomplish great things and make a lot of money for everyone . . . and you spend half your life in the sack!" Lawrence was smiling, but there was an element of consternation in his complaint.

it seemed, could exist indefinitely on three to four hours' sleep per night.

By the time Robert Six's Continental Airlines had acquired Pioneer Airlines in the mid-1950s, and along with it Harding Lawrence, Lawrence's work habits were already well formed. As he would be overly fond of saying over the next twenty-five years, aviation was his vocation and his avocation, an all-consuming passion. Lawrence was never the type of executive who watched the clock, looking forward to golf games, tennis matches, outside civic clubs, or organizational meetings. By the time he had come to Braniff, his sense of excitement and pride in simply accomplishing the corporate goals he set for himself and his organization was the driving force behind his personality. Lawrence thoroughly enjoyed being a dynamic, knowledgeable corporate executive who could, in the same maverick fashion as his mentor, Bob Six, determine a best course of action through his own analysis of whatever corporate challenge was at hand and then take immense pride at having bucked the tide of tradition or skepticism when he succeeded. By his own admission he was a "numbers man," a leader who relied on having the maximum amount of information and who acted only with a plan. It was simply Lawrence's ability to understand what the numbers could mean better than the average executive and his talent for formulating unique courses of action based on that understanding that would make him look like a gambler so many times in his career.

As a corporate officer and a nonpracticing lawyer, Harding Lawrence knew it was the responsibility of an airline president of a publicly held carrier to work with his board and his senior management, keep his people extremely well informed, and listen to all well-supported ideas and opinions. But Harding's model of a modern major airline leader had been Bob Six, and despite Six's soft-hearted personal warmth, his style of management was autocratic if not dictatorial. Six also had a propensity for salty verbal expression that could "batter a barn at forty paces." Harding Lawrence's own style reflected much of Bob Six, though in a somewhat more refined way.[2]

---

[2] Harding Lawrence from his boyhood had possessed a burning desire not only to acquire the finer material things in life, but more importantly to acquire the knowledge and the *savoir-faire* to appreciate them. In later years his love of French art and the modernistic works of Alexander Calder would reflect this passion.

Lawrence's personal dedication to his job at Braniff was total, and he was well aware that he expected no more from his well-paid senior people than he did from himself. He also knew, as he had expressed to Ed Acker in asking him to join the Braniff executive team, that in trying to change the work habits of the existing team, he would have to "educate" them to the new ways—*his* new ways. Just as Bob Six had "reared" his senior people at Continental from green junior managers into senior managers, Lawrence was determined to direct and guide the professional, managerial maturation of his people. In fact, he fully expected that sometime in the early 1970s he would be able to become more of a teacher than a manager, stepping more into the role of a chairman than a chief executive officer. By then, Lawrence assumed, his executives would understand how to run the airline his way.

Six had accomplished the structuring of Continental's management through the stable years of the 1950s, working in an airline he had created and controlled from the first. Lawrence, on the other hand, had torn like a Texas tornado into the middle of an overly lethargic organization that was lagging behind the ever-increasing pace of the industry challenges of the midsixties. Lawrence didn't have the same luxuries of time and familiar surroundings to work with, and his attempts to use some of the same techniques he had learned from Bob Six—"rearing" senior people rather than hiring proven talent and replacing nonperformers—would be a seed of future disaster that he could neither see nor detect in the late sixties.

By the summer of 1967, with substantial growth and profits behind him and great things ahead, it was too soon and there was simply too much to do for Harding Lawrence or his executives to spend much time in leisurely examination of his overall management philosophies and how they were working. Lawrence had encountered enough trouble trying to penetrate the provincial attitudes he had encountered throughout the company—the inability of middle and lower management especially to see what the military calls "the big picture"—the "brass ring" of international status to be grabbed ten to fifteen years down the road if the proper groundwork were laid.

The new Braniff president's personal style of talking and dealing with his employees reflected a genuine interest and concern, and a personal friendliness that was not feigned. But Lawrence could change in a split second from pleasant conversation to a fiery expression of dissatisfaction, then return to pleasant conversation again, often leaving the poor employee's composure in ruins. To Lawrence, it was no more than an honest and forthright expression of disapproval, upset, or unhappiness with what the man or woman had done or reported. It bore in his mind no relationship to his personal regard for the employee, though to the employee it was often regarded as a violent personal attack, and this latter view of Lawrence became the accepted, inaccurate image of him throughout the ranks of the employees, union and management alike.[3]

Lawrence didn't "beat up" all his executives. Those who were careful to present him with well-supported facts and information—especially those who were recognized experts in their fields (such as Ed Acker, Tom Robertson, and even Executive Chef Willy Rossel)—never received Lawrence's wrath. Of course, different people react to the same event with different perceptions, especially when the ego and self-image of an executive or manager is at stake. The stronger men, the ones possessed of self-assurance, could field Harding's style with little trouble. For instance, Ed Acker—widely rumored to be the only Braniff executive who could and would "talk back" to the boss—was not alone. But too many others, especially those who felt out of their league in Lawrence's presence, developed their own defense systems for dealing with him, ranging from hiding bad news and problems in their divisions or simply lying to him, to developing nervous habits, some of which would grow to serious proportions over the years.

Lawrence's style and the reaction of many of his senior people imposed a "leader oriented" structure on what was supposed to be a bureaucratic structure, and instead of managers, vice presidents, and department heads conducting themselves in accordance with the responsibilities of their position, too often they conducted themselves and their divisions in accordance with their view of what Lawrence wanted, and what would keep them personally (and their job longevity) as safe as possible. "Cover your ass" became the watchphrase in Braniff management during the late 1960s.

Imposed on such problems then were the tremendous expansion

[3] As Lawrence said to Northwest Regional Sales Manager Jim Huff in Portland, Oregon, one day as Lawrence arrived from Dallas, "I want to apologize, Jimmy, for the last time I was here." Huff looked at him as they walked up the jetway. On the last visit Huff had been present when Lawrence publicly dressed down one of the local station managers for not knowing his station's performance statistics. "You don't have to apologize to me, Mr. Lawrence." "Well, I know that, but I still apologize. My people tell me I can be a real sonofabitch when I want to!" Huff, an engaging and direct fellow, smiled at Lawrence and replied, "Yes, sir, you sure can be."

and disorienting changes that, basically, by mid-1967 had transformed Braniff into a new carrier with indigenous if confused middle and lower managers. Thus there was a great need to determine who among those managers were really qualified in the new scheme of things, who should be dismissed or demoted or retrained, which experienced managers with proven track records from other airlines should be hired, and which people from lower positions would have the intelligence and the capabilities to be brought up into management, properly trained, and groomed for better things. One of the greatest problems created by the expansion was that Braniff's junior and senior management were simply too overwhelmed with the job of expansion to do any of this.

Instead of an orderly system, there was little or no quality control imposed on the hiring of new managerial people, too little firing or dismissal of those who couldn't handle the new challenges of their jobs, and no methods of evaluating formally who should stay. There simply wasn't time. Quite a few of the pre-1965 managers left or retired, taking with them vast quantities of knowledge gained from long experience. There were no attempts to keep them on as consultants or to construct any other method of transferring their skills to new people.

Formal professional training courses for senior and junior executives, managers, and lower-level directors were another major deficiency that would play such a pivotal role in frustrating Lawrence's attempts to retire from a stable, world-girdling airline of first-rate quality. Under Chuck Beard's administration there had been regular management training courses, usually conducted by business professors from such schools as nearby Southern Methodist University. These courses, however, took the time as well as the concentration of the participants, and all their time was required on the programs of growth and change. Such luxuries would have to be put off to a quieter time in the future—a time that never came.

When Lawrence had taken control in 1965, the Greatamerica people felt that the Braniff South American operation should be shut down or sold. The routes were limited to the West Coast of South America and included only exemption authority to operate out of Miami, which was a key to making the system profitable. Regardless of its potential, to that date the system had been losing small amounts of money annually and stagnating with a noncompetitive, piston-powered fleet. Instead of making an uninformed decision, Lawrence had taken a ten-day inspection trip into the region in late 1965 to see for himself, and he returned convinced the area was a gold mine for Braniff, provided they could obtain additional gateway and route authority from the CAB, adding at least some eastern cities in South America (Buenos Aires was the only one then served); put the right jet equipment on the routes; and develop a marketing campaign for South America.

There was one quick fix available: Panagra (Pan American Grace Airways) and its experienced people in South America. Panagra was an airline with a split personality—owned half by W. R. Grace & Company and half by Juan Trippe's Pan American, an arrangement that had led to monumental and continuous fights between the two owners through the years. Braniff had tried to get approval to acquire part of Panagra in 1963, since it was Braniff's chief competitor in South America and since the bitter, dirty-tricks-style competition they had thrown against Braniff had been costly to combat. That, however, had failed when (as usual) Pan Am and Grace couldn't agree. Finally in late 1966, Lawrence, Greatamerica, and the Braniff Board decided to try again.

Grace's interest was purchased rather quickly for $15 million, but Pan Am's Juan Trippe was in no hurry to sell his half. After a frustrating series of treks to New York to negotiate with Trippe and hours spent listening to his rambling tales of early aviation, which he used as a stalling tactic to avoid the necessary bargaining, Lawrence finally managed to get him to agree to the same price for his 50 percent share as Grace had accepted—$15 million. With quick CAB approval Braniff began combining the systems in late 1966. By early 1967, Lawrence had directed the sale of surplus Panagra aircraft, consolidated the tax benefits, and ended up making enough from the deal to pay for the $30 million purchase price in its entirety.

The flights to New York to spar with Juan Trippe had given Lawrence an added bonus—more opportunities to get together with Mary Wells, whose highly successful new agency was headquartered among the towers of Manhattan. He and Mary had been seeing each other quite a bit since the start of the push to develop and market Braniff, and despite Lawrence's quandary over his marital status—his estranged wife, Jimmie, and their children had lived in Dallas since the move from Continental's Los Angeles headquarters—and the not-so-subtle disapproval of some of the people connected with Greatamerica back in Dallas, Lawrence counted the days between their meetings. If his computerlike mind ever wandered in these heady years of empire building, it wandered to thoughts of her.

In returning from several of those trips, when the aircraft was completely full of paying passengers, the forty-seven-year-old airline president would ride in the cockpit jumpseat of one of the Braniff BAC-111s after politely asking the captain if he could do so. The pilots would remember such flights as pleasant and uneventful as Lawrence often would ask questions and seem to enjoy the ride. In fact, most of the Braniff people who came in contact with him during that period came away with good memories of the encounter, but there were exceptions. As with any chief executive, one bad encounter is worth a thousand rumors, and Harding Lawrence had dressed down more than one lower-level employee since his arrival, usually, so he thought, with just cause.

A similar return from New York to Dallas on a Sunday evening found Lawrence walking down the concourse at New York's Kennedy International Airport in a disgruntled mood. Several things had gone wrong so far that night, including an encounter at the front counter with one of his ticket agents whose slovenly demeanor, flippant attitude, and lack of preparation with Lawrence's trip pass had caught the president's attention and his wrath. As Lawrence approached the gate for his Dallas flight, he was in no mood to be trifled with.

Joanne Miller had passed by the same counter an hour earlier, eager to get to the gate in time to get a good position on the standby list. She and the five women with her were all new reservationists for Braniff based in Dallas who had just passed their sixth month with the company and received their first round-trip pass. Joanne and her compatriots had joined Braniff in great degree because of the élan of its vibrant new image, and although their first six months had been a rather perplexing exercise of little instruction and much on-the-job self-training, their enthusiasm for their new company eclipsed the problems. In fact, that enthusiasm was the primary reason for the trip. Although there was no official encouragement from within the management group for them to become familiar with other areas of the operation, Joanne, her compatriots, and many other new, starry-eyed employees spent many lunch hours, weekends, and evenings just touring around various areas of Braniff. One night she had spent almost all evening watching the mechanics at Love Field take the seats out of quick-change Boeing 727's to get them ready to fly cargo to New York and Chicago (Braniff was one of the first airlines to operate successfully the passenger-by-day, cargo-by-night concept with the Boeing 727-100). It was thrilling to be a part of such an avant-garde, pacesetting airline.

The departure lounge at the gate was almost filled with passengers, and it began to look doubtful whether Joanne and her friends would be able to get on, since they were flying on a standby basis and could go only if there weren't enough paying passengers on the flight. During that afternoon they had enjoyed New York's sights and sounds and taken time to visit Braniff's New York reservations center, where they compared notes with the other reservationists, getting a feel for their view of the operation. It wasn't the most glamorous way to utilize a first pass, but for people vibrantly in love with their company and curious about what made it work, it was fun. It made them feel part of a big and important enterprise. Before they had left the "rez" center, the other reservationists had teased them on how lucky they were to be flying back home on that particular flight, since the dynamic new president of the airline, Harding Lawrence, was to be on board.

Joanne had never seen Harding Lawrence in person. In fact, she had yet to meet anyone who had, but she was looking forward to it. Many of the dynamic things he had done with Braniff in such a short period had caught her attention and had been part of the attraction of applying to work for Braniff. She had seen pictures of the handsome airline chief, but when he actually walked up in person to the gate agent at the podium not fifteen feet from where she was standing, she didn't recognize him at first. Suddenly, however, the volume of the conversation at the podium increased, and it became clear to everyone in the departure lounge who the well-dressed gentleman with the booming voice really was.

Lawrence had expected the flight to be full. That is why he had exercised his privilege as a key executive to fly positive space—first class. He would occasionally move back to coach when first class was to be filled with full-fare passengers, but Lawrence spent his time on airplanes working, and the added privacy and elbow room of first class was to him a necessity—in the best interests of the company. Consequently, when he walked up to his gate agent he wasn't prepared to hear that he was wait-listed in coach and might not get on. He had to get to Dallas on this flight. The incompetence of the statement was too much, and on top of it, the man wanted to argue with him—the boss of the airline—about whether or not he would get a seat on the flight.

"I WILL get on! You understand that, idiot? I am the president of your goddamn airline, and I WILL get on! And don't *ever* try to put me in coach when I've reserved first class. . . . The president of your airline is flying first class on this flight. . . . Is that crystal clear?"

"Mr. Lawrence, sir, what I'm trying to tell you is that the flight is oversold—and I'm not sure we have space for you or any company passenger, and first class is filled with—"

Lawrence banged both fists down on the podium, jumping up off both feet simultaneously and repeating the explosive manuever four times for emphasis "I . . . WILL . . . GET . . . ON!"

The agent stood silently at last, mouth open, oblivious of the dead silence in the waiting room, which was by now filled with over fifty passengers, all of whom were shockingly aware that the outburst from the direction of the podium came from none other than the president of Braniff International.

Joanne turned her head in confusion and folded her ticket in her hand in case any of the people around her might think she was associated with this airline. She heard rather than saw Lawrence rush past toward the jetway, presumably to take his seat in first class.

"My God!" she thought, "that—that's the fabled president of my new company! My God!"

The Image of a Legend

CHAPTER 5 Harding Lawrence looked like an airline president, according to the press. With his square-cut jaw and bushy eyebrows and deep, melodious voice tinged with a hint of Texas regionalism, Lawrence looked—in the words of one magazine writer—"as if the Ashley Famous

Agency had sent over someone to play the part of a dynamic airline president."

What's more, Lawrence had long had the self-confidence and the determination to be an airline president, or most anything else he might decide to become. His drive and workaholic dedication were rapidly becoming legendary in the industry, but folks around his hometown of Gladewater in East Texas weren't the least bit surprised.

Harding Lawrence had been a boy of eleven when his father and mother and two brothers moved a boxcar of hotel furniture from the dusty, limited prospects of Drumwright, Oklahoma, to the promising hamlet of Gladewater, where they set up a workingman's hotel on South Main Street. As oil gushers began blackening the skies around the riverbed to the east of Gladewater in early 1931, the tiny town itself exploded into a bustling frontier-style economic oasis in which Moncey and Helen Lawrence and their boys would be able to ride out the Depression. It was an exciting period of noise, frenetic activity, and promise, an inspiration to a handsome young boy whose self-confidence and determination were already apparent by 1931.

Harding by age fifteen was known as a serious-minded though not humorless student with average grades who had begun working at various grocery stores in Gladewater since the age of eleven but who would be remembered mostly for his jobs in several drug-stores—especially when he worked behind the soda fountain. He was so frugal that several years later, when his mother needed an operation the family couldn't afford, young Harding had the money and paid the bill. To his older brothers Don and Eugene, their little brother was a bit of a tightwad with his money.[1] He was also not a kid to be trifled with: If Harding was pulled into a fight—an unusual occurrence—he could be counted on to finish it with a fierce determination and unbeatable ferocity that instilled as much fright as physical damage in the opponent.

Unlike some men of his generation, whose driving quests for power and wealth reflected a poverty-ridden, unhappy childhood of

[1] It would be ironic that even though Lawrence, as a corporate leader, continued to be very frugal by nature (as demonstrated, for instance, by his iron-fisted control of Braniff's "head counts" of personnel over the years and his insistence on personal approval of a myriad of company expenditures), he would be viewed as a lavish spender by many of his employees, the press, and the public.

the Depression and a desperate need for security and self-esteem, Lawrence came from a close-knit, loving family of stable, if limited means. That stability engendered a self-confidence that would follow him throughout his professional life.[2]

Moncey Luther Lawrence, who died in the early 1950s, had worked as a schoolteacher in Oklahoma as well as serving as pastor of churches in Perkins and Yale in that state, and his literacy and polished, dignified bearing—his thespian capability of holding the rapt attention of his parishioners—provided a model for young Harding.

Harding graduated from Gladewater High School with a mediocre grade record, but over a year ahead of schedule at age sixteen. After two years at Kilgore Junior College in nearby Kilgore, Texas, where his academic average was high enough to earn membership in the honors group (Phi Theta Kappa), he enrolled in 1939 at the University of Texas in Austin. When World War II broke out, Harding Lawrence became involved with a civilian flight school in Terrell, Texas, operated under contract to the military to train British pilots and run by Texas aviation pioneer W. F. Long (also known as "Mr. Love Field"). The school was an important defense activity, so Lawrence remained there as a link trainer instructor, and as Long recognized the potential of young Harding Lawrence, he was moved up to manager and later to overseeing the maintenance department. It would prove to be a turning point.

Harding had always intended to be a lawyer, and consequently had enrolled at the University of Texas Law School after getting his B.A.; but as the war ended, one of the organizers of the flight school offered him a job with a tiny commuter airline named Essair (later Pioneer Airlines) in Houston, Texas. Harding took the job, figuring he could complete law school at night while working. While he was destined to get his law degree, the legal profession was not destined to get Harding Lawrence. The romance of commercial aviation lured him away.

Back in 1928, while the Braniff brothers were busy incorporating their airline in Oklahoma City, and Harding Luther Lawrence

---

[2] Harding was close to both his father (a minister of the Christian Church who had become disillusioned with preaching) and his mother, who ran the Lawrence Hotel in Gladewater until her death in the late 1960s. She resisted all attempts of her successful youngest son to move her into the luxurious quarters he had built for her in Dallas.

was eight years old and attending elementary school in Drumwright, Oklahoma, the northeastern city of Youngstown, Ohio, routinely recorded the birth certificate of one Mary Georgene Berg.

The little girl from Youngstown would grow up blond and beautiful, attend Carnegie Institute of Technology in Pittsburgh for two years, marry a young New York art director named Burt Wells, and begin a career as an advertising copywriter whose accomplishments and name—Mary Wells—were to become legends in the advertising business by 1967.

Mary Wells was no more an overnight success than the Oklahoma-born airline executive she would meet at Continental Airlines in 1964, Harding Lawrence. Her career did begin with a lucky break in 1950 in the form of a job with Macy's in New York, but talent and hard work earned her the position of manager of fashion advertising in just two years.

At the age of twenty-four, in 1952, she jumped to the heart of the advertising field and joined McCann-Erickson, Inc., one of the more prominent ad agencies in town, as copy group head. By 1957 she had been hired by what she would later describe as "the best advertising school in town," Doyle Dane Bernbach, Inc. The years in the trenches learning the advertising business began to pay off. By 1964, richly talented and intelligent and accompanied by a reputation for innovative thinking and thoroughness, Mary Georgene Berg Wells had become copy chief and vice president of the agency, making $40,000 per year. By that time she was also newly divorced with two adopted daughters, Pam and Katy. At that juncture in her career Jack Tinker and Associates hired her away from Doyle Dane Bernbach at $60,000 annual salary to work in the "think tank" they were putting together. Within the next six months she would become one of the prime architects of the highly successful Alka-Seltzer campaign ("Plop, plop, fizz, fizz . . ." and "No matter what shape your stomach's in . . .") and begin work in Los Angeles on some of Continental Airlines' advertising at the direction of forty-four-year-old Harding Lawrence, who was married with three children—two boys, State Rights and James, and a girl, Deborah.[3]

[3] When asked once why he named his first son State Rights, Lawrence replied, "Oh, that . . . I think the time I got to name him, the time he was born, it was in the mid-1950s and it was a great national issue . . . the issue, I mean, was state rights vs. national rights and the strong federal government. It appeared state rights were on the wane, so to speak, most being usurped by the federal government. Like most names, he's stuck with it, unless he wants to change it and he hasn't done that yet. . . ." (June 1977).

Lawrence had dealt with many advertising people before, but he was particularly impressed with the Tinker group's fresh approach—and equally impressed with the poised young lady with the pulled-back blond hair and the penetrating eyes who seemed to be able to follow his thinking on every point. Lawrence was used to having to backtrack and explain things to people as patiently as possible, but with Mary Wells it wasn't necessary. She had a certain style and refinement about her—a certain mystique—that Lawrence found captivating. They got along beautifully, but the relationship was all business.

In the midst of the tempestuous mental preparation that Lawrence began doing for his move to Braniff, the problem of image and advertising had an easy solution: He had been and still was impressed with the Tinker people (and, of course, the stylish young lady named Wells), so when the time came to recommend a dynamic new ad agency for Braniff, the Tinker group was at the top of his list.

Although 1965 was something of a blur of nonstop work and creative energy as Mary and her people put together the history-making "end of the plain plane" campaign for Harding Lawrence and Braniff, the year brought them together on business many times in Dallas, New York, and elsewhere—always with a never-ending agenda. During 1966, however, with the campaign off to a wildly successful start, there were more lunches and dinners with just the two of them—potentially innocent meetings considering the vast corporate enterprise in which they were both engaged, but fateful nonetheless. Harding was falling very much in love with her, and the feelings were, by all indications, mutual.

In early 1966 Mary had been offered a new, long-term contract with Tinker along with a substantial raise, which threatened her creative independence: Mary Wells resigned, and along with her went two other key members of the Tinker group, Dick Rich and Stew Greene. After a week of sifting through the gratifying offers that started coming in from other agencies the moment the word circulated through the Madison Avenue community that the three of them were available, the trio decided suddenly to start their own agency and maintain their creative, entertainment-tinged commercial style.

Back in Dallas, through a third party, Lawrence heard of their departure from Tinker and the new venture, canvassed his executives and Board, and decided that the people who had built the most successful airline ad campaign in history were to be followed just about anywhere they wanted to go. Braniff switched to Wells Rich Greene, Inc., and became their first client with an instant $6.5 million in billings. The company was so new, Lawrence had trouble finding their temporary phone number—the embryonic Wells Rich Greene, Inc. had rented a suite of rooms at the Gotham Hotel in New York while trying to find an office.

The scope of WRG's instant success could be measured in their billings (the amount of advertising in terms of cost placed for their clients by an agency in a one-year period). Within three months of existence, WRG hit $30 million in projected annual billings, which in turn instantly placed the fledgling agency in the top fifty. Madison Avenue was stunned.

The hoopla over Mary's "end of the plain plane" campaign for Braniff had made the new agency possible. Never before had an airline been marketed with such dynamic force or such immense coordination. The campaign made Braniff, in the words of one CAB member, "the most talked-about airline in America," and Mary Wells and her people the most talked-about advertising agency in New York. The "Golden Tail" campaign at Continental in 1961 (Mary Wells and the Tinker group were not responsible for that one) had been an impressive departure from the boring, institutional advertising most airlines had done previously, but it was nothing compared to the staggering scope and the financial effectiveness of the Braniff campaign. With the new "Easter-egg fleet" (a reference Lawrence hated) and the stewardess wardrobe of up to seven different Pucci uniform combinations in iridescent colors stripped off progressively—and sometimes teasingly—during a flight (known as the "air strip"), the girls heard every conceivable joke (such as the designation "Pucci galores"), but the seats were filling with fascinated passengers, and Braniff's profits were climbing.[4]

---

[4] The television ads were highly effective and entertaining attention-getters, and the fact that they were somewhat provocative raised only mild protests. One tag line for a TV spot featuring the "air strip" ended, "Does your wife know you're flying with us?" Probably the best-remembered ad featured a little old lady ("LOL" in airline passenger service jargon) sitting in her colorful Braniff seat, happily stuffing everything from silverware to blankets into her oversized carpet bag. As the sweet, grandmotherly type drives across the screen on a Braniff baggage tug pulling the Boeing 707 behind her, the announcer intones: "We're glad you like us, but please, let's not get carried away!" Braniff had a distinct increase in the loss of silverware, blankets, and the other inflight equipment as soon as the ad aired.

Wells Rich Greene had other clients, of course, and they too got the benefits of the innovative, free-wheeling creativity of Mary's people, but the star client was still Braniff. To the airline whose campaign had made her company wealthy and famous, Mary devoted much time and attention. To its president she began devoting more and more of her personal life.

Early in 1967 a young attorney fresh out of SMU Law School, Samuel D. Coats, acquired Harding Lawrence as a client for the purpose of divorcing Mrs. Jimmie Lawrence.[5]

In September 1967 the Lawrences got their divorce. Two months later, in a civil ceremony held in the Mairie, the town hall of Paris, France, Mary Georgene Wells, chairman of the Board of Wells Rich Greene, Inc., brought an end to the rumors swirling around New York and connecting her romantically with her client airline president Harding Lawrence—by marrying him.[6]

The marriage was clearly a loving one from the first, though the realities of corporate commitments and distance immediately made it a logistics nightmare. Following the wedding, they announced that they would be living in New York, Dallas, and a ranch in Tucson. In practical terms, while they bought and completely refurbished a house in the Turtle Creek area of Dallas, Mary lived in New York during most of the week and Harding lived in Dallas, mostly at Braniff. Their constant commuting between New York and Dallas to be together whenever possible made them familiar figures in the first class sections of Braniff's New York–Dallas flights.

Late one evening on such a flight to New York, Lawrence sat

[5] Sam Coats at that time had no connection with the airline business, but the friendship he developed with Harding Lawrence would come to haunt him some fifteen years later, when he found himself in Lawrence's old corporate bunker as a Braniff senior vice president, listening to the financial shelling—the sounds of threatened corporate destruction—getting closer and closer.

[6] One of the honored guests at the wedding, and Harding's best man, was the owner and creator of Greatamerica Corporation (which held more than 80 percent of Braniff's stock), Troy Post. The previous months had been rather momentous for Post as well: He had just sold his Greatamerica and along with it his ownership of Braniff to Jim Ling's LTV Corporation in exchange for an issue of LTV debentures called "The Fives of '88," which were to pay a 5 percent interest rate and be redeemable in 1988, whence came the name. The use Jim Ling would make of Greatamerica would eventually imperil "The Fives of '88" and Post's fortune, which had already been jeopardized by an ill-starred and slightly naive attempt to build a plush resort in Mexico (Tres Vidas). Post would also find himself thoroughly at the mercy of a fellow Board member of Braniff and a powerful behind-the-scenes manipulator, banker Robert (Bob) Stewart III, chief executive officer of Dallas's First National Bank, later to become First International Bancshares, Inc.

down in the first class section of one of the company 727's in his usual seat, 6C, and found himself across the aisle from a senior Braniff flight attendant, who was deadheading to New York. She introduced herself, and Lawrence (after stowing his briefcase under his seat for a change—he usually worked his way to New York) ordered a Scotch and began chatting with her. As the brightly colored green 727 (Mary had called it the *Super Pickle* in a recent speech to a Houston civic group) began its climb for the trip to Kennedy International Airport, Lawrence turned to the subject of his new wife and what an incredible lady she was. As the flight progressed, he talked on and on about Mary, extolling her virtues, her intelligence, her business acumen, and most emphatically how much he loved her.

When at long last he fell silent, the mesmerized employee looked at her watch and realized they were almost in the descent for landing in New York. Lawrence had been talking for over two hours on the same subject.

She left the airport that night feeling very good (as she had told him before leaving the airplane) about working for a company led by a man who loved his wife as much as Harding loved Mary.

The More Conservative Risk

CHAPTER 6 In the afternoon of May 3, 1968, the radarscope on the flight deck of Braniff Flight 352 was showing a solid line of thunderstorm cells dead ahead, about forty miles south of the Dallas area and blocking the flight's straight-line access to Dallas's Love Field. Captain John R. Phillips, a capable and well-respected forty-six-year-old Braniff veteran, sat in the left seat at the controls, flying this leg of their flight schedule from Houston to Dallas. Captain Phillips and his crew (copilot John Foster and flight engineer Don Crossland) had been through this area several hours earlier. At that time there had been clear skies and no problems, so confronting this angry wedge of black clouds on the way back had been a surprise, and they'd been looking at it since shortly after leveling at twenty thousand feet. This sort of weather was depressingly typical of Texas in the late spring.

The line was ahead of them now by about thirty miles, and the other flights were going around it to the east. That was the best method of dealing with a thunderstorm—avoid it—but it also meant as much as five to ten minutes more flight time and a late arrival at the gate.

John Phillips was aware—perhaps too aware—of a clock on the forward bulkhead of his aircraft's passenger cabin in plain view of his passengers; it was ticking inexorably toward the scheduled arrival time at the gate. Braniff had come up with another bold new promotion called the "fast buck," which would result in every passenger on board getting a company chit redeemable for one dollar if the crew didn't make it to the gate at the destination airport within fifteen minutes of scheduled arrival time—which was when the alarm on the clock was set to ring.

The "fast buck" campaign was another innovative and controversial idea emanating from Wells Rich Greene, Inc. and Braniff's marketing people, and its purpose was to point out in dramatic fashion that Braniff was, for the most part, an on-time airline at long last. The company had propelled itself out of an embarrassing sixth place in the industry to second place—from 74 percent on time to 89 percent. However, the public, remembering the past propensity for delays, still regarded Braniff as perpetually late. Lawrence and his new wife were sick of the image, especially since it was no longer justified, and the "fast buck" campaign was designed to do something about it.

The media took a predictably skeptical viewpoint. The campaign, they said, would end up costing Braniff an incredible amount and simply show up the airline's inadequacies (in fact, this was encouraged by the advertising, which warned that Braniff could lose as much as $1.5 million). Lawrence was confident his people could perform, so he authorized the campaign and worked hard to enlist companywide enthusiasm to make it work. With the entire passenger cabin betting against Braniff on each flight, the drive to get there on time was hard for the ground or flight crews to ignore.[1]

[1] In terms of its cost, the campaign was a success. The company had budgeted around $100,000 in "fast buck" payouts; the final figure was less than $110,000.

The three-month-long campaign had started on April Fool's Day of 1968. Until May 3, even many of the Braniff employees found it fun.

Captain Phillips knew they were already pushing the time limit. They had departed the gate in Houston on time, but the takeoff had been delayed by other landing airliners. With the bad weather ahead and all the other flights deviating around the ugly buildups, the passengers would probably win their money on this trip. Nevertheless, he wasn't inclined to take any chances if getting there faster meant tangling with the black heart of a thunderstorm cell. Phillips had flown for Braniff seventeen years. He knew all about avoiding thunderstorms.

Suddenly however, staring intently at the phosphorescence of his radarscreen for the best way to go, Phillips thought he saw a black area he felt was a "hole"—an area of reduced turbulence between the worst cells. It looked safe and passable.

"It looks like there's a hole up ahead to me," Phillips remarked, working the knobs of the radarscope.

Foster looked at the scope and nodded. "Yeah."

Phillips decided to head that way. Just another of the hundreds of decisions an airline pilot has to make on every flight.

Back in the passenger cabin a group of eighty passengers, many of them Dallas businessmen returning from business meetings in the Houston area, were reading, drinking, and talking—enjoying the sight of the two young stewardesses in their wild Pucci prints as they served drinks and snacks from the rear first class section to the front of coach. The flight had been relatively smooth so far, so there was no cause for concern when Phillips's voice came over the PA system.

"Folks, this is Captain Phillips. We expect to be at the gate on time in Dallas at four fifty-eight P.M. Now, we've got a little line of thundershowers ahead of us and I'm going to take us a bit to the west to keep the ride smooth and comfortable for you.

"I'm going to turn on the 'seat belt' and 'no smoking' signs at this time, just in the event it's a little choppy in the area. Our radar is working quite well and we're going to be able to go under and to the west of all the thundershowers, but they'll be visible to you on the right side of the aircraft. So please fasten your belts now for us."

Phillips put down the PA microphone and looked at Foster. "I *guess* I can go under," Phillips said.

The whitish "echoes" of the storm on the radar set were nearly filling the screen as Phillips leaned over the scope once more. There was a knob on the radarscope labeled "contrast." When turned full up, it caused the area of worst possibile intensity in a storm to appear on the scope as a black area—a black hole. Of course, when that feature is not used, a genuinely clear area between thunderstorm cells can appear exactly the same—as a small black hole. If the pilot using the scope had the "contrast" function on (also known as "iso-echo" or "contour" on some aircraft) and didn't know it, the worst area might appear to be the clearest. Because of the scope's location to Phillips's left, Foster didn't know whether the captain was using the feature or not.

Whatever the nature of the "hole" that Captain Phillips had seen, the Braniff Electra, with eighty passengers and five crew on board, was now aimed squarely at it.

The Electra with its four powerful Allison turboprop engines and stubby, rigid wings had been a workhorse for Braniff since its introduction in 1959 as the company's first jet-powered aircraft. Despite the crash of another Electra near Tell City, Indiana, in the late fifties, and the crash of a Braniff Electra near Buffalo, Texas, on September 29, 1959, the aircraft was basically a good one. As a result of those accidents, the Electra fleet had been grounded and the unique cause of the problem discovered and corrected. Although the public was still somewhat jittery over the aircraft, the memories of those troubles in the late fifties were fading.[2]

The powerful jetprop suddenly hit the black wall of clouds sur-

[2] Both the Tell City and the Buffalo crashes were the result of a technological flaw in the Electra related to the rigid wing. The tremendous gyroscopic forces of the spinning turbines, propellers, and gear-box assemblies on each engine would begin to set up a harmonic vibration and interaction with the rigid wing spar at certain high cruising speeds. The gyroscopic wobbling in conjunction with minute cracks that had developed in the wing spar, undetected by maintenance procedures then in use, would cause the spar to react like a giant tuning fork. The harmonic interaction would rapidly grow out of control until the engines on that wing would literally tear themselves off their mountings, disintegrating the crack-riddled wing at the same time. An incredible job of technological detective work and reassemblage of the wreckage of both crashes was required before the cause was discovered, and by changing the rigidity of the wing spar in certain places, the problem was cured. In the meantime, all Electras had first been grounded, then released for flight at reduced cruise airspeeds. No further crashes were attributed to this problem, which was essentially a result of the Electra's wing representing the edge of new, advanced aerodynamic technology. The cost to the airlines that operated the Electra was high—not only from lost use because of the grounding, but also due to avoidance of the aircraft afterward.

rounding the hidden cells and began to pitch and buck. It was 4:45 P.M.—thirteen minutes to scheduled arrival at Love Field.

Captain Phillips told his engineer to turn on the engine heat (anti-ice system) and told Foster to ask the center controller if he had any reports of hail in the area just ahead. At that moment the flight was under the control of the FAA's air traffic control facility known as Fort Worth Center.

"No three fifty-two, you're the closest one that's ever come to it yet—I haven't been able to . . . anybody to . . . well, I haven't tried really to *get* anybody to go through it . . . they've all deviated around to the east."

Phillips could see nothing but clouds out the front of the blunt-nosed aircraft as the intensity of the turbulence increased.

Foster was about to reply, but Phillips raised his hand to caution him not to.

"No—John—don't talk to him too much. I'm hearing his conversation on this. He's trying to get us to admit we're making a big mistake coming through here."

The yawing and bouncing of the aircraft were getting severe—cups and glasses began to depart their owners' hands in the passenger cabin, becoming small missiles flying around above and below the seats. The two flight attendants hurriedly strapped themselves in, apprehensive over the severity of the turbulence.

In the cockpit, Phillips was having increasing difficulty reading the instruments when the sounds of high-speed impact with an area of heavy rain or hail filled his ears. Foster was looking at the radar too. "It looks worse to me over there."

Finally, Phillips had had enough. He could imagine how frightened—frozen with fear—his eighty passengers must be back there. It was getting frightening up here, too. He began a bank to the right that began to steepen—10 degrees, 20 degrees—as he tried to hold her attitude level.

Phillips almost yelled at Foster, "Let's make a one-eighty!" (reverse course). Foster grabbed the mike and asked the center for permission as Phillips steepened the bank to the right.

Suddenly the rate with which the Electra was rolling to the right increased—through 60, 70, 80, and 90 degrees. The nose dropped sickeningly as a result of the wild wind currents and updrafts in the thunderstorm cell they had penetrated. Within the space of a few heartbeats Phillips was wrestling with a major "upset"—in aviation parlance, an "unusual attitude." The Electra's nose was pointed down at nearly a 40-degree angle, the bank angle was over 110 degrees—and the aircraft was essentially diving toward the ground in a tight right spiral, the altitude readout unwinding rapidly on the bouncing and vibrating instrument panel.

Phillips tried to roll the aircraft back to the left while pulling on the yoke—trying to get the nose up. The G-forces built up beyond 2.5 to 3.5 and higher as he pulled harder and retarded the throttles to idle, desperately trying to get back to stabilized, level flight. A large aircraft like the Electra could cover the distance between ten thousand feet and the surface in almost no time in a steep dive; Phillips knew that with cold certainty.

The G-forces built up to over 4.2, causing the faces and limbs of the passengers and crew to feel tremendously heavy. In the confusion of the moment, John Phillips may not have realized what happened next, but the top of the right wing of his Electra crumpled upward and the entire wing (along with engines 3 and 4) ripped off the fuselage, washing the tail section with jet fuel, which promptly ignited in a ball of flame. The still-intact fuselage, with only the left wing still attached, began an uncontrollable dive to disintegration at several hundred miles per hour into the soggy Texas terrain near the small town of Dawson. The only sounds on the cockpit voice recorder from the time the wing departed to the end of the tape were those of multiple alarm bells and warning horns inundating the doomed cockpit with a cacophonous death knell as the three pilots helplessly watched the ground rush up to kill them. Captain Phillips, married, the father of two boys, along with the rest of the eighty-five crew and passengers, ceased to exist on impact. The "fast buck" alarm clock never rang.

Although the tragedy near Dawson on May 3, 1968, rocked the Dallas community (as well as the Braniff community) and gathered a dark cloud of public distrust over the Electra once again, it would be the last fatal aircraft accident that Braniff International would ever have—despite all the expansion to follow over the next fourteen years and the ripe opportunities for mishaps provided by the hostile flight environments of South America, Europe, the Pacific, and "tornado alley" in the midwestern United States.

In great measure that is an accolade to the aeronautical professionalism of Braniff's pilots and all those who trained, maintained, and supported each of their flights. In another vein, to paraphrase what Ernest Gann pointed out so well in *Fate Is the Hunter*, it is a recitation of the confluence of good people, good equipment, good training, and good luck.

The Dawson crash had the predictable impact on Braniff's traffic—a temporary and moderate decrease in the load factors, especially those related to Electra flights. But the summer vacation season was on and the public jitters over the propjet faded once again. The "fast buck" campaign ended quietly (all airline advertising for that carrier is suspended traditionally for a decent interval after an accident). There was never any overt causal connection made—nor justified—between Captain Phillips' decision on which route to take and the desire to make a scheduled arrival.[3]

No one associated with the pilot group would have believed for a minute that Phillips would have openly compromised safety for the promotional campaign, yet the desirability of a scheduled arrival probably crossed his mind in those critical decisional microseconds as he looked for acceptable routes on his radarscope.

Harding Lawrence and Ed Acker, neither of them fans of the Electra, couldn't wait to get rid of the propjet fleet. They had been building a fleet of Boeing 727's to replace the Electras, and as 1968 drew to a close, they had some pivotal decisions to make on future flight equipment that could conceivably make or break Braniff.

In early 1969 Braniff received the route award for nonstop Dallas to Honolulu service, which the company started with the Boeing 707-320's—the same long-range, four-engine jetliner it was using for Military Airlift Command (MAC) charter flights in the Pacific. Braniff would need greater seat capacity in the future, however. Even though the rest of the industry was skeptical, Lawrence knew Braniff could assemble enough Hawaii traffic from all over the Midwest and Southwest daily through its Dallas hub to fill a direct flight. (The critics were considering only the traffic that the Dallas-Fort Worth area could generate.) For such a route, then, something more

---

[3] The National Transportation Safety Board, after a lengthy reconstruction of the accident and the aircraft pieces, concluded that the "probable cause" was: " . . . the stressing of the aircraft structure beyond its ultimate strength during an attempted recovery from an unusual attitude induced by turbulence associated with a thunderstorm. The operation in the turbulence resulted from a decision to penetrate an area of known severe weather."

than 130 seats daily would be needed, and the 300-passenger 747 fit the bill. Two of them were ordered for delivery in 1970, but only one was actually accepted and put in service, on January 15, 1971. The second—an all-green 747—was traded back to Boeing for two 727's.

There was a more substantial decision to be made, however, as Braniff phased out the last of its piston fleet and planned the demise of its Electras and BAC-111's. That impending decision concerned a new generation of jumbo jets that many airlines, such as competitors American and Delta, were ordering for future use on domestic routes: the Lockheed 1011 and the Douglas DC-10.[4]

Lawrence appointed a committee within the company to study the aircraft and how they might fit into Braniff's fleet plans, but he was worried about the cost. Although Braniff was becoming more profitable every year, it was still 80 percent owned by LTV, which was in increasingly desperate trouble as a result of its purchase of Jones & Laughlin Steel, and just what LTV might do with or to Braniff was worrisome. In addition, there was a recession looming on the business horizon, and Braniff's traffic predictions were beginning to slip.

When Lawrence assembled all the facts, it appeared that to bypass the 260-passenger "junior jumbos" could be extremely hazardous if the public embraced them with open arms and began choosing such aircraft over flights using the 130-passenger 727. But it also was apparent to Lawrence that to purchase a small fleet of the DC-10's or 1011's would put a heavy strain on the company's financial plan. Harding Lawrence had strict ideas about what his debt-to-equity ratios should be and how much long-term debt should be carried. Such a fleet would put those figures out of limits, although it certainly could have been done if he and his Board decided it was necessary. Regardless of how he would appear a decade later, Lawrence, by his own admission, was a "numbers" man. He was not in the habit of gambling with his company's financial position.

[4] Both the 1011 and the DC-10 are intermediate jumbo jets with three engines (one mounted in the tail section like a 727, the other two under the wings) and a passenger capacity between 250 and 300. When the order books were first opened in the late 1960s, the price tag on this type of jetliner was about $15 million apiece. The price of a 747, on the other hand, was close to $30 million. A Boeing 727, by comparison, cost about $6 million and could carry 130 passengers at the same speeds.

Although the Board could overrule but seldom did (Lawrence's positions and decisions were well discussed and supported), it was principally Harding Lawrence's final decision. After much agonized consideration, he decided to take the more conservative risk and bypass the 1011 and DC-10 in favor of a standardized fleet of Boeing 727's—both the normal and the new stretched 727-200 version. Braniff, he reasoned, could put two 727's on the Dallas to New York run with two departure times and a combined total of 260 seats against a single American Airlines DC-10 with one departure time and 260 seats and do it for just about the same operational cost. In addition, he felt the business traveler would appreciate the convenient choice of departure times more than the crowded jumbos. It would be far less expensive to beef up the 727 fleet than to buy the new equipment. And if he was wrong (as he told his Board), "We can always buy the damn things later. It's getting rid of airplanes you've bought by mistake that's far more dangerous."

Lawrence and Braniff would weather a firestorm of scathing criticism in the industry for failing to buy the new aircraft, but within the next few years it would be Braniff who had the last laugh—all the way to the bank.

In the meantime, however, the go-go image that Braniff had achieved was being damaged by both the failure to purchase the exciting new jumbos and more ominously by the plight of LTV.

By the end of 1969 LTV had slipped in the public eye from the status of an exciting, omnivorous conglomerate busily acquiring and spinning off corporations through the Byzantine planning of its undefeated chairman, James Ling, to that of an embattled house of cards under siege. Since LTV owned over 80 percent of Braniff's stock, Braniff was viewed publicly as merely an arm of LTV. If LTV was in danger of collapsing, to the public it appeared that Braniff must be in danger of collapsing as well.

The climax of LTV's troubles and Braniff's image problems came just six months later, in the summer of 1970, with a palace revolt of sorts in downtown Dallas at the LTV Tower. The change of command that resulted would also change the ownership of Braniff and have far-reaching implications for the airline.

A group of powerful Dallasites, including Braniff Board members Bob Stewart (chief executive officer of First National Bank) and Grant Fitts (chairman of Gulf Life) brought their conspiratorial plans to depose LTV creator Jim Ling to a successful conclusion. Ling had imperiled LTV after the purchase of Troy Post's Greatamerica Corporation by breaking that company up and using the proceeds from the sales of the parts to buy Jones & Laughlin Steel. The "J & L" acquisition was Ling's undoing. Not only had he smashed headlong into a brick wall of eastern resistance and resentment (LTV's and Ling's methods were not well thought of in traditional corporate circles), he had also managed to draw a massive Securities and Exchange Commission antitrust action and lead LTV into a serious cash crunch in 1969. Ling's conglomerate was based on massive cash flow to service the various debts created by all his purchases of other corporations. When the cash level dropped, the price of LTV's stock dropped, and those LTV stocks and other LTV obligations (such as the infamous "Fives of '88") secured a disproportionate number of business loans in Dallas, including those of Troy Post. The chain reaction of events imperiled Post and imperiled Bob Stewart and his First National Bank. Stewart, always a manipulator, joined with Grant Fitts to correct the situation. Ling was removed, Ed Acker (briefly considered as a possible LTV president) joined the LTV Board, and a settlement was concluded with the SEC requiring LTV to divest itself of a corporation called Okonite and an airline called Braniff.

The feeling among Braniff's people during the late 1960s and 1970 was that LTV had been bleeding Braniff of cash and that the loss of cash was causing all the furloughs of Braniff personnel and cutbacks. Although there was some utilization of Braniff's tax credits (since LTV owned more than 80 percent of Braniff, LTV could do such things), there was no proof that LTV was bleeding the Braniff accounts. Braniff's main problem was the image of being an adopted corporate child of a disintegrating giant.[5]

The LTV divestiture would free Lawrence and Braniff from hav-

---

[5] Lawrence and Ling knew each other, but there was no warm, abiding friendship between the two hard-driving men. Ling, in fact, handled Lawrence with great caution. In the years following LTV's acquisition of Greatamerica and Braniff, Ling would complain on several occasions about Lawrence's activities, but almost never to his face. After Mary and Harding's marriage, Ling worried out loud to numerous friends and associates about the apparent potential conflict of interest in having the president of Braniff married to the chairman of the ad agency that took a percentage commission of the airline's ad revenues each year. Lawrence had written his Board members beforehand about the wedding and the potential technical conflict, but there was no complaint. Ling, who didn't join the Board until the January following the marriage (1968), never approached Lawrence directly on the subject. Ling professed to be worried more about the potential for derivative stockholder

ing a single major owner for the first time. It meant the company would now have the freedom to chart its own course in every way—and the future, as Lawrence saw it, was unlimited. Achieving the status of a worldwide airline would simply be a matter of time.

Lawrence, who was now chairman of the Board (Ed Acker had become president when LTV consumed Greatamerica), had basically succeeded in rebuilding Braniff International into an entirely new airline in terms of route structure, profitability, image, and potential. He had not, however, had sufficient time to discover that the senior executives he was trusting to keep the management structure at the middle and lower levels effective and vital were failing him.

Lawrence had never actually ordered his vice-presidents to reorganize and revitalize the middle and lower levels of Braniff management—he assumed that his executives would be aware of the problems and would handle them without his having to do their jobs for them. He was busy with the overall strategic structure, and though he did involve himself in too much of the minutiae, he expected his executives to handle the majority of the internal organizational problems, unaware that too many of them couldn't.[6]

Since the senior staff neglected to tackle the inherited problems in middle and lower management (especially in the service areas of the Dallas operation) and Lawrence did not detect their failure, Braniff's managerial infrastructure continued to weaken. The undesirable nature of being a low-paid, untrained, and unsupported low-level Braniff manager was illustrated all too graphically when the Brotherhood of Railway Clerks union was displaced by the Teamsters, who gave managers who had started as union men the option to return to the protection of the union contract. There was a veritable exodus. The people had received too little training and too little

---

lawsuits, none of which were ever filed. The problem solved itself within a year when WRG resigned the Braniff account and took on TWA in Kansas City.

In another instance, Ling privately professed to be outraged about a new contract request from Lawrence, but despite his powerful position as chairman of LTV, Braniff's parent company, he couldn't bring himself to face Lawrence down. The omnipotent conglomerate builder merely told Lawrence he'd see about it later, then tabled the issue.

[6] Years later in a CAB deposition, Lawrence would describe his need to be able to trust his subordinates to handle the details unassisted: "But a lot of things are done that I don't know about—that are marvelous, and I encourage them on it; but we do have a very effective group of people, they have tremendous latitudes of authority—if they would come to me with a decision on everything that goes on, then I would not have them, they would not make themselves available, nor would I work for anybody where I had to take everything to them."

support to feel any sense of permanency as managers, and they wanted no further part of it.

To the many Braniff people who had joined at the lowest levels and had plans to move up into management someday, the arrival of the Teamsters and the resulting turbulence was disturbing (though Lawrence welcomed the change from the hardened "work rules" attitude of the BRC). There was an influx of new managers to take the place of those who had returned to the union-protected positions, but too many of them were hired without the proper screening or qualifications, no experience, little if any training, and low pay. At the same time, there was still a core of pre-1965 lower and middle managers throughout the company who had adjusted just enough to the new regime to survive but who had not and would never be qualified for their positions. These people, plus the newly hired managerial people, were pitted against what would be several years of growing militancy on the part of certain already disgruntled union members, many of them longtime employees—men and women whose attitudes were destined to calcify into near-hatred of Braniff. In all too many cases when rank-and-file Braniff employees complained of having to put up with horrible managers, their complaints were justified.[7]

[7] The people in middle and lower managerial positions who could not handle their jobs or their people were in the majority in the operational areas of Braniff's Love Field in Dallas and later DFW Airport, but in the minority in other areas of the company. Especially in the outlying stations all over the United States there were a host of fine, accomplished managers who performed with the highest professionalism over the years. The incapable ones, however, had a tremendous effect throughout the company.

A Pretty Expensive Game

It was March 1, 1972, and the election-year excitement of the presidential race was already permeating Washington, D.C. as Harding Lawrence entered the headquarters of the Committee to Re-elect the President—Richard Nixon's fund-raising headquarters.

Braniff, as all major U.S. airlines, "lived" at the pleasure of the Civil Aeronautics Board, whose members were political appointees. The widespread perception within the Nixon circles in Washington had been that from 1968 on, Harding Lawrence of Braniff was a staunch supporter of Democrats.

There wasn't supposed to be a correlation between such an onus and CAB route awards, but in the reality of Dick Nixon's Washington, such a reputation was damaging. The fact that Braniff's route system was suddenly being subjected to additional, costly competition at the behest of the CAB may have been an independent, coincidental development—but no one accustomed to the political games in the nation's capital, or familiar with the insular attitude of the Nixon administration, would believe that. Neither, for that matter, did Lawrence nor Ed Acker.

The re-election of President Nixon seemed a sure bet. Lawrence and Acker both wanted Braniff thought of by the Nixon people as a company filled with Nixon supporters (which, in fact, it was). Accomplishing that image was worth $5,000 of personal money apiece.

As Lawrence walked into the "CREEP" headquarters, he was carrying $10,000 in cash—perfectly legal, individual political contributions, which he proceeded to give to Maurice Stans when ushered into his office.

Stans quickly counted the money and looked up at Lawrence

with a slightly hurt expression. "We sure appreciate this very much, but—uh—you know, Harding, politics is a pretty expensive game these days. We've been having to spend a bundle to get the message out—to combat these Democrat inroads into the President's record. We were kind of hoping that you folks—you and your wife, for instance—could do a lot more."

Lawrence was astonished. Neither he nor Ed Acker had ever given so much money to a political campaign before, and Stans wasn't even appreciative despite his words.

Stans went on. "You know, we've got some people giving a hundred thousand, a hundred fifty thousand—and we need every cent of it."

"Well, we're, you know"—Lawrence interjected a small, rueful chuckle—"we're poor folks down there in Texas compared with those hundred-thousand-dollar people . . . just peanut farmers and all, Maurice. We just can't go into anything like that."

Stans fixed him with a friendly gaze and smiled as he held out his hand to bid Lawrence good-bye. "Well, see what you can do for me, okay?"

"All right, I sure will."

"We'd like to have you on the team."

Lawrence left Washington for Miami on the next leg of a packed business trip. Stans had made him feel like a cheapskate, and for $5,000—$10,000, counting Ed's money. The response was incredible!

When the Braniff chairman returned to Dallas headquarters on March 4, he and Acker talked over the situation. Acker was equally amazed.

Bob Burck, vice president for public affairs who handled a wide assortment of political liaison affairs for the company, was called in as well, and the three men over the period of the next few days decided "Braniff's" contribution would be $50,000, of which $10,000 had already been paid. Lawrence and Acker left to Burck the problem of getting the extra $40,000 before April 6, 1972. On that date a new reporting law was to go into effect, and they didn't want a public airing of any contributions.

The initial $10,000 had been perfectly legal. What happened next was not. Burck enlisted Vice President for Operations John Casey, who huddled with Vice President for Latin American Division Charles South, who in turn made arrangements with Regional

Vice President for Panama Camilo Fabrega, who sent a courier north from Panama City with the $40,000 in U.S. currency. On April 6, 1972, Harding Lawrence, Ed Acker, and Bob Burck walked into Stans's office in Washington and delivered the extra contribution in cash. The Braniff men had no intention of letting Braniff be "on the outs" with the Nixon administration.

The problem was, the $40,000 was corporate money, and corporate campaign contributions were illegal.[1]

Forty thousand dollars should leave a hole in the corporate books rather difficult to hide. Somehow John Casey, Charlie South, and Camilo Fabrega had done it—and rapidly. (Lawrence would profess later that he thought the company had taken out a bank loan that individual officers would repay later—making the $40,000 personal contributions.) Casey, in fact, had created an account receivable entry in Braniff's books for $40,000—money supposedly due from a personal holding company (CAMFAB) in Panama owned by Fabrega. Casey had then caused a Braniff check to be issued to Fabrega and listed as an "advance for expenses and services" for $40,000—which Fabrega had cashed, sending the money north by courier. There was no bank loan.

Ah, but where in South America did Braniff generate the money to repay CAMFAB's $40,000 "debt" to Braniff's accounts? The question arose in the minds of several people close to isolated portions of the operation who, at the time, had no idea what was going on. The answer would be the genesis for the onslaught of a consumer complaint and a grandiose CAB enforcement action three years later in the wake of Watergate—a complaint that would bring to light a system of off-the-books tickets used to combat ruinous, illicit competition from foreign carriers in South America and used in this isolated instance to repay CAMFAB's debit on the Braniff books.

Back during 1969 the highly successful expansion program at Braniff had begun to slip as a recession gripped the country. Braniff

---

[1] The contribution would be repaid a year later by individual Braniff officers as personal contributions—after the company got in trouble. Braniff was by no means the only airline to make such "contributions." American Airlines, for instance, also ended up in an unwelcome spotlight as a result of such a move. As Harding Lawrence would say later on, "We weren't the only ones in the whorehouse—so to speak!"

still ended the year with a profit, but at $6.2 million it was less than half of what Lawrence had told Jim Ling (at cash-strapped LTV) that Braniff would produce. The predictions of traffic and profit were changing by the week (the same uncertainty that would face Lawrence ten years later) as Braniff watched as much as $45 million in potential revenue drained away by additional competition on previously protected routes and watched the recession eat away at the number of discretionary travelers.

Lawrence had weathered the storm by playing both chief executive and his favorite role of teacher, showing his senior team how to batten down the corporate ship for the recessionary gale ahead. He had been through four previous recessions at Pioneer and Continental and knew well what was required. The most visible result was contraction: Braniff shrank from thirteen thousand employees to just over ten thousand during the period (Delta is the only major carrier in the industry who protects its people during cutbacks and tries never to furlough. Braniff—like most—would furlough people without blinking.) The rank and file were already working amid the confusion of a new union (the Teamsters); new, untrained managers; and constant expansionary changes. Suddenly they were also faced with contractions, furloughs, and dislocations.[2]

Though no one in the senior group was happy with the necessity of furloughs, few paid any attention to the human impact of the resulting turbulence, or the managerial impact. The resentment in the ranks of agents, mechanics, pilots, and flight attendants alike at being thrown out of a job without so much as a letter of sympathy planted seeds of discontent that would haunt Braniff for years. The fact that thousands of corporations take the same callous attitude didn't ameliorate the effect on Braniff's people.

The recession was centered in North America, but there was also a monstrous problem eating away at Braniff's new, combined South American operation. The competing foreign carriers were leaching

[2] Under a union seniority system, when the company eliminates positions at one station, anyone who loses his position in a particular "base" or "station" can relocate to another city and "bump" a worker junior to him, who can also go somewhere else and "bump" someone more junior, and so on until the lowest man is forced out on furlough. Although it protects those who have been with the company longer than others, the system can create massive disruption in families and life-styles. Most large companies—Braniff and Lawrence included—look on such problems as self-generated. In other words, those who demand a union and a seniority system must live with the results.

away Braniff's business by bribing the travel agents with extra commissions—brokering seats on unfilled aircraft at any price they could get—giving away a host of complimentary extras to the travel agents and others in the industry and in local government, and in doing all this, flagrantly violating IATA rules.[3]

From a profitable year in 1968, Braniff's South American operation had slipped into the red in 1969. Something had to be done.

Braniff had taken the right course even before acquiring Panagra in setting up South America—it had hired South Americans to run the operation and provide the cabin crews for the aircraft (the pilots were regular Braniff pilots—all North Americans). The indigenous managers and regional vice presidents knew what it took to survive in their own countries, so when carriers such as Aerolineas Argentinas and APSA began courting the travel agency business in violation of IATA rules, the Braniff people in South America understood the challenge and what would be required to meet it.

Tom Braniff and Chuck Beard had been faced with such problems years before. The South American and North American views of what constituted monetary morality are different, but Tom Braniff and Chuck Beard had a strict, unbreakable rule against using money to change opinions (outside of advertising). Their rules kept Braniff "clean as a hound's tooth" but an outsider in the ways of the South American business world.

In 1968, however, Braniff and Panagra's merger was too much for the competing foreign carriers to accept, so they determined to run Braniff out. By 1969, numerous alarms had been relayed to Charlie South in Dallas, who in turn was keeping John Casey updated on the problem. The Braniff group tried everything it could think of—including IATA complaints and direct pleas to the offending carriers to cut it out, as well as many rebuffed requests to the U.S. government for help. Nothing had worked. Finally, in mid-1969, South and Casey went to Executive Vice President Ed Acker with a plan. The meeting lasted about fifteen minutes, was quite

[3] The Geneva-based International Aviation Traffic Association is essentially a legal cartel, which before the late 1970s wielded tremendous power in setting fares and competitive rules throughout the world in international travel. For a member carrier to violate the IATA rules would mean stiff fines that the carrier would have to pay. Unfortunately, the lack of legal power akin to the U.S. CAB's power in American airspace prevented IATA sanctions from forcing an end to the sort of abuses Braniff was facing.

informal—and did not include a specific outline of what they planned to do. They had a problem, they thought they knew how to fix it, and they could do so without getting the company in trouble. Acker approved without further explanation. His most serious worry was about violating IATA rules, since he didn't think they could end up in violation of U.S. law in playing the same game of extra commissions. Ed Acker wasn't enthusiastic about abandoning Braniff's traditional clean reputation, but the bottom line had to be put back in order.

What resulted was a system of off-the-books tickets issued to the South American stations and sold to raise the cash necessary to fund the extra commissions, paid transportation, and other incentives paid to the South American travel agents, who then began to turn back to Braniff. Over the next four years the program raised nearly $750,000, which increased Braniff's revenue in South America by at least $13 million during the same period. Acker was told no more details, and Lawrence wasn't told at all.

In July 1973, at the height of the Watergate investigations, the federal hounds closing in on Richard Nixon's administration and rooting out the dark corporate wrongdoing associated with the re-election campaign were presented with the voluntary disclosure by Braniff that the $40,000 payment had been made—and subsequently, just that summer, refunded to the company by various "contributing" executives. The company was charged with a misdemeanor, and Lawrence along with Braniff pleaded guilty and paid fines of $1,000 and $5,000, respectively. Unfortunately for Braniff, that was only the beginning.

That "debit" owed by CAMFAB in Panama to Braniff to cover the $40,000 hole had been repaid by the sale of off-the-books tickets—a special batch sent to Camilo Fabrega specifically for that purpose and not connected with the anticompetitive practices campaign as such. As soon as that information surfaced in the resulting CAB probe, the question was certain to arise: If Panama, then where else? It was just a matter of time, and sure enough, the small incendiary "bomb" exploded in the self-flagellistic post-Watergate witch-hunts sweeping Washington in 1974 and 1975 (the national *mea culpa* orgy of purity crusades featuring legions of righteous young people out to eradicate hypocrisy for all time in the business world).

A Ralph Nader enterprise known as the "Aviation Consumer

68

Action Project" had been hovering over the CAB's proceedings like a stern Puritan, intent on rooting out miscreants in the system. On January 30, 1974, they filed a lengthy complaint against Braniff with the CAB, detailing the $40,000 transaction. The CAB initiated a major investigation. Braniff's executives, including Ed Acker, tried not to present the CAB with road maps to the Braniff anticompetitive practices campaign, which had by then been terminated. Within the bounds of sworn testimony, they attempted to paint the CAMFAB transaction and the tickets sold to cover it as a totally isolated instance. The investigators, however, found the right questions to ask, and the entire anthology began to unfold. Lawrence and his people thought at the end of the CAB's initial probe that the damage control had been effective and that the CAB would accept their promise not to repeat such ticket programs and leave it there. On March 12, 1975, however, the CAB's Enforcement Division filed a major action against Braniff that they fed in condensed detail to the press, charging widespread violation and falsification of CAB reports and, in effect, asked the CAB to consider opening a route case to parcel out Braniff's South American routes to other carriers, or in the alternative, revoke Braniff's certificate to operate as a scheduled air carrier.[4]

Lawrence and his senior people were thunderstruck. They had never anticipated such a broadside. Lawrence ordered a complete internal investigation into all that had transpired, "day by day, memo by memo" to get to the bottom of it. He had, he said, not found out about the anticompetitive practice campaign until August 1974. Acker had never told him.

---

[4] As any aviation attorney in Washington knows, such language is excessive—but common nonetheless. Whatever the ultimate result of the complaint, Braniff's people weren't likely to be put out of work because of misconduct of the management (if there had been such). The public and the press, however, often do not understand such things. To the average citizen it seemed, as reported eagerly by the media, that the CAB had caught Braniff in a nefarious and illicit plot involving bribery and corruption in South America, and Braniff was likely to be put out of business as a result. It was another classic example of how the media can overstate the effective implications of a governmental legal action and, by so doing, create great public-relations damage for a possibly innocent company containing thousands of totally innocent Americans. It was an equally classic example of how effectively the consumer organizations and the overly zealous among enforcement divisions of federal agencies can inflict far more damage with a public announcement of an action than with the action itself. In such a "contest," the targeted company is adjudged guilty in the public eye *because of* being charged.

The real tragedy highlighted by all that transpired was the painting of the ticket scandal, which was essentially a self-defensive effort, in the darkest, most evil terms. Wrongdoing should certainly be disclosed or prosecuted when it is genuinely illegal, but American corporations dealing abroad are not necessarily dealing with competitor companies or people in foreign governments who share our national structure of ethics and legal constraints on what we call bribery. It is difficult, if not sometimes impossible, to be successful in competing in such foreign trade while acting in accordance with accepted standards and legal constraints in the United States.

In addition, Braniff's position of having been forced to resort to self-help pointed up how terribly neglected it had been as an American business in need of assistance by its own government. In a decade of growing concern of balance-of-payments deficits in the United States—a true fear that U.S. businessmen were failing to make the effort to compete abroad—a plea for help in enforcing the same business moral standards Braniff would later be tarred for violating went unheeded by the CAB, the State Department, Congress, and the White House. Braniff was left to solve the problem alone and then threatened with corporate extinction when it did just that.

As the CAB's zealous young attorneys in the Enforcement Division eagerly jumped on the case, Braniff found itself in the middle of an exasperating battle. What was more ominous, however, was the loss of political position. Harding Lawrence understood political reality very well indeed. His understanding (as well as that of Ed Acker—less experienced but astute nonetheless) had prompted them to want to "get on the team" with the Nixon administration. Now, with a Democratic administration looming ahead as a possibility at the end of Gerald Ford's term, Lawrence and Braniff were tarred with the image of having been Nixon supporters and Watergate-era offenders—and this when Lawrence's master plan for a worldwide route system depended on the largess of the government and the White House.

In all other respects Braniff had been doing wonderfully, with consistently improving profitability, a decreasing debt-to-equity ratio, and operating revenues that had topped $500 million per year by the end of 1974. What's more, Braniff's fuel contract, negotiated on a long-term basis at a slightly higher-than-industry-average cost in 1973 to the amusement of the rest of the industry, had given the airline the fuel to fly through the dark days of the Yom Kippur War and the Arab oil embargo with surplus fuel. Other airlines cut flights while Braniff added them. In the recession of 1973–74, Lawrence's decision to standardize his fleet with the 727 and forsake the junior jumbos proved to be a masterstroke—other airlines' DC-10's, 1011's, and 747's were being parked in Arizona and New Mexico storage areas for lack of use, and even his old carrier, Continental, was in deep trouble trying to get rid of their surplus big jets.

To sail through a period that had seriously imperiled a host of other major airlines and then be assaulted with such an enforcement action by the CAB was extremely upsetting. Lawrence consulted with all his Board members, filling them in at great length on what had actually transpired in South America, and he and the Board appointed an outside accounting firm to provide an independent audit. There was always the worry that someone could be "ripping off" Braniff internally.

Lawrence had almost relaxed his workaholic schedule several times during the period of 1971–74, thinking he had his senior executives sufficiently well trained to handle things and secure in the knowledge that Ed Acker was on the job. Now, however, Lawrence jumped back in with a vengeance. Clearly the alarm bells had rung.

Little Room for Error

CHAPTER **8** There are, as yet, few if any "South Americans." There are Colombians, Peruvians, Chileans, Argentines, and Brazilians. You'll also find Ecuadorians and Bolivians, Paraguayans and Uruguayans, but almost no residents of our huge neighboring continent to the south who will characterize themselves as part of a common political confederation—or even regional confederation—known as "South Americans." There is a great measure of nationalistic pride in the people of most of the various nations on the South American continent, and while they may appear to the uninitiated tourist to be merely one grand repository of natives in their "quaint and colorful costumes," they are in fact separated by wide gulfs. This also means that the people in each such nation, bound by their own history, ancestry, and cultural threads, in many cases running farther back into the mists of history than ours, simply cannot understand why their sometimes arrogant brethren to the north insist that they, North Americans, possess the true faith when the subject of ethics— especially ethics in the affairs of money, government, and enterprise—is broached. The truth is, the United States' attitude against the use of money to influence other people directly, especially those in official positions, is an attitude shared by only some of the European countries, Japan, Canada, and a scattering of others. It is not necessarily the true faith of this planet. Just as we are free to practice our ways, they are free to practice their ways, whether it creates moral difficulties for our companies or not.

Of all the cultural, legal, and bureaucratic differences a U.S. business must deal with in South American nations, the local tax systems present one of the thorniest challenges. If an airline such as Braniff made too much profit, there was both a tax system and an overabundance of outstretched hands waiting to take their not-so-insubstantial share. Therefore, it was not terribly smart to show too large a profit in any South American station. This is not to suggest that reports to host foreign governments should be falsified but to point out the wide latitude of choice available under the acceptable (CAB-approved) method of airline accounting for such an airline to make its own decisions regarding the allocation of nonoperating expenses.

Operating expenses involve the cost of fuel, the cost of the crews, the ticket counter personnel, the meals, the fees, or any other expense that can be attributable to the flight operations of the airline. Nonoperating expenses include such things as the cost of the headquarters operation and many other categories not directly related to operating, marketing, or supporting the company's flights. In a system such as Braniff's, with a domestic and an international division as separate elements, certain portions of the nonoperating expenses generated in North America can be attributable legitimately to the administration of South America. How an airline decides what percentage to use for such allocated expenses is their business as long as it bears some relationship to reason. Braniff's people were masters in knowing how much to allocate to South America to show a profit, but not too much profit.

It was as a result of this practice that South America, the one division of the airline that could generate tremendous profits because of the high fare structure, would appear on paper to be a loser. To the man who would come riding to the attempted rescue of the airline eight years later—a man who admitted he knew nothing of South America and did not have time to learn—the entire operation was an albatross. The decision he would make based on nearly fourteen years of supressed-profit reporting (and his predetermined prejudice against international operations) was destined to do irreversible damage to the company and the many years of expertise that had gone into building the safest airline operation over the South American continent.

That safety record was not easily achieved. Braniff's South American system pilots had to contend with less-developed airports, air traffic control personnel of questionable competency, language barriers (English is used in international flying throughout the world, but local accents often destroy the ability to understand the local controllers), and—worst of all—the mighty Andes, one of the most spectacular chains of mountains on Earth. The Andes mountain range runs from Tierra Del Fuego at the southern tips of Argentina and Chile to the Caribbean—a distance of nearly 4,500 miles—with peaks above 20,000 feet in some areas. That one factor of altitude has always been the most dangerous aspect of South American flying. In the days of propeller-driven airliners, just getting over the mountains from east to west was a problem, but that was largely solved with the high-performance capabilities of modern jetliners that can cruise above 30,000 feet. Operating through high-altitude airports, however, will always remain a challenge—and airports such as 8,000-foot Bogotá, 9,000-foot Quito, and the highest commercial airport in the world, at 13,404 feet overlooking La Paz, Bolivia, had been served by Braniff for thirty years.

High-altitude airports are inherently dangerous. That may be considered an axiom in aviation. It doesn't matter how long or how well constructed the runway or how good the electronic navigation and approach equipment, a high-altitude airport is an open invitation to disaster, especially in the face of any inattention by the flight crew.

The basic reason for this is that the air is thinner, meaning that fewer air molecules exist in a given space than at a lower level. Thus, in order to achieve flight, a fixed-wing aircraft (which must have a given volume of air molecules moving over its wings' surface in a given period of time) must move faster through that more rarefied air in relation to the ground to build up enough lift to enable it to leave the ground and achieve sustained flight. Not only do the higher ground speeds create a problem, but higher temperatures in summer months are a problem as well, spreading the effective molecular concentration farther and raising even higher the effective speed required (this is called density altitude—the higher the temperature, the higher the density altitude). When there has been a disturbance of the air in the vicinity due to weather, such as a thunderstorm, the changes in airspeed that can occur to a large aircraft on takeoff or landing can cause wind shear, which can be far more difficult to react to and fly through safely than the same problem at sea level. (As the 1982 tragedy of the Pan Am crash in New Orleans demonstrated, wind shear can be lethal at sea level; at high altitude it is magnified.)

El Alto Airport, on the altiplano (high plains) just west of La Paz, Bolivia, is, as mentioned, 13,404 feet above sea level. Jet engines accelerate slower at those elevations—it takes longer to build up airspeed—and the difference in the response to the controls of a heavy four-engine jetliner such as the DC-8-62 is remarkable. Whereas at lower altitudes the response is very quick to any control input—any movement of the control column by the pilot—at La Paz at approach speed it is very mushy—somewhat like the difference between driving a car on an ice-covered road (with the tendency to fishtail), and the feel of a car on a dry surface.

On takeoff from El Alto, a DC-8-62 cannot be loaded to the same weight it can handle at sea level, because even with a 13,000-foot runway (nearly 2½ miles long), if the aircraft is heavily loaded there isn't enough room to accelerate it to a high enough speed to enable it to lift off safely from the runway surface and sustain flight.

In fact, although the DC-8-62 at the sea-level elevation of Lima, Peru, can lift over 330,000 pounds (a full load of passengers and baggage and enough fuel to fly nonstop to Los Angeles), at La Paz the maximum weight, depending on temperature and a few other variables, is down to around 220,000 pounds. There is, however, one more critical point: the airspeeds. V1, which stands for Velocity 1, is the speed at which the aircraft is technically committed to the takeoff. After that speed it is presumed to be going too fast to stop safely in the remaining runway distance. It's used as a dividing line between the point in the takeoff at which a problem—engine malfunction, electrical problem, or otherwise—might justify an aborted takeoff, and the portion of the takeoff after V1 in which almost nothing would justify trying to stop, because of the calamitous certainty of leaving the runway surface at the far end while still on the ground.

VR stands for velocity of rotation. A jetliner is suspended on three main wheel assemblies. In most jetliners, as in most jet aircraft, merely rushing down the runway at and above flying speed won't cause the aircraft to leave the runway. There will be lift on the wings sufficient to support most of the aircraft's weight, but more lift will be needed to begin a healthy climb into the air. To climb, the wing surface needs to be canted upward at a higher angle than it has when the aircraft's nose wheel is on the runway along with the main wheels. To get that wing angle higher, the nose has to be lifted off the surface of the runway, and that can be done only when there is sufficient forward velocity over the ground—and thus sufficient air flowing over the tail surface (the elevator)—to give the pilot the control effectiveness to pull back on the yoke and cause sufficient downward pressure on the tail, which in turn causes the nose to lift up and the wings to attain a greater angle—which increases the lift. This manuever is called rotation. That VR speed is the optimum speed (not too fast, not too slow) at which the pilot should begin pulling back on the yoke (the control column) of the aircraft, to lift the nose wheel off the runway and cause the increase in lift that will in turn cause the aircraft to lift off and achieve sustained flight.

Those speeds are vitally important even at sea-level airports. If the pilot rotates at too low a speed, he increases the aerodynamic "drag" on the aircraft and sets up a situation in which he will need more distance to attain flying speed. If he rotates too late, he will have traveled farther down the runway than was necessary. Therefore there is a middle ground, and it is the flight engineer who calculates in his charts the optimum speed at which to rotate, the VR.[1]

At El Alto, calculation of the exact rotation speed can be a matter of life and death. The distances required are magnified, and if a DC-8 is rotated 15 knots too soon (at 115, say, rather than at 130), it may cause the runway required to be greater than the length of the runway remaining—meaning that the aircraft may not be off the

[1] On Braniff, as with most U.S. airlines, the second officer/flight engineer is always a pilot.

ground when the last of the concrete passes under the main wheel assemblies.

All this is predictable, and all of Braniff's flight crews and second officers in particular were extensively trained on the vital importance of getting those figures exactly right, from the correct page of the performance manual, and then rechecking to make certain the figures were correct. In addition, at La Paz, the captain or first officer was also charged with the responsibility of checking over the flight engineer's work, and on top of all of those precautions stood the comforting fact that the vast majority of the Braniff pilots operating the South American flights were very experienced in that area and, based on that experience, would have a gut instinct of what the speeds should be for a given weight. Therefore, if the captain was given a data card with a significantly incorrect speed on it, he would almost always know, instantly, that it was wrong.

With such experience and checks and balances and training and professionalism, Braniff operated routinely in and out of the highest, most dangerous (in terms of altitude problems) airport in the world.

There is one more problem with high-altitude airports—the need of the human body for oxygen. At about 13,000 feet, for one not used to living in such rarefied air, a slight degree of hypoxia (reduced awareness and judgment resulting from too little oxygen to the brain) usually occurs after about thirty minutes.

Braniff's pilots were required to breathe 100 percent oxygen from thirty minutes prior to departure from La Paz, regardless of how they felt. The reason centers around the fact that different people will be affected in different ways, but without the use of on-board oxygen a pilot can become sufficiently hypoxic (and be sufficiently unaware of it) to make significant mistakes reading his charts and checking them. One night in 1974, that is precisely what occurred.

The 220,000-pound Braniff DC-8 (at its maximum weight for this altitude), bound for Lima under a canopy of stars in the most crystal-clear night sky imaginable, rolled onto the first section of the runway with the flaps properly set at 12 degrees and advanced power. The captain, copilot, and flight engineer had been on the ground about an hour and didn't feel they needed to breathe any oxygen before departure. They were feeling fine and sharp and had been here many times before.

A small piece of paper called a data card and containing the numbers for the takeoff rested on the center pedestal in front of the throttles, over one of the radio control heads—the place the crews normally kept it. As the speed built up and the airspeed indicator on the captain's panel came off the peg, he glanced down and re-checked his V1 and rotation speeds, which the copilot was to call out when reached. As it indicated on the data card, at 122 knots of airspeed (over 145 knots of ground speed) the copilot called "Ro-tate," and the captain pulled back on the yoke.

The aircraft felt much heavier than usual; the response to the pull on the yoke was minimal, but finally he managed to get it into about an 8-degree nose-high attitude. And there it stayed.

They had used up over 9,000 feet of runway, and the red lights marking the end of the 13,000-foot strip of concrete were coming up fast—at over 165 miles per hour. The DC-8 was still rolling along on its main wheels, nose reared up into the air at an 8-degree angle, airspeed indicator now hovering just above 120 knots, and not ac-celerating. The captain pulled harder, bringing the nose up a bit farther. Still the red lights grew brighter—and the main wheels stayed on the ground. The heartbeats of all three men quickened slightly, but at such a tense moment, the problems at hand are han-dled quickly but routinely. There is no time for panic, even if that were the normal response of a seasoned airline pilot to a rapidly deteriorating situation—which it is not.

There was now less than 1,000 feet of runway left. The nose was as high as 9 degrees, the indicated airspeed still around 120, and the main wheels were still on the ground. Nothing but blackness seemed to exist to the west of the two red marker lights—nothing but the blackness of the altiplano, fortunately flat as a West Texas pasture between the end of the concrete and the shores of Lake Titicaca 10 miles to the west.

Just as the red lights disappeared from view, the captain did the only thing there was left to do—he pulled hard on the yoke and "yanked" the nose of the giant airliner as high as he could without contacting the tail skid.

As the last vestige of concrete passed beneath the wheels, they had gained a couple of feet of altitude, enough to clear the red lights at the end—but no more. The aircraft was now airborne in "ground effect," a cushion of air compressed by the huge mass of metal screaming across it and tenuously holding it above the surface.

At the captain's command "Gear Up," the copilot reached up with his left hand and raised the gear handle. The huge gear doors on the main gear opened, increasing the drag momentarily and canceling any acceleration as they hung suspended over—nothing. There was nothing visible in front of them in the blackness.

The gear thudded into place on the uplocks and the doors closed at last. The captain was holding as high a deck angle as he dared, watching the airspeed finally, slowly, begin to increase, watching the vertical velocity indicator (rate of climb) and keeping it slightly positive, and watching the radio altimeter (an extremely precise instrument that gives the altitude of the aircraft above the surface with accuracy better than plus or minus 2 feet) showing first almost nothing, then 10 feet—moving ever so slowly upward.

The 220,000-pound machine full of people and baggage and fuel was now screaming along barely off the ground over the flat Bolivian terrain, barely clearing unseen fences and small rises in the landscape, caught in a position in which the deck angle was so high, and the resulting drag so great, that even the thrust of all four engines at maximum power was barely able to keep the airspeed from dropping. The aircraft was leaving a wake of dust and dirt behind it as it skimmed over the ground.

Finally it began to accelerate and gain 20—then 30—then 40 feet. The captain relaxed his back pressure ever so slightly and let the nose drop a tiny bit, which lowered the drag coefficient and made the thrust of the straining turbojet engines greater than the overall drag—and at that moment he knew they would make it.

As the climb-out finally became normal and the DC-8 passed through 2,000 feet above the surface with flaps retracted, the effect of the adrenaline began to overpower the slight hypoxia that had influenced them, and with limbs beginning to shake slightly (and an oblivious load of passengers who never suspected a thing was wrong, never suspected they had almost been in the middle of a monstrous aircraft accident), they yanked out the books and recalculated the speeds.

There it was. For the weight and the temperature, 140 knots was VR. They had horsed it off 18 knots early, and nearly, well . . . The prospect of what would have become of their craft settling down in the dirt on the other side of those lights at 165 miles per hour was too frightening to go into. All three of them knew that if the captain had been too abrupt—dropped one ounce of back pressure after they had lifted off or increased it any—they would be on the ground right now. But his skill deserved mixed accolades—he had checked the airspeeds without oxygen back at the ramp, too. All that skill, all that experience had canceled out a simple but potentially fatal mistake. At Lima the craft would have stagnated a bit on speed, then gone right on with the takeoff. At La Paz, the margins were so thin, there was little room for error—the error they had made.

Braniff had operated in South America for decades and had never had a fatal accident. The experience Braniff had gained—the position it maintained as the largest U.S. carrier on the South American continent—constituted assets of almost inestimable value (especially the Braniff South American employees). Within a few years, however, they would be thrown away for a few million dollars.

Since the initial shock had worn off in 1966, Dallasites were used to seeing the bold colors of Braniff's aircraft slicing cleanly through the sky over the city, but the strange apparition that had rolled out of the Braniff hangar on Lemmon Avenue in the fall of 1973 was the wildest color scheme anyone in the area had ever seen—and another example of Harding Lawrence's drive to instill style in every possible corner of the operation.

Alexander Calder, the modern artist who invented the stabile and the mobile as art forms, had been persuaded by Braniff to use a DC-8 as a "canvas"—to create a flying work of art to celebrate Braniff's South American service. The artist worked on models of the DC-8 for six months for a $100,000 fee before presenting Braniff with a wild, colorful design of bright-colored circles and ellipses along with some more esoteric doodlings for the engine cowlings. The design was transferred to ship number 1805, with no mention of Braniff's name on the surface of the aircraft. The name "Calder" appeared in script, however, just aft of the nose. The idea was a moderate success as a gift of sorts to South America, where it flew in those colors throughout the Braniff South American system for the following seven years.

Style was more than an advertising concept to Harding Lawrence and Mary Wells Lawrence. It was a way of life. The colorful, fashionable style of high living on two continents with homes in Arizona, Dallas, Acapulco (Braniff-owned), New York, and their palace on the southern coast of France, combined with Mary's position as chairman of Wells Rich Greene and Harding's chairmanship of Braniff International, made them pacesetters—a storybook couple—jet-setters (in the language of the day). Just as Mary sought to keep her company stylish as well as profitable, her dynamic husband was determined to raise Braniff to an unchallenged position in style of service, style of equipment, and style of attitude.[2]

Consistent with the Lawrences' goal for Braniff's image, one of the ad campaigns launched in 1969 was built around the theme "If you've got it—flaunt it!" The chairman and his wife may have had "it," but Braniff didn't quite have "it" together. By the beginning of 1975 the problems still festering and unaddressed in the lower- and middle-management ranks were creating inconsistent service that kept the complaint levels high and continually blocked Lawrence's attempts to have his people deliver what the company's advertising was promising: the best airline service in the world.

Also in 1975, on September 30, and much to Lawrence's dismay, Ed Acker submitted his resignation as president of both Braniff Airways, Inc., the airline, and the new holding company that had been set up to hold all the stock of Braniff Airways, Braniff International, Inc. In March 1976, a proposed agreement for a consent decree was reached between Braniff and the CAB to conclude the off-the-books ticket problem for a $300,000 fine, thus settling the issue. The timing was very suspicious, and the rumor that Acker had "taken the fall"—resigned as a sacrifice to the CAB so they would settle the enforcement action—would persist for years. Acker, however, maintained that he simply wanted to run his own company, and at Braniff that wouldn't be possible for some time, since Harding Lawrence and Braniff seemed inseparable. As a result, Acker decided to move on, and he accepted the presidency of Transway International in New York. The lingering doubts over the years of just what his motivation for leaving really was have been fueled by

[2] In fact, Lawrence honestly felt that he was spending more money on maintaining a style in the best interests of Braniff than he was collecting in the form of his $300,000 annual salary. Although such sentiment was likely to be greeted with scorn by many of his employees (who felt he was enjoying the good life at their, and the company's, expense), Lawrence's incredibly dedicated work schedule and his twenty-four-hour-a-day role as the prime representative of Braniff was extremely helpful in regaining and maintaining political and business favor over the years as well as setting the Braniff "image." In many respects, Lawrence *was* Braniff. His always-on approach to his stewardship of the company created a sort of corporate *"L'état c'est moi"*—in the language commonly attributed to Louis XIV.

the fact that going from the presidency of Braniff—even under a strong chairman such as Lawrence—to the presidency of a company such as Transway was a step down. Despite the appearances, the CAB action (which Lawrence was angrily prepared to fight with a vengeance) wasn't settled as a direct result of Ed Acker's departure, but Acker knew his leaving would make things easier. He also had to know that the CAB's enforcement staff was determined to get him or Lawrence or both. If they succeeded, one of the likely penalties would be forced removal from an executive position with any certificated carrier for several years. Acker's departure from Braniff could be seen as unrelated, or could be read as the sage and prudent move of a superlative executive who might be preserving his option to return voluntarily to the airline business by voluntarily leaving it at the right moment.

Suddenly Lawrence was on his own. Braniff was essentially its own company, and with Ed Acker gone, the last vestige of connection to Greatamerica and LTV seemed to go with him. Moreover, Lawrence's source of internal executive control (on which he had always been able to rely) as well as his most trusted source of financial advice was also gone. Lawrence alone would have to move the airline toward the worldwide system he had envisioned and groom some of the other senior executives to move into Ed Acker's shoes. Harding Lawrence had no way of knowing that neither his nor Ed Acker's shoes could be filled.

Strategic Decisions

CHAPTER **9** Harding Lawrence had been in the ornate hearing room before, but he'd never been the star attraction. The Aviation Subcommittee of the Senate Commerce Committee had picked this Thursday afternoon, June 17, 1976, to continue its hearings on the Kennedy-Cannon airline deregulation proposal. Senator Ted Kennedy was more or less an interloper in the proposal. He had come in to put his name on the legislation after Senator Howard Cannon had developed it.

A long line of airline executives including Lawrence had been invited to Washington to give their viewpoints on why the current regulatory system with the Civil Aeronautics Board in control should or should not be retained, and to what degree the protected route system should be opened to free competition. Kennedy and Cannon—both Democrats—were having a delightful time stealing a traditionally Republican point of view: the advocacy of less governmental interference with business. The proposal, however, was scaring the hell out of most established sections of the industry— with the notable exception of United Airlines.

The specter of deregulation had Lawrence very worried. In its purest form, deregulation would allow free route entry and exit and quick certification for any new company that wanted to be an airline. Lawrence felt that Braniff was still too small to survive the predatory response it could expect under deregulation from competitors such as American Airlines, Delta, and United.

Reading from a prepared script, Lawrence looked up for a moment and surveyed the sparsely populated hearing room, noting that only Howard Cannon and his aides seemed to have been interested enough to show up. Cannon—who represented Nevada— was out to get more air service for his state. What his proposal might do to the rest of America's airline system probably wouldn't be of as much concern to the senator as the question of whether it would benefit Las Vegas and Reno. Then too, Cannon had become a believer in the theories of Professor Alfred Kahn. Kahn, who had little practical experience in the airline business, had worked out a theoretical structure in which an unfettered airline industry in unlimited competition would end up providing better service at lower fares to the nation—following a "period of adjustment," which could be a bloodbath of sorts for the weaker and the smaller carriers. Kahn had remarked that one or more bankruptcies might be expected if the bill were passed and that such events might be desirable. That's precisely what Lawrence was worried about. Braniff was still squarely in the category of the "smaller" trunk carriers.[1]

[1] Kahn firmly believed that under the tight regulation that had governed the industry since 1938, there was little incentive for U.S. airline management to be truly competitive. The fare the CAB would allow on a given route segment was structured to provide a small profit (a given percentage calculation). To arrive at that

Lawrence looked back at his script and began reading his presentation:

> We expect that Braniff [if the bill passed] would find itself with additional competition on at least twenty-two of its own best twenty-five markets—Dallas/Fort Worth to New York, to Washington, to Miami, and to Honolulu are certainly four examples. Carved into little pieces, these profitable markets would soon be loss markets.
>
> Existing carriers could expand their operations to entirely new cities at the yearly rate of five percent of system operations. Some simple mathematics will show you that a four-billion-dollar (per year) carrier expanding its system at five percent per year would soon blanket a one-half-billion-dollar airline no matter what it did. Efficient or not, profitable or not, smaller airlines with smaller fleets and smaller financial reserves would not be able to stand up under these pressures for long.
>
> Then what? Dismemberment and a few remaining large monopoly carriers?

Lawrence paused again as he thought of his statement to a similar subcommittee in the House the previous month, and a remark

---

fare, the direct, operating cost of flying that route was figured and added to an allocated portion of all the other nonoperating administrative and labor costs of the airline (under an allowable CAB formula). The CAB would then determine that if the cost was, say, $100 per passenger, the airline would be allowed to make $6 per passenger, and thus the fare would be $106 per person. Any additional hike in salaries for the union workers of an airline, or any addition to the management team could become part of the basic "cost" calculation over which the CAB would allow a fare that "assured" a profit. Kahn's objection to this system was that the airlines had permitted higher and higher salary settlements and let their management ranks grow larger and excessively compensated because they knew they could pass on the cost to the airline passenger. Thus, he reasoned, there was no incentive under the existing system to cut fares and increase worker productivity and raise the load factors. Kahn and his advocates pointed to small, no-frills, high-frequency, low-fare—and financially successful—regional carriers such as Southwest Airlines in Texas and PSA in California as proof of their theories. Neither of those two carriers were regulated by the CAB at that time, since they flew entirely within their respective states. In many respects, however, it was a comparison of apples to oranges. The intrastate carriers were serving only the choicest of short, intercity routes (and thus no crew overnighting), using newly formed labor forces that, due to the contributory interest in starting the enterprise and the absence of unions at that stage, cost roughly half as much as the labor force of an established carrier.

he had made that this whole idea was so totally "off the wall as to be incomprehensible—unless the true purpose of [this bill] was to let the industry destroy itself in a bloodbath for a few years so that the government would be forced to come in and pick up the pieces— and form a federally operated monopoly airline system." The joke around the industry was that such a federal animal would be labeled "Flytrak" and run with the efficiency of the Postal Service.

> When these hearings have separated fact from opinion, I cannot believe that unregulated competition will become the national policy for the air transport system. I believe that these hearings will turn the focus instead on constructive regulatory improvements which the air transport system needs to resume its role as a catalyst in the development of the foreign and domestic commerce of the nation.

As Harding Lawrence flew home from Washington, he knew only too well how vulnerable his airline would be if such a bill passed. His master plan for expanding Braniff to a major national and international carrier was essentially on track, but he had to have more time. He had neither the route system nor the financial war chest to take on American, Delta, United, or Eastern in a battle for Braniff's bread-and-butter routes.[2]

Lawrence's airline in the summer of 1976 was considered highly profitable and very well run from a strategic point of view, despite the growing middle- and lower-management problems. Critics in the industry had to acknowledge, albeit grudgingly on occasion, that Harding seemed to know what he was doing and seemed to be able to stay in the black even during hard times. In terms of annual revenue alone the airline had grown to five times its 1965 size. The team of Lawrence (providing the strategic leadership and control as chairman) and Acker (providing the sage corporate financial direction as president and—effectively—chief financial officer) had worked brilliantly. Ed Acker's departure, however, had been a watershed. When he left, Lawrence lost a prime source of experienced

---

[2] In 1975 a high percentage of Braniff's routes were still monopolies, or devoid of effective competition. Such routes as Dallas-Fort Worth to Kansas City, Dallas-Forth Worth to Minneapolis-St. Paul, Dallas-Fort Worth to Denver, and Dallas-Fort Worth to Seattle-Tacoma were Braniff territory.

financial planning, a prime connection with the major financiers of the country, and his right-hand man.

Lawrence had always retained the final word, but Ed Acker traditionally had been a major voice in any significant corporate decision. The two men were the best of friends who respected each other, and it was obvious that Lawrence had been turning over more and more of the daily executive administration of the company to Acker in the same manner as Bob Six had slowly slipped into the role of chairman at Continental.

Ed Acker had originally come on board as Post's and Greatamerica's inside man at Braniff (at the insistence of Lawrence), and there had been a line of communication between Acker and the outside corporate parent of the airline that had given him in realistic terms a far more important status than his title as executive vice president might indicate. Then too, "Eddie" (as Lawrence commonly referred to him) had originated both the idea of Greatamerica acquiring Braniff, and the idea of Braniff acquiring Harding Lawrence. When LTV bought Greatamerica, they seem to have acquired by inheritance Ed Acker's direct line of communication, as evidenced both by Acker's sharing of Board positions on many of the insurance companies previously owned by Greatamerica and subsequently sold by LTV (American-Amicable Life, Gulf Life, and Franklin Life Insurance companies), and by his being one of the men turned to as a possible LTV chief executive by the "junta" that ousted Jim Ling from his ailing LTV in 1969.

Harding Lawrence, as a result of Ed Acker's outside ties, always felt Acker's presence to a greater degree than that of anyone else in the senior officer ranks, and he felt those ties to be a stabilizing advantage to him. To lose "Eddie," then, left a large hole in the organizational structure that had brought Braniff so far. With neither Ed Acker nor a corporate parent, it was entirely Lawrence's show.

Lawrence would certainly have no trouble running Braniff in Ed Acker's absence in terms of overall executive control, but he needed a strong and accurate source for corporate financial planning in Acker's stead. Lawrence did not have Acker's hands-on experience as a financier. He needed a good finance man, and he tried to obtain one in the person of Edson (Ted) Beckwith, who had been Acker's assistant with the title of vice president and treasurer.

Beckwith was an excellent financier who believed himself Ed

Acker's equal in strategic financial planning, though under Acker's stewardship Ted Beckwith had been only the "nitty-gritty" man, following in Acker's wake. C. Edward Acker's financial *savoir-faire* was a tough act to follow, and in too many quarters Ted Beckwith was perceived as a lightweight. It had been Ed Acker who knew (personally and professionally) the Walter Wristons and the David Rockefellers of the financial world, but Beckwith had been trotted out to negotiate the details. The betting in major financial circles was that he wouldn't last six months as Harding Lawrence's finance man, though that was too harsh a judgment.[3]

With Ted Beckwith designated to take over Ed Acker's functions in corporate finance, Lawrence needed a replacement for Acker's duties as president of Braniff, but for the next two years he would occupy the post himself as chairman, president, and chief executive officer. Executive Vice President for Sales, Service, and Operations John Casey assumed he would be elevated to the position of president within a year or so. When Lawrence eventually named Russ Thayer as president and chief operating officer (in 1977), Casey's friendship with Thayer disintegrated along with his hopes for the office. Lawrence needed someone to groom as a replacement, but Thayer would prove a disappointment. Casey's pique at being passed over, meanwhile, would manifest itself in further isolation of the various sections of the company and further contribute to the isolation of Lawrence himself from the true picture of what was transpiring in the depths of his airline.

If, in fact, Harding Lawrence had listened to no one but himself, as was widely believed to be the case within the company, some of the strategic decisions he would make in the critical years to follow might have been drastically different—and less disastrous. But Lawrence was a planner, a leader who needed massive amounts of information and a comprehensive plan to operate effectively. The

[3] Beckwith's prime liability was his method of approaching other finance people. He used only a "hard" position from which to negotiate, and his propensity for compromise in an atmosphere of give-and-take was minimal. Although that works very effectively when negotiating from strength, it becomes a handicap when favors are needed. Some of the positions Beckwith took with the bankers during the good years when the company finally took out some unsecured bank loans (most of Braniff's large, long-term borrowings for equipment had been from insurance companies) would come back to haunt him when times subsequently became rough. It would be the absence of Acker, though, more than the presence of Ted Beckwith, that would hurt.

chairman never avoided making strategic decisions, but such decisions required the careful informational support his senior people and their subordinates were supposed to be providing. Many of those same people had long since risen above their maximum level of executive competence, their Peter Principle level, so much of that underlying information and support was badly flawed. Many of the pivotal decisions that would prove so damaging in the future were based on such flawed information and advice.

Strong, autocratic leaders in corporate life do not by definition create a senior staff full of sycophants and self-protective, marginally competent executives. Corporate chairmen such as Harold Geneen of ITT can have legendary tempers and strong, autocratic control of their staff meetings and their staff and still surround themselves with capable performers. The one significant difference between Harding Lawrence's form of control and that of a corporate leader like Geneen is the willingness to fire. When a leader like Geneen threatens to get rid of a man if he doesn't perform, he means just that, and he will follow through. The senior ranks may be in constant upheaval for years but eventually will be filled with strong, capable performers who can both stand up to the boss and perform to his satisfaction. Contrary to the image so many Braniff employees had of him, one of Harding Lawrence's most significant faults as a corporate leader was his softhearted reluctance to fire his people (or demote them to a level they could handle) no matter how incompetent they were. "When you hire people," Lawrence once said, "you marry them and they're there forever, and that's the reason you're very cautious in hiring people."

Lawrence had been brought up in Bob Six's organization in which executives good and bad were molded into effective managers—"reared" in the industry. Lawrence saw no reason why the men around him at Braniff couldn't be handled in the same way. Before 1975, any executives dismissed at Braniff were dismissed by Ed Acker. After Acker left, none of the key people were shown the door (with only a few exceptions), though perhaps a third should have been.[4]

[4] In addition, an executive faced with a massive medical (or in one case, emotional) problem could be assured of compassion. Lawrence refused to let the money run out for one of his people when he was in need. One officer of another airline, examining Braniff's books in a potential merger probe, said, "I've never seen so many former vice presidents still on a payroll!" One of the cases he was referring to in-

The trust Lawrence put in his senior people—the concept that however bad they might be, they could be molded into better executives—was encouraged by his lack of knowledge of just how incompetent some of them really were (empty suits, as some vice presidents were known in later years). Although there were a host of good, capable people in senior management, their accomplishments were always imperiled by the incapable ones who had learned how to hang on.

Lawrence had no practical way of knowing how deep the problem ran because of a monumental managerial error: Braniff had virtually no method of formal evaluation for its management, senior or junior. None. Executive position was based on loose verbal communication of unsupported and politically tainted opinion. This one fact, by itself, was sufficient to imperil all Lawrence was struggling to build. It virtually assured the institutionalization of mediocrity, and a ferocious system of political intrigue and self-protection in the executive ranks. If Harding Lawrence saw much of this, it was by accident. The people most involved struggled mightily to keep him from the truth.

Although these organizational problems in the executive suite would have far-reaching influence on Braniff's ability to survive and flourish as a corporation, its ability to survive and grow as an airline that promised superior service would depend in part on the attitude of that average fellow with a briefcase and a business trip asking his secretary or travel agent to book a seat to Tulsa (or Seattle, or Honolulu, etc.). All too often as the 1970s progressed, a fleeting memory of inconsistent service would interpose a negative loyalty: ". . . and Linda, book me on anyone but Braniff!"

---

volved a gentleman in the throes of terminal cancer whose sick leave would have otherwise run out. When Lawrence was told of any employee facing a major problem—especially a family problem—he was a "soft touch." That attitude, though, was never perceived at the union levels. Although Lawrence might hear of an executive problem, he was seldom told of anything directly affecting the rank and file as individuals, and Braniff had virtually no system for dealing with any individual human problem suffered below.

Biting the Hand

CHAPTER 10 A balky ADI (attitude deviation indicator, the modern version of what used to be called an artificial horizon) on the panel in front of Captain Herb Rustad in Ship 299, a Braniff 727-100 series aircraft, had kept the bird at the gate in Minneapolis twenty minutes past the scheduled departure time of 8:00 A.M. for Flight 51. The flight was due to make a stop at Kansas City's new International Airport (MCI) before proceeding on to Dallas-Fort Worth Regional Airport (DFW), and the delay was sure to be felt down the line, since each station usually took every minute of their allotted "ground time" to get the flights unloaded, loaded, fueled (if necessary), serviced with meals, and out of the gate.

It could be done faster than schedule, but only if the pilots really pushed, and from the pilots' vantage point, communications with the operations people was strained enough (they usually kept their distance, separated by a glassed-in enclosure adjacent to the pilots' lounge). When the bird was on the ground, it belonged to the agent and the station, and they weren't interested in any pilot telling them how to run their show. Of course, when they waved a flight out the gate a few minutes late, or took more than the scheduled ground time, the gate agents could be the epitome of friendliness in asking for "schedule"—essentially asking the captain to fudge the actual time, and report an on-time departure where a delay, and all the appropriate paperwork and chastisement from above, would normally ensue. It was a standard phrase on Braniff—more or less a joke, but used nonetheless—"Aw, they're good ole boys—give 'em schedule."

The managers of the various outlying Braniff stations were used to catching hell for any delays because their vice presidents in Dallas would catch hell—usually from Vice President for Operations John J. Casey at his morning briefing at the Love Field maintenance base.

John Casey, an engaging Irishman from Boston who never shed his regional accent, perpetuated a morning ritual in which the various operational department heads (or their next in command) would sit down around a large conference table at 7:30 A.M. and try to shift the blame for anything that had gone wrong in the previous twenty-four hours to each other. It didn't have to work that way—the meetings could have been highly productive exchanges aimed at how to prevent reoccurrences of problems encountered in running an international airline. Instead, it had degenerated to an exercise in futility—a miniature inquisition in which Casey (who attended quite a few of the meetings but never chaired them) could growl at and belittle whoever happened to be representing a department involved in causing a problem. It was as if Casey were intent on having his own version of Harding Lawrence's staff meetings (at which John Casey would be chewed out on many occasions by the chairman). One of Casey's favorite methods of displaying his disgust was to get up and stalk out the doorway of the conference room, slamming the door as hard as he possibly could in the process. It was almost a therapeutic release for John Casey, but it instilled in his people a profound and weary disgust. Troubleshooting and creative, energetic problem-solving had to take a backseat to survival. Only an idiot would volunteer a problem at the morning briefing. In any position under Casey, one learned early that survival meant, individually and departmentally, covering one's ass.

As suspected, Flight 51 left the MCI gate that partly cloudy and very warm July day 21 minutes behind schedule and headed for DFW with Rustad doing his best to make up time.

On board the flight one of the first class passengers caught flight attendant Dee Thompson by the sleeve.

"Excuse me—I'm supposed to go on to Shreveport on a Delta flight that leaves at eleven forty-five, and it looks like we won't be in Dallas until eleven-thirty or so—and I've got people in Shreveport who're going to meet me, so I can't miss the flight. Is there some way they can hold that flight?"

Thompson, a gregarious and enthusiastic veteran flight attendant well versed in such problems, knelt down in the aisle beside the passenger, a gentleman of perhaps sixty in her estimation, obviously nervous about his connection. "Sir, I'm not sure how late we'll be, but if there's any way we can get you over there, we will. I'll have the flight engineer—that's our second officer, one of the pilots—call ahead for a company car to run you over there when we land. Be back in a minute."

Thompson walked forward and knocked on the cockpit door, slipping in when the engineer opened it from within.

"Okay, guys, need some help on connections. I have a fellow in first class trying to get to a Delta flight to Shreveport at eleven forty-five, and I've already had three other passengers ask Debbie in coach about other connections on us—and I need a cart for an LOL [Little Old Lady] in 23B going to Honolulu on 501."

The engineer looked up and smiled. He had been writing the information down as she spoke. "I think we can arrange that. Give me a few minutes, Dee. We're still not in radio range."

As the 727 began the descent over Lake Texoma for approach and landing at DFW, the engineer began talking with Dallas-Fort Worth operations, the large control center in the basement of the Braniff terminal.

"Regional ops, Fifty-one."

"Howdy, Fifty-one, it'll be gate five this morning. What's your estimate?"

"Looks like eleven twenty-five—and I've got some connect problems."

"Go ahead, sir."

"Okay, we've got a gentleman going to Shreveport on a Delta flight at eleven forty-five—we need a company van curbside to take him over there—and I need gate information and departure times on Ninety-five to Seattle, One to San Antonio, Sixty-eight to Denver, and Seventy-seven to Tampa—also, we need a cart and special assist for an LOL going to Honolulu."

A minute passed while the coordinator assembled all the information. "Okay, Fifty-one, no problem on the van, tell your passenger to go curbside, we'll take him over to Delta. Okay on the LOL to Five-oh-one, special services will meet you. Ninety-five goes out of Gate Seven at eleven twenty-five—we'll misconnect that one—tell your passengers to go to a ticket counter for rebooking. Flight One to San Antone is out of Fourteen at twelve noon—no problem. Sixty-eight to Denver is out of Gate Fifteen at eleven twenty-five, you'll misconnect that one, but they can go on Flight Seventy at twelve twenty-five. And Seventy-seven to Tampa's out of Gate Eighteen at eleven thirty-five—tell your passengers to go straight to the gate and they'll hold her."

The orange 727 taxied off the runway with Rustad doing his best to minimize the taxi time and turned into the huge ramp area bordering the outside perimeter of the semicircular DFW Braniff terminal (a half mile in length), nosing smoothly into the gate. The maintenance man helped park them, then disappeared under the aircraft as the crew ran the shutdown checklist and noticed that the jetway just outside the cockpit to their left was vacant. There was no agent to open the door.

Dee Thompson was noticing the same thing. With the passengers all beginning to stack up behind her in the aisleway behind the cockpit, she was looking through the small circular window on the forward left door of the jetliner—trying to spot an agent. Two of the "close connect" passengers were getting out of their seats and watching her, wondering why the door wasn't open.

Thompson opened the cockpit door as the engineer was reaching for it. "Hey, we don't have an agent!"

"I'm already calling Dee—hold on. Regional, Fifty-one."

"Go ahead, Fifty-one."

"We're in Gate Five and don't have an agent, and we're full of close connects, as you know."

"We'll call him again, sir."

The outside agent who was supposed to meet Flight 51 was in the process of half walking, half running down the jetway. The damn flight had been in several minutes and he knew it—but thanks to whatever sadist put the schedule together, he was supposed to park another flight three gates away, open their door, go open their rear stairway, and then get down here to park Flight 51, which had nosed in at almost exactly the same moment. Braniff was too shorthanded to have anyone else around to take care of the other flight. At least it always seemed that way to him (though he knew that half the problem was the refusal of so many of the agents to help each other—if it wasn't their gate, it wasn't their problem!).

The agents on the ticket counter were the same way in too many cases. They were too busy drinking coffee and complaining about Braniff management to walk ten feet and help a snowed-under fellow agent. The good ones were sick and tired of picking up the slack—sick and tired as well of being overworked into perpetual overtime (even though the money was good), and tired of some of the inept managers who couldn't seem to approach a problem without threatening to fire someone.

He was used to the problems, but it never got any easier. When he had joined the company in the late 1960s, he'd been very enthusiastic and interested in making Braniff the best. But he'd been kicked so many times—he'd been frustrated so much—he wasn't too sure he cared anymore.

The agent opened the door of Flight 51 and waited for the inevitable onslaught of exiting passengers, and the upset flight attendants and pilots angry at him because he couldn't be in two places at once.

Thompson and the engineer were doing all they could to keep any ruffled feathers from getting more ruffled, but a five-minute delay to open the door was hard to overlook. Rustad and his copilot, Clem Zang, grabbed their flight kits—"brain bags"—and headed out the doorway when most of the passengers had departed. They and the engineer had about an hour before flying Flight 132 back to Minneapolis.

The engineer was standing with Thompson in the concourse, just outside the gate, disgusted. The special services cart, always promised but seldom delivered, had failed to come again, and their passenger, the LOL, whom Thompson had helped by the arm all the way from the aircraft and was still supporting, was looking confused. On top of everything else, the Delta-bound passenger was coming back in from the curb (at DFW the distance from the center walkway of the concourse and the gates to the driveway, or "curbside," is less than fifty feet). Obviously he hadn't found the van that was to take him to his flight at the Delta terminal, which was nearly a mile away and at least seven minutes by car.

The engineer put his bags down in the jetway entrance. "Sir, why don't you come back in here a second and let me get on the phone and figure something out." He half ran back inside the terminal and dashed over to the baggage service phone, with the passenger following at a distance.

In the entrance to Gate 5, Dee Thompson had given up on special services and seated her LOL passenger in a purloined special services wheelchair she'd found nearby (in the absence of the electric cart). She was pushing the lady toward Gate 12 and Flight 501 when the special services agent (a woman with hard features and a sour attitude whom Dee had been forced to deal with before) flashed past on her electric cart—ignoring Dee's efforts to flag her down—scattering passengers with a small horn as she headed for what would be a deserted Gate 5.

Hurriedly flipping through the DFW airport directory for the number of Delta operations the engineer had finally found it and discovered that the Shreveport flight had been delayed. There was plenty of time. He, however, was running out of time. He had to get to his outbound gate and preflight the aircraft they would be flying back to Minneapolis. Nevertheless, as so many Braniff people from many different departments would often do, the engineer escorted the passenger down to the Airtrans station (from which automated trains transfer passengers between the far-flung terminals of the huge airport). The Airtrans would take about twelve minutes to get the man to Delta's facilities, and the Braniff van was still nowhere in sight.

"Sir, I'm awfully sorry for the communications breakdown—obviously our people found out about the Delta delay and somehow didn't get the word to us—I hope you'll forgive us." The engineer put one of his own quarters in the slot of the turnstile guarding the entrance to the Airtrans waiting lounge and motioned the man through. "Now, take the yellow train, sir, and it'll take you right to Delta's terminal—get off there and ride the elevator to the lobby level. There will be Delta people in red coats there to help you to your flight. And please come back and fly with us again."

The man smiled and waved. "I sure will. I appreciate all the help. Are you one of the agents?"

"No, sir, I'm one of the guys who flew you in from Kansas City. I'm a pilot."

The man looked shocked. "Is that right? Well . . . uh . . . thanks again! Geez, you people are serious about service!"

The flight engineer for outbound Flight 132 to Minneapolis-St. Paul (MSP) headed back up the escalator to the terminal, checking his watch and calculating how much time he had left to preflight. As he entered the terminal he saw the missing Braniff van pull up in front of baggage area A—only twenty minutes late.

The line in front of Gate 13—departure point for Flight 132, nonstop to MSP, had begun gathering by eleven forty-five. The flight was oversold today according to the computer readout, and the agent was already having a difficult time. Of course, he had lingered over coffee, seeing no sense in getting behind the podium too early. Judging from the size of the line and the demeanor of some of the people in it, he should have come sooner.

He was quite used to getting to the counter late—it put off the agony of dealing with the damned abusive public. He knew he had a tendency to pick fights with passengers (and had been reprimanded several times due to passenger complaints), but if the damned ivory tower managers had to put up with the daily abuse he had to face, maybe they'd understand. "Nearly fifty years old, overweight, underpaid, overworked, and too many years in this chicken outfit to quit," he had told one of the lead agents the previous month. Of course, there had been a time when it was fun—but that was long gone. One of the managers had told him his problems came from having a "low self-image." He knew it was true—he wasn't good with the passengers—but a decade of being threatened and lied to by management, who considered him stupid and worthless anyway, had finally done the trick. If that's what they considered him to be, why try to be anything more? Besides, Braniff had never given him a minute's worth of training on how to handle angry people— so he usually ended up getting angry as well, and that's what always got him in trouble. It was their fault.

He realized he'd been deep in thought and ignoring the passengers. He began arranging his counter and his ticket envelopes in neat stacks, stamping them one by one with the flight number and date—while the line of passengers stood and waited with growing impatience, tickets in hand.

Clockwise down the corridor of the expansive, stylish Braniff terminal, Bob Clark, one of the customer service agents, waved to the engineer (whom he knew) of Flight 132 as the young pilot hurried by with his flight bag. Clark was the type who almost never let problems get the best of him on duty, since dealing with problems and upset customers was his main job. Having just finished a half-hour marathon effort to get a misconnected young army private re-ticketed and delivered to the right gate for the San Antonio flight, Clark had left him in the capable hands of one of the best DFW agents, a woman whose smile and poise were perpetual. He was aware of the vast gulf between different factions of the public-contact people in the terminal—he had discussed it many times, even with outsiders such as the Minneapolis-St. Paul-based engineer he'd just passed. But he knew that the majority of the people were doing a damn good job, concerned and careful with their customers and hardworking. The others ranged from incorrigible to disillusioned, and it was nearly impossible to fire any of them.

Spotting a young child with tears in his eyes and looking lost, Clark altered course to help him.

Captain Herb Rustad had been passing the time between flights in a typical ritual—a trip down to the basement crew room to talk to whomever might be around, check the crew bulletins, sign the flight release for the next leg, then back up to the concourse and a quick turn through one of the four convenience shops located at equal intervals along the length of the terminal. Rustad had his brain bag now and was headed past the line toward the entrance to the jetway to do his cockpit preflight. This was a turnaround; since he and his crew were based in the MSP pilot base, they would all be home tonight. Well, at least he would. The copilot and the engineer were commuters—pilots who lived in one city and commuted several times per month to the city in which they were based to fly their trips. They'd be in hotels tonight.

As Rustad disappeared through the jetway doorway, the mood at the podium at the gate was becoming testy. Acidic comments from the people in the line had already floated to the agent's ears. They were tired of waiting in line, and the air conditioning in the terminal wasn't quite keeping up with the summer heat shimmering just outside on the broiling concrete ramp. The agent loosened his tie a bit—then unbuttoned the collar of his shirt, leaving the tie loosely in place. He still had his coat on, but it was showing significant signs of wear. He hadn't sent it to the cleaners in a month.

As the agent worked through the first of the line, assigning seats and handling the ticket coupons, a stylish lady in an obviously expensive suit walked up to his counter, ahead of all the others who had been waiting in line, demanding his attention.

"Excuse me. I'm supposed to be on your flight to Chicago this afternoon, and I'd like to go a bit earlier. Can you tell me where to go?"

The agent looked up and caught her eyes. He didn't feel very possessed of a sense of humor today, but damnit, that was a wonderfully tempting straight line. He would, indeed, like to tell her where to go, but he thought better of it. "I can't do it here, ma'am, but go down to the ticket counter by Gate Twelve and they'll help you."

He went back to the ticket he was working on, only to find another individual—this one a man in a business suit—standing in front of him. The guy had jumped to the front of the line, too.

"Where do I find the Tulsa flight?"

"Look at the monitor, sir, the TV monitor."

"Hey, can't you look it up for me? I'm gonna miss it."

"No, sir, I'm sorry—I can't right now." The agent was still looking at the ticket he had been holding.

"Look, I don't know this airport too well, and I've already tried to find an agent and you're the only one around. So come on, where is my Tulsa flight?"

"They're usually around Gates Thirteen or Fourteen, sir. Please just check one of the monitors."

The passenger looked at the lady to his left whose ticket the agent had been working on. "Can you believe this?" he asked. Then to the agent he said, "Okay, where do I find one of these so-called monitors? Point one out to me."

The agent put down his pen. "I'm in the middle of working a flight, sir, and I don't have time."

The volume level of the man's voice was increasing. "Hey, fella, you want my business on this crummy airline? I don't care what you're working on. I'm one of your customers and I need some information."

That did it. He had been angry all morning anyway, and this jerk was the last straw. "Listen, friend, I don't give a damn whether we have your business or not. You're breaking into my line—with a stupid question—and I don't have time to fool with you. Now either go find yourself a TV monitor or an agent who isn't busy."

"I want your name, buddy."

"You can copy my name tag—and spell it right!"

The infuriated passenger stomped off to find someone to complain to as the agent got back to his tickets, ignoring the comments from down the line.

"Did you hear that guy? Typical airline treatment."

"Typical *Braniff* treatment."

"I can't believe the rudeness of that agent."

"They oughtta fire that guy!"

To Err Is Human—Except in the Airline Business

CHAPTER **11** Airline customers tend to be fickle. Like a co-quettish, adolescent girl, the allegiance of most passengers will shift like the wind in the face of lower fares, different departure times, different aircraft, or indifferent service. A business traveler may fly an airline such as Braniff for years before a problem occurs, but as a result of a lost bag, a botched connection, a lost reservation, or a myriad of other potential problems, only a forceful and professional attempt to make amends will rescue his or her business for the future. Present such a person with indifferent attitudes or lackadaisical, uninterested effort to solve his or her problem and you have created an enemy—a passenger who will consciously avoid your airline and, what's worse, communicate to anyone who will listen how lousy and incompetent and perpetually late, etc. your airline always is. In many parts of society this is known as slander. When the relative merit of airlines is the subject under discussion, however, there is no restraint. One wave in a sea of smooth service and on-time arrivals can leave an airline's reputation in irreparable ruin with that one customer (and whomever he or she can influence).

The various departments of an airline that are charged with monitoring and influencing the public's perception of their carrier (usually public relations, marketing, advertising, and those sections that handle complaints and compliments) live with this awful truth and do their best to combat it. Sometimes a furious passenger can be soothed with a deeply conciliatory letter; sometimes it takes a financial adjustment (in rare and specific cases). Once calmed from his or her towering rage, however, the customer's cocktail conversations will probably still include a scathing (and often shamelessly embellished) recanting of the horrid affair.

98

The best method of preventing a steady diminution of a carrier's reputation starts with trying to prevent the problem to begin with. Since airline travel is inherently vulnerable to delays (for weather or maintenance or because of Air Traffic Control delays, for example) and inherently vulnerable to human mistakes (lost bags, lost reservations, lost tempers), the problems and the angry passengers will occur. Couple this to the reality that as a nation and a people we have become far less considerate in our conduct toward one another—especially toward those employed by a company whose services we are patronizing—and you have, essentially, a guarantee that on any given day, at any given point of public contact, any given airline is going to need to worry about soothing the ruffled feathers of at least a few passengers, even if the problem that caused the upset is entirely the passenger's fault.

Most airlines handle this with training. They train people for special positions called by different names at different carriers (passenger service, supervisory services, special services, passenger service agents), but their reason for existence is to turn a problem into the opportunity to leave the passenger feeling good about the carrier again, despite whatever went wrong. A certain amount of native intelligence, affinity for other people, and innate psychology are essential ingredients for someone in such a position, but the one indispensable factor in creating an effective employee in such a position is training. Without training you're gambling on native ability alone, and not all people are that gifted.

Additionally, you hand-pick the people according to their capabilities and psychological makeup. Even if there is a union involved (and there almost always is), you still screen the people who want such positions.

Braniff's violation of the maxims was nearly total. No training— no effective screening—and precious few supervisors who had such passenger-service duties. In fact, no significant training course would be offered to Braniff's agents in public-contact, problem-solving positions until the spring of 1981, when a small group was put through a "Dale Carnegie course." The results of that effort were immediate. The agents who received professional guidance through the course on how to turn irate passengers into happy customers for the most part began enjoying the challenge. There were exceptions, but overall the course was an instant, verifiable success. The tragedy is the realization that archrivals American and Delta had been giving their people similar in-house courses for years. Braniff's personnel department, which was ultimately responsible for hiring and training programs, maintained no effective centralized control of either throughout the late 1960s and 1970s.

An angry passenger in a Braniff terminal was face-to-face with the rawest of elements in most cases: an untrained, unprepared agent who had none of the sophisticated defense systems to protect his or her feelings—to guard against taking passenger abuse personally—and who, as a result, was likely to reach a breaking point and strike back at the most important element in the airline equation: the passenger.

Despite the lack of people trained to take care of problems in passenger relations, despite its violation of the maxims, Braniff still managed to maintain fairly good relationships with its passengers (repairing damaged feelings, damaged luggage, and upset business passengers while generally maintaining a professional demeanor) because of the native abilities and the professional determination of many of its people. Despite an abysmal lack of training, despite rough edges and working relationships with many managers who were distant, hostile, and void of any respect for the individuals they supervised (especially at DFW), a large and significant number of Braniff public-contact employees (union and nonunion alike) did the job the way they thought best and tried their damndest always to represent Braniff as a company they themselves could be proud of. The accomplishments of these good, professional people were the backbone of Braniff's business—the first ones and the last ones to handle Braniff's all-important customers as they came and went from Braniff's flights. The fact that such employees did so much with so little and under such pressure was, in retrospect, astounding.

Most of the passenger-service difficulties historically centered at DFW, and at the Love Field terminal before DFW opened in 1973. Several other Braniff stations in Texas and Oklahoma (Tulsa) were also hotbeds of employee discontent and passenger-service complaints. The farther the station was from the Dallas area, however, the better it seemed to be. The principal reason for this was the greater stability of the management of outlying stations, which usually made them happier places in which to work. Such people also were distant from the daily pressures of DFW. Later in the 1970s, as Braniff added new cities at a rapid clip, the bright-eyed innocence of some of the new, enthusiastic agents in such new stations as Fort

Lauderdale, Florida, and Oakland, California, provided a refreshing change. To veteran Braniff people, dealing with such new stations was like dealing with a different airline.

Because of the realities of airline life and the way passengers react to the slightest affront, the problems created by those employees in public-contact positions who couldn't rise above the handicaps cost the company incalculable millions of dollars in lost revenues over the years, especially at DFW, where its exposure to the public was greater, and any problems were sure to affect more passengers. This is true for any airline in its home city. For instance, if Braniff had 100 daily departures to Delta's 20 daily departures, and each airline had an identical 90 percent on-time rate, Braniff would have 10 delayed flights to only 2 for Delta each day. If each delayed flight represented (on average) 75 unhappy passengers, in one day Braniff aggravated 750 passengers, while Delta inconvenienced only 150. This is why Delta has greater image problems in its home city of Atlanta, United at Chicago and Denver, Eastern at Miami, and so on. It also means that an airline's home airport is the one location that should be as nearly perfect in passenger-relations capabilities as is humanly possible. But at Braniff, DFW—its showplace and home port—was the worst station in the Braniff system.

Braniff had lost a significant percentage of local loyalty in the burgeoning Dallas-Fort Worth metroplex (as the area calls itself). Too many businesspeople especially, with and without just cause, used Braniff as their favorite whipping boy when the subject of airlines good and bad was broached in their presence. Too many local people complained of surly agents, lost bags, long ticket counter lines, snippy personnel, and other aggravations. There were too many people in the area as well who would fly Braniff only if it were the last possible choice between getting there or losing their job. There was still some local loyalty, but it had been eroded over the years while American Airlines was working very hard to build their image as the businessman's airline with highly trained and consistently professional public-contact people. All this provided one of the links in the chain of problems that would ultimately resemble a causal chain of corporate destruction.[1]

Sometimes the difference in hating Braniff or loving Braniff was

---

[1] The test of a link in a causal chain is whether—if removed—the same ultimate result would have occurred at the same time and place. By that test, the diminution of local passenger loyalty to Braniff forged a small link, but a link nonetheless.

simply the sound of a pleasant voice on the telephone, and the one department full of Braniff people who never worked in person with the public but shaped their first impressions of their airline were the reservationists. Like so many other nonflying elements of the company, the lack of training, lack of coordination and consistency, the politics, and the small empire one manager in particular was trying to build in Braniff "rez" left the individual reservationist on her own. Without support, without many elements of basic respect, and without training or guidance, the good ones carried the load.

Brenda Mize, wife of Braniff Captain Harold (Tiny) Mize, was enjoying her day. It was cool in the reservations center (which occupied a good percentage of the upper-floor office space over the hangars at the Braniff maintenance base), and she had completed several hours of talking to friendly people. Upset folks and grouches weren't too common, but they could spoil your whole outlook for the day when you had to deal with one.

Wearing a lightweight headset, she was plugged into her station, facing a computer terminal. The rules had become more and more "Mickey Mouse" in the past number of years, and she was particularly incensed that she had to raise her hand even to get permission to go to the ladies' room. She knew many of the other airlines such as Delta and rival American had similar rules, but it was irritating nonetheless. The most difficult part of the job was the pressure to take as many calls per hour as possible. The management of reservations insisted on measuring the performance of their reservationists largely in terms of how many calls they took per hour and how long they were plugged in. There seemed to be little emphasis on the way the calls were handled, and with many new faces coming into "rez" and receiving almost no instruction, not all of the people were representing her airline the way they should.

The management structure above her was also an irritant. Her immediate boss was one of the so-called assistant managers, many of whom had come up from being a reservationist—out from under union protection—to be in "management." Their function was theoretically to roam the floor and provide guidance and help with questions or situations the reservationists might be faced with and to see that the people toed the line, followed all the rules, and got the highest possible calls-per-hour rating. The assistant managers however, were too busy fighting among themselves, playing dirty tricks on each other, or trying to look better than their rival assistant managers to provide much help to the reservationists they supervised. The managers over them who headed the Reservations Division of Braniff appeared to encourage rather than squelch the infighting. They were fond of pitting their assistants against each other—apparently on the theory that it made for better performance in a competitive environment.

Braniff "rez" had not been a happy "shop" in many years, but (as was all too typical throughout the lower- and middle-management ranks of the company) management didn't seem the least bit interested in talking about problems or suggestions—they were primarily interested in keeping the call-per-hour rate as high as possible so they could present impressive productivity figures to their vice president and thus cover themselves. The object of selling the product had long since disappeared as one of their priorities.

Brenda reached up and punched up another call.

"Braniff International, good afternoon!"

"Uh, yes, I'm calling about your flights to Hawaii—to Honolulu. You do go there?"

"We certainly do, sir, in the grandest style you've ever seen, aboard a beautiful orange-colored Boeing 747, the biggest airliner in the sky. When are you interested in going?"

"Well, we want to go out and spend a couple of weeks there—it's a vacation my wife and I have been wanting to take for, oh, gosh, maybe twenty years and haven't had the time. We'd like to leave August fourteenth."

Brenda punched up that date and the number 501, the Braniff 747 flight to Honolulu. "It's available that day all right, sir. That's you and your wife, first class, to Honolulu and back?"

"Uh, no—coach. I don't think we need the extra space."

"It's a lot more than extra space, sir. Let me tell you, my husband and I flew out there recently and went first class and the service was magnificent. Our people wine and dine you all the way in this beautiful front part of the airplane, where it's the quietest—and there's an upstairs lounge you can wander up to. Even if you just go one way first class, it's well worth it. If you've been waiting this long for the trip, you owe it to yourself!"

Brenda loved selling, and she was in classic form with this customer. What's more, she could tell from talking to him that they really would love the front cabin and the pampering. It was a fantastic way to start a Hawaiian vacation. She disliked selling someone something they didn't need, but this sort of situation was different. Braniff's Hawaii 747 first class service was legendary, as she knew firsthand.

"It's really that good, is it? That different from coach, I mean?"

She proceeded to tell him more about the airplane, about seeing Diamond Head for the first time from the orange 747, and struck up a friendship with the man who, forty-two minutes later, asked her to confirm him and his wife in first class on the way over—which, of course, added hundreds of dollars to the fare.

"Mr. Watson, will you do me a favor? When you two get back, will you call me here at Braniff reservations—my name is Brenda Mize—and tell me how you folks enjoyed it?"

"I sure will, Brenda. Thank you so much."

"Thank you, Mr. Watson, and have a wonderful trip!"

Two days later she was called into the office by her assistant manager, who had monitored the call.

"Brenda, we're giving you an unsatisfactory on that call because you failed to use the proper phrase, 'Thank you for calling Braniff.' Also, you had only a total of three calls in one hour with that long one. That just won't do!"

Brenda Mize looked at the woman and shook her head.

"Don't you get the point? I sold them two first class tickets to Honolulu on 501. Who the hell cares how I signed off?"

"You're missing the point, Brenda. We're—"

"*I'm* missing the point? Did you hear me? First class tickets— two of them. We're supposed to be selling Braniff seats here. What I sold was certainly worth an extra thirty or forty minutes of my time. It sure pays more than my salary for an hour!"

"Brenda, consider yourself warned!"

It was early September when Mr. Watson, the customer, called back to say what a wonderful time they'd had on the flight to Hawaii and back and how right she'd been about the first class. It was also September that a curious little scene of three minutes' duration occurred in reservations. Harding L. Lawrence, chairman of the Board, walked through.

He simply opened the door at the eastern end of the room and walked through—nodding to an occasional reservationist who happened to look up and stumble in midsentence. His hair was silver-gray now, and as the media were saying more and more often, no one looked more like an airline president than Harding Lawrence.

The chairman did not stop, just looked around slowly as he strolled to the western end of the large rectangular room, opened the door, and walked out.

The confusion he left behind him was incredible. The assistant managers, who had frozen in their tracks at the sight of him, almost knocked each other down trying to get to their managers to tell them what had transpired. None of the chiefs were there—which meant that they hadn't known he was coming. Whenever there was a rumor Lawrence was coming, the place went on battle alert, all the floors were cleaned, all the desks were arranged just so, and everyone was instructed on how to act. The visits were few and far between, but never had he just walked through.

One of the reservationists called a friend of hers in another part of the company—a forbidden personal call, but what the hell, it was an unusual day.

"I've seen him, and he actually exists!"

"Who?"

"Harding! I never really—*really*—believed he existed before today, but he does, and he's got blue eyes!"

Gaudily Colored
Aircraft from the Colonies

Braniff Airways was forty-eight years old (forty-six as a corporate entity) in 1976. The nation was two hundred. The celebrations that had been planned for the Bicentennial year provided the perfect backdrop for another metamorphosis of image for Braniff. In 1976 Lawrence would bring his airline another notch closer to the level of style and fashion, elegance and exclusivity that he epitomized. The first step involved a reprise—Alexander Calder was once again flown to Dallas.

Calder had been intrigued in 1973 with the idea of painting Braniff's DC-8, and once accomplished, that flying artwork had gone on to turn heads all over South America. The critical reviews of the idea had been good, so Lawrence decided that the Bicentennial year called for a special Braniff contribution—a Calder painting riding the skin of a Boeing 727 and titled "The Flying Colors of the United States." For another $100,000 fee, "Sandy" Calder set to work on four scale-model 727's, and produced four different versions, one of which was picked by a committee of art critics from the East Coast at Braniff's request.

As with the DC-8, it was the technical expertise of the people in Braniff's maintenance section that did the job of copying the painting from the scale model to the actual aircraft—a job they performed in several weeks of work in the Braniff hangar at Love Field (part of the maintenance base building) under the periodic inspection of Calder himself. The plane, when finished, was a typical Calder—a wild and happy pattern of reds, whites, and blues in the form of stripes of different widths undulating from the front to the rear of the craft, on top of and beneath the wings, and once again, an esoteric rendition of something on number 3 engine that appeared to be a snake.

There was one problem. Somehow, someone had chosen Ship 408 (a Boeing 727-291, the stretch series), as the Calder aircraft. That particular 727 had started its professional life as a Frontier Airlines jetliner but had been purchased by Braniff in the late 1960s. While they owned it, Frontier apparently had assaulted some of the roughest runways in North America with the poor airplane. Although it was quite safe and totally airworthy, it had a personality all its own, from the wrinkled skin on the lower rear of the fuselage just aft of the wings (which worried so many newly hired flight engineers on walk-around) to her old-style pressurization control system (the reliable but somewhat antiquated pneumatic type used on all the original, short 727's). In addition, it was, in aviation parlance, a "hangar queen"—an aircraft that has an inordinate number of maintenance write-ups (seldom serious, just vexatious and constant). Finally, according to the pilots who had to put up with her across the Braniff system, she flew "funny," sort of "sideways." In cruise, at altitudes of about thirty-five thousand feet, it was hard if not impossible to get her trimmed to where a pilot would need almost no pressure in any direction on the controls to keep her boring straight ahead.

And then there was the matter of Calder's "snake" on number 3 engine—the pod-mounted engine on the right rear beneath the T-tail. Although the audacity of the colors and the design obscured it from the general public, to the employees it was a hilarious reminder that the old bird was, from a maintenance point of view, "snake-bit"—and the name *Sneaky Snake* (coined in part because of a whimsical novelty song on the charts at the time) gained momentum. Other than the big orange 747—Ship 601—which was referred to alternately as *Fat Albert, Big Orange,* or *The Great Pumpkin*—*Sneaky Snake* was the only other Braniff craft in the jet age with a distinct personality and an individual name.

From the public-relations point of view, however, *Sneaky Snake* was a smashing success. With appropriate planning and good advance work, a crew of management pilots spent many of the days of 1976 touring various Braniff cities, doing low flybys with the Calder aircraft (which did not have Braniff's name on it, only Calder's giant signature over the front left door area) and presenting it to various city fathers—in honor of our national celebration of the Bicentennial. The entire idea had been another characteristically innovative and effective marketing move. It was highly cost-effective as well—the company could never have purchased the widespread publicity it received. Lawrence and Braniff were becoming famous for such unique promotions.

By the end of the year, Braniff was able to issue the startling proclamation that the Calder 727—as artwork—had been seen in person by more people than any other work of art in history!

While Braniff's flight crews were joining in the festivities of the year with their own "Bicentennial minutes" on the PA's, the Calder aircraft became a familiar sight at airports all over the Nation—often mistaken for a wild, private aircraft, but recognized as the Braniff flying artwork just as many times.

Of course, there were the derisive comments, too, such as that from the cockpit of an American Airlines 727 that had taxied around the corner of the concourse at Oklahoma City's Will Rogers World Airport one afternoon. Spotting the brightly colored Calder 727 sitting at the Braniff gate, the American pilot keyed his microphone on ground-control frequency and asked simply: "Circus in town?"

In fact, it was just the opposite. The era of circuslike fashions and colors for Braniff's flight attendants and aircraft, which had thrust Braniff into national recognition twelve years before, was about to give way to something much more subdued, much more elegant. Since the flight attendants and the passengers were getting tired of the ten-year-old design of the Pucci uniforms and the bright, pastel colors of the Girard aircraft interiors, Lawrence approved the hiring of the current rage in American *haute couture*, Halston, to design new uniforms for the entire airline and new interiors for the aircraft. The new interiors for the aircraft featured a far more subdued, boardroom look, with genuine leather seats as the central point of uniqueness. The entire package was called the new Braniff "ultra" look, and in early 1977, to introduce it, Braniff threw a huge, extravagant party in Mexico called "Three Nights in Acapulco." The internationally reported affair was a sort of corporate "coming out" party, with an elegant Braniff as the debutante—a celebration of the Halston designs, the new interiors, the new "ultra service" and "ultra" look, and a celebration of the company's record-setting profitability.[1]

Over three hundred guests were flown in from around the world for the Acapulco party—jet-setters and "beautiful people," as they were called in the press. The affair was shamelessly contrived, shamelessly extravagant, and shamelessly successful in establishing the desired image—that there was no airline on Earth as stylish, pacesetting, and internationally sophisticated as Harding Lawrence's Braniff International.

Most of the Braniff employees read of the company-funded extravaganza in a multipage, full-color spread in the next Braniff inflight magazine, which had been renamed *Flying Colors*, in keeping with the new slogan, "The Flying Colors of Braniff International"

[1] The company had turned in a 64.6 percent increase in profits for 1976, earning $26,369,000 after taxes on revenues that now topped $679 million annually (recall that Braniff in 1965 was a $100-million-a-year company).

The "ultra touch" was introduced in the airline's 1976 annual report: "Braniff . . . not only is profitable but has an unusual route structure which is based, in large part, on business travel rather than pleasure travel. In fact, some 70% of Braniff passengers are business travelers. They respond to more service not less service, better treatment not poorer treatment, more comfort not less comfort. Braniff's opportunity, then, is to give its own air travelers what they want rather than what others think they want, in other words to give them superior quality in passenger service. Braniff perhaps can never aspire to be the biggest airline in size, but it can attempt to set new standards of quality in the airline business and, specifically, in everything a passenger touches, sees, tastes, and experiences."

(or as it was known on the Latin American routes, *Los Colores Triun-fales de Braniff*—the triumphant colors of Braniff). Although many Braniff people were impressed, many others were disgusted, and a large number wondered about the obviously lavish cost. As had been the case so often in the past when new campaigns or promotions were announced, the company failed to tell the employees (who would be administering the promised services to the public) much about it. Suddenly Braniff was spending hundreds of thousands of dollars in Mexico to announce Braniff "ultra service," and none but a few managers in any department had been given any instruction in what "ultra service" was supposed to be. When at last a "road show" training course of considerable quality was put together, it was quite effective. The problem was follow-up. As with too many Braniff programs in the past, it was a one-shot training course. Instead of revitalizing the airline's service capabilities, it provided a momentary flicker of excitement, then was forgotten by the employees—flight crews and ground personnel alike.

And what of the promotional money? That, in fact, was brilliantly spent. Lawrence had a personal rule about never spending more than ten cents to make a dollar. Considering the publicity value alone of the Acapulco gala (and the fact that half of the expense was paid for by the Mexican Ministry of Tourism), the party probably produced at least ten times as much value as its cost. Although many of the chairman's "social" expenditures over the years looked foolish to the employees, the majority were highly cost-effective.

Braniff's propensity for throwing money around (as the local press called it) did extend to the employees every so often. On the western edge of DFW Airport, Braniff had begun work on a lavish new world headquarters complex that was going to house all the executive offices and flight training facilities as well as a hotel. Lawrence had also included in the design what amounted to a small country club, with a golf course, swimming pools, racquetball courts and tennis courts, a gigantic gymnasium, and other features, all of them available without fee exclusively to any Braniff employee. As the chairman would point out after its completion, no airline had ever built such a lavish playground for its people. In fact, though, it saved money by consolidating the company functions such as training. In addition, the complex was built with a local airport bond issue at just over 6 percent, cost $7.42 per square foot to operate, and utilized the acres of land behind the complex without cost.

Harding Lawrence, as surprising as it would seem to many of his employees, many of whom held a different image of him, truly believed that the most important assets of the company—what actually constituted the company—were the Braniff people. He may not have felt a warm, personal kinship with the average Braniff employee, but he firmly believed that his stewardship as head of the company meant that he worked for the employees as well and had a responsibility to look after their welfare even if he hated to part with the money. He knew what too many corporate leaders have forgotten over the years—that the aircraft, the facilities, and all the other "assets" referred to in annual reports and banking transactions were worthless without the people and their expertise to mold them into an airline. Lawrence's belief in this as an axiom came both from his background at Continental (and Bob Six's attitude toward "his" people) and from Lawrence's own family background. (This concept, however, would be foreign to those who would follow him as president in the troubled years to come.) The chairman didn't communicate it to the rank and file very well over the years, and he certainly neither had nor deserved a reputation for being especially generous with the company's cash, but there were some overt examples, the lavishness of the world headquarters being only one of them.

Long before Lawrence arrived from Continental, Braniff had been giving out service pins (a tiny set of wings with various stones set in the middle) for employment anniversaries of ten, fifteen, twenty years and up (at five-year intervals). It was a tradition, and for the wearer, a badge of pride—but over the years no one had found a more ceremonious method of presentation than a quick handshake and photographs in the boss's office. When the pin was for twenty-five or more years with the company, its presentation seemed to call for a bit more pomp and circumstance. In the late 1960s, an employee committee suggested an annual awards banquet for all honorees of the year, and Lawrence surprised everyone by not only embracing the idea, but also doing so with typical Lawrence style.

Braniff began throwing an annual extravaganza. The honorees and their families (if from an outstation) would be flown into Dallas and put up at one of the finest hotels in town the night before, then treated to a reception, a sumptuous dinner, wine, entertainment, congratulations, and an open bar. Lawrence and most of the senior officers would usually attend the bash, and for the honored employees and their families, it would be a genuine night to remember—a high point in their careers. The tradition that was established became well appreciated and well respected. It was on such a night that Bob Annear, one of the pilot crew schedulers from Minneapolis, was so honored on his twenty-fifth year with the airline.

Annear, who was single, brought his close friend Ginny Linder, who had been head of the flight attendant base in Minneapolis for several years. She had met Lawrence before, and remembered listening to him talk about Mary Wells Lawrence all the way to New York on a late evening Braniff flight. But she was still in awe of him. As Annear prepared to get up and go over to the open bar near their table, Ginny pulled at his sleeve and pointed out the imposing man standing in front of it—Harding Lawrence. "You're not going up there now, are you? Harding's up there."

"Who cares? I've never been impressed with upper management. I mean, he's just a man." Annear got up and walked over to where the chairman was standing.

"Excuse me, Mr. Lawrence, I'd like to get to the bar here, please."

Lawrence, who had been talking to another company executive, stopped and looked at Annear a moment without speaking. "You're from Minneapolis, right?"

"That's right."

"You're—ah—you're a pilot scheduler up there, aren't you?"

Bob Annear was surprised. He'd met Lawrence once before, but that had been years ago on a quick inspection trip.

"Yes—in Minneapolis. But how—"

"I thought so!" Lawrence said, smiling. "I remember meeting you some years back."

Annear felt a bit flustered. "I hope you'll excuse me, but I just wanted to get a drink."

"Oh, I'm sorry!" Lawrence said, smiling again and gesturing toward the rest of the huge ballroom. "You know, this is kind of dumb—this is for the employees, our honored guests, and here we are hogging the bar. Please, go right up there and help yourself."

Annear got his drinks and returned to Ginny at the table, grinning from ear to ear.

"I don't believe you did that!" she said.

"What the hell, he's just like I am. He just makes a lot more money, that's all."

Annear was still grinning when the evening ended hours later.

The next morning at the Braniff Building, Lawrence stepped into the elevator with one of the people from public relations.

"That was another beautiful party last night, Mr. Lawrence. Didn't you think so?"

Lawrence gave her a withering stare as the doors opened at the tenth floor.

"Yeah, but I wonder if it's worth all that money," he said with a growl as he left the elevator and stalked down the hall toward his office.

All the pieces seemed to be falling into place in Lawrence's view. It was the summer of 1977, the Halston uniforms were being deployed throughout the flight attendant ranks, the new leather seats were being installed as fast as maintenance could handle the job, and the beautiful new solid-color paint scheme for the 727's and the DC-8's was finally coming on the line—elegant, subdued colors of dark brown, dark blue, and six others, with the name "Braniff" in script. The company had just received its first new route award in several years and by July had added service from Denver to the heart of Delta's territory—Atlanta, along with Denver–Oklahoma City and Denver–Miami. Congress was hotly debating the deregulation proposals of Kennedy and Cannon, but passage still seemed uncertain. Many of the unions and most of the carriers were working in the same cause, creating a blizzard of letters and telegrams to Capitol Hill demanding the death penalty for the deregulation proposals. The letters and telegrams were coming from tens of thousands of airline employees (and their friends and families) across the nation fearful of what would become of their jobs and their industry if the bill was passed and the dire predictions of doom came true.

Lawrence was engaged in another battle at the moment. He wanted London. He was determined that Braniff would be the first carrier to fly nonstop from Dallas to London, and he had pulled out all the stops to secure the route, which was now under consideration by the CAB in response to a new set of bilateral agreements with Britain. Braniff's application had first been filed in 1974, but had then awaited the glacial movement of the CAB and the State

Department. The United States under Carter's administration was systematically renegotiating many of the international treaties that permit American-flag carriers entry abroad and permit foreign carriers access to U.S. airports. Now, with the door flung wide and foreign carriers hungering for entry to the heartland of the United States, new ports of entry such as Dallas-Fort Worth, Atlanta, and Kansas City (not hamstrung by the air-traffic problems of New York, Chicago, and Los Angeles) were open to U.S. carriers as well for reciprocal access to the foreign destinations. Braniff had jumped into the fray instantly with a renewed London application, promising a startling array of cut-rate fares on a 747 if the route was granted. The competition was fierce, and the other U.S. carriers (including American Airlines) who were competing for the route were making much of the fact that Lawrence only had one jumbo and therefore couldn't possibly service the route.

In the end it was going to be a political decision, and despite the recent setbacks (the Nixon campaign contribution problem), Lawrence was still a master at understanding the political system and how to handle it to Braniff's best advantage. It was, for instance, no coincidence that the former chairman of the Democratic Party's National Committee, Bob Strauss (a Texan), had been elected recently to the Braniff Board, though he resigned within months due to other commitments.

When the decision was reached, the CAB in their "wisdom" awarded the route to Pan American. Lawrence put the airline on full "battle alert." He was *not*—repeat, *not*—going to lose that route! President Jimmy Carter suddenly began receiving a small avalanche of mail and telegrams from Braniff's friends and employees, as well as interested community leaders and politicians throughout the Southwest. While Lawrence and several senior staff members flew to Washington to lobby the White House directly, Carter's staff was being told by a wide range of sources (including congressional) that it made no sense to let Pan Am serve the route since Pan Am possessed virtually no "feeder" system at DFW.

Much of the traffic Braniff could generate would come in on Braniff aircraft from all over the Braniff system in the Midwest and Southwest. Pan Am would have to generate all their London-bound traffic from just the Dallas-Fort Worth area, or have their passengers laboriously transfer from other carriers in other far-flung parts of the sprawling DFW airport complex. It didn't make a damn bit of sense—in the language of countless telegrams. Additionally, the CAB had contradicted itself in that they had awarded Delta a London route from their home city of Atlanta (where they had feeder capability as well), TWA a London route from Kansas City, and Northwest a London route from Minneapolis-St. Paul. The allegation that the CAB had pointedly ignored Braniff just to throw a bone to Pan Am and that such action was inconsistent with the awards to other carriers in their home cities was used to bloody the name and alleged "wisdom" of the CAB as the campaign continued to batter the White House.

On an international route award, the CAB does not make the final decision. Their "decision" is merely a recommendation to the White House. It is up to the current occupant of the Oval Office to take the time to make a sage decision on who should get the golden apple. In this case, after due consideration (which had to include the political implications of imposing a New York-based carrier on Texas), Carter decided that Braniff was indeed the proper choice and overturned the CAB's decision. Harding Lawrence had his route!

While William T. Seawell, a retired Air Force general and chairman of Pan Am, screamed foul and petitioned the White House for a review of the decision, Braniff began preparations for a European debut. New sales offices were opened in London and the Continent, new lavish inflight menus and service additions were designed, and a gigantic inaugural celebration in the grand style of Braniff was planned on a scale that would have done justice to Busby Berkeley.

Although the assault on the White House had been a *tour de force,* the assault on London began as a "tour de farce" thanks to the British.

For some reason, Lawrence and the senior people he sent to London to set up the arrangements for the new route thought the British should be as excited at the prospect of a direct Braniff air link to DFW as Braniff was. To put it mildly, the British were "underwhelmed." Those Britons who were familiar with Braniff to any degree remembered it as a brash and flashy carrier from that probably still uncultured state of Texas, where only Neiman-Marcus could pass their muster (never mind that the TV show *Dallas* would take Britain by storm two years later and result in the presence of Stetsons in place of bowlers on British heads in Trafalgar Square). British Airways, after all, was not being allowed to fly to the hinterlands of, pardon the term, "Big D." Only British Caledonian Airways was allowed in the state of Texas, and then only in Houston. That was decidedly insufficient to justify the excitement of Queen and country, so it was a less than enthusiastic response that Braniff people received when they approached Her Majesty's government on the subject of which British airport would be open to Braniff. Certainly, Braniff indicated, the British wouldn't mind if Braniff flew into Heathrow Airport (the main international airport just west of London).

In fact, the British minded very much indeed, thank you. The upstart operator of gaudily colored aircraft from the colonies would do quite well at Gatwick, if you please, and the appropriate paperwork was begun by the appropriate ministries to institutionalize the decision.

Gatwick is a relatively quiet airport twenty-seven miles south of London and twenty-five miles distant from the worldwide connections provided at Heathrow. Harding Lawrence hadn't the slightest desire to be stuck at Gatwick. He wanted to fly to London, not the English countryside (lovely as it is). This was to be Braniff's gateway to Europe, and despite the fact that Gatwick was the home of British Caledonian Airways and did provide connections all over the Continent, Lawrence felt the decision would hurt. The war was on.

First, he went to the CAB for help. Since the members of that theoretically independent body had just suffered the humiliating experience of having been overruled by the President, they were somewhat less than enthusiastic about jumping into a further controversy on Braniff's side. In fact, Lawrence got no support at all from the CAB or the State Department. If Braniff wanted to fly to London, they would have to land where the British told them to land. The British objections were centered around explanations of severe overcrowding at Heathrow (and in that they were technically correct) and a questionable verbal agreement that the U.S. bilateral negotiator had made with his British counterpart at the termination of the "Bermuda Two" talks: Any U.S. carrier chosen for London service that was not already flying into Heathrow would fly into Gatwick. It was not part of the treaty, but the British were holding America's feet to the fire on the point, and Lawrence was asking an embarrassed U.S. government for help which, if given, would spotlight still another sophomoric mistake by the Carter administration.

The true motivation for the severity of the British resistance, however, had more to do with considerations of who was going to tell whom to do what in whose country, than which airport had more empty gates. Braniff could have been accommodated had the British Ministry of Aviation so desired.

With virtually no support from his own government, Lawrence ordered the preparations begun for entry to Gatwick as he plotted a new campaign to get Heathrow.

On March 1, 1978, Braniff Ship 601, otherwise known as the *Great Pumpkin,* touched down at Gatwick with a full load of dignitaries and Braniff brass, wives, members of the press, and an ample selection of politicians. There were 244 people in all, brought over and put up at Braniff's expense for the weekend at the Savoy in London.

For the departure from DFW Braniff engaged the service of an old English-style "town crier," and on the ramp at Gatwick the welcoming strains of music came from the Queen's Windsor Barracks Regiment Band (the only donated part of the affair)—a welcoming gift from the British government after all. When the weekend festivities were over and the guests had all been returned to Texas, the final tab came to about $350,000, though one newspaper would later erroneously peg the cost at $2 million.

Now, however, the British had discovered another ripe issue of contention: Braniff's discount fares. Neither British Airways nor British Caledonian Airways had any desire to give away their product, and the fare structure the U.S. Civil Aeronautics Board had approved for Braniff to use was far too low in the British view. This time the U.S. government was in the fray on Braniff's side. In fact, Braniff was caught in the middle between the two governments as they fought over the obscure meaning of a portion of the bilateral agreement and whether Britain had to accept the American fares. While the "row" was in progress, Braniff had to delay the start of service for three long weeks.

Finally, on March 18, Braniff's first live London flight departed for Gatwick, carrying passengers at the discounted fares. The British had lost the skirmish over the low fares, but Braniff had lost the war over Heathrow. Her Majesty's government might be forced to honor a treaty obligation, but it would jolly well not be dictated to by a mere airline.

The amazing aspect of the new London service was the fact that it was operationally profitable within the first sixty days. The load factors, even with the cut-rate fares, were significantly high, and the cargo Braniff carried in the hold of the giant 747 almost paid the operating expenses alone. It was another boost to Braniff's reputation as well. There was no lack of local pride that Braniff had become a true international carrier (many people had never regarded the South American system as qualifying Braniff for "international" status—possibly because the routes did not originate from DFW).

In August 1978, as the traffic continued to build on the shiny new London route, Lawrence went to a cocktail reception given by Gene Bishop, chairman of the Mercantile Bank of Dallas, for a newcomer to the local business community, a fellow named Howard Putnam from United Airlines' Chicago headquarters. One of Southwest Airlines' founders, Lamar Muse, had just been fired by Southwest's Board as president, and Putnam had been brought in to take over. Lawrence came to look the new man over.

After being introduced, Lawrence took Putnam aside.

"Is it true that United increased the productivity of the fleet by flying more hours and flying more efficiently—and that by doing so you effectively increased the size of the airline by 28 percent without buying another airplane?"

Putnam looked at Lawrence in admiration. "That's exactly right!"

Lawrence didn't smile. He was coming to a point. "Do you know that the size of that increase alone is the size of Braniff today?"

Putnam didn't answer.

"It concerns me for the future that if deregulation comes, what will happen to an airline like Braniff? Will we just get swallowed up by someone else?"

Putnam replied that he didn't know, but he could see that the prospect existed.

"Well, if deregulation comes," Harding continued, "I don't think it will last very long. I think there will be a window, and then people will try to reregulate. And"—he lowered his head slightly, striking a determined and conspiratorial pose—"Braniff will be ready!"

Lawrence had a look in his eyes that Putnam had seldom seen in anyone. It was obvious that he meant exactly what he had said.

Howard Putnam went home thinking of that statement and of the look in Lawrence's eyes. Whatever was going to happen, it was obvious to Putnam that it wouldn't catch Harding Lawrence napping.

*   *   *

On October 19, 1978, the Congress of the United States passed the Airline Deregulation Act of 1978, and the lines began forming at the CAB building within hours to apply for the dormant routes.

The lights in the executive offices of Braniff at Exchange Park in Dallas began burning into the night. The pressure was on. That window was open.

Today London, Tomorrow the World

CHAPTER **13**   While the members of the Civil Aeronautics Board grappled with the dormant-route applications in the last week of October 1978, including Braniff's request for 626 of them, Lawrence flew to New York to attend a formal dinner of the Wings Club (an aviation business and social organization of which Lawrence was a past president) along with a group of other airline chiefs who were the collective guests of honor for the evening. Lawrence found himself seated at the head table between United Airlines President Dick Ferris on his right and American Airlines Chairman Al Casey (Braniff Vice President John Casey's brother) on his left. As the evening progressed, Lawrence and Ferris became engaged in a slightly contentious discussion over whether Braniff could keep the promise it had made to the public and the CAB that its new service from Seattle and Portland to Honolulu would be started with a 747 by the end of October.

Braniff had jumped into the new market along with several other carriers (including United) when Pan Am filed for authority to abandon the route. Braniff promised new low fares and the use of a 747. Ferris's United was planning to start the new route by November first with a DC-8-61 (the super-stretch DC-8), since United couldn't get an extra jumbo for the route until December.

Unlike the period in the early seventies when 747's, DC-10's, and 1011's were being parked on desert airfields from lack of need, the airline business in 1978 was booming, and there was no ready supply of the giant airliners for lease or purchase. If United—the largest airline in the Free World—couldn't find a jumbo for the route by November 1, Harding Lawrence and little Braniff certainly couldn't find one, regardless of Harding's well-known bravado and reputation for achieving the impossible.

"Harding, there is no way—*no way*—you're going to be able to keep that promise about starting with a 747 unless you lease one, and there aren't any available to lease!"

"Well, we'll see," Lawrence replied, grinning slightly.

"Would you care to make a small wager on it?"

Lawrence thought about it a second, then turned back to Dick Ferris: "I have been known to make a small wager on occasion. How much would you like to lose, Dick?"

"One hundred says you can't find a 747 to lease by November first!"

Al Casey leaned past Lawrence's left elbow to where he could see Ferris. "Dick—don't bet him!"

Lawrence just grinned.

"It's a sure thing, Al. He can't do it. I know the location of every 747 in the world, and there simply isn't one for him to lease!"

Lawrence extended his hand and Ferris shook it to seal the bet. "You're on, Dick. One hundred."

Al Casey was shaking his head in disbelief. He leaned past Lawrence's elbow again, nearly dipping the sleeve of his tux in his plate.

"Dick, you damn fool! I told you not to bet him. I leased him a 747 before dinner!"

When the $100 check arrived on Lawrence's desk the following week from Dick Ferris, Lawrence endorsed it over to Ferris's sons and had Marion Drinkard (his longtime secretary at Continental and Braniff) prepare a letter to the two boys that said in part, ". . . I hate to inform you of it, but your father is squandering your inheritance! You'd better prevail upon him to stop making foolish bets. The enclosed check is for you fellows. Buy yourselves something fun."

Lawrence's people had advised against Braniff taking the Seattle/Portland to Hawaii route. Lawrence wanted anything he could get in the Pacific (to give the company additional toeholds for the future) and theorized that Braniff could begin the flight sequence in Dallas (DFW), pick up more passengers in Seattle and Portland, and then fly on to Hawaii, picking up equally good loads for both areas on the return trip. The idea refused to take into account the warnings from Braniff's own sales people in Seattle that Northwesterners wouldn't like the resulting schedules (or the overnight return from Honolulu). Braniff started the flights anyway—ahead of United—and began flying a nearly empty 747 back and forth. In midspring they acceded to the anguished protests of the northwestern sales force and changed the schedule to provide a same-day return from the islands, but that cut out the single-plane Dallas traffic (there was no way to make a DFW–Seattle–Portland–Honolulu and back round trip work on a daily basis with one aircraft). With no feed from the Southwest, Braniff couldn't generate enough originating traffic from Seattle and Portland to break even. In July, Braniff pulled out—seriously damaging the credibility of its sales force in the Northwest, which had been trying desperately to convince area travel agents that Braniff wouldn't pull out.

In early November the CAB made its decision on the dormant routes. Brushing aside with undisguised disdain Braniff's grandiose request for 626 routes, it granted 67. The attitude among most of the CAB members was that there was no way Braniff and Lawrence could begin even a fraction of those 67 routes in the allotted time of 45 days. The CAB was wrong.

In the period between mid-1974 and October 31, 1978, a staggering total of 588 new pilots had been hired—a 48 percent increase! Braniff suddenly announced in early December of 1978 that it would bring on an additional 300 pilots and 300 flight attendants by early spring for the massive increase in scheduled flying time resulting from all the new routes. With much of the new service to start by December 15, there wasn't time to hire and train the aircrews, so Braniff's existing pilots and flight attendants agreed to increase their flying hours drastically for a 4-month period. Whereas the pilots usually flew a maximum of 75 "block hours" per month, the company (with the full approval and cooperation of the unions) raised the maximum to 90 hours per month for a 4-month period (which was still below the FAA maximum).[1]

---

[1] Contrary to popular belief, airline pilots do not work only 75 hours per month. The "block hours" are those from the time the aircraft begins the pushback or taxi-out sequence at the gate to the minute its wheels come to a stop at the destination gate. None of the massive amount of duty time necessary to position for, prepare

The flight attendants raised their maximum duty times too, and while the hiring got under way in full force, Braniff's aircrews, flushed with the excitement of their company's phenomenal growth, enthusiastically jumped to the task.

So did the ground forces. New agents had to be hired and positioned at all the new stations around the system, which also had to have ticket counters, local telephone numbers, service contracts for fuel and cleaning, and catering of the inflight food. Local airport clearances, baggage handling facilities and personnel, local sales agents, and regional managers had to be selected and positioned, and what seemed like a thousand other details had to be handled. It was no wonder that the executives of most other major carriers around the nation looked at the Braniff situation in late November and smugly assumed that at last Harding Lawrence had bitten off too much: There was virtually no way an airline the size of Braniff could start up so many routes in such a short time with such a small cadre of management people and operational crews—and even if Lawrence could get it done, there was no way it could be done smoothly and professionally.

It was also no wonder that those same executives were all but dumbstruck when on Decembr 15, 1978, in one 24-hour period, Braniff International successfully initiated 32 new routes involving 16 brand-new cities that Braniff had never before served. It was (as the next year's annual report would crow) "the largest single-day increase by any airline in history!" By damn, ole Harding had done it!

But what had he done—beyond the incredible feat of logistics? In his view, he had positioned Braniff in one quick move into some new markets it had been trying to secure for years. True, some of the

---

for, and connect with the periods in which "block hours" are running is included. International pilots often fly only 8 to 10 days per month, but during that period they rack up all of their 75 or 80 hours of "block time" plus all the other duty time. The average domestic-route pilot usually needs about 15 on-duty days a month to log the same number of hours. Whether international or domestic, however, the "duty days" may be as much as 15 hours long. The average 8-hour-per-day office worker in the United States puts in about 175 hours of "on duty" time per month. The average airline pilot averages between 160 to 240 hours of "on duty" time per month (not including personal commuting time for those who don't live in their base cities). The accusations over the years that airline pilots are semiretired in terms of work hours are obviously ridiculous. In Braniff's case in late 1978, the crews were paid on a per-hour basis, so they were paid proportionally more for flying 90 hours per month. However, the number of days each pilot was away from home each month also increased dramatically.

routes into some of those markets were bad, but at least Braniff would be serving the targeted city (such as Jacksonville, Florida; Orlando, Florida; and Birmingham, Alabama). Second, he had done it for comparatively little cost, considering the traditional start-up costs of a new route into a new city. Many of the new segments were "add-ons" (such as Cleveland, Ohio, served by a flight that normally stopped in Chicago; or Albany, New York, served by one that normally terminated at Kennedy International Airport in New York City), and the additional crew and fuel costs were very small.

Lawrence had, however, spent a significant amount of cash in a very short period of time to get things done overnight. At least some of that money could have been saved if more time had been granted to the executives and managers who were told to hit the road and not come home until their assigned cities were ready to operate flights. Some of the leases they tied Braniff into were shamelessly expensive and had to be renegotiated—or different suppliers substituted—within months.

More significant, however, was the problem of scale. All the normal operational problems had been scaled up to even more unmanageable proportions by the astounding, overnight expansion of December 15. The normal mistakes in timing, servicing, providing crews, and dispatching the network of aircraft were magnified. Confusion, though admirably limited, crept into the operation. The least of the problems were such gaffes as flight attendants forgetting which city they were landing in as they made their welcoming announcements, and the plight of the pilot and flight attendant crew schedulers who were about to lose their sanity trying to keep the airplanes and the crew members matched up.

In the midst of all this frantic activity, the people who ran the flight attendant department and the people hiring and training pilots were under incredible pressure. A total of 117 pilots were hired in November, 121 more were hired in December, with 100 more to be hired in January. Because Federal Aviation Agency requirements dictate precisely the training sequence a pilot must go through to join the line pilots as a flight engineer, there was no way to shorten the amount of training required or the length of time it took. For this reason there was a pressing need for the remainder of the pilots to agree to extend their flight hours to 90 hours monthly.[2]

[2] Braniff could hire and ready a new pilot for "line flying" very rapidly because it had a ready source. "BESI" (Braniff Educations Systems, Inc., a subsidiary) pro-

The flight attendants are not as tightly governed by the Federal Aviation Agency regulations, and thus it was possible to cut their school almost in half. Over 300 new employees, men and women, had been hired by the end of January. They were rushed through the abbreviated school, adorned with Halston outfits and Hartman flight luggage (at their own expense), issued their service manuals, given a check ride, and turned loose on the line. As the old joke goes, it was a case of "Yesterday I couldn't even spell 'flight attendant,' and now I are one!"

Yet again, a quick cure begat a more serious problem. A steady deterioration of the quality of Braniff's inflight service began that did not escape the attention of the media nor the eye of the passengers—even those in the new cities that Braniff had just begun to serve.

Braniff's "ultra" service was a joy to behold on paper, but translating it into reality took a great deal of hard work by flight attendants. They had to follow a myriad of procedures often in a tiny galley, in sequence, working with and beside each other, carrying and returning the trays bearing the food and drink to up to 130 passengers on flight segments as short as one hour (such as DFW to Kansas City). All this was done on one's feet, and while some of the longer flight segments provided time to sit down (and even loaf), the "service," as the airborne meal or snack is called, required poise, skill, experience, compatibility, diplomacy, and patience—not to mention stamina and strength.

There is very little likelihood that even carefully screened people (300 in this case) are all going to be capable of such performance within days of their graduation from a training course that itself has been compressed and minimized. There were also problems with compressing the screening process and hiring so many in such a short period of time. Incapable people could and did slip through, as did a few whose attitudes from the first moment belied any inten-

---

vided would-be commercial pilots with a course costing $5,000 that would give them one of the qualifications (a flight engineer license earned in the Boeing 727) that Braniff, the airline, required as a minimum for pilot applicants. Since thousands of ex-military pilots were looking for airline jobs in the midseventies, and since almost none of them had this type of license, BESI made millions—much of it in Veterans Administration benefit money—providing the type of training that most other airlines provided free to pilots after hiring them. It was a morally reprehensible exercise in shameless exploitation of the unlimited supply of pilots and the VA benefits—but it was highly profitable for the company.

tion to work for a living. The majority, of course, were good, young people doing their best, but the predictable problems began occurring almost as soon as they went on the line.

Amateurish announcements, botched "services," spilled food and drink, and one flight attendant who couldn't remember how to open the forward door of a 727 in Tulsa one February afternoon were just some of the examples.

The vast majority of the inflight services and the performances of the people old and new were marvelous, given the situation and the confusion. But the problems that did occur, even though they were corrected in large measure as the months went by, brought the public perception of Braniff down a notch from where the glamorous expansion had placed it—thanks in no small measure to the merciless reporting of the media.

Still, Braniff's people had managed an incredible feat. The size of the airline and its operations had increased over 30 percent in a few short months, and now even its new Concorde service was ready to begin (subsonically). It was a shame that the breadth of the achievements was somewhat obscured by the problems in quality, but in the parlance of aviation, "A thousand 'Attaboys' are wiped out by a single 'Aw, shit!'"[3]

An executive of United Airlines in Chicago remarked to a Braniff pilot one afternoon in late spring 1979: "You guys did in ten days with the Concorde what it would take our bureaucracy ten months to do. Hell, we'd take ten months just to complete a feasibility study. How you did it so understaffed is incredible!"

That's exactly the reason Braniff was able to do it.

Braniff had traditionally kept its middle-level manning lean— keeping only a handful of people in certain departments where other airlines had thirty or forty or more. For example, the eight-man office in charge of technical performance and flight manuals, headed by a fellow named Jerry Albers, had as its counterpart at

[3] To date Braniff was the only U.S. airline ever to operate the Concorde. After overcoming unbelievable legal, regulatory, training, international, and financial difficulties, Braniff pilots and flight attendants began flying the craft at subsonic speeds from Dulles International Airport near Washington, D.C. to DFW Airport daily after the Air France aircraft had come in supersonically from Paris. The following morning another Braniff crew would return it to Washington, where the French crew would take over and fly it (and the Braniff passengers) back to Paris. On alternate days the interchange airline was British Airways, and the European origin/destination was London's Heathrow Airport.

American Airlines several departments containing a total of over fifty people. Albers was under Chief Pilot (and Senior Vice President) Captain Bill Garbett's area of responsibility, and this section accomplished the equally incredible task of solving the technical problems—as well as the paperwork and training headaches—created by the new agreement among Air France, British Airways, Aerospatiale, and Braniff for Braniff to operate the Concorde. A challenge to the legal, regulatory, technical standards, flight standards, publications preparation, and flight-training capabilities of Braniff that could have taken the better part of two years was done in six months, and in the same period of time in which Lawrence hired three hundred pilots, started Seattle service to Honolulu, began thirty-one new routes in twenty-four hours, and won a $100 bet from Dick Ferris.

The reason the company could move so fast was the lack of organizational restraints. The same problem—different divisions and sections of the company becoming so isolated that their organizational line of communication and authority bypassed the formal organizational chart and went directly to Lawrence's office—also enabled nearly instantaneous accomplishment of tasks a normal bureaucratic corporate structure would need weeks or months just to plan. The year 1978 brought out the few benefits of this structural weakness in Braniff's system. It also demonstrated the incredible depth of energy and commitment of so many of those people whose areas of responsibility were seldom recognized by the outside world, or even by other members of their company.

Many of those deserving and highly effective people who accomplished so much for the company would nevertheless (because they were technically management) be tarred by the image of the confused, ill-trained, and failed majority of the company's middle management. Such a result is unfortunate but merely a measure of how disastrously ineffective so many managers were at that level. The good people were there—struggling with various degrees of effectiveness to figure out how to excel in their tasks regardless of the lack of support, lack of guidance or training, or the inordinate confusion of the political games constantly being played within their managerial level. They were the valuable ones, and they were in the minority.

On May 4, 1979, when United's people walked out on strike and grounded their behemoth airline, Braniff's Tom Robertson and staff once again beat a path to the CAB, this time to apply for temporary Los Angeles–Honolulu authority. Due to CAB General Director Mike Levine's unauthorized but effective decision to speed up the deregulatory process and award just about any route to any airline that asked for it, Braniff was getting close to an award of regular Pacific authority to such destinations as Guam, Hong Kong, and Singapore (with applications to Seoul and Tokyo as well in the hopper). The CAB granted the temporary Los Angeles–Honolulu route almost immediately to Braniff and several other carriers (to pick up United's traffic while the strike lasted), and another instantaneous Braniff route start-up was under way.

Braniff already had terminal support and ticket counter facilities at Los Angeles and Honolulu, so the depth of the effort required for this new route was more limited in scope. Pilot and flight attendant schedules had to be reshuffled, a maintenance facility had to be contracted for at Los Angeles (TWA ended up doing the honors), and more advertising had to be formulated to let people know Braniff had invaded the market as another $50 million 747 came off the line in Everett, Washington, just in time to go on the new route.

For Braniff, the new flight meant a new toehold in the area and the opportunity to get positioned for the long-sought Pacific routes Lawrence had been lusting after for many years—routes it had flown ten years before as a contract carrier for the Air Force's Military Airlift Command (ferrying military troups and dependents to and from the Far East).

For the previous two years, a negotiating team acting on the orders of President Carter to renegotiate the expiring bilateral air treaties with many nations had been pursuing a policy of "open skies"—essentially trying to force the new American concept of deregulated routes and deregulated price structures on the other nations of the Atlantic and the Pacific. What the new strategy did in fact accomplish was to fritter away a cornucopia of valuable routes from many foreign countries to major airports in cities all across the United States, while in return giving U.S. airlines the "right" to pay exorbitant landing fees, suffer under ruinous ground service costs at remote gates, and put up with "dirty tricks" ranging from government harassment to outright operational sabotage (as in South Korea) as they tried to fly from cities all over the United States into crowded central foreign airports such as those in Amsterdam, Brussels, Frankfurt, Seoul, Hong Kong, and Singapore. The foreign governments and their often subsidized national carriers wanted to fly into the heartland of the United States, but they weren't excited about having to accept additional U.S. airline competition into *their* heartland. The idealism with which the bilateral treaties were concluded by the U.S. team ignored any possibility that the trade-offs might be unbalanced.[4]

The new agreements did give carriers such as Braniff a crack at routes that would have been nearly unattainable a few years before. At the same time, many of those routes were long and "thin" (in terms of revenue), and profitable operation depended on more than fast establishment of service, low fares, or fancy inflight meals. If Lawrence was worried about these drawbacks in the heady summer of 1979, however, he showed no sign of it.

In fact, in April Lawrence had recorded for all Braniff employees a slide/tape presentation entitled "Deregulation and Braniff." In it he spoke of the "specific plan" the company was following as simplified into points A, B, and C:

A: We seek routes domestically and internationally that will let us assemble or collect passengers who will then flow to and through the rest of the system.

B: Logical expansion of our international route system will thus give us a balance from an economic standpoint. When domestic business is slow, perhaps Europe will be strong and vice versa. Having the South American routes has proved of great financial assistance to Braniff at several times during the past ten years.

C: With the proper routes and balance within the system, the key is connecting the international passenger flows over the domestic gateways, connecting the domestic and international passenger flows so they feed each other, and connecting passenger flows within the domestic system at the hub cities.

Many, including other airlines, have asked how we were

---

[4] Not only would Braniff face incredible governmental harassment in places like Hong Kong and Singapore, but in Seoul, South Korea, it would be fighting a rearguard action against an unfriendly government that thought little of threatening the government-monopoly travel agency system in South Korea with dire action if they booked passengers on Braniff instead of Korean Air Lines, and directing a campaign of outright thievery against Braniff operations at Seoul's Kimpo Airport. For instance, Braniff's 747's, when cleaned by ground crews contracted from Korean Air Lines, would regularly be stripped of all the paper products (including toilet paper) from the aircraft.

able to add so much service so quickly. Some, including Braniff employees, have asked why we wanted to do it. There are even those who ask whether Braniff has taken on far more than it can handle. The answer to those questions is that we were ready for deregulation and we are following a very specific plan. The ultimate objective: growth and size as the key to Braniff survival combined with the best service to customers as the key to Braniff success.

Now, how were we able to take on so many new markets in so short a period of time? A major contribution to flight time was secured by increasing utilization from 8.5 hours per day to 9.5 hours per day, which gave us the equivalent of 14 additional aircraft. Some evening flights were extended to new cities. Some frequencies were reduced. But the catalyst was being able to move small increments of capacity around sufficiently to begin service.

If we are successful in all our efforts, then we will be selling all the world on Braniff and selling Braniff to all the world.

Why is growth one basic objective of our plan for Braniff? The answer is that growth of the airline means profits, and profits mean strength, stability, and security in this new era of free competition, when airlines can fly anywhere. The point is that airlines without growth and profits will be smothered by competition. They will not be able to remain in business as independent airlines. To be a surviving and successful airline, we must be strong. To be strong requires profits. To be profitable we must continue to grow. We must secure *and keep* more and more passengers. Keeping the passengers we have and the new ones who try us out then becomes the key to everything. Keeping passengers means our people who deal with our customers must provide service as good as or better than any other airline or our customers will go to those other airlines who fly the same routes.

Only the airlines who are strong and who have the best service will prosper under deregulation. It is as simple as that.

On July 3, 1979, Braniff began serving Guam and Hong Kong; Seoul, South Korea, on September 15; and Singapore on October 31. Schedule changes were coming fast and furiously now. The company was spending incredible sums with every change just to reprint the general schedule (which was distributed all over the system at ticket counters and in the aircraft).

The flow of cash into the Pacific basin reached frightening velocity with the need to set up all these new stations and enter into all the required new contracts, hire all the necessary people, and do all of it seemingly overnight. In the meantime, the European expansion was moving just as fast—and wasting money just as blindly.[5]

Lawrence was reaching for an immediate worldwide system. Among all the other new routes and applications, Braniff had applied to fly direct from DFW to Bahrain in the Persian Gulf (Lawrence felt there was enough southwestern oil traffic going in that direction to justify it). The plan was to extend the Pacific routes as soon as possible south to Australia (the applications were already in), and westward to Bangkok, Thailand, and on to India. The next move would be to link Bahrain and India and secure Braniff's position as America's newest round-the-world airline.

There was a story going around the industry by late 1979 that the CAB had finally told Braniff to go to hell—and Lawrence had promptly applied for the route!

---

[5] While the amounts spent on the domestic system expansion were high, they were not ruinously excessive (though some of the gate leases at various airports locked the company into expensive payments for facilities that would not be needed if the route were later abandoned). In the Atlantic and the Pacific, however, the drive to get the stations set up "yesterday" meant that cost was, essentially, no object. Service contracts, gate and office space, and local personnel were acquired with little thought of the future. (Employing local people in such countries was a special problem, since under the laws of some of those countries Braniff was required to compensate laid-off or terminated workers for up to a year, along with full benefits.) In the event Braniff's entry into such a new station didn't work out and the route was dropped, the expenses would continue. Facilities leased in many locations bound Braniff to payments for years, regardless of whether the gate or office space was used. In addition, different airport authorities and competing airlines that provided gates and services made sure Braniff paid dearly for what it received (which was often inferior), and the demanding manner of many of the Braniff sales and services people angered the locals and drove the prices even higher. In Frankfurt, for instance, Braniff ended up with an office high in the airport terminal building in the most inaccessible location possible, until a German-speaking American— a former Lufthansa employee—was hired and sent over to smooth the ruffled feathers and secure more cooperation. In addition, some of Braniff's sales people began enjoying the effectively unlimited expense accounts in this wild and unsupervised period. In one instance—again in Frankfurt—management-level sales personnel had a contest to see who could spend the most money partying in town in one evening on expense account!

It was Pan Am's application to abandon its Boston–Europe service that once again sent Braniff's people down the well-beaten path to the CAB to apply for that market. It was decided in the executive suite that Boston would make a good East Coast international hub, and would position Braniff for a Boston–London route, and thus more applications were deposited on the counter of the CAB's docket section. Again, there was little resistance. Braniff had not become the darling of the CAB—it was simply the CAB's new policy to give away just about anything to just about anyone.

By June 1, Braniff orange 747's, many of them leased while the new ones were being built, were flying from Boston and DFW directly to Paris, Brussels, Amsterdam, and Frankfurt. The number of trained 747 crews had reached unprecedented proportions, and Braniff had over 2,200 pilots on the payroll where there had been only 1,350 four years before. As with the Pacific, the setup of the new European stations was done in haste, and diplomacy was ignored in too many instances.

It has been said that an airline route—domestic or international—is like a separate business. It may be a part of a massive airline system, but it has to be started, introduced, nurtured, managed, sold, and developed like a subsidiary company if the route has any hope of becoming profitable. Lawrence's theories justifying his monstrous growth of Braniff didn't totally discount this, but in the light of the perceived necessity to grow under the gun of deregulation, his view of the dynamics of the new order and the airline system he was creating to deal with it was fascinating. In the final analysis, it was also characteristically unique.

Braniff, along with Delta, had pioneered the idea of the "hub-and-spoke" concept of airline route systems. The theory of such a system (as Federal Express has contemporarily reproven in small-package service, and many other airlines are now copying) is that the least expensive and most efficient means for collecting people at one spot and delivering them to another when a multiplicity of cities is concerned, is to transport them through a central point, or "hub." For Braniff, DFW was its main "hub," and Kansas City was being expanded as its second.

What Braniff was up to with many of the dormant-route authority segments it had been awarded (the thirty-one new routes started on December 15) was a new refinement Lawrence had adopted to augment the "hub" principle. Basically, if you could add a city one stop past your present end-of-the-line station, such as Albany, New York, tacked on to the Dallas–New York City service, your costs would be minimal and your break-even factor for the route between New York City and Albany would be correspondingly low. The brilliant twist, however, was the recognition that passengers who were carried from Albany through New York City and on to other more distant Braniff destinations were paying many times the cost of an Albany–New York City ticket. As Lawrence explained it shortly after starting Albany service, "The new segment, Albany to New York, produced an average of fifty-one passengers on board, which was less than break-even. However, the seventeen passengers [from Albany] traveling beyond New York had purchased tickets for more distant Braniff destinations. When you take the *total* dollar amount of the tickets of those seventeen longer-distance Albany folks, you'll find it's a hundred ninety times the coach fare from Albany to New York. In other words, from the standpoint of Braniff revenues, those same seventeen generated as much revenue as if we had carried a hundred ninety local passengers from Albany and let them get off in New York. Add that to the average fifty-one passengers on each one of those flights, and the new segment to Albany is flying with an equivalent revenue yield of two hundred twenty-one passengers on each trip for an aircraft that holds a hundred thirty. Thus it was profitable right from the start."

Although this approach worked domestically, the rationale didn't quite translate to some of the foreign destinations.

In the Pacific, Lawrence had long believed that due to the large oriental population in South America and the great amount of trade, there was a large demand for travel between such places as Buenos Aires, Argentina, and Santiago, Chile, on one hand, and Seoul, South Korea, or Tokyo, Japan, Hong Kong, and Singapore, on the other. If that were so, then a carrier who could flow traffic up the West Coast of the South American continent direct to Los Angeles and then across the Pacific in one hop to the Orient could gain a major market share and establish its dominance. In other words, it didn't matter how much competition Braniff would have across the Pacific; there would be enough traffic that only Braniff could carry in a single aircraft all the way from Buenos Aires to Singapore to justify the route and the intermediate stops.

The second cornerstone of justification for the Pacific routes was the expectation of eventually receiving landing rights in Tokyo. In

Lawrence's view, when Tokyo became a Braniff city, any money spent on maintaining a marginal Pacific operation in the meantime would be worth it because the company would have established a solid marketing "presence."

What the theory didn't take into consideration was the financial staying power of the foreign carriers to outlast Braniff in any fare war they might start. This, coupled with expensive harassment and the rising cost of fuel, resulted in the loss of between $25 million and $50 million in the eighteen months of Pacific flying, including some of the astronomical costs of setting up stations such as Singapore, which was dismantled a mere six months after opening, despite the best efforts of Harding Lawrence's son, who had struggled hard to develop the new market overnight.[6]

Jim Lawrence was twenty when he attended the Parisian marriage of his father, Harding Lawrence, to Mary Wells in 1967. By the summer of 1979, at age thirty-two, Jim Lawrence had become vice president for Pacific and Asia for his dad's airline. Well qualified by education and a personable young man who related well to the other officers and employees of the company, Jim Lawrence was also mindful of the implied questions about nepotism and whether he really deserved his salary. Though such questions are inevitable, it was at once ironic and unfair that the Lawrences be confronted with them. Unlike many corporate executives who discourage or ban more than one member of a family from employment with their corporation, Harding Lawrence had traditionally encouraged father-son, father-daughter, husband-wife, etc., employment when the family member was properly qualified, and over the years numerous families held two and even three or more Braniff employees. In one instance in late 1979, Braniff Captain Willard Hayes was able to take his retirement flight to Seattle and back in command of a 747, with his two Braniff pilot sons serving as first officer and second officer. Jim Lawrence was the only one of Harding Lawrence's five children to join Braniff on a full-time basis, though one of his daughters worked for the company during one summer.

[6] Harding Lawrence vociferously disagrees with these loss estimates for the Pacific, estimating them at under $10 million. The company's figures show a loss of over $85 million for the Atlantic and Pacific operations during that time frame, however, but it is unclear how much came from each sector.

At 11:56 A.M. on May 11, 1980, Jim Lawrence sat in a window seat in first class watching the runway at Los Angeles International Airport drop away with unusual speed as the brand-new Boeing 747 SP he was riding in soared over the sand dunes at the western end of the runway and out across the shoreline. The Lufthansa 747's that Braniff had leased, especially Ship 611, usually lumbered off the runway near the very end—giving the passenger an uncomfortably close view of those dunes. This new beauty, however (Ship 603), had fewer seats and power to spare—as well as all the other attributes of a shiny new aircraft. It had cost Braniff $53 million.

Several hours after departure, with the aircraft at thirty-nine thousand feet over the North Pacific on the way to Seoul, South Korea, one of the pilots stopped by Lawrence's seat to invite him up to the cockpit.

Captain Johnny Cole and First Officer Jack Sallee were manning the controls when Lawrence came in and sat down next to the second officer. The three pilots were all commuters to Braniff's new (and very senior) Los Angeles 747 base.

"How are you gentlemen doing up here?" Lawrence asked.

Captain Cole swiveled around, sitting sideways on his left seat as Sallee monitored the aircraft, and answered Lawrence enthusiastically in his gravelly voice.

"We're fine. Fine. Everything okay?"

"Absolutely. Except that I'm going to be on here until Singapore, and I'm going to have to go right to the office when I get in."

"How's it going out here for us?" (The aircraft was carrying fewer than a hundred people from Los Angeles to Seoul.) "We making any money with the small loads?"

"Well, as the chairman says, it takes a little while. I've been trying my best to get some of these problems solved out here so we can get the loads up, but it's an uphill battle. In Singapore, for instance, our competition is Pan Am, and they've got these new, special recliner seats in first class that all the local American businessmen, and for that matter most of the business travelers, really like. I've been screaming at Dallas to get off their duffs and order those seats for this bird and our other SP, but they won't do it. I can't fill up first class going up against Pan Am with those damn seats."

"How much are they?"

"Around forty-two hundred apiece, but they'll pay for themselves rapidly. I know I could fill that first class section of ours on every flight if I had those seats."

Jim Lawrence moved in a bit and warmed to his subject.

"See—these fellows tell me, 'Jim, I'd love to fly Braniff—I think you guys are great, and I know your service is great, but damnit, I need to get some rest on the way and I can't do it in a regular first class seat.'"

"Any chance Dallas will change their minds?"

"I don't know. I know I don't see all they're considering, but they don't have any idea what we're up against out here. Most of the places don't want us in here, and to get anything done is a major job of yelling and demanding and threatening, and then seeing the whole thing botched up. We're making progress, but it'll be a while."

Lawrence and the engineer began talking about the performance of the fabulous SP they were flying and then about an idea the engineer had for an airborne teletype or telephone system to cater to the caliber of executives who fly this type of route first class and who need to stay in touch.

"Well, y'know," Lawrence said, "the problem with that is that if you can reach the ground, the ground can reach you. That means DFW could reach us up here, and that also means the chairman can reach us by phone. It's better if the chairman can't reach you all the time!" He chuckled.

Jack Sallee, a six-foot-two Texan turned northwestern rancher, turned around slightly and asked Lawrence in a slight Texas drawl, "You think we're gonna make it out here?"

Jim Lawrence looked him in the eye, then looked down, apparently in thought. When he answered, he looked up and out the window. "I—don't know. We're sure spending a lot of money."

A short while after Jim Lawrence had left the cockpit to return to his seat, the engineer turned his seat forward and leaned over the center pedestal where both his compatriots could hear him.

"It's kind of strange, but did you notice? This fellow is Harding's son—Harding is his dad—but when he refers to him, it's only as 'the chairman.' Never 'Dad.' Just 'the chairman.'"

The Best and the Biggest

CHAPTER 14 "I don't understand where Harding is going with all this, but I tell you what. If he did decide we were going to fly to hell and back, I'd bid the trip!"

That sort of statement was common in the incredible fall of 1979. Intensive discussions in break rooms, offices, airborne cockpits, galleys, hotel coffee shops on three continents, and favorite watering holes all over the Braniff system focused on the question "Do we have any idea what we're doing?" The usual conclusion was, "If Harding says we can pull it off, then I guess we can."

The "older heads"—people of all job descriptions who had been around Braniff since at least the late 1960s—were fond of ending such discussions with worrisome references such as "No more rumors till after the merger" or "We're hiring again, so when's the furlough?" With the worldwide company communications system and the speed of a jetliner to spread "the word," a new rumor started at breakfast in Seattle (for example) would probably be the topic of dinner discussion that evening in New York, Boston, and Miami, and on its way to Europe, Hong Kong, and Buenos Aires as well.

Most of the rumors were juicy (but often totally inaccurate) items about more expansion, new destinations, or new, significant changes in the inner structure of the company, and they had a positive effect on some of the least content of the Braniff people. No matter how demoralized or disappointed an employee had become with the company or its managers, the vibrancy of the rumors seemed to be able to reach them, instilling almost a renewal of the fierce pride Braniff people had traditionally had in their company— a sort of Braniff "spirit" that transcended all the problems and could exist despite abysmal hatred of management.

Lawrence's record of having repeatedly "gambled" and won—having perpetually snatched victory from the jaws of defeat despite the initial scorn of the airline industry each time—reassured those Braniff employees who tended to have misgivings about the unbelievable expansion. After all, Lawrence had transformed Braniff into a carrier fourteen times its pre-Lawrence size in terms of revenue, six times its original size in terms of ASM's (available seat miles—a measure of the company's route mileage), and three times its size in number of employees. He had also taken them through several recessions, the LTV period, and the fuel crunch of 1973 and had been right every time. The corporation had made money every year but one and now owned the newest fleet in commercial aviation. The rank and file might not love him, but most respected his ability as a pacesetter in commercial aviation. Of course, that same impressive list of accomplishments sustained and justified the confidence of the Board of Directors (as well as the disparate group of insurance companies and banks that would ultimately be unmasked as the closest things to "villains" in Braniff's corporate life—Braniff's long-term lenders).

Yet, confidence or no confidence, empty airplanes the size of a 747 are hard to ignore. Even the most starry-eyed new employee could see that the load factors on the new routes weren't to the break-even level, even though they were the highest in the company's history (an overall average of 56.3 percent against a break-even point of 59.9 percent). The crews who flew the Pacific were well aware that they had the plane to themselves on too many runs to be making money. With the confident rhetoric coming from the fabulous new world headquarters, though, few of the Braniff people spent much time worrying. It was a lot easier to enjoy the new benefits and the corresponding prestige of working for a dynamic, fashionable international carrier that could take care of itself.

Suddenly agents and cargomen and mechanics who had hovered around the lower levels of seniority for years found themselves able to bid for choice positions. Pilots who had been bottom flight engineers in 1973 were now checking out as captains on the 727 in 1978 (an unprecedented speed of progression for airline pilots with a major airline), and some of those who had joined in 1975 were flying as engineers on the 747's and alighting in exotic destinations.

The more experienced among the flight attendants were finding that their new seniority entitled them to stable patterns of flying and a chance at the glamour routes: working the first class sections of the 747 from Dallas to London, or to Frankfurt, Amsterdam, or Paris.

For the executives of junior and senior rank right up to the senior vice presidents, the picture seemed rosy as well, though it would have seemed less so had they faced the reality of how inadequate they were as a group to control and operate an airline of such size. Certainly some very worried vice presidents faced the problem, but so many of the others were too busy enjoying the prestige (and the fatter executive salaries) to be overly concerned. It was exhilarating to work for an airline that had clawed its way into prominence through sheer force of will—the will of Harding Lawrence (and the hard work of approximately ten thousand people, now closer to fifteen thousand). If Lawrence's drive had brought the company this far, who were they to worry about the future? Then too, Lawrence was finally authorizing an infusion of new, more qualified executive management talent into the company, partially through the use of "headhunters" (personnel agencies who specialize in the placement of high-level corporate executives). So for the worried ones who saw the problems, there did appear to be hope that they would catch up and it would all work out.[1]

Suddenly it was possible for Braniff employees and their families

[1] The influx of new managers resulted from Harding Lawrence's belated realization of how many "empty suits" he had in key positions and how alone he really was. He had complained bitterly to several of the new men as they settled in that he had a "plan," but it wasn't reaching the lower ranks—and his calcified, uncommunicative senior officers in operational, sales, and service areas were to blame. The number of senior executives who were at least two levels above their maximum level of competence was frightening. It was late in the game for Lawrence to see the truth, but at least he was beginning to understand, and he expected the new people to solve the problems.

To those new executives hired in this period, joining Lawrence's Braniff was an exciting challenge—made all the more so by Lawrence's stem-winding interviews with each one under consideration. New executives with proven track records at other airlines came into the company impressed with its accomplishments and full of enthusiasm and ideas, and promptly ran into the brick wall of realization that before they could get on with conquering the world, they had to work to conquer and then modernize the chaotic management structure they had entered. That would prove more of a challenge than some of them had bargained for, since the modern management techniques they were used to using were foreign to Braniff. As one of the new people was told by a longtime senior officer when he tried to use a group discussion approach in making a decision: "This is Harding Lawrence's airline. He built it—he runs it—and don't ever kid yourself, he is the only real authority around here!"

to get away to fabulous destinations on their own airline—and for a pittance: as little as $17 per person. Braniff's employee pass privileges were very liberal, thanks in no small measure to Harding Lawrence's acceptance of the proposition that there are few employee benefits available in corporate life that cost as little and are appreciated as much. Braniff people could now fly to Hong Kong or Seoul, London or Paris, Frankfurt or Buenos Aires, and this was very significant: One of the reasons people put up with some of the trying and discouraging aspects of some of the jobs in commercial aviation is for the greatly discounted travel. It is, in a very real sense, part of the compensation of the job.[2]

The new scope of Braniff's system also helped to cause and to compensate for a curious and significant strategic error committed by Lawrence and John Casey in the summer of 1979. Airline employees throughout the industry traditionally have been able (through reciprocal agreements approved by the CAB) to secure free or reduced-price tickets on carriers other than their own, and Braniff had participated in such programs. These are known as "interline pass privileges," which provide a means for the average airline employee to fly all over the world for affordable fares. Suddenly, with Braniff approaching the size of a major carrier, Lawrence and Casey decided to reduce drastically the capability of other airline employees to get interline privileges for small service fees anywhere Braniff flew.[3]

The rest of the industry was aghast and infuriated. Each airline's reservationists have many chances in any given day to steer passengers headed to final destinations not served by their airline to another carrier. If a reservationist with United Airlines, for instance, has a choice of connecting a passenger at DFW with either Delta or Braniff, how that reservationist feels personally about Delta and

---

[2] Efforts by the IRS to tax those pass benefits as income—efforts temporarily defeated in the late 1970s—ignored several legal and practical aspects of airline "non-revenue" seating, the most important of which is that the seat would have been empty otherwise, and thus is of no value to the company. Therefore, to put an employee in that seat for a small pass fee (which covers processing, a meal, and the minuscule increase in fuel consumption of the aircraft for carrying the added weight) gives the employee something that is valueless to the airline but quite valuable to the employee.

[3] Harding Lawrence remembers John Casey as the instigator; Casey remembers Lawrence as the one who thought up the change. In any event, Lawrence had the final approval, and Casey implemented it.

Braniff will inevitably influence her decision. If Braniff has just told her (collectively and institutionally) to go to hell, she's not welcome on board without paying up to 50 percent of the normal fares, it's not hard to guess which airline will get the connecting passenger. This began happening to Braniff all over the United States and South America. Braniff made itself persona non grata in the minds of thousands of reservationists, and signs began appearing in such reservations centers saying "Don't Book Braniff!"

Lawrence and Casey apparently had taken the self-destructive step in order to get rid of the large group of interliners who were flocking to Braniff's new domestic and overseas destinations using Braniff interline passes. Both Lawrence and Casey, however, knew that the crowds weren't costing Braniff anything, since partial fares and pass fees were being collected, but they cited statistics on the high percentage of interline travel on Braniff as if the company were somehow being victimized. In addition, both men knew that Braniff people would be unable to obtain interline passes on other carriers the minute the change took effect, but the growing "Braniff is alone—Braniff doesn't need anyone!" syndrome had begun to develop as a theme in the chairman's mind, and it dictated that Braniff employees wouldn't need any other airline—they could go anywhere on Braniff. Vice President for Sales Walter Conrad had lobbied against it and had warned of the consequences. Now, suddenly, Braniff was losing incalculable millions in revenues from connecting passengers, and load factors that had already been in trouble dropped farther.

By the time the reality had sunk in that Braniff had bloodied itself unnecessarily with what amounted to a gratuitous insult to the rest of the industry, the losses had been significant, and the stigma that remained even after a hasty retreat and partial reinstatement of the interline privileges refused to die. There were reservationists at other carriers who refused to book Braniff forever thereafter, regardless of what apologies were issued. The industry interpreted the episode in an even more damaging light. It confirmed to many that not only had Braniff grown arrogant, but also its arrogance had reached astronomical heights. In the airline industry where coexistence is difficult without friends—even bitterly competitive friends—alienation of the sort Lawrence and Casey managed to achieve with the interline pass fiasco was unarguably and significantly detrimental.

In 1978 the new world headquarters complex had opened at DFW Airport after overruns had doubled the price of the facility. The $75 million cost was paid for through an Airport Authority bond issue, and Braniff took over as a long-term lessee for nearly $800,000-per-month rental. The sprawling low-rise complex included the executive offices (all furnished and decorated identically by a Houston decorator who demanded that the walls contain nothing but a single Calder painting) plus a sumptuous penthouse for Harding Lawrence, who was now literally living "over the store."[4]

The complex was another element of pride for the employees. The Spartan decor (it was described as Mediterranean) held some excesses, such as the several-thousand-dollar matched pair of genuine Greek olive trees flown in from Greece for an enclosed courtyard (and promptly killed by the harsh Texas winter), but overall there was a recognition that this structure represented a level of independence and achievement that all could be proud of. In addition, it represented a psychological guarantee of permanency. No airline with such a complex labeled "world headquarters" could be other than invincible.

Braniff's people were certainly aware that the blemishes still existed in the operation. The attitude of many of the agents at DFW and some (though not all) of the outstations still ranged from testy and antagonistic to rude and abusive (at worst), but there now seemed to be more of a reason to try, and even the radicals had found in the expansion a reason to work a little harder to treat passengers a little better in case their job might get a little easier in the future. Of course, none of the problems with the poor, untrained first-level managers had been solved or even addressed—just pushed aside in the scramble to expand. The new executives brought in to clean up the problems were still trying to get oriented.

Everywhere a Braniff employee looked in late 1979, however,

[4]The penthouse would also draw fire from Lawrence critics within and without the company, though he paid nearly $2,000 per month to the company to use it. He had originally looked into the idea of building such a facility over Braniff's terminal on the other side of the field, reasoning that the time saved in commuting was time devoted to the company. With the world headquarters penthouse, he was able to stay on the job from dawn to midnight—though that would later create the erroneous image of a bunker philosophy. (Indeed, it wasn't long before the complex had acquired two irreverent nicknames: "The Bunker" and "Fort Lawrence.") In terms of additional executive hours on the job, Lawrence's penthouse made significant economic sense.

there were signs and suggestions, symbols, and evidence that kept repeating the same message: We are the best—we are going to be the biggest—and this company (and by inference everyone working in it) is great. The signs were everywhere. A cursory glance at the TV departure screens at DFW presented a vista many had thought would never be seen under the name of Braniff: departure times, gates, and flight numbers printed next to city names such as Frank-furt, Paris, Amsterdam—nonstop.

There was even that sort of "we are the greatest" attitude in the new (and abortive) advertising campaign that broke about then with the central tag line "We'd better be better, we're Braniff!" It was an unfortunate double-entendre. To many employees it con-firmed the attitude "Of course we're better (than anyone or any-thing else), we're Braniff! Why would you even ask?" To many customers who had firsthand experience with the service problems that were the growth pains of an enlarged operation, the ad line meant "We haven't been too good up to now, folks, but from now on we're going to have to be better than we were." Tragically, either connotation was disastrous![5]

The employees, of course, wanted to believe the first connota-tion—that Braniff was by nature superior—but in doing so, espe-cially when manifested by the minority in public-contact positions who couldn't handle their jobs properly, the public began to get a greater feeling of employee arrogance than ever before. The reac-tions could be seen in the complaint letters, too many of which be-gan with variations of the same line: "You'd certainly better be better, Braniff, because in my experience you've got nothing to be arrogant about now!"

Complimentary letters still poured in, of course, most often for flight attendants. (Some, such as Braniff flight attendant Floyd Cor-sey, received so many "sunshine" letters the company stopped counting.) But the number of complaints over all areas of public

[5] In defense of the campaign, which was conceived by Wells Rich Green (which had once again acquired the Braniff account), the point has been raised that after the campaign started, the load factors increased in greater percentage than the in-crease in available seat miles (domestically), and therefore the campaign should be considered a success. If traffic gains were realized through the campaign—and that appears to be the case—they were realized at the expense of the future. A time was coming when Braniff would need all the friends it could get, and the "better be bet-ter" campaign had helped alienate at least some.

contact were much too high to justify an ad campaign saying "We'd better be better . . ." In fact, with 13.04 passenger complaints per 10,000 passengers (as recorded by the CAB for all of 1979), Braniff was ranked as the most-complained-about airline in the business.

Lawrence had tried throughout his fifteen years at Braniff to get the airline's inflight and ground passenger-service functions as close to perfection as humanly possible. Although inflight responded, passenger services had defied all attempts: Throughout the company it was still the weakest part of the operation, especially at DFW.[6]

Braniff's inflight services, however, ranked close to the best in the business—but Harding Lawrence had a zero tolerance for any deviation from his view of what excellent inflight service should be. He couldn't see the slightest reason for being satisfied with failures, whether it be a drink mixed incorrectly or a meal served out of sequence. Neither was the chairman hesitant about letting his people know—on the spot—when he felt they had screwed up. His propensity for dressing people down instantly whether in a crowded passenger cabin or otherwise had generated an anthology of horror stories, most of them embellished as they were passed from employee to employee, and most of them describing in lurid detail Lawrence's explosions on the aircraft. The stories had become so frightening and pervasive that many flight attendants who had never seen the chairman were terrified of flying with him.[7]

Most of the stories were of wild, explosive outbursts often involving tales of trays and glasses being tossed at, or past, or to a flight attendant who had served the wrong drink, let the entrée touch the vegetables in a meal service, served coffee to the chairman

---

[6] The large number of protected monopoly routes that Braniff had traditionally served contributed to the casual attitude of many passenger-service agents both in the past and into the mid-1970s. As long as Braniff had little competition, there was no need to fight for every customer.

[7] Employee fear of the big boss is certainly not uncommon in a large corporation run by a strong and charismatic leader, but in Lawrence's case the frightening rumors and tales of close encounters with his disapproval resulted in some very aberrant employee behavior. Flight attendants frequently called in sick rather than work a trip with the chairman on board, even though they had never had an incident with him. Flight attendant supervisors would brief a crew scheduled to fly with Lawrence just before departure and scare them half to death—thus guaranteeing a botched meal service and an apprehensive group waiting for the promised blowup.

in a Styrofoam cup rather than china, or any number of variations. When the stories were traced to the source, however, there was often a basic episode of unchairmanly behavior, but just as often it had been shamelessly enlarged upon. Predictably, some elements of the press would fall victim to the bizarre allure of the resulting third-hand stories.

Even flight attendants who had worked many pleasant flights with the chairman on board, and who had never seen him upset or loud (and they were the majority), were very cautious. Most station managers as well knew to be careful about preparing the flight Lawrence was scheduled to leave on (even if the rest of their flights that day went begging). It all made good sense to the employees. No one in his right mind wanted a row with the chairman.

On July 3, 1979, as the pressure of the mounting losses was beginning to eat at Harding Lawrence, he stepped on board one of his new 747's in Paris, France, heading for Boston and in no mood for anything less than perfect service from his people. The massive expansion wasn't working well so far. The company was losing money on his very flight, and he was convinced the inconsistent service the press had been lambasting was one of the causes. Lawrence's reactions during the next three hours would provide another juicy tale of infuriated high jinks with the chairman at thirty-five thousand feet.

Of the four Braniff flight attendants working the first class section of the fabulous 747, it fell to supervisor Wen Ann Sun and Sharon Turbovitch to ready and serve the dessert service—which (according to their carefully studied service manuals) was placed on one of the rolling carts and pushed through the first class cabin, row by row. Since there was limited room on the service cart, one of the managers back in Dallas had decided on an improvised solution for the fruit bowl: the flight attendants were to use an empty champagne bucket instead, place it on the cart, and fill it with fruit. By the time Sharon and Wen Ann pushed their cart next to Lawrence's seat, the chairman had already expressed his irritation over several aspects of their service. Each of them, as a result, was on edge.

Lawrence looked at the fruit in the champagne bucket. To him, it exemplified everything that was going wrong with the 747 service—little details his people couldn't seem to get right that made the difference to him between truly professional, polished service and poor, amateurish attempts. The chairman was incensed. He reached out and picked up a banana and an apple and half threw, half dropped them at his feet.

"Damnit, what the devil are you doing with fruit in the champagne bucket? A champagne bucket is for champagne bottles! This isn't a fruit bowl. Don't you people know how to do anything right?"

Lawrence's booming voice was clearly audible throughout the first class cabin and into the first area of coach. The two flight attendants picked up the fruit, apologized, and beat a hasty retreat to their galley, leaving Janet Dewey and her coffee and cappuccino cart next in the aisle—next in line to deal with the chairman.

Janet was nearly shaking in her chic Halston shoes. She had been just behind her two friends as the hapless apple and banana were deposited by Harding on the carpet, and she had heard his objections while watching the expression of disgust on his distinguished, imposing face. Harding Lawrence was larger than life to most Braniff folk, and now it was her turn to face him. She knew—she just *knew*—that something on her cart wasn't going to be to his satisfaction.

Quickly she went over in her mind all the manual-mandated details of the service, and somewhat reassured that everything was right, she pushed the cart to Lawrence's seat.

"Excuse me, Mr. Lawrence, would you like some coffee or cappuccino now?"

Lawrence looked up at her—that same expression of disgust and pained exasperation filling the airspace between them with the promise of impending doom. Janet Dewey tensed and braced for the verbal impact she could see was coming.

"Young lady, don't you know you never do the coffee service until after the dessert service? And you use demitasse cups, not breakfast-size cups!" Lawrence's voice seemed even louder than before. He didn't realize it, but heads were turning in his direction all over the first class cabin.

"Mr. Lawrence, everyone has had coffee. Everyone has asked for coffee."

Lawrence shook his head. "I want to talk to your supervisor right now, and I want to see your service manual!"

Wen Ann Sun, the senior flight attendant, came over and Lawrence lowered his voice to begin discussing with her the things he hadn't liked.

The remainder of the flight was marked by a few other minor encounters (including an unsuccessful attempt by one first class passenger from France to discuss with the chairman his treatment of the flight attendants), and when the 747 taxied up to the gate at Boston's Logan International Airport, the four nervous and upset flight attendants in first class lined up next to the departure door and braced for a parting broadside from Lawrence—who smiled at them instead as he stepped off. "Thank you very much, ladies—a very nice flight!"

They were stunned.

When Lawrence got back to Dallas, memos began to fly and angry telephone calls were made, and as in all organizations possessing a strong leader, the ball began rolling downhill—getting bigger as it descended. The chairman wanted the manuals changed, the people responsible for training in the Boston flight attendant base to correct the problems, the meal service revised, and never—*never*— was a champagne bucket to be used for anything but champagne again![8]

That same week, Lawrence walked through the flight attendant lounge at the DFW terminal, appalled at the shabby appearance of what had been a stylish lounge. He removed personal notices from an overloaded company bulletin board, yelled at the supervisors, and stormed out thoroughly disgusted with the parting remark, "Only pigs could live like this!"

The grapevine version of the Boston flight escapade naturally escalated. Before it had fully saturated its way through the ranks, Lawrence was throwing the fruit-filled bucket itself across the first class cabin. In fact, of course, he never moved the bucket—just a doomed apple and banana dispatched to an uncertain fate on the carpet beneath his feet. The story became one more indication of the chairman's violent unpredictability, and his foray through the untidy flight attendants' sanctuary didn't help the image a bit.

As had been the case so many times before, it wasn't so much the reality of what had occurred—what Lawrence had done or said—or even whether he was right that was important. It was the image it created in the minds of the employees and how they in turn

[8] He stunned the flight attendants on that Paris-Boston flight once more, however. He sent them a letter of apology when he discovered that the procedures they were using had come from an improperly written manual. To the first class crew of Flight 603, it was all very confusing.

reacted within the scope of their job performance that mattered. In fact, the lack of communication between and among departments and levels of the airline, vertically and horizontally, made Braniff effectively a loose amalgamation of little companies within a large one, none of them really cognizant or supportive of each other's role. Braniff employees in different jobs had radically different perceptions of the nature of their company—as radically different as the perceptions of the proverbial three blind men trying to describe an elephant by touching different parts of the beast. At Braniff, the lack of communication kept the employees "blind."

As 1979 drew to a close, the enthusiasm over the huge expansion and the overconfidence engendered by the "better be better" campaign seemed to obscure the fact that the new expanded Braniff had been built on an unstable foundation. Erroneous images of a worried chairman on the rampage (rumored to result from growing frustration at the red ink) were distant rumbles of thunder in an otherwise blue sky. The future looked great, and most employees wanted to keep it that way.

In truth, of course, the sand beneath their feet was being leached away by the flow of the money draining into the Pacific and Atlantic and to the accounts of the oil companies for hundreds of millions of dollars in jet fuel. Those who felt they might be standing on the brink of a hidden abyss didn't want to look down. As the figures would later prove (even to the Board), it was Braniff's equity—its financial lifeblood—that was flowing away in rivulets, and unlike Pan American (which had hundreds of millions of dollars of equity in subsidiary corporations and a huge building to cash in), Braniff's equity was limited in dollars if not in ambitious prospects.

But for most employees of Braniff International, 1979 looked like tall cotton.

The First General Alarm

The first general alarm of impending financial disaster was sounded in the early fall of 1979.

In its March 19 edition *Business Week* magazine had run an article full of glowing praise for Braniff's expansion ("Braniff Is Making the Most of Deregulation"). Suddenly, the October 29 edition sprang forth with a hand-wringing report that alarmed the business and financial community and helped depress Braniff's stock with dark predictions of the company's future ("Indigestion Brings Financial Woe to Braniff"). In the Dallas-Fort Worth area the local newspapers awoke to the possibility of a good story of corporate travail in their backyard.

In October 1979, a vitally important $75 million preferred stock issue was placed on the market to raise the cash needed for the new aircraft coming down the line in Seattle. (Braniff had a squadron of 747's and 727's on order—over $700 million worth of aircraft in total.) On October 6, however, Federal Reserve Board Chairman Paul Volcker announced a change in the nation's monetary policies, throwing the financial markets into confusion and Braniff's stock issue out the window. The buyers wouldn't buy, and the issue was postponed and later canceled. The $75 million would have been merely a small bandage to cover a small wound in the body of the company's overall financial plan. Without it, though, that wound began to grow larger as the far-flung Braniff operation continued to bleed at the bottom line.

The Singapore route had opened on October 31, 1979. On May 15, 1980 (four days after Jim Lawrence's return flight), it was closed. The load factors on too many flights had been ridiculously low, just as in the remainder of the Pacific system. Braniff was losing

147

nearly $1 million a week on the operation, and that was too much to hide by allocating it to the South American system's expense column (which had been done at first).

In the Atlantic system, Braniff's massive expansion into Europe consisting of direct flights from DFW and a series of flights to Europe from Boston were doing better than the Pacific system in terms of load factor but were still falling below the break-even point. What was doing the most damage to both systems and raising the break-even load factor beyond reach was the cost of a rather vital element in the airline formula: fuel.

Braniff had long-since expanded beyond its normal fuel supply contracts into what is loosely called the "spot market." In the Pacific and Atlantic especially, the thirsty 747 fleet was guzzling fuel costing upward of $1.20 per gallon and higher. The domestic fuel prices were damaging enough (Braniff's main supplier, Texaco, was one of the highest priced in the industry), but with the Atlantic and Pacific fuel bills, Braniff was tens of millions of dollars over budget.[1]

Domestically the CAB did nearly nothing to help. Braniff and a host of other carriers were begging for permission to raise fares fast enough to stay up with the steadily climbing fuel costs, but the same agency that couldn't wait until the ink was dry on the Airline Deregulation Act before throwing route regulation to the wind (without waiting for the law to authorize it) was continuing its ironclad regulation of fares. All the U.S. carriers were hurt by the foot-dragging, but Braniff—being far more exposed than most—was damaged to a greater extent.

Other problems had assailed the company as well during 1979. For one, American Airlines had decided to move their headquarters to the Dallas area. Whether they smelled Braniff's blood in the wind is uncertain, but they undoubtedly recognized an opportunity to move in on the imagined deregulatory riches of the Sun Belt. They began building their DFW operation into a major hub—their first, since traditionally American had been a coast-to-coast, long-haul carrier that avoided hub systems. Braniff was still the largest operator at DFW, but suddenly American began nose-to-nose competi-

[1] For 1979 alone Braniff suffered a fuel price increase systemwide of $137,390,000, of which only $53,925,000 could be recovered by fare increases—leaving the airline overbudget on fuel by $83,465,000, or nearly twice the corporation's entire loss for the year. For 1979, Braniff's total loss was $44,330,000. If the $83,465,000 overage on fuel cost had not occurred, the company would have ended the year with a profit of $39,135,000.

tion on many of the traditionally protected bread-and-butter routes that had contributed so much over the years to Braniff's profitability.

As American packed the boxes in New York for the move (much to the consternation of New York Mayor Ed Koch, who did his best to get them to change their corporate minds), there were at least a few at American who realized the depth of the gamble Braniff had taken, how much it was financially exposed in growing so rapidly. Some of the executives at American *had* to have some idea what would happen if Braniff's master plan failed, and further, what opportunities that would open for American—if American was ready.

The Federal Aviation Administration also got into the act of damaging Braniff, charging maintenance violations for which a fine of $1.5 million was asked. The transgressions involved several improperly deferred routine maintenance items that had been allowed to remain deferred as three subject aircraft flew in daily, regular service. The huge figure was computed by taking a small basic fine and multiplying it by the number of flights. It was actually a very innocuous violation, but whereas the FAA's people would have normally handled the matter in a quieter atmosphere (seeking the type of cooperation that had traditionally marked its relationship with the various trunk carriers and that usually accomplished vastly more than contentious litigation), Braniff had the misfortune to be dealing with a new and different FAA.

This Federal Aviation Administration was being led by a man who apparently could neither appreciate nor understand the role of cooperation in the FAA's regulation of the industry. Langhorne Bond, another Carter appointee with limited qualifications for his position, had, in the opinion of some, destroyed every last vestige of mutual trust and cooperation between the FAA's people and the air carriers. By the time Reagan would fire him (as the new President took office in 1981), the utter destruction Bond would bring about would, by best estimates, take at least ten years to repair. Bond had a penchant for loud enforcement proceedings and seemed to encourage his inspectors to file violations and use the press to publicize them to force the carriers into embarrassed compliance. That was the same technique used on Braniff.[2]

[2] Bond's attitude toward airline pilots appeared to be particularly hostile. At one point he searched for months to find a senator or congressman who would introduce a bill containing—among other things—criminal penalties and prison sen-

There were problems deep within Braniff's maintenance department, to be sure. Too many little things had been shoved to the future to keep the utilization rates high in accordance with Lawrence's plans. But Braniff was decidedly not flying unsafe aircraft, and the violations could have been easily and effectively solved without the circus of damaging publicity eagerly sought by Bond's FAA.

With the public already alerted to the fact that Lawrence's mighty leap for worldwide status was in trouble, the FAA's timing, shrill publicity, and posturing hit at the worst possible moment—almost as if it had been precisely and maliciously calculated to damage Lawrence, who, it was rumored, had failed to show Bond the proper personal deference in previous contacts. Very few laymen understand such complex maintenance matters enough to see through such publicity. To the average citizen, the fact that the FAA in all its alleged wisdom felt strongly enough about the seriousness of Braniff's maintenance shortcomings to demand $1.5 million in fines must mean that Braniff's maintenance was poor and Braniff's airplanes were unsafe. Such conclusions are sufficient to scare away customers, and that's exactly what they did—at a time when Braniff could least afford the loss.

During a period in which corporate executive communication was more vital than ever to solve the problems, the breakdown of communication with the chairman had worsened. By the early fall of 1979 the weekly executive staff meeting had become an exercise in futility. Lawrence could seldom get a straight answer from most of his top people. Whether Lawrence could recognize the shadow boxing or not, he kept holding the meetings until early 1980. After that there would be a weekly notice to each of the secretaries from Marion Drinkard (Lawrence's secretary) that the meeting had been canceled. In the final analysis, it was a loss to no one.[3]

---

tences for any pilot violating certain FAA procedural regulations. The FAA finally had to introduce the bill on its own; no one in Congress would touch it.
[3] The seriousness of the breakdown in communication with the chairman was typified by the degree to which some of his senior people began to cut him entirely out of the "loop" of executive communications. When inflight services was told to cut the amount and quality of the food service on the Pacific runs to save money, the

By the early spring of 1980 cash was getting short, and Braniff was facing the harrowing prospect of having too little cash in the accounts to pay for the new aircraft that would be delivered in the summer. If they ended up unable to meet a delivery deadline, it would generate stiff contractual penalties with Boeing and a worsening of the financial community's perception of Braniff's problems. A $100 million preferred stock issue was prepared, this time for private sale. In order to make it attractive enough to sell, though, Braniff was forced to attach warrants (essentially coupons that give the holder the right, for a set period of time, to purchase a specific amount of the company's common stock at a set price). The warrants, if all were exercised, would result in the purchase of nearly 14 percent of the company's common stock. Even with the warrants, it would be an uphill battle to sell the stock, and by April, only $35 million worth had been sold (though many of the remaining shares had been placed). Then it fell apart all over again. The worsening cash position of the company triggered several provisions in the conditions of the stock sale that effectively released those who had contracted to buy the additional shares (but had not yet completed the purchase) from their obligation actually to do so.

Genuine concern began to give way to hard-core worry. Vice President for Financial Services Edson Beckwith—now in the position of having to go hat in hand to some of the same people he had treated with withering disdain in better years—managed to beg a

---

head of that division (Staff Vice President Andy Hoffman) asked if Lawrence knew of the cut. The answer was "no." "Well, gentlemen," Hoffman told them, "if we cut this prized service and the Man finds out—well, I'm not going to take the fall. You get his authorization, and then I'll cut it. Otherwise, no." The projected savings amounted to several million dollars. No more was said. The service was retained, but when the latest cost figures for the Pacific service were presented to Lawrence, they showed the money as having been saved when in fact it had been spent. In the same time frame, Lawrence asked Hoffman to look into getting some "disco"-type music for the aircraft music systems. President Russell Thayer came around later and told Hoffman: "Hey, Andy, the guy's crazy. Forget it!" Several weeks later Lawrence asked how the project with the disco music was coming. "Fine, Harding," Hoffman answered, "I'll have a sample for you soon." Hoffman beat a path to Thayer's office. "Russ, you told me to forget it—now the Man's asking when it'll be ready." Again Thayer told him to ignore the chairman. "Hey, Andy, don't worry about it. He'll forget it. It's a dumb idea." When Lawrence asked once more a week later, Hoffman finally got busy and secured a sample tape of disco music that he delivered to Lawrence, who promptly ordered it incorporated in the fleet. The "Man" hadn't forgotten, and customer feedback later confirmed it as a good idea.

$100 million short-term loan. It was a 4½-month finance package with the first staggering payback of $30 million due on July 31. Quietly, within his Braniff Place office, Ted Beckwith began working with the figures and reached the chilling conclusion that with the losses continuing as they were, Braniff might not have enough cash to make that first payment on July 31. He told several of his fellow officers, but he didn't tell Lawrence—not yet, at least. The figures might change. The summer traffic might cut the $6 million-per-month operating losses.

The annual stockholder meeting for 1980 (covering fiscal year 1979) was held on May 7 in the new auditorium of Braniff's world headquarters. In addition to the presentation of the annual report, a slick, professional publication with a blue cover outlining all of Braniff's global routes, Lawrence gave a carefully compiled presentation complete with slides and graphs showing the corporation's financial performance figures from 1965 forward. It was almost like a campaign presentation—a plea for the assemblage to consider and keep in mind how far Lawrence had brought Braniff since 1965, how much money they had made, and how sound his stewardship of the airline had been. (The figures clearly showed just that.) Lawrence's opening statement was a concise summation of not only the achievements, but also what he and the company were doing to stem the losses.

Along with the annual report, the first-quarter report for 1980 had already been issued, and it showed a $22 million loss—less than half the loss of the previous quarter.[4]

Braniff, obviously, was still hemorrhaging, but hopefully at a slower rate. Even though the company's lenders were making worried noises from New York and elsewhere, and some of the Braniff Board were worried that perhaps Lawrence needed faster contraction of his fabulous new route system, the need for emergency action wasn't yet clear. After all, Harding had been right so many times before.[5]

---

[4] The fourth quarter of 1979 had shown a loss of $51 million, and therefore there was hope that things were improving. In 1978 the airline had made a whopping record profit of $45 million, but the overall loss for 1979 of $44 million almost wiped that out. (There had been a small profit in the first part of 1979, so that, coupled with the fourth-quarter loss of $51 million, equaled a net loss of $44 million.) The gross revenues in 1979 were over $1.4 billion.

[5] Nevertheless, three of the strongest outside directors—Stewart, Post, and Bass—

When Lawrence had formulated his plans to seize the opportunity to grow out from under the shadow of deregulation, he had pinned the attempt on a combination of moves that carried certain interlocking risks. The central element was the purchase of Boeing jetliners. The exposure of the company in terms of existing orders for new aircraft soared from $186 million in 1978 to $792 million in 1979—an increase of $606 million. (Some of those orders were far in the future and cancellable without significant penalty. The majority were hard commitments). To buy all those aircraft, the senior debt package was increased from $348 million in 1978 to $578 million in 1979. The figures sound staggering, but if the interest rates remained below 15 percent ($170 million of that long-term money was tied to 2 percent over the prime rate) and if the traffic on the expanded route system held up well enough to generate the cash flow to pay the operational expenses, Braniff would have no trouble. The wild card was fuel, which no one believed would climb from under $.40 per gallon to over $1 per gallon. Even that disaster could have been countered if the economy had remained strong, or if the CAB had permitted immediate pass-through of fuel increases, or both. If the fuel prices and the interest rates began climbing at the same time the economy began declining, Braniff would have one viable fallback position: the sale of surplus aircraft to raise cash to make up the difference. If the used-aircraft market went to hell too, the long-range formula would be in mortal danger. It was a "worst possible case" consideration that couldn't possibly happen—and promptly did.

Ted Beckwith had been right. The cash wasn't there for the July 31 payment of $30 million. Lawrence dispatched his people to press negotiations with American Airlines to rapid conclusion for the sale of fifteen surplus Boeing 727-200's. The sale was concluded in late July for $8 million apiece, which infused $120 million into the coffers just in time to meet the payment deadline.

The press pointed with great alarm and total misunderstanding

formed an informal watchdog committee that was said to be merely for the purpose of "seeing the company through these difficult times." In fact, it was an emergency awakening of these members to the fact that the Board might be exposed to legal liability if the company got into more desperate straits—especially since they had been in lockstep with Lawrence all the way and had been very lax as a watchdog group. They suddenly jumped in to find out how bad things really were and what could be done. In effect, it was an early manifestation of impending panic.

to the sale as the desperate act of an airline selling off its "best" assets. That was dead wrong—and dead right. "Desperate act," yes; best assets, absolutely not. Those dear, departed 727-200's were the oldest in the company's fleet. Some of them, in fact, were the hangar queens of the airline—sister ships of *Sneaky Snake* (old 408). Their elimination in favor of the remaining, newer models lowered the average age of both Braniff's fleet and American's fleet! Additionally, the press reports that the aircraft had been sold for half price (as compared to the alleged market value of $16 million apiece) was totally misleading. Although $8 million apiece was a bargain-basement price, there was virtually no way in July 1980 that any airline was going to pay as much as $16 million (or, for that matter, even $12 million) per plane for such aircraft, especially with the flight hours logged on Braniff's jets.

The erroneous press reports fanned the flames of the alarmist concept that Braniff was, in fact, a very financially troubled company. Lawrence was worried. He knew that such reports could trigger a self-fulfilling prophecy, assuring that Braniff would become a genuinely financially troubled company. All it would take would be a sufficient undermining of the confidence of the travel agency community and the traveling public.

During one of the summer meetings of the Braniff Board of Directors, the subject of dire press reports about Braniff and the effects they were having boiled to the surface. Herman Lay (chairman of PepsiCo and one of the founders of Frito-Lay and a longtime Braniff director) needled Lawrence throughout lunch about the adverse publicity.

"Harding, you've got to counter those stories. You've got to do something!"

"Well, what do you suggest, Herman?" Lawrence replied in a loud voice. The group had been served lunch in the boardroom adjacent to Lawrence's penthouse apartment in the new world headquarters. Lawrence had tried for the previous hour to convince Lay that he was doing all that could be done. Lay and the other directors were becoming increasingly nervous over the sea of red ink washing around the company's financial foundations, and worried that Lawrence wasn't contracting his new system fast enough. The rock-steady confidence they had maintained in Lawrence's prodigious abilities was being shaken, and the sniping of the business press was getting to Lay in particular.

"What I suggest, Harding, is that you damn well do something about it!"

The discussion flared into a loud argument as an exasperated Lawrence charged through the double doors separating the boardroom from his penthouse—with Lay following close behind. The sounds of raised, angry voices wafted through the closed doors for about ten minutes before Lay and Lawrence returned to the rest of the group and continued the meeting.[6]

The boards of most publicly held corporations have certain practical limitations on how much control the members can exercise over internal corporate matters and even long-range decisions. Braniff's Board was no exception. Most directors were elected to it because of their individual prominence in the business community, their original ownership position in the company, or their political value to Braniff. Such people are usually very busy individuals with a lot more to occupy their days than just the problems Braniff International might encounter. In addition, many of Braniff's directors sat on at least one other board (and in the case of Lawrence, Stewart, and Lay, sat on each other's corporate boards).[7]

There is really nothing inherently wrong with this sort of interlocking relationship among directors. In fact, it gives a corporation greater stability, and greater capability to secure financing and other

[6] The Braniff board consisted of eleven outside and three inside directors in 1979–80. Harding Lawrence, Russ Thayer, and John Casey were the insiders. The outside members were Mrs. Anne Armstrong, former U.S. ambassador to Great Britain; Perry Bass, millionaire Texas oilman; R. Mort Frayn, Sr., chairman of his own commercial/legal printing and publishing firm in Seattle; Noel Gayler, a retired U.S. Navy admiral; Mrs. Pamela Harriman, socially and politically prominent trustee/director of a long list of public-service organizations; Mrs. Albert D. Lasker, a New York philanthropist; Herman Lay, chairman of the Executive Committee of PepsiCo; L. F. McCollum, Jr., millionaire Houston oilman and investor; W. Sloan McCrea, a prominent Miami banker; Troy V. Post, Dallas millionaire investor and the man who—as owner of Greatamerica Corporation—is responsible for bringing both Ed Acker, and through him Harding Lawrence, into Braniff in 1964 and 1965, respectively; and Robert H. Stewart III, Board chairman of First International Bancshares Corporation of Dallas and probably the strongest, most manipulative Boardmember.

[7] For instance, Bob Stewart, chairman of the Board of First International Bancshares Corporation of Dallas (corporate parent of First National Bank, one of Braniff's lenders), was also a director of NCH Corporation and PepsiCo, Inc., Herman Lay's company. Herman Lay, of course, was a Braniff director as well as a director of Stewart's First International Bancshares. Harding Lawrence was also a director of First International Bancshares (both Lay and Lawrence left the First International Bancshares Board in 1980).

benefits arising from a "good ole boy" network of corporate friends. It can, of course, be subject to conflict-of-interest problems—such as those that would later drive Bob Stewart (lender) off the Braniff (debtor) Board when loans to Braniff became questionable. But the main problem is that people who are this involved, this busy with other companies as well as their own interests simply do not have the time to become experts in all of them. When, as in Braniff's case, a strong, trusted chairman with a superlative and profitable track record provides his directors with a constant flow of information, a form of complacency sets in. None of the Braniff outside directors were experts in the airline business; thus the temptation to provide only cursory oversight to Lawrence's decisions was great. Then too, there is the "gentlemanly" factor—the reciprocal courtesy and re-spect shown by one corporate leader to another, especially when they sit on each other's boards. To seriously question the chairman in good times on matters in which he is an industry-acknowledged expert would be to insult him. In the case of the Braniff board, the urge to question Lawrence's strategy didn't arise until late in 1979, and coming as it did after so many years of agreement and support, Lawrence considered such questioning an implication of sudden loss of trust—and that was irritating. Harding Lawrence, ever the teacher, had tried to instruct his Board as well as inform them over the years. To have them suddenly lose faith indicated they hadn't been listening—hadn't learned anything about the airline business.

Of course, the majority of the outside directors really tried their best, putting uncounted hours into the task of overseeing Braniff and doing everything they could to help, even if they had found no reason to disagree with Lawrence over the years. Out-of-town di-rectors such as Anne Armstrong, Sloan McCrea, Mort Frayn, and even Pam Harriman and Mary Lasker tried their best to be fully participating members. But it was the longtime Dallas-Fort Worth area directors—members of the executive committee such as Perry Bass, Herman Lay, Troy Post, and Bob Stewart—who were the core of the Board. It was these sage businessmen who should have at-tained an expertise in the business of Braniff—as extensive an ex-pertise as any outside director can ever be expected to attain in a business wholly unrelated to his professional training.

Some Braniff outside directors, however, were so relaxed about their responsibilities that they neglected to attend meetings, or left early, or otherwise never fully executed their responsibilities as watchdogs of the stockholders' interests.

It took nearly a year of red ink to spur Braniff's outside directors to question openly the company's course of action, but that was far from unusual or improper. It was very reasonable for the Board to have supported Lawrence up through 1979 (in what would seem to some to be a "rubber stamp" fashion). After all, they had examined the same data and studies that Lawrence had provided; they had considered the same arguments about the threat of deregulation and Braniff's need for growth; and they had not just ratified the chairman's decisions, they (along with Lawrence) had *made* them. They weren't a "rubber stamp" board. They held equal responsibility for the effect of the decisions they made along with the chairman. And, of course, the most critical decisions—to buy 747's and add routes and senior debt—were made when no one but a confirmed Cassandra would believe that so many things could ever go wrong at once. Later, though, when the most powerful among the directors woke up to the danger facing Braniff, the mature, professional, tempered reaction of these men would be to panic. The decisions they would make under the gun of the lenders and the tide of red ink were as much out of ignorance of the realities of airline operations as from fear of default.[8]

The Honorable Way Out

CHAPTER **16** In July 1980 Harding Lawrence faced the fact that the cutbacks he had begun as early as May 1979 were not enough and that he would have to take a meat-ax to his beautiful route system and the newly swollen ranks of his company. Reluctantly he began a new, massive cut of the domestic routes effective September 1—most of the routes

[8] The frightening aspect of this for American corporate life is that the lack of expertise and attention of board members—the failure to perform as a sophisticated, independent "watchdog" (and the tendency to elect directors for political or honorary purposes)—is more common than not throughout the public corporate boardrooms of the nation.

and the cities added in the great dormant route grab of less than two years before—and drastically cut flights out of Kansas City, dropping it out of the category of a "second hub" for Braniff. Internationally, Lawrence closed down all but a bare-bones operation to Seoul and Hong Kong in the Pacific. In Europe, Braniff discontinued the nonstop Dallas–continental Europe flights, leaving only Dallas–London, and continued to serve Frankfurt and Brussels as an add-on to Dallas–London. Paris and Amsterdam were abandoned, but their costs, as predicted, continued. In South America, 747 service was slashed, and even little Manaus, a turn-of-the-century rubber baron's boomtown along the Amazon River in the interior of northern Brazil, was dropped.

By October 1, it was obvious that the Pacific system was too far in the red and too assailed by the fare-cutting tactics of Northwest Orient and Pan Am (as well as foreign carriers) to survive. In addition, Braniff had failed to win a route to Tokyo, the goal that Lawrence had cited as his justification for maintaining an expensive, losing Pacific route system—a presence in the region. Without Tokyo, there was no justification. With great reluctance he gave the order to pull out, announcing an official suspension of service to preserve the authority for the future—if there was to be one.

The furlough list for Braniff pilots and flight attendants was distressingly long. The pilot force alone went from twenty-two hundred to seventeen hundred, dumping most of the people hired in the previous two years. As more senior people used their seniority to bid for the positions that remained, usually in other cities, the resulting turbulence was incredible as they were transferred all over the United States. Some families bought and sold three homes in three different cities in as many years, chasing first the expansion and now the contraction.[1]

Ticket agents and baggage handlers and others under union seniority protection were also transferred and forced to commute to

_____

[1] The elimination (or addition) of a single pilot position in any category can cause as many as five pilots to change their base to other cities. Basically, each city that has a crew base has its own ranking of pilots within that base. For instance, the Denver pilot base for Braniff might have 60 pilots: twenty captains, twenty first officers (copilots), and twenty second officers (flight engineers) assigned. These pilots all have a specific seniority number on the basis of the date they were hired. When a base contracted or was eliminated, the pilots in that base weren't necessarily furloughed. If even the lowest-ranking second officer was more senior than a pilot in another pilot base in another city—such as DFW—he could bid into that base

distant stations (or move their families). All around the Braniff system a mood of impending doom began to surface where cautious to swaggering confidence had been just a year before.

The naysayers had been right: After the hirings, the furloughs were indeed right around the corner.

The national press was in full cry after the story of how Braniff—the proud, confident, "flamboyant" cappuccino airline from Texas—was having to tuck in its tail and run for financial cover after all. The pressure of the losses, the worried Board members, and the dithering lenders (who were burning up the phone lines from New York with questions) bore down on Harding Lawrence day by day as he increased his work schedule to practically twenty-four-hours a day, seven days a week, and tried tirelessly to construct a plan.

Lawrence had always been the sort of executive who could accomplish almost anything provided he had a sound plan based on good information. To formulate a sound, usable plan, however, he needed two things that were no longer possible to secure by the fall of 1980; valid, truthful information from *all* his people (concerning the status of the company's operations), and some stability in the industry—in fuel prices, interest rates, and economic decline.

Though there were senior executives (such as Vice President for Financial Services Ted Beckwith and Vice President for Finance and Control Neal Robinson) who were trying to alert him to what they saw as the true state of financial peril Braniff faced, Lawrence was planning for the long-range goals and had little patience with dithering about what he saw as temporary problems.

Lawrence had a plan, but it was changing daily. The fuel prices, the overall wild card, were making a shell game out of the job of predicting anything with certainty. In some weeks the fuel prices and the resulting profit-and-loss projections would change daily, and even retroactively (since fuel used a month before often would be billed at a higher price than had existed on the day of purchase).

---

and "bump," or displace, that other pilot, who in turn could go to another base containing a more junior pilot and displace him, and so on until the last pilots left had no positions left to "bump" into. They were the ones—the most junior pilots—who ended up furloughed in a cutback. In the meantime, captains were bumping first officers who were bumping second officers all over the system—all of them changing cities in the process. Toward the end of 1981, most pilots at Braniff would simply elect to commute to work—sometimes as much as three thousand miles. The base staffing was changing literally monthly, and no one could know for certain where he or she would be departing from the following month.

The other element of the planning was based on the original "fall back" position—the great escape clause that if all else failed, Braniff could raise cash by selling airplanes, used or new. If that could be accomplished, the company would indeed pull through with no more than a close scare and a scarred reputation. If, however, the 747's couldn't be unloaded (they cost over $50 million each), the only hope left to avoid a future loan default would be more borrowing—but the lenders had effectively cut off Braniff's credit the previous spring when the company fell below cash and equity requirements of the loan agreements.

Thus Harding Lawrence sat in his office in the world headquarters and charted the company's course through the next few months and years—based squarely on the assumption that the aircraft could be sold. Russ Thayer, who had been a disappointment as a chairman-in-training, was now assigned the specific task of unloading 747's—anywhere, to anyone, for anything reasonable. Through his efforts the company did manage to sell its second special-performance (the short-body) 747 to Aerolineas Argentinas, which infused enough cash to help with some of the other obligations to Boeing, but by that time there were three new, brightly colored 727's in Braniff markings sitting unclaimed on the delivery ramp at Boeing Field in Seattle. Braniff couldn't pay for them.

Russ Thayer's strong suit was marketing, not playing the tough corporate leader. During the summer he had done a series of commercials for television promising the world that he'd "Take it on the chin" before he'd cut Braniff's excellent inflight service (despite the fact that Braniff had cut fares to match new low-cost competitors such as Texas International and their "peanut fares"). On August 20, 1980, Thayer (at Lawrence's direction) sent a five-page letter to all Braniff employees to counter the "financially beleaguered" rumors. There were so many news leaks from the executive suite and the employees during this period that Lawrence knew the letter would find its way into the hands of the press almost instantly. He had had it written with that in mind. It was for public consumption as well as to calm employee jitters.

Thayer began,

Much has been written and spoken by the press about the financial losses of the airline industry in the fourth quarter of 1979 and the first half of 1980. The losses recorded were the worst in history for the airlines and your company was no exception. As a result the press and others have been speculating and guessing about the effect on individual airlines. Those guesses, based often on misinformation and bad assumption, have in turn produced still more rumors and just plain gossip. The results of these oftentimes irresponsible acts produce uncertainty unnecessarily among our employees. Unfortunately, Braniff has been the subject of some of these misinformed statements and rumors, so we want to bring you up to date. . . .

Braniff is a financially sound company. Braniff is not in a "financial hole."

It helped, but it didn't fully still the butterflies collecting in the stomachs of those in the ranks who could see the empty aircraft and the less-than-profitable load factors. The employees worried about whether the Thayers and the Caseys—even Lawrence himself—*really* knew what they were doing. The Braniff people were trapped below decks. Only the officers could see the horizon.

The letter wasn't an outright lie. If the aircraft could be sold and the fuel costs didn't continue into orbit, Braniff would be okay. Whether it was or wasn't in a "financial hole" was a matter of semantics and guesswork. What it clearly was (as Beckwith and Robinson and several others tried in vain to get Lawrence to accept) was a financially *imperiled* company.

On the same day, August 20, Lawrence held a news conference at Braniff headquarters in the boardroom, to which he had invited a long list of print reporters including *Business Week, The Wall Street Journal, Forbes,* and the young business reporter from the *Dallas Morning News* with whom Lawrence had spoken so often, Dennis Fulton.

On the appointed day, Harding Lawrence, flanked by Ted Beckwith, John Casey, and Russ Thayer, sat at the head of the large leather-covered conference table in the stark-white boardroom and tried to convince them all that Braniff was financially sound.

Perfectly dressed, groomed, and composed, chain-smoking his usual cigarettes—Benson & Hedges (an early and satisfied Wells Rich Greene client)—Lawrence began by going down a long outline of Braniff's situation and the master plan, which included heavy emphasis on the continuing sale of jetliners. He discussed the fleet planning and how Braniff's fleet was one of the newest and most cost-efficient in the industry and how Braniff had always been in the business of buying and selling aircraft, so aircraft sales were not evidence of "panic"—simply part of the ongoing plan.

In painting a convoluted explanation of why Braniff was not a financially troubled airline, he explained that the principal element of the plan for buying new aircraft was to use the cash generated by depreciation to pay for them. The reporters were lost. Lawrence explained it in greater detail, showing how the amount of the 1979 total loss for Braniff as a corporation ($44 million) included the amount of depreciation charged off for that year ($77 million). "Therefore," he explained, ". . . you subtract the 77 million dollars from the 44-million-dollar loss, and you no longer have a loss— you've got a 33-million-dollar gain." The reporters were still mystified. Lawrence tried again, explaining that the $77 million had been spent years before to buy airplanes; the money was already gone. On the books in 1979 it was charged off under depreciation, and that depressed the so-called bottom line at the end of the year. But Braniff still *had* that $77 million of cash in 1979. It was *that* money that was used to buy new airplanes! Lawrence pointed out that over the next few years, the amount the company was scheduled to pay on the long-term debt to purchase airplanes would be less in each year than the amount to be charged off to depreciation. "Therefore, depreciation in effect pays for the new aircraft."

After a long series of increasingly skeptical questions, it was obvious the assembled reporters hadn't the slightest intention of accepting—or understanding—what Lawrence was saying.[2]

---

[2] In fairness, it may have been that too many of them were aware that if the losses continued and grew greater, the explanation would make no sense anyway. Even if the airline had $50 million in depreciation, a $150 million loss would mean a net cash drain of $100 million. The point was: Braniff didn't have the net worth to continue bleeding like that, with or without depreciation. Too many of them, however, simply didn't understand the concept. What Lawrence was saying was essentially correct—but they apparently hadn't sufficient knowledge of airline economics to appreciate it. The various articles written as a result of the conference demonstrated their ignorance of the point. One article in *The Wall Street Journal* (January 6, 1981) described the conference as "emotional" and said that Lawrence had "alternately cajoled, joked with and shouted at reporters for what [he] considered unfair publicity on Braniff's financial problems." In fact, Lawrence never once broke character, lost his temper, or shouted at anyone present—although he had plenty of reason to do so in the following weeks when he read the resulting articles and realized the press hadn't believed a word of it.

To them, Harding Lawrence was trying to deny the obvious. Here was a famous airline chief—one who had been successful, and therefore had become an instant target the minute he had stumbled—sitting on a command bridge that was already sinking below the waterline of financial viability. This high-and-mighty corporate chairman who made so much more than they did was trying to tell them, confidently, that there was no hole in the hull.

Braniff, in fact, could remain afloat if it could sell airplanes rapidly. Unfortunately, the market had all but dried up in the face of the recession and the hideous fuel prices throughout the world. Since only the Arabs had sufficient resources to buy such aircraft, Russ Thayer packed up and began chasing will-o'-the-wisp Arab customers all over Europe.

Lawrence dropped one other comment in that news conference that many of the reporters did pick up. He said that he didn't envision his position with Braniff being the same in 2½ to 3 years. The reporter had asked about retirement, but the genesis for the question had come from a wildfire rumor that had swept through the Dallas-Fort Worth area—a rumor that Lawrence was going to step down, and Bob Stewart was going to take over. Both men vigorously denied the rumor when it rippled through the press. The origin of the item was never disclosed, and despite some whispering, there was no evidence to indicate that Bass or Lay or Post—or Stewart himself—had planted the rumor to send Lawrence a message.

Harding Lawrence, in fact, was getting very weary. Nothing he tried seemed to work. His senior people were avoiding him, the advice he had received in many cases was flawed, and the press was nipping at his heels. Competition was increasing everywhere, and the damn fuel prices climbed daily. As soon as he thought he saw a way out, the facts would change and the projections would have to be plumped up (written to show greater yields than his people believed would occur) in order to show any possibility that the company could make it through the recession. The worst aspect was the fact that since the deregulation bill had passed, the rules of the game had changed, and it had destroyed the predictability of the system he had operated in for over thirty years. No longer could he depend on a specific reaction to a specific marketing stimulus. It was wild and unpredictable, this new system. Harding Lawrence couldn't control this game, and he damn sure didn't like it!

On October 25, 1980, the third-quarter reports hit the papers, and though Lawrence was able to point to the small profit of $18 million, he had to admit it was from a capital gain on the sale of 727's ($61 million). The operating loss was $22.7 million, and the press didn't miss the distinction.

In search of long-term solutions, Lawrence launched in November "Operation Turnaround," which was to include employee participation to the extent of a 10 percent pay cut. One singular story emanating from an employee meeting held to discuss the measure was used to kill it. According to the report, which circulated throughout the company, the chairman had ridden to the meeting in the company Lincoln Continental, driven by the company chauffeur. The sight of the $300,000-per-year chairman climbing out of the chauffeured Lincoln to ask his already shell-shocked (and, in their opinion, underpaid and overworked) union people to slash their wages by 10 percent did not—to understate the response—"go over." That one report, regardless of its veracity (Lawrence does not remember such an incident), when spread by union opponents throughout the ranks, probably created sufficient animosity toward Lawrence and the 10 percent pay-cut proposal to kill it without further consideration.

Lawrence had a significant and basic credibility problem in trying to sell the pay cut. If he told them the truth—just how bad things really were (which he didn't fully believe himself)—the information would instantly leak to the press and the public and come close to starting that self-sustaining cycle of diminishing public confidence that could cost the company hundreds of millions of dollars and ultimately bankrupt it. If, on the other hand, he told them there was no problem, they'd never agree to take a pay cut. What he tried, then, was the middle ground, explaining it as a precautionary move. Unfortunately, the people were more upset than scared at that point, and with the dissidents in the Teamsters ranks snarling against it, the idea was doomed.[3]

By early December Russ Thayer had fled town chasing 747 customers but the airplanes weren't selling, and the fuel costs were

[3] The Teamsters had won an "UNCOLA" clause in a late 1977 contract—"unlimited cost-of-living allowance." With inflation nationwide at 8 to 9 percent, such increases could be handled by Braniff with ease, and indeed, the projections of Vice President for Personnel Terry Schrader, which showed the item to be financially viable, were based on much lower inflation rates. When the national inflation rate began to climb into double-digit range, however, the cost of each raise became very

rising. Lawrence was determined to ride it out. He wasn't about to retreat and destroy all he had created over the past few years. The economy would improve, the fuel cost would eventually go down, and Braniff would survive. But he was becoming increasingly interested in the idea of Braniff surviving without Harding Lawrence. His dream of retiring from a world-girdling carrier of immense profitability was tarnished badly. Now he dreamed of a change in life-style—a chance to be rid of the continuous turbulence and frustration (he had discussed retirement with some of his directors several times over the previous two years). The whole situation saddened him. He had built an empire for the people of Braniff, but they weren't appreciative—and judging from recent experience, if he left, they probably couldn't handle it. He had tried to teach them how for fifteen years, and apparently they hadn't learned a thing.

The 747 operation had never run from DFW with the smoothness the chairman expected. During that period he would inspect the departures personally—not interfering, merely standing and observing, trying to get a feel for what needed correcting. Some of the senior pilots sitting at the gates, high up in the 747 cockpits, would spot their silver-haired chairman standing behind the large glass window of the gate area as they pushed back for London or Honolulu—standing like Ahab watching the great white whale (orange in this case) and longing for control over it and all aspects of the incredible system he had done so much to create. He had brought Braniff so far—was it just to watch a bunch of panicked people dismantle it? It obviously gnawed at him, but other than a few lonely vigils at the gate, it didn't show in public.

Stories would be written concerning Harding Lawrence during this period, questioning whether he was really in control of the corporation and whether he was viewing things realistically—as well as a few suggestions that he had lost his grip on reality. The chairman was upset and frustrated, but he was decidedly not out of control, and he had decidedly not lost his grip on reality. His reliance on the ever-changing plans as proof that the company wasn't in dire

---

high. Since a new adjustment—a raise of nearly 10 percent—was coming up in late 1980, Lawrence was asking the Teamsters (some six thousand strong) to forgo that raise. The other unions (of the pilots, mechanics, flight attendants, dispatchers, etc.) had no such clause (although some of the contracts did have scheduled raises for January 1981). Therefore, the union that could most afford to take the cut was the one that eventually turned it down—the Teamsters.

trouble—his attempts to persuade even himself that the 747's could be sold and the rapidly approaching loan payments met—were a bit surrealistic in light of the data that came across his desk daily telling the tale of deteriorating load factors and yields. But his planning, however flawed, was still an ongoing attempt to gain control of a situation that simply defied solution.[4]

Almost every one of the elements required to make the expansion program a success had failed—as had the fallback position of aircraft sales. There was no way he could have foreseen it.

There was also no way he wanted to let his creation be torn apart; yet the directors were upset, the press was chewing on him, and the red ink continued to flow. He knew the last quarter would hold no profits and the next spring would be more of a struggle. There had to be a better way.

Finally, in mid-December, Lawrence announced what he hoped could be a solution: the beginning of serious merger discussions between Braniff and Frank Borman's Eastern Air Lines—another sick man of the industry. It was, possibly, a way for him to put Braniff in good hands so he could depart. The combined debt of such a merged behemoth would be $1.9 billion—as the press quickly pointed out—but even if it constituted grasping at straws, he was at least doing something positive. Lawrence knew the discussions would take at least a month to complete, and with the Christmas season approaching, perhaps the business would improve a bit. Meanwhile, he continued his nonstop work schedule as senior executives such as John Casey tried to stay out of his way.[5]

On December 22, 1980, a delegation of bank and insurance company representatives—representatives from Citibank, Bankers Trust, Aetna Life & Casualty Company, Prudential Insurance Com-

[4] In fact, Lawrence had made very substantial strides since mid-1979 when he had begun bringing "new blood" into the operational areas of the company's senior management—and they in turn had brought in more qualified people below them. "PAWOGS," an acronym standing for Passengers Arriving WithOut baGS, had been a traditional Braniff problem. In 1978 Braniff ranked twentieth in this category out of twenty major carriers—last place. By 1980, Braniff was third best of twenty. Equally important was the direct revenue saved. In 1978, the costs associated with reuniting angry passengers with wayward bags totaled $13 million. In 1980, it cost Braniff only $6 million.
[5] Harding Lawrence had lost faith in Group Vice President John Casey by 1979—partially because of his brother Al Casey's accession to the chairmanship of American Airlines and American's increasingly threatening posture of competition toward Braniff. Casey's position on the corporate organizational chart was

pany of America, and Mutual Life Insurance Company (some of Braniff's largest long-term lenders)—flew in from New York. Their spokesman was Robert Ferguson, right-hand man to Bankers Trust Company Senior Vice President John Blevin. There at the world headquarters to meet them was the Executive Committee of the Braniff Board of Directors. The subject was Braniff's future, and whether it even had one—a determination the Fergusons and Blevins of the financial world felt they would soon control. Braniff had $37.5 million in loan payments due in two months, and the lenders suspected Braniff would have to strain to meet them.

Bob Ferguson carefully laid out their concerns to Bob Stewart, Perry Bass, Herman Lay, and Troy Post, being very cautious not to use language that would seem to demand Lawrence's resignation while effectively demanding just that. Among the financial problems, there was a personal one. The lenders felt they had been misled and betrayed by Lawrence, and they wanted him out.[6]

The message was basically simple: There had better be drastic changes in Braniff and its management to cut the losses and restore profitability, and they had better occur rapidly. Despite the fact that existing management wanted to hang on to as much of what was created as possible, the losing parts of the operation had to be cut—

---

changed. Instead of most of the airline's corporate departments reporting to him along with the operational departments, Casey was left in charge of the operational areas only. Lawrence had warned Casey not to discuss company matters with his brother, but he knew the two Caseys still talked frequently, and he suspected classified Braniff information might be finding its way to American through that conduit. The "leaks" in the Braniff executive suite were rampant during that period. Within twenty minutes of the end of a staff meeting in which any sensitive marketing information had been discussed, that information would be in the hands of competitor American. For his part, John Casey was tired of being yelled at every time Lawrence saw him during the past few months. In November Casey had started dropping into various executive offices during the day and chatting about nothing in particular for hours—admitting he was hiding from Lawrence.

[6] As would become clear in the next two years, the lenders were attempting to influence the corporation—effectively take control—without legally taking control. When the major banks and insurance companies became frightened in mid-1980, they began to pressure Braniff for some security, since all of their loans were unsecured notes and agreements. In October and December 1980, Braniff mortgaged its entire fleet to the lenders to provide security for over $455 million in loans. If the lenders had unduly influenced the decisions of the corporation before or after, they would imperil their secured position in the event of a bankruptcy. Therefore great care was taken to appear not to be taking control of the airline, even though in practical terms their trip on December 22 and the results it had were morally if not legally a clear seizing of control.

now. The "concerns" amounted to "demands"—demands they were pretty certain Harding Lawrence was not prepared to accept.

There was one large meeting involving the inside Board members as well, who were then asked to leave. Finally, later in the afternoon, the Executive Committee and Lawrence talked it over—the parameters, the possibilities, the "demands." In addition to the lenders, he was being confronted with a panicked board.

Lawrence thought back over the years and the accomplishments, the good calls and the bad, and all the people he had worked with. He was very concerned over the state of the industry and disgusted with the backboneless response of some of his oldest business friends in the face of young Bob Ferguson from Bankers Trust. Suddenly it just didn't seem to be worth it. Harding Lawrence had contributed too much to put up with the indignities they were demanding of him—the effective relinquishing of control to a group of young bankers who held none of the gentlemanly, professional concerns of the previous generation of bankers he had dealt with. If these bastards wanted to take over so much, they could have it—he could see where it would probably end anyway. Neither the bankers nor his Board could run it and understand it as he did. Jim Ling had been pushed out the doorway of LTV in similar fashion—encouraged "in the best interests of the company" to step aside in the midst of a crisis. But Ling only knew how to build a conglomerate—not run one. Harding Lawrence knew both how to build an airline *and* run one. He wasn't expendable.

Harding looked out the large windows of his penthouse over the sculptured ponds and reflecting pools of Braniff's world headquarters and for just a moment felt a rush of relief that maybe he could be free for the first time in decades—free to travel, be with his family. His often-repeated words kept coming back to him, though: "Braniff is my vocation as well as my avocation." Just as quickly the sadness of ending such a wonderful career like this flooded in on him, and with bitterness he turned back to his guests with a reply.

Harding Luther Lawrence would retain the dignity he had earned in thirty-five years as an airline man. He had built this building—this airline—this corporation. He had walked into it proudly, and he would walk out the same way. He would resign.

The following morning, with Vice President for Public Relations Jere Cox at his side, Lawrence gave a previously scheduled interview to a magazine reporter, giving not the slightest hint of the seismic change that had occurred the day before—not a single indication that he would be taking early retirement and resigning effective December 31.

An era ended on that date—December 31—as Lawrence climbed the outside steps of one of the Braniff jetways at DFW and boarded a flight for Acapulco, with *Dallas Morning News* reporter Dennis Fulton sitting with him for an exclusive interview. As they gained altitude southbound in the cold December sky, Lawrence waxed philosophical, calm and collected as he talked of a new life ahead and how he was unsure what he was going to pursue. Fulton realized as he listened that Lawrence wasn't going to discuss whatever had happened to precipitate his departure. If Harding Lawrence were to cry for the past—or for paradise lost—he would do so in private.

For the first time in 15½ years, Braniff was without the leadership, the teachings, and the control of Harding Lawrence, and neither the company nor the Board members who had been so quick to grease the skids for him knew exactly what to do. As the marvelously Byzantine workings of the corporate empire Jim Ling had built stood as a mocking challenge to the would-be rescue attempt of those who had deposed him in the face of looming insolvency, so too at Braniff, the far-flung, stylish airline that Harding Lawrence had created with the Braniff people stood in mocking defiance of anyone who might pretend to the throne—attempt to grab the helm—or try to avoid the deadly shoals of corporate shipwreck looming just ahead. Curiously enough, the key player in the wresting of LTV from Jim Ling had appeared again in the last hours at Braniff: Bob Stewart. He (along with the other activist ouside directors) had rushed to the rescue in the face of pressure from the banking community whence he came, but Stewart was more visible to the world in general, especially after the rumor of his accession of the previous summer. As the teletypes chattered out news of Lawrence's startling departure, Stewart's name came up in conversations from Buenos Aires to Seattle. Was it now to be Chairman Stewart?

The Demon Is All Too Real

The dingy streets of Lima, Peru, just after midnight are a depressing sight. The heavy coastal mists that enfold the grimy walls of decaying buildings and trash-filled, vacant lots impress a desolate feeling of dustiness and gloom over what was once one of the most magnificent of the European-style cities of South America.

In the first hour of Wednesday, December 31, 1980, First Officer Jim Maxwell and his two compatriots began the next leg of their week-long trip, a flight to Los Angeles, by sitting uncomfortably on the cracked, vinyl seat covers of a ramshackle taxi. Cool, dank night air blew through the partially opened front windows as they rumbled through the vacant streets on the way from the downtown area to Jorge Chavez Aeropuerto Internacional. Half asleep, they watched the well-remembered vistas of broken, rubble-strewn neighborhoods of unfinished cement-block houses lighted dimly by an occasional neon street lamp, and they waited for the unkempt façade of the airport terminal to come into view. As usual, they had tried to rest in their rooms all evening before getting up with the ten-thirty wake-up call, grabbing a quick cup of coffee, and climbing in the taxi. Such midnight departures were disorienting.

Once in the airport, the familiar route through the terminal and behind the Braniff ticket counters led them down the darkened edge of the main ramp to a drab crew room ten by twenty feet deep.

The crew room was dominated by several desks strewn with papers—teletypes from Dallas and other points on the Braniff system. Being in the system meant being in another world—one linked principally by the teletype machines at every Braniff station. The stacks of yellow paper, some many days old, were the lifeline of information—the tenuous thread of official linkage to the real airline for which they worked, the one headquartered so far away in

Texas. For the international pilots of Braniff, reading every last one of those yellow teletype messages was a compulsion.

"Jesus Christ, look at this!" Maxwell had picked up one of the yellow sheets, holding it close enough to verify what he had started to read to the other two. "DFW, DECEMBER 30TH . . . HARDING L. LAWRENCE ANNOUNCING HIS RETIREMENT FROM ACTIVE MANAGEMENT AFTER 39 YEARS IN AVIATION AND 35 YEARS IN THE SCHEDULED AIRLINE INDUSTRY SAID TODAY THAT HE HAS RESIGNED AS CHAIRMAN OF THE BOARD AND CHIEF EXECUTIVE OFFICER OF BRANIFF INTERNATIONAL CORPORATION AND BRANIFF AIRWAYS, INC., EFFECTIVE JANUARY 1, 1981!"

The other two pilots closed in to see for themselves, reading over Maxwell's shoulder the rest of the text, which chronicled Lawrence's career with Braniff and his plans to "travel extensively" in the next several months.

"Who's taking over?"

"It doesn't say. Maybe that Board member Robert Stewart. There were rumors about him last summer possibly replacing Lawrence."

"That must mean the merger with Eastern is definitely on . . . they couldn't get Lawrence out with dynamite otherwise."

The captain put his hat on the table and rummaged through some of the other teletypes. "Hey, here's one from Lawrence."

DFWGWBN 302242DR
ALL OFFICES/PLEASE CONVEY THE FOLLOWING PERSONAL MESSAGE TO ALL BRANIFF PERSONNEL.
AS YOU CAN SEE FROM THE COMPANY ANNOUNCEMENT WHICH PRECEDES THIS PERSONAL MESSAGE I AM RETIRING FROM ACTIVE MANAGEMENT AFTER ALMOST 40 YEARS IN THE INDUSTRY WHICH YOU AND I SO DEARLY LOVE.
MY THOUGHTS EXPRESSED THERE ARE ENTIRELY ACCURATE. I HAVE PARTICULARLY ENJOYED MY YEARS WITH THE VERY FINE PEOPLE WHO ARE BRANIFF.
YOU ARE GREAT AND DEDICATED PEOPLE AND YOU AND YOUR COMPANY WILL DO WELL. YOUR TRACK RECORD IN SERVING THE PUBLIC AND THE PUBLIC INTEREST IN OUR ALMOST 16 YEARS TOGETHER IS A PROUD AND ENVIABLE ONE.
IT HAS BEEN MY PLEASURE TO HAVE SERVED WITH YOU. BEST WISHES AND KINDEST PERSONAL REGARDS.
HARDING L. LAWRENCE

The second officer, who had made it to Boeing 727 copilot before the cutbacks started, shook his head. "Well, Frank Borman, here we come, I guess. Two billion dollars of combined debt. We'll join the "moon man" and go happily bankrupt together!"

"What were those suggested new names you mentioned yesterday?" asked Maxwell.

"Someone had written them on my fuel panel. Either 'Beastern' or 'Eastniff'!"

Braniff was confused. From the Board of Directors to the rank and file, it was an uncomfortable interim, fraught with uncertainty. The announcement of the Braniff-Eastern merger talks in early December had injected an ambivalent mixture of optimism and regret into the thinking of agents and mechanics, pilots and managers alike. The thought that Braniff's financial ills might be alleviated by such a merger didn't fully obscure the realization that between the two airlines, Eastern in name and management certainly would be the surviving entity, and Braniff would disappear into the maw of the Miami-based giant. Then too, most Braniff people were sufficiently aware of Eastern's continuing saga of financial woes to know that a Braniff-Eastern marriage would be a confederation of invalids at best—a debt structure of sufficient magnitude to frighten any financier.

The thought that Braniff might cease to exist in the absence of a merger, the unnamed fear of the rank and file, and a subject taboo to management—that bankruptcy might lurk ahead—had not as yet been elevated from the status of a nightmare to that of a realistic threat. Only a handful of the senior executives and a couple of members of the Board had actually looked that demon in the face, and whether Harding Lawrence had recognized it too was uncertain. The fact was, of course, that the demon was all too real.

In the view of most of the rank and file, the so-called contract employees (mechanics, agents, pilots, flight attendants, and all the others working under a labor agreement), the past year had been a depressing assault of furloughs, dislocations, and closed stations amid the continuing litany of the press chanting the preamble "Financially Troubled" before the name Braniff as if the corporate name had been changed to that. It was a depressing period—paradise lost, indeed—and the morale had crashed from optimism to a shuddering depression. The majority struggled to maintain their service at the highest, or even better, levels, sensing that if the company had ever needed an improvement in service, now was the time. But they were all fighting the gloom that comes from watching reality trample a dream and trying their best not to acknowledge the nightmares and the demons that arose in their place. Things had to get better.

But now Lawrence was gone, and while the vast majority of Braniff's people traded rumors and speculated about what his retirement meant, the members of the board were running up longdistance charges trying to decide what to do.

Robert Stewart was sitting in his office on the fiftieth floor of the First International Bancshares Building in downtown Dallas on a Friday, the day after New Year's, talking to yet another of the outside directors.

"Yeah . . . like I told Sloan and Herman and Troy . . . I really don't need this right now in my life . . . I really don't want to take this on. I don't think it would be right for me or the company. I mean, I appreciate the vote of confidence, but the Executive Committee is as much as I want to handle."

The wrangling had begun on December 23, and almost everyone's first choice had been Stewart. Bob Stewart, however, had been in the saddle of First National Bank, which had become First International Bancshares, for over ten years, and at the age of fiftyfive and the peak of his successful career the thought of tackling the merciless monster that the Braniff problem had mutated into was something he was determined to resist—not that he hadn't considered it.

By January 3, and with a Board meeting set for January 7 in Dallas, the press had begun speculating on Lawrence's successor, raising Stewart's name along with that of John Casey, but most prominently they were speculating over the possible appointment of Russell Thayer, who was president of Braniff. The Board was sure of only one thing: Thayer wasn't the man for the job. A pleasant and cultured gentleman, a Princeton graduate, married to a member of the Mellon family, Thayer was far too weak an executive for such a position. Thayer's area of expertise was marketing, but in his position as president he was known as an "empty suit" among many of the newer of his fellow executives for his propensity to change positions with the prevailing wind. His friendship of many years with John Casey had cooled considerably when Thayer was promoted in

1977 to president (a post Casey had coveted and one that was at best undemanding under the strong leadership of Harding Lawrence; Casey had remained as group vice president over most of the airline's operations). Now to have his name hoisted to the masthead by the papers along with Casey's, both as potential heirs-apparent, irritated Casey even further, especially considering the fact that while Casey had stayed and weathered the wrenching emotions of Lawrence's sinking ship through December, Thayer had indulged in a month-long escape—what turned out to be a wild-goose chase to Europe trying to find buyers for Braniff's surplus 747's. Whether it had been a worthwhile effort or not (and Thayer had in fact been ordered to concentrate on selling those new, undeliverable 747's), Russ Thayer had spared himself the agony of the last days at the bunker and was still out of town as Stewart and the Board talked into the evenings of early January, looking for a leader.

Retired Navy Admiral Noel Gayler had joined the Braniff Board in 1976 after his retirement as naval commander-in-chief for the Pacific. A cultured officer of medium height, piercing eyes, and weathered features, the admiral had shown up at Braniff headquarters just after Christmas and had been the most visible of the Board members as he worked to help sort out the financial picture and coordinate with the other outside directors. With Stewart's refusal, several of the outside directors wanted Gayler to take the post, but at age sixty-six, heavily involved in writing and consulting, including a continuous liaison with the Navy Department, Gayler couldn't be tempted either.

In the opinion of most of the Board there wasn't time to go outside the company or their own ranks for a new chairman and president. With the March 1 deadline pressing in on them for the payment of $37.5 million that the company didn't have, a leader who knew the problems and knew Braniff and its operation had to be found immediately.[1]

Even if an outsider could be found, the transition time to bring

---

[1] Braniff actually had that much cash, but if it had been used to pay the amount due, the operating-cash cushion available would have been severely squeezed and the capability of the airline to stay ahead of its bills—a capability that had already been sorely strained with many small suppliers finding their bills unpaid for three and four months on thirty-day accounts—would have placed it in peril. All it would take would be three aggrieved creditors acting together to plunge the company into involuntary bankruptcy.

him up to speed would leave a void of leadership that could be disastrous. The lenders were too diverse a group, and already too upset, to be trusted to defer easily those debt payments that would soon be due, and the aircraft that might have been sold to raise cash to pay them simply weren't salable in the deteriorated airliner market of early 1981. In addition, since the entire fleet was now mortgaged to the lenders, selling a mortgaged airplane would require their approval.

The field was narrowing to John Casey, but a number of the outside directors were very uncomfortable with the idea of giving him the job. John Casey was considered a good operations man, but his experience with the world of high corporate finance was limited at best, and part of the Board felt strongly that the principal demand of the job of chairman would be to orchestrate the high financial manuevers that would be required to keep Braniff flying. After all, Braniff had total corporate liabilities of just over $1 billion and a senior (long-term) debt of $578 million and was still bleeding at the bottom line—hemorrhaging, in the metaphor of the financial press. True, Casey was a friendly, congenial fellow who got along famously with other executives of other companies throughout the industry, and he could probably be expected to relate as well to the financial people, in normal times. But these were not normal times. There was considerable and dangerous anger among the handful of bankers and insurance company people who confronted Post, Stewart, and Bass across the table at the world headquarters on December 22 and growled their demands through Robert Ferguson— demands that were designed to result in Lawrence's immediate departure. They were not in a congenial, cooperative, or forgiving mood. They had lent Braniff under Lawrence hundreds of millions of dollars in good faith on the basis of what had turned out to be inflated projections of earnings and profits. Some of these people, especially the insurance company representatives, felt they had been lied to. What Braniff needed now to deal with these upset lenders was someone with a high degree of financial expertise, and Casey did not have it.

The Board meeting was two days away, and John Casey, prompted by the continuous discussions, had been frantically preparing a plan of how he would go about reorganizing the management structure if the rest of the Board turned to him, which looked increasingly probable. Casey decided to simplify the layer just below the top, and instead of the cumbersome and confusing mix of senior and regular vice presidents reporting to the chairman, he sketched out the three posts of executive vice-presidential rank over operations, marketing, and finance—a *troika* of chiefs to whom most of the rest of the airline would report.

For Executive Vice President for Operations he penciled in the name of William Huskins, an organizationally oriented executive then overseeing Braniff's maintenance functions as a senior vice president, who had been hired away from Donald Nyrop's Northwest Orient Airlines in Minneapolis the year before. Casey and Huskins got along well.

Under the title Executive Vice President for Finance, Casey wrote in Ted Beckwith's name. Beckwith was the sharp-tongued, rank-conscious finance man with wheeler-dealer tendencies who had tried hard to serve Lawrence's needs for creative financial structures after Acker left in 1976, and though Casey didn't care for Beckwith and felt somewhat threatened by him, with Lawrence gone only Beckwith had the knowledge of where the cornerstones lay in the Byzantine financial structure they had built. In addition, Beckwith had been on the front line with the lenders all along. To switch now would invite trouble. Casey felt he could recommend Beckwith enthusiastically to the rest of the Board despite his personal reservations.

Marketing was a problem. Perhaps the best marketing man Braniff had was a man Casey privately detested—Neal Robinson. A younger man, Robinson was a dedicated realist—one of the few new executives around Braniff who had consistently held his ground with Lawrence, even though on more than a few occasions when trying to convince the chairman of the company's perilous financial situation he had been ordered to ". . . get back downstairs and stop meddling in corporate affairs that don't concern you!" Robinson also possessed a self-assurance and a brusque manner that could alienate people. Tall, given to a modish hair style, and often angry, Robinson was not someone Casey wanted on his senior team. He had, however, little choice. Robinson's talents were significant, and not the least among these were those of cultivating the politically powerful. Casey was aware of Robinson's close friendship with several members of the Board's outside directors, including Mrs. Pamela Harriman.

John Casey sat down with several of the other executives privately in the days before the Board meeting and asked if, in their opinion, he could trust Robinson. "What I mean, is, will he turn on me like he did on Harding and undermine me? Or can I trust him?"

In the final analysis, though, Casey knew he couldn't approach the rest of the Board with a proposed list of his senior team if Robinson's name wasn't there for a sufficiently powerful position.

On January 6, Casey was told by Bob Stewart that he would be named chairman, chief executive officer, and president, provided he agreed to certain conditions. First, he would not get a contract and would be expected not to ask for one. Only William Huskins was then still working on a contract basis, and in the opinion of the rest of the Board, it wouldn't be fair to the remainder of the senior people to protect only Casey with one.[2]

Second, Casey had to agree to work very closely with the Executive Committee, of which Stewart was chairman. Stewart and the others had discussed Casey's plans for his management team, and there was general agreement after some hesitation.

Russell Thayer was stripped of all pertinent executive power and named vice chairman of the Board—a nearly useless position at best. Subsequent speculation in the press would point to his long association with Lawrence as the reason, but he was no more tainted than Casey. There was simply unanimous recognition that those executive skills he might possess were insufficient in such a crisis. It would be nearly a year before Russ Thayer would line up another job (with Pan Am) and resign.

The Board met as scheduled on January 7 and confirmed the arrangement unanimously (Russ Thayer made it back from Paris the same morning just in time for the meeting). Each of the directors was well aware that the company's situation was so dangerous there could be no open disagreements within the Board. Much of the business of such a diverse group of strong personalities is done by phone and private contact anyway, but now more than ever, it

[2] Senior management contracts (also sometimes called "golden parachutes" when they include guaranteed compensation provisions) are common throughout corporate America. Harding Lawrence had been hired pursuant to such a contract in 1965, which had been renewed to 1990. Lawrence, with urging from attorney Alan Stewart and others, had voluntarily terminated his contract (which was for $300,000 per year plus other accrued compensation totaling nearly $700,000 dollars per year) and agreed to take early retirement instead, which netted him $306,000 per year.

was important that the Board members be united and unanimous on the record.

As the meeting broke up, several of the directors wandered into what was called the directors' lounge, but what in fact had become Lawrence's living room, connected by double doors to the board-room. It was hard to believe Lawrence wasn't still there. For fifteen years he had *been* Braniff, and every inch of the headquarters offices reflected him, from the Calder paintings to the stark white walls. As the word was passed to the press that John Casey had been named to the vacant posts, Lawrence's implicit influence if not his presence in the world headquarters environment he had created seemed ines-capable.

The teletypes began chattering out the news all over the shrink-ing Braniff system again, and the yellow sheets found their way to photocopying machines and bulletin boards in minutes. The re-sponse ranged from stunned disbelief to more guarded optimism.

"John Casey, that sonofabitch! God save us!"

"With Casey in there, I know we're merging with Eastern. He could never be more than a caretaker."

"Look, he may have been a bastard in Operations, but he's never had a chance really to lead before. Let's give him a chance!"

"Hey, Casey's a good fellow. Let's hope he can handle it."

A Different Brand of Anger

CHAPTER 18 As John Casey began moving into Lawrence's outer office in Braniff's world headquarters at DFW on January 8, 1981, the well-loved secre-tary and de facto "den mother" of the Miami-based Braniff pilots, Pam Shone, placed still another of Miami Chief Pilot Ken Mase's news summaries in the crew room briefing book—this one with more news concerning the naming of Casey to the chairmanship of Braniff.

Mase, a former Navy pilot who had joined Braniff in 1966, had been elevated to chief pilot of the New York pilot base in 1979 and then appointed to take over the all-important South American base in Miami with the retirement of the highly regarded Miami chief pilot, Captain Joe Dean, who had become a fixture. Dean's act was hard to follow. Warm and gentlemanly, he had run Miami's pilot affairs with a fatherly touch. Though far younger than his predecessor, Captain Mase had risen to the challenge with his person-to-person, hands-on management style of constant communication. Ken Mase's methods had resulted in a very smooth operation, even though the pilots had been rotating literally by the hundreds in and out of the Miami pilot base as the monthly base reassignments heralded the agonizing contraction of the pilot force.

To Mase, communications was the key, and as he had in New York, Mase worked hard at making sure his pilots had instant access to every scrap of information he could obtain. A "CPR" (confirmed pilot rumor) book stood on one end of the counter filled with the latest newspaper clippings, magazine articles, and anything else— good or bad—which might have an impact on the people. Mase's methods were unique to Braniff as a company, not just unique to the management of pilots. While the traditional attitude among middle management had been to guard inside information carefully and keep it from the rank and file, Mase's method was to tell all, and the record of his style of management spoke for itself: an unheard-of, total lack of disciplinary actions for over fourteen months.

On this particular day the Miami crew room was full of pilots between flights, including Captain Fred Davis, who was reading aloud selected comments on Casey's accession.

"Here's one from *The Wall Street Journal:* 'While the lenders and the chief financial officer grapple with the financial woes, Mr. Casey can concentrate on improving another of Braniff's serious problems: poor morale. Quote, Braniff hasn't been a very happy place to work for a long time, end quote, a Braniff insider says.'"

"Amen"—the response from one of the captains on the far side of the room. "And who helped make it that way? None other than Mr. John J. 'Fire the Sonofabitch' Casey!"

John J. Casey had been senior vice president for Operations, and as such he was in charge of the flight operations personnel—pilots, flight attendants, maintenance, and several other functions. In the 1970s he had been elevated to group vice president by Lawrence, becoming the ultimate reporting authority for sales, inflight services, customer services, and most of the corporate functions, though in 1979 he was effectively demoted back to control of just the operational areas. The pilots knew Casey from long association, and with exceptions, there had been little love lost over the years. It was well known that Casey's explosive temper would ignite when confronted with any problem associated with the flight crews, and the most common epithet of all was his traditional directive to fire the offending pilot. Casey knew very well it wasn't that easy. To fire a pilot, even if he deserved to be fired (which was sometimes the case), required a long routine of preparation and careful handling of the case in strict accordance with the pilot's contract. That's why he could so easily issue such a directive time and time again. He was protected from having to face the possibility that his subordinates would actually do it. It gave him a dramatic emotional outlet to demonstrate his frustration with the delay, or the incident, or whatever had sparked his ire.

The trouble with such displays is that reports of them inevitably filter down to the ranks. In the case of the pilots, whose skills are essentially nontransferable (due to the inflexible nature of the different seniority systems in different airlines, pilots are effectively married to their airline), such alienating displays are counterproductive because they're taken very seriously. Coming from a man like Casey, whose skills and experience are transferable to any other carrier in aviation, such words are a declaration of arrogance and contempt. This had been Casey's method over the years, however, and as he took the helm, the bitter memories of past outbursts smoldered in the minds of many of Braniff's most senior airmen as well as in the recollection of many other people in various areas of operations who had been on the receiving end of a Casey tirade.

John J. Casey, a five-foot-ten Irishman, was born in Boston, attended MIT, took graduate engineering work at Cornell in 1942, and subsequently entered a branch of what was the forerunner of the CIA, serving during the war in several foreign locations. With professional credits that included American Airlines and Seaboard World Airlines, Casey joined Lawrence at Braniff in 1968. One of the few senior Braniff executives involved in the community, he participated heavily in the Boy Scouts programs in Dallas and had become socially prominent in Dallas by the mid-1970s. Casey's capabilities included a great capacity for the enjoyment of individual contact, and he had friends at the most subterranean of levels in the company. His principal flaw was an echo of one of Harding Lawrence's personal millstones—his temper knew few reasonable bounds. Casey was perceived as being either a prince of a guy or a "sonafabitch," depending on whether a fellow Braniff employee had gotten to know him in an *ex officio,* friendly basis, or had been on the receiving end of an episode of pronounced displeasure.

Casey's explosions were quite different from Lawrence's brand of anger. Most executives, however badly beaten up they may have perceived themselves to be after a Lawrence tongue-lashing, usually had the impression that the chairman had known exactly what he wanted to accomplish with the explosion. In most cases they were a theatrical event, staged to impress a point on the hapless subordinate with indelible poignancy, or to intimidate him or her to a calculated degree.[1]

Casey's style, on the other hand, was to notice when something went wrong and then to rant and rave almost deliriously, getting lost in the histrionics of the moment—apparently from acute frustration.

Like author Robert Serling's description of Continental Airlines chief Robert Six in Serling's book *Maverick,* Casey "had a heart as big as a whale's" and genuinely cared for his friends, as long as they remained friends. But to be an employee under John Casey did not by itself entitle you to the protection of being a friend.

Casey had been reasonably effective as head of the company's operation functions over the years, but his breezy, freewheeling style prompted one subordinate vice president, on the eve of his own appointment as a senior vice president, to say privately, "I've watched John Casey for years, and I still don't know what a senior vice president is supposed to do."

Casey took great pleasure in his contacts with friends throughout the aviation industry and would keep a junior executive waiting on the other side of his desk for fifteen or twenty minutes while Casey talked expansively to another airline man in New York or Los Angeles or Denver. He especially relished the calls from his brother, Albert Casey, chairman of American Airlines. John Casey would

[1] In 1979, while interviewing future Vice President Jeff Krida, Harding Lawrence asked him for a definition of "leadership." After listening to Krida's carefully stated answer, Lawrence leaned over: "You know how I define leadership? I'm a damn good actor and I 'con' the hell out of 'em!"

put his hand over the mouthpiece of the phone and whisper con-spiratorially to whichever subordinate was seated in his office, "It's Al!"—then go on to talk for a half hour. Of the two brothers, John was the older, and to watch his brother selected from another indus-try to pass him by as chairman of a major airline—and one that was hurting Braniff at that—made John more than a little anxious to prove he was capable of at least as much executive responsibility.

John Casey's personal pride, then, was substantial at taking the helm at Braniff, despite the conditional nature of the coronation and the fact that his fellow Board members were nervous about his abil-ity to handle the job. Al was only the chairman over at American. John was chairman, president, and chief executive officer at Braniff. Were the times less perilous, there was speculation that his head could well have expanded to accommodate all three hats.

Casey hit the deck running, calling his executives at all levels in for meetings on the new regime and instilling a refreshing burst of communications that gave real hope and a genuine thrill to many of the sales, services, and operational people based outside Dallas. As Captain Ken Mase wrote in the briefing book for his pilots in Miami:

> I am excited and encouraged to see the new attitudes, the openness and frankness, the willing spirits, the receptiveness of management to listen and communicate, the new stream-lined management concept instituted by Mr. Casey and the cooperative spirit displayed by employees at all levels. This is not to downplay the seriousness of the financial dilemma that is facing us in the next few months or the responsibility that we must grasp in our day to day treatment of our cus-tomers.
>
> We must continue to work even harder than before. I am proud of the Miami pilots because of the constant feedback that I am receiving concerning your sensitivity to the per-sonal greetings you are giving to our customers. I am count-ing on each of you to think and fly safely. Then to meet those customers in flight, make the PA announcements, be in the doorway on enplaning and deplaning and go to the boarding lounge to greet our customers.
>
> You can turn our customers into "Braniff Boosters" by your actions. We must do it—we have no choice!
>
> I'll keep you informed.
>
> K. J. Mase

The senior and junior officers of Braniff regarded Casey's accession as an opportunity. To some, it was an opportunity to manipulate—corporate political games were a well-established custom at Braniff—but to most of the others, it became an opportunity to get their ideas across at long last, ideas on how to improve Braniff's product.

The good middle-management people and those one step up from the unions regarded the change nervously, hopefully, wondering if Casey would suddenly recognize their plight. The automatic raises for the contract employees had finally boosted union wages far above their old salaries, and the good managers who were left were trying hard not to become demoralized, especially the ones fighting the battles at DFW, which for a junior manager was akin to a combat assignment, since the Teamsters delighted in trying to emasculate the managerial authority of any new manager as fast as possible.

There was a war on at DFW, the showplace of the Braniff system, which had become an unbelievable rat's nest of radical union discontent and hatred of the company on the part of too many public-contact employees. These were the people who formed the front lines of Braniff's increasingly desperate attempt to win the hearts and dollars of the traveling public, and with such people in the lead, Braniff might not have a prayer.

Crass, Inept, Nasty, Rude, and Lazy

CHAPTER **19** Billy McCutcheon, Braniff's DFW customer service manager, sat at his dining-room table in his North Fort Worth home and reread the letter. One of Braniff's first officers, a fellow named Jerry Todd, had become so fed up with the sloppiness and uncaring attitude of Mc-

Cutcheon's agents at Braniff's DFW terminal that he had committed the ultimate sin—he had sent a scathing letter of complaint to another department of the company, McCutcheon's department. Traditionally in Braniff, such effrontery would earn the offending pilot or flight attendant or mechanic the status of target—the complained-of person or department would backtrack through the chain of command to the complainant's vice president who, embarrassed, would chastise his subordinate, and so on down the line. Instead of a productive response, the hapless complainer would often find himself in trouble.

McCutcheon had seen the entire rotten process of intradepartmental self-protection as it grew through the late 1960s. He had started as a ticket agent in Lubbock and worked his way up to the managerial ranks while watching the progressive hardening of union attitudes against the company and any moving target labeled management. He had also seen the paranoia of many managers and vice presidents ferment into such a fortress of self-protection that no complaint from outside about anyone or any function within that department could be allowed to stand unchallenged, lest it imperil the leaders of that department or reach Lawrence's attention. Though there were constructive exchanges of criticism constantly, all too often a complaint would engender a protective-reaction counterstrike aimed squarely at the complainer.

Now he, Billy McCutcheon, ex-agent, ex-Teamster, had the god-awful mess at DFW, and he was determined to change it.

He was convinced that the key to that process lay in first acknowledging that it was a disaster, especially in terms of horrid customer service and poor attitudes among the public-contact people. The position he held had destroyed good managers before him, but in the late summer of 1980, after having the job for two months, he was beginning to make headway.[1]

First Officer Todd could be assured of a compliment not a counterstrike. After all, what the pilot had to say was dead right.

Todd had flown on his Braniff passes to Chicago from DFW and returned using an interline pass on American Airlines: He had been

---

[1] McCutcheon's position placed him in charge of all the ticket agents, gate agents (inside and outside), lead agents, section managers, passenger service representatives, special services employees, and all other public-contact personnel and their managers at Braniff's huge, semicircular DFW terminal.

impressed and saddened by the tremendous difference between his company's people and those of the competitor. American's personnel, he had noticed, were professional in all their contacts with their customers:

Driving home from the airport, pondering the pleasant experience I had just taken part in, I thought of all the times during the past thirteen years of observing or standing in Braniff lines with as many as twenty or more people in them. Many times there was only one agent to serve them. Some of these agents have appeared to be indifferent, emotionally detached or just plain rude. In retrospect, if I were offered the same passes from American that I receive from Braniff, I would choose to "non-rev" from the American terminal. I would make that decision due to the friendliness and efficiency of their public contact employees. Three months ago while flying out of DFW we had a mechanical just prior to departure. A fat and sloppy agent with his shirt-tail out in the back, picked up the P.A. microphone and said in an almost incomprehensible Texas drawl, "Folks, this airplane is no good, and y'all hafta go back to th' waitin' lounge." What is a first-time passenger to think of such a comment? In my opinion, we have too many public contacts who are emotionally or intellectually not suited to stand before the discriminating public traveler.

I sometimes wonder if the Company is aware of the number of times we pull into the terminal on time only to have to wait five or ten minutes for the agents to pull the jetway to the aircraft so the passengers can leave. When we stop the aircraft, we shut down the engines and block-in for time, so the Company probably isn't fully aware of the problem. Every good thing that the flight crew and the flight attendants have done is negated and erased in the passenger's mind who has been standing in the aisle.

In summation, and in my opinion, the Halston uniforms, the leather interiors, the Beef Wellington, and all the cups of coffee in the whole world with brandy in them can never take the place of expeditious handling of our customers by professionals who are truly concerned and discriminating in their contacts with the travelling public. I have taken the

185

time to write this letter because I really do care about my Company, and I believe its content to be true based on thirteen years of observing our operations on our domestic system.

The public contact employees at DFW are for the most part the worst in the entire Braniff system. I thank you for reading this letter, and if there is anything I can do to help get this message to the right people, please don't hesitate to call me.

Sincerely,
Jerry Todd
First Officer/Braniff International

McCutcheon, mad as hell over the truly lousy customer-service problems Todd had observed, deleted Todd's name from the letter, then pulled out a pad of memos, slammed them down on his dining-room table, and began writing:

MEMO
BRANIFF INTERNATIONAL

To: All Public Contact Employees
From: W. McCutcheon
Subject: Attached Letter
Date: August 18, 1980

The attached letter was written by a Braniff First Officer. Although this does not describe many of your fine efforts, it is indicative of how we are perceived in the eyes of many. I am pleased he took the time to describe what he saw, as it should open many of your eyes as to what is needed to return Braniff to profitability and prosperity for all of us.

McCutcheon paused, then looked again at the stack of yet-to-be answered complaint letters alongside Todd's. McCutcheon had tried before to tell the people at DFW how bad things were—show them, for instance, that Braniff ranked dead last in CAB passenger complaint ratings against Delta's first-place position. They refused to listen. Braniff had led all other airlines in June and July on-time performance, but its passenger service was rotten. McCutcheon began writing another memo.

MEMO
BRANIFF INTERNATIONAL
To: All Public Contact Employees
From: W. McCutcheon
Subject: Company Rules
Date: August 18, 1980

On March the 7th, 1980, you were provided with the following addition to your employee's handbook under "customer complaints":

Employees who work in customer contact positions at Braniff are required to provide the highest quality of service to Braniff customers. Any employee who is unfriendly, discourteous, or impolite to Braniff customers, or otherwise does not project an attitude of total service, will be subject to disciplinary action for failure to satisfactorily perform his duties. Disciplinary action will range from a letter of warning, to termination, and may be considered a major infraction depending on the severity of the act, as determined by the appropriate company representative.

Many of you have not taken heed of this advisory. During my weekend "pleasure" reading (of passenger complaint letters), your actions have been described in the following manner: curt, crass, bad attitude, inconsiderate, inept, inhumane, nasty, non-professional, sarcastic, rude, lazy, and unpleasant.

As a professional and as one who is being paid good wages to serve our customers, these types of descriptions represent a deplorable approach to your basic responsibilities as customer service agents. There should be little doubt what is expected from you in serving our customers, and there should be no doubt what the consequences [will be] for not providing good services at all times.

If you don't have a good attitude, Get One! Don't leave home without it!

MEMO
BRANIFF INTERNATIONAL

To: All Public Contact Employees
From: W. McCutcheon
Subject: Status of the Company
Date: August 18, 1980

In the Wall Street Journal to the local newspapers, it is no well-kept secret that our Company has lost money for four successive quarters, or 69-million dollars for the first half of 1980. There should be little doubt left that our problems are severe, and each of us must act at once. In our deregulated skies there remains only one difference: personalized service. Each passenger must be given superior service each time we come in contact with him. How? A warm smile . . . sincere effort to serve the customer using empathy at all times, and "thank you" for his or her business. Simple enough? Absolutely! It all starts with personal pride, followed closely by corporate pride. Pride will beget confidence, confidence in ourselves and our customers, and confidence in our Company.

Put your best foot forward at all times. Look sharp. Be proud to display your name badge. Think positive. The results will be beneficial to all of us and make DFW the best station in the United States.

When McCutcheon arrived at his office at DFW on Monday morning, August 18, 1980, he had his secretary type all the post-dated memos he had written the day before and place them by mid-morning on the various bulletin boards in the halls and break rooms throughout the IBT (International Brotherhood of Teamsters) working areas of the terminal. The reaction was immediate and furious. McCutcheon would later dub them the "Jericho memos," because as soon as they were issued, the walls began to crumble.

By the end of the day, the shrill level of fury of the agents and their Teamster representatives had exceeded anything McCutcheon had ever witnessed on either side of the management fence. Delegations trooped in and out of his office enraged at the gall of the pilot and the effrontery of McCutcheon to believe such lies. Scrawled comments, many echoing the same obscene descriptions the Teamsters were spouting verbally about the letter, the memos, and management in general, began appearing in the margins of the posted memos themselves. More ominously, the strong-arm revenge mentality of some of the less refined members of the group—many of them union stewards and case-hardened radicals—began plotting their revenge. They were going to find that "goddamn lying sonofabitch pilot" if it took a year. The tiny spaces in the posted copies of the letter where McCutcheon had excised all references to the first officer's name became mocking, gaping holes to the leaders of the group.

It was painfully obvious to McCutcheon and the lower-level managers who worked for him that they had a near revolt on their hands. Officially and as a group the Braniff public-contact employees at DFW absolutely refused to believe anything could be wrong with their performance. And if, they grumbled with clenched fists and gritted teeth, there was anything wrong with their performance, it was the company's fault, not theirs. They were the downtrodden, mismanaged, kicked-around, and overworked victims of the company's crass exploitation. They could see no farther than that. The idea of taking individual or even collective responsibility as a group for their actions with regard to how they treated the customers and helped sell the product was simply not an issue. The attitudes of these people had deteriorated over the years to the point that objective evaluation of their own job performance was impossible.

Naturally, not everyone in the agent group felt that way. There were a large number of motivated, pleasant, professional agents who, left to their own methods, would have matched any counterpart at Delta or American in customer-service positions of any type. The disastrous truth of the matter, however, was that even the good ones were so intimidated and dominated by the vitriolic company-hatred of the radicals within the agent group that they would rather risk being fired than try to oppose the idea that virtually anything management said or did was by definition an unjustified affront or an attempt to harass.

The roots of the problem ran back many years, beyond DFW, back to Love Field, whence too many of the bad apples had come. It ran back to the lack of training for agents, lead agents, and their managers, back to the overall company neglect of what might be called the front-line management structure, and the inability to get rid of the people who couldn't or wouldn't perform. It was a result in part of hiring people from noncontact jobs without screening them to determine whether they had the intelligence or the temperament to deal with the public. Finally, it stemmed from the inescapable fact that far too many agents who should have been fired years before had been allowed to stay on, treating Braniff's passengers with disdain, Braniff with distrust, and their jobs as gifts from the Teamsters.

It wasn't easy to fire a contract employee, and that was a matter of protection for both the company and the union people. Defense against arbitrary termination of a career with a company is one of the valuable functions of a union contract relationship. At Braniff, however, the all-important training of lower-level managers on how to fire an employee who truly deserved to be fired had never existed. Too many times the attempt was botched, and after several weeks or months of wrangling between the union and the company, the offending individual would be put back to work with all his back pay. In effect, the manager who did the firing had cost the company unnecessary time and money, and in the end had simply reinstalled a problem behind the ticket counter, an individual now radicalized in attitude against the company despite what had amounted to a paid vacation. What was worse, the manager, if not disciplined or transferred himself for the mistake, would have lost a great deal of whatever authority and credibility he might have achieved with his employees. Since he had obviously been wrong, the incident would be considered another example of how the company harassed its contract people and how effectively the union could override such managers.

Without training and support from upper management, the smart young, junior manager would quickly see the counterproductive effect of trying to tangle with the union people and would cease trying. Why take a chance if it wasn't appreciated or supported from above? The ranks of the radicals thus increased, and the inability of management to manage became nearly total. Before the efforts of 1980 at DFW, the Teamsters had been the de facto management of the agents, and passenger service was a concept foreign to them and the dangerously poor personnel they protected.

Many of these worst agents—the radicals—had become union stewards. Again, certainly not all held such crass viewpoints toward their responsibilities, but in the majority of cases where the DFW agents were concerned, the Teamsters had become an integral part of the problem—a cornerstone in the fortress of union self-protection standing between Braniff's efforts to build customer loyalty with consistently professional service and the reality of what really occurred on a daily basis at DFW: an abysmal and continuous show of arrogant neglect and disdain for the Braniff passenger.

To point out these problems to the group as a whole, however, was to trigger an unsophisticated, primal rage among a few union leaders who acted as if the Teamsters signed their paychecks. The hunt for the mysterious first officer had gone into high gear by late September, and even some of the agents over at American had joined in the detective work, going back through their computer flight lists to find what Braniff pilots flew from Chicago to Dallas during the targeted month. McCutcheon had no idea of the scope of the search, but the end result would be one of the most childish displays of mindless vindictiveness ever committed by a group of public-contact airline employees who claimed to be professionals.

In the meantime, McCutcheon was making headway in his attempts to weed out properly the unsalvageable agents, retain and remotivate the rest, and push through one particular project that had met instant resistance from the rank and file. As with his prior experience as a section manager in 1976, the agent group resisted change even when it would simplify and ease their jobs. The gospel according to the Teamsters was that the company couldn't be trusted; therefore, any suggestion that came from management was a plot.

In its simplest terms, Vice President Doug MacArthur and Customer Service Manager Billy McCutcheon wanted agents who could greet the passengers as they came out of the jetways on arrival. It seemed like such a simple thing—American and Delta had been doing it for many years. At Delta, the red-coated passenger service people wouldn't even wait to be asked for help. Their method was aggressively to walk up to deplaning passengers and ask if there was anything they could do. The practice was in no small measure responsible for Delta's extremely low complaint rating and high degree of passenger loyalty.

In the fall of 1980 it was painfully obvious to everyone that Braniff could ill afford to hire additional employees. So the idea arose to eliminate the outside agent's duty of walking all the way to the rear of an arriving 727 to open a small panel under the tail and extend the rear stairway. If he was free from this duty, he could position the jetway, open the door, and then walk up the jetway ahead of the passengers to position himself to help them and answer their questions.

The additional task of dropping the aft stairway had been added to the outside agent's duties back in the sixties at Love Field when Braniff began flying 727's. The agents had resisted it then but had quickly adopted the task as their own, and despite the presence of cargomen, mechanics, catering personnel, and others around the aircraft who could have easily been trained to accomplish the mindlessly simple job, the outside agents hung on to it as if it formed the entire rationale for their employment.[2]

McCutcheon began the battle to convince them that their company needed the additional public contact and that their jobs would not be reduced in number because of it. He began holding meetings with his people in all sections and lobbying Teamster Business Manager Schlinke, who tried repeatedly to table the issue until the rank and file agreed to it. In the panicky atmosphere of early December 1980, however, it was becoming increasingly clear to McCutcheon that time was running out. He attempted to make his contract people see that their careers were in jeopardy because their airline was in jeopardy and that any further delay in drastically improving the quality of passenger service could be fatal. Many listened, a few understood, but with too many of them McCutcheon ran headlong into a fresh memory of Lawrence's request for a 10 percent pay cut amid his public denials that Braniff had any financial problems. Their company wasn't in financial trouble—Lawrence had said so himself; so management, including McCutcheon, was simply lying once again. The agents had neither the time nor the patience to

[2] In effect, those agents who bid for the outside-agent job were said to be "on their way to cargoman" because of the extremely limited opportunities the job held for contact with the public. Other than meeting the flights with the jetway, opening the door, dropping the rear stairs, and reversing the process on departure, outside agents could simply disappear on an extended coffee break the rest of the time— they had no other formal duties. To eliminate one small task and substitute another, that of greeting deplaning passengers, was scarcely a case of overworking the agent. There were many outside agents who diligently helped the inside agent with the check-in and boarding procedures and who would jump in to help in a section or gate that wasn't their own when another agent was snowed under. All too many, however, regarded such extra effort as unnecessary at best, and another example of company attempts to undermine their jobs at worst. Helping each other for the good of the company was a foreign, laughable concept to too many.

listen to him, especially considering the approach of Christmas and the closely guarded fact that one of their number had finally hit the jackpot. They had isolated the offending letter writer, one Jerry Todd. With this clandestine victory, the plans for revenge went into high gear. Management nonsense about financial troubles and alleged passenger-service problems could wait.

At 7:26 A.M. on the Sunday morning of December 14, 1980, beneath overcast skies and a brisk north wind, Braniff Flight 379 turned off DFW Runway 35 Left and headed for Gate 19 at Braniff's terminal. In the first class section was the new wife of one of the pilots (they had been married four months) who had flown with her husband on his layover trip the night before to Corpus Christi, Texas. Such trips, with a Braniff family riding on passes and the father or mother flying as a crew member were somewhat traditional and usually very enjoyable. For the pilot's wife seated in 1A on Flight 379, however, what had been a delight was about to become a nightmare.

As the Boeing 727 nosed into Gate 19 and shut down, the captain—who had gotten word over the radio—turned to his copilot. "Apparently you did something very wrong. There's going to be trouble when you get off."

As they ran the shutdown checks and packed flight maps into their flight bags, the copilot noticed that the jetway was full of Braniff agents in uniform. They had been carrying a light load of passengers from Corpus Christi, and as they filed out the front doorway, the copilot put his arm around his wife and stepped out amid a crowd of angry, scowling faces and cold, hateful stares. First Officer Jerry Todd and his wife began the walk through the jetway to the terminal between a gauntlet of hysterically infuriated agents and a thundering chorus of boos and jeers and profanity ("You've flown your last Braniff pass, you motherfucker!" "You'll never get on at my gate again, you sonofabitch!"), raised fingers, obscene signs, shaken fists, and shouting, angry, purple faces of the nearly 150 male and female Braniff agents who had assembled from all over DFW to ambush Todd and punish him for his letter. Startled, embarrassed, unsure what to do, Todd pushed his wife through the gauntlet of jeering, uniformed hecklers toward the terminal, with the crowd closing in behind them as they moved, doing everything but spitting on him.

With he and his wife both in tears, confused and shaking, he emerged into the terminal and tried to turn and talk to a few of the agents, who simply shouted him down as they walked past back to their various posts and breakrooms. Todd, shaken and humiliated, began trying to apologize to the jeering mob individually, but none of them wanted to hear it. They had accomplished their grand purpose for which three months of unremitting effort—effort far in excess of what many of them had put into their jobs in years—had been expended.

The ringleaders had covered their tracks by staying home and trading their Sunday duty days so they would be off-duty and seemingly blameless when the ambush was carried out. No one could decide who to discipline, so no one was punished. Much later it was discovered that one of the best of Braniff's junior managers, a man named David Hare, had known of the upcoming ambush and had been too intimidated to report it or prevent it.

As Braniff International entered the most deathly critical eighteen months of its fifty-three-year existence—a period in which every customer, every dollar, every ounce of passenger goodwill could change the balance point between survival and bankruptcy— the showplace of the airline was staffed with people such as those who had abused Jerry Todd and his wife. They had grown into a vitriolic cadre of individuals who would rather demean and belittle a legitimately concerned fellow employee and reduce him to tears than admit that maybe, just maybe, there was some truth in his criticisms.

As one of the complaining customer letters had said, ". . . with people like yours at DFW, you don't need competitors. You'll run yourselves out of business!"

Casey at the Bat

20 As John J. Casey took over as head of Braniff International on January 8, 1980, his priorities for immediate action were based on several clear and certain truths. First, the lenders were in control, and they had seized on the idea of a 10 percent pay cut (similar to the one that had failed two months before) as a gesture they wanted to see the employees agree to before there was to be any discussion of slipping the payment date for the $37.5 million of principal and interest due March 1. In the absence of some sort of quick merger agreement with Eastern, which was still a remote possibility, the payment date had to be considered unavoidable. Braniff had to face it and therefore had to dance to the lenders' tune.[1]

Second, the key to getting such a pay cut from the employees was securing the agreement of the Teamsters (since they were the one group that had voted down the idea the first time around) and the mechanics' union, the International Association of Machinists (IAM). Braniff's Teamster employees, nearly seven thousand strong, represented the crux of the discontent in the ranks. The previous fall's angry, overwhelming vote of rejection was a good indication of that. Therefore, Casey had to win over the Teamsters, or any one of the lenders could, and might, hand Braniff a letter of default on the

---

[1] The major lenders, who had become secured lenders with the granting of the mortgage on Braniff's fleet, were desperate to keep the company alive at least until the first ninety days after the granting of the security interest had expired. If the company should go bankrupt and liquidate before that point, their security interest would be worthless. They were controlling the company by mid-January, when they had forced Braniff into a financial maneuver involving the sale of a new 747-SP (Ship 603) to a specially created holding corporation for $32 million, over $6 million under book value. The proceeds were paid to the lenders.

morning of March 2. God knows what might happen after that, but an involuntary bankruptcy filing under Chapter 7 and dissolution of the company was a possibility.

Casey knew he had only about five weeks to alter a case-hardened attitude of distrust that had taken years to build. He waded into the morass immediately and put his senior people to work on a profit-sharing/salary reduction program—an idea similar to one used at Eastern whereby all the employees, including management, contribute a certain percentage of their pay each month—in this case, 10 percent. Unlike Lawrence's rejected plan, Casey's was leaning toward one that would refund everyone's contribution along with a percentage of excess profits if the airline ended a year firmly in the black with an operating profit.

Before Casey hit the campaign trail to sell the idea to the Teamsters and the rest of the contract employees, he settled the $1.5 million maintenance enforcement action with the FAA for $250,000 in an incredible scene in Washington, D.C.

Casey felt that Langhorne Bond's personal involvement in the Braniff maintenance case was a result of his pique at Harding Lawrence, so he figured that Harding's departure would open the way to concluding the matter with a small fine. Casey flew to Washington and picked up one of the Arnold and Porter attorneys before walking in to Bond's office at FAA headquarters.

"You know I could run this up to ten million in penalties, don't you?"

Bond was watching Casey for his reaction, which was immediate and offended. "That's ridiculous!"

"Well, how 'bout a million?"

Casey couldn't believe it. Bond was acting as if he had Braniff by the throat. Braniff could easily fight the action in court, but Casey had just wanted to get rid of it.

"No way! No way will we pay a million dollars!"

"Okay, just a minute." Bond walked into the next room adjacent to his office and returned two minutes later with a folded slip of paper, which he handed to Casey as if it were some sort of sealed envelope on a game show. Casey opened the slip and found a handwritten figure: "$500,000." Apparently Bond had no intention of treating this seriously. He was supposed to be discussing what amount would be appropriate to satisfy the just concerns of the United States government. Instead Casey was dealing with a frustrated Monty Hall! John Casey demurred again, and they eventually agreed to $250,000. It had been an unbecoming display.

The Reagan administration was just settling into the White House, and the hostages from the American Embassy in Iran were on their way home at long last when the announcement of the FAA settlement was released on January 24 and promptly buried on the back pages of most of the papers. The extreme damage to Braniff's safety reputation that Bond's people had achieved with their shrill, publicity-seeking enforcement action ended with a whimper. The violations, after all, were more technical than substantive. How many passengers the episode had scared away and how many dollars failed to flow into the company's accounts as a direct result were impossible to calculate. The inexcusable aspect of the FAA's action was that no damage should have occurred. Had the matter been handled as problems with other airlines in the past, before Bond, Braniff could have been shocked into even faster compliance through quiet, internal ultimatums from the agency to the company with nary a headline.

Among the other links in the ever-lengthening chain of revenue-depressing troubles draped around Braniff's corporate neck, at least one link had been forged by Bond's FAA.

On January 27 another shock wave rolled over the company. After some extended conversations between Casey and Eastern Chairman Frank Borman, Eastern formally notified Braniff that the merger was off—their Board wasn't interested in looking any further. What had killed it was a combination of things. The negative response of the Eastern and Braniff lenders to the gigantic debt structure that would result was probably paramount, but the lack of interest of Braniff's lenders in a quick Braniff debt restructure to pave the way for a merger was also a negative factor. Then too, there were the all-important worries about whether Braniff's coveted South American route system could be transferred intact to a merged Braniff-Eastern. The CAB had been rumbling that new route hearings might be necessary, and that would destroy the value of the deal for Eastern. Finally, Borman had expressed concern over the large numbers of pilots and other Braniff personnel, senior in hire date to Eastern's people, who were on furlough. Merging the seniority lists could furlough some of the Eastern personnel and damage the relationship of trust Borman had been working so hard to build with his employees over the past few years. Borman and Casey agreed to hinge the explanation of the call-off of the merger talks on that point. As reported in the *Dallas Times Herald* on Wednesday, January 28, 1981:

BRANIFF, EASTERN END TALKS

Braniff International Corporation and Eastern Airlines Inc. have broken off merger discussions because they could not countenance the personnel layoffs a merger would have necessitated, it was announced Tuesday.

John J. Casey, Braniff Chairman and President, said the decision to end the merger talks was arrived at mutually and that staffing considerations were the "overwhelming, basic reason for breaking off discussions."

Casey said he and his management team are "delighted Braniff will remain an entity."

The reaction throughout Braniff was surprise—many people in the company had already resigned themselves to what they saw as the inevitability of the upcoming merger, and some of the leaders of the various unions had already begun taking steps to protect the seniority lists of their membership when the merger occurred. Now it was off, and with it, a certain degree of relaxation disappeared. There had been the feeling that Eastern was to be Braniff's "white knight," its savior from financial doom, and with that feeling in the background, it was more difficult to persuade people that paycuts or any other concessions were really needed.

There appeared to have been little opportunity for Casey to have had much influence on the outcome of the merger talks, having been in office only a few days, but some people in the industry privately expressed their suspicions that perhaps Casey, having now been installed as the chief, wasn't too interested in presiding over the demise of his position. Casey's statement that the management team was "delighted Braniff will remain an entity" fueled the speculation. No one knew exactly how he meant that, or why he said it.

With or without the merger, Braniff would face massive problems. Now, with it off, there was only one direction to go: The debt had to be restructured and the operating losses reversed or the company was dead. Casey had to get that message across now more than ever, and the clock was ticking.

198

John Casey's strong suit had always been his ability to relate to people on a warm and friendly basis when he desired to do so. The majority of his subordinates before the end of 1980 had never had the opportunity to enjoy such concerned attention from Casey, but now that he was chairman and now that the company's survival hinged on winning the friendship and influencing the trust of the diverse group of good and lousy employees alike who made up the Braniff membership of the Teamsters throughout the airline, Casey initiated the most energetic "trust me, I'm your friend" campaign of his career.

The Teamsters represented nearly seven thousand Braniff employees. The vast majority of these people were basically good professionals, despite the normal human variances in capabilities, education, personal qualities, and attitudes resulting in no small measure from the company's longtime system of flawed lower management, nonexistent training, and the most damaging practice of all: placing people in public-contact positions solely on the basis of seniority—with no screening whatsoever. Many of those not in public-contact positions, many of the reservationists and the outstation agents, were of the highest caliber. The cynical, company-hating attitude of the DFW agent cadre certainly involved a small minority of the Teamsters—but that minority had done great damage to their company.

The Teamsters union was not the only one with people who had lost sight of their responsibilities and reason for existence. Members of the mechanics' union, the IAM, were just as virulent in their refusal, as an entity, to acknowledge the basic need to keep the company healthy. Though they approved the 10 percent pay cut both times, their leadership was guilty of trying to sabotage the plan on both occasions. With the deadline approaching in February of 1981, Jerry Emmell, the general chairman of Braniff's IAM (and employed by the IAM, not Braniff), was quoted by the press as saying, "I don't give a damn whether they [Braniff] go under or not! I'll just go get a mechanic's job with Texas International."

Even the pilots' union, the Air Line Pilots Association (ALPA, the most professional of the airline unions, which is run by line pilots rather than non-Braniff business managers), despite their unhesitant approval of both episodes of the pay cut, had begun to rumble loud and long that the company had always depended on being able to stampede the pilots into any concession. Increasingly, in the view of ALPA's leadership and that of many pilots, the company was trying to place the financial mistakes of management on their backs, blaming their higher salaries for an unrealistically large share of the airline's losses. The attitude that was developing was destined to create a major problem within a matter of months, when negotiations for a new contract for the pilots got under way in the valley of the shadow of bankruptcy.

Casey began inviting union leaders in to see the company books—trying to give them a clear idea of just how frightening a dilemma the airline faced. He told them as he had been telling the press that until he took over, he had had no idea of just how bad things were. The statements, widely quoted in the newspapers, were somewhat incredible for the man who had been in essentially the number two executive position of the company (Russ Thayer spent most of his time in marketing, while Casey ran the operations under Lawrence). In addition, John Casey had been a member of the Board during a period in which the realities of a billion-dollar debt and a decreasing cash flow had shocked the Board into action. Casey would be quoted later in the year, on April 7 in *The Wall Street Journal,* as saying, "I didn't even know that we were running out of cash. The way it was set up before, there was only one person who knew the total picture." Speaking about the panic sale of the older 727's to American the previous summer, he said, "I looked at it as the sale of surplus planes because we had the new ones from the factory coming down. We were paying debts, but with money from selling assets." In light of the press coverage and editorials in the aviation trade journals at the time, Casey's attempts to say that he didn't know what was going on are believable only in the sense that he didn't have a sufficient grasp of the complex financial matters to understand the figures fully.[2]

Taking constant potshots at Lawrence, Casey began an urgent round of meetings with the employee groups at the DFW terminal and elsewhere around the Braniff system, trying to explain the near-

[2] Casey was something of a babe in the woods when it came to high corporate finance and the subsidiary corporations Braniff owned. Speaking of Ted Beckwith's structuring of those corporate entities (which structure was not unusual among large corporations), Casey would later say, "I spent a month trying to figure out . . . what I called the house of cards . . . the financial structure that he had built up for Harding . . . fantastic structure, and I kept talking about [how] I've walked from one room to another, was the way I pictured [it]."

desperate status of their company, the need for the pay cut/contribution plan, and trying with increasing success to sell them on the idea that things had really changed and Braniff management could now, perhaps for the first time in a decade, be trusted. It was an effective "we're all in this together" campaign, and he was gratified at the positive reactions. In addition to the instant cheers that would consistently greet his announcement of the sale of the company limousine Lawrence used, the dismissal of the chauffeur and valet, and the ongoing attempts to get rid of the Acapulco residence, Casey was promising the rank and file an honest, open-door policy. "Write me!" he invited. "I'll read the letters personally, I'll take the time to make sure your problems are looked into and, if possible, solved, and I'll make sure that no one gets chastised for letting me know when something needs correcting. If you find a leaky faucet, someplace we're wasting money, tell me." The employees were encouraged, and the feeling began to grow even among the hard-core dissidents that maybe Casey would behave differently as the chairman than he had as head of operations. Maybe the man could be trusted.

John Casey was quite sincere in his statements. He really did intend things to be different. One of the impressions he fostered, however, was that Lawrence had never had an open-door policy toward direct employee contact. That just wasn't true. Harding Lawrence in effect had always had an open-door policy to letters and problems from the ranks, especially since too many of his senior people simply stopped telling him about any problems below. The trouble was that few lower-level employees were brave enough to communicate with him directly. The times that problems were brought directly to Lawrence, especially if the complaint had merit, things happened, albeit not always with sustained success. Too often the senior management would thwart a change they didn't like by telling Lawrence one thing and then doing another.

Casey didn't concentrate only on the Teamsters, although he spent a great amount of time seeking their support, even making the rounds of the ticket counters and breakrooms at DFW. As he warmed to his subject and became more confident of the reception he was getting in such meetings, Casey's efforts broadened to include people from most every area of the operation, from clerical, pilots, technical training, and flight attendants to reservations, sales, and the outstations. The Teamsters as a group were still resistant to the idea of the 10 percent pay cut/contribution plan, but he was making inroads. Throughout the company there was an increasing awareness that the peril Braniff faced was real.

As Beckwith shuttled back and forth to New York trying to hammer out a deferral agreement with the diverse lending institutions, the deadline inexorably approached.

On February 24, the company released the 1981 results and braced for a firestorm of reaction from the press, the lenders, and the public. Braniff had achieved revenues for all of 1980 of $1.45 billion, but even with those revenues, it had managed to lose $128.5 million, $20 million of which represented the dumping of previously amortized, unrecoverable start-up expenses into that one year.[3]

Compared with a 1979 loss of $44.3 million (on 1979 revenues of $1.35 billion), the company appeared to be awash in red ink. Braniff had lost in two years an amount equivalent to every dollar of profit it had earned since January 1973.[4]

On February 26, the company had to announce that it was going to skip paying dividends on three series of Braniff preferred stock. It

[3] Harding Lawrence, watching from afar in retirement, felt Casey was being a "smart-ass" by trying to sweep away some of the debts of the Lawrence years in one cascade of red ink. What the possibly gratuitous addition of the $20 million start-up expenses did accomplish was to distort further some of the basic measures of the company's financial health and help trigger more restrictive provisions in the various loan agreements. Most of the overall loss, however, stemmed from the massive operational cash drain of 1980.
[4] Braniff had been a highly profitable carrier under Lawrence before 1979, with 1970 the only exception. The net income (profit) figures for the company since 1965 were:

1965	$9,448,000
1966	$17,816,000
1967	$4,751,000
1968	$10,416,000
1969	$6,249,000
1970	($3,058,000)
1971	$8,619,000
1972	$17,151,000
1973	$23,151,000
1974	$26,137,000
1975	$16,021,000
1976	$26,369,000
1977	$36,692,000
1978	$45,230,000
1979	($44,330,000)
1980	($128,500,000)

was a technical default that Beckwith was scrambling to rectify.

With the events of that week and the rumblings throughout the airline industry over Braniff's staggering losses coupled with the collapse of the merger talks with Eastern, Casey had a chastened audience at last among the employee groups. He had been hammering away at the message that the 10 percent profit sharing/salary reduction plan was optional only if shutting down the airline was one of the options the employees wanted to consider. Once again the pilots and the flight attendants, along with some of the smaller union groups, had given their approval. The Teamsters and the IAM remained. Now, however, he had their attention.

As soon as he had finished dictating the letter to accompany the copies of the salary reduction plan to the employee mailboxes, John Casey ordered another message spread verbally through the ranks urgently and immediately: "We're shutting this airline down and locking the doors forever on Tuesday, March third, if the Teamsters and mechanics don't approve the plan by Monday evening! This is not a threat . . . this is a promise."

The Teamsters and the IAM were to vote in each of their stations, and since there simply wasn't time to go through the usual ballot process, which could take weeks, each station was to phone in the results of its polling to its respective headquarters. The Teamsters would vote first on Monday, and Casey would await the word by phone at the world headquarters. The lenders would wait in New York, San Francisco, Seattle, and numerous other locations of the banks and insurance companies that stood ready to destroy Tom Braniff's airline.

On Friday, February 27, John Casey, who knew well how to manipulate the company rumor mill, made a brilliant move of self-sacrifice at precisely the right moment in exactly the right way. Amid the grumbling and the grousing that shutdown threat or not, the Teamsters weren't going to give anything more, Casey sent a simple note to Braniff payroll, which was staffed by Teamster clerical employees. The note directed them to reduce to zero and cease paying the $180,000-per-year salary of Braniff management employee John J. Casey. The chairman was reducing his pay to nothing indefinitely to lead the way in making a commitment to the company.

One of the key officials of the department received the one-page memo, read it, read it again, and stood up.

"Holy Christ, look at this!"

The attention of most of those in the office focused on him, and the noise level dropped.

"Casey wants his salary cut to nothing!"

There was a count of about ten before anyone moved. Then, simultaneously, half the men and women in the office jumped up to come over and see for themselves, and the other half picked up their phones to dump the word into Braniff's high-speed rumor mill. The attitude among the Teamsters began changing.

The whipsawing of positive and negative attitudes throughout the ranks over the weekend ran the gamut from concerned support to *macho* bravado. First this group and then that group were going to reject overwhelmingly (or approve overwhelmingly) the measure. One employee would rate the chances of his station's approval at near zero, the next at near 90 percent. The confusion was even worse for the rest of the employees—the non-Teamsters—who felt like hostages. Those who had heard the shutdown threat tried to buttonhole any teamsters they knew for support.

Monday dawned, the shifts began voting, and tense people with Braniff ID's in their wallets waited all over the system. By midafternoon, Marvin Schlinke relayed the news to Casey.

"It looks like you got the message through to them, Mr. Casey. It's sailing through by an eighty percent margin."

Next came the IAM, which voted that night. They had tried to keep Casey from speaking to their members but had finally relented a week before. As the balloting got under way, it looked to John Casey as if he had lost it. The reports that the mechanics were going to vote it down overwhelmingly even made the evening news.

Just after midnight Casey got the results. The IAM membership had just barely approved, and Casey had his 10 percent pay cut by a slim 56 percent margin.

In accordance with the deal Beckwith had wrenched from all thirty-nine lenders, employee approval of the pay cut meant automatic approval of the forgiveness of principal and interest payments until July 1, but by no means was the crisis over. The insurance companies especially wanted it understood with crystal clarity that by the end of June, Braniff had better have an acceptable plan for restructure and a vastly changed operation producing, or on the verge of producing, a profit. It was either that or pay up as of July 1, and as Casey and the Board knew only too well, there was scant chance of coming up with the cash by then. The only choice was restructure. The airline had simply contracted its operations too much to produce the revenues to make such payments on such a massive senior funded debt.

Although Casey was relieved at the union endorsement and personally proud that he had been able to bring it off, he knew he couldn't relax. He sat there awhile that Monday night and thought with increasing nervousness of how much had to be done in only four months. He had never been a finance man, as too many analysts had been pointing out in the previous few weeks. Now he had to lead the company out of this deadly morass, and as his chief lieutenant he had Ted Beckwith, who was increasingly trying to go his own way. Beckwith bridled at taking directions from Casey, and Casey was never quite sure what he was up to with the lenders.

In one case, Casey had taken the lead. One Texas insurance company had balked to the very last on slipping the payment date, threatening to tumble Braniff into what everyone assumed would be the black hole of bankruptcy. John Casey had borrowed a corporate jet and one of Bob Stewart's bankers, First National Bank President W. Tack Thomas, to fly down to Galveston in early February to see the head of American National Insurance Company. Braniff owed them about $5 million, and the lender was adamant in its stance toward Braniff: Our money or your (corporate) life! Casey literally begged the head of the company to agree to the deferment. "You *can't* do this to people in Texas . . . put ten thousand Texans out of work! New Yorkers could do it, but you're a Texas company!" Under such direct pressure, the insurance man relented but made it clear that things had better improve on the bottom line.

Braniff had a reprieve from the lenders, but it also had a new deadline, and both had been very difficult to get. What would be equally damaging was the fact that the entire affair had given Braniff's main competitor a potent weapon. In the final analysis, another link in the chain of corporate destruction had been forged.

A Chill of Apprehension

CHAPTER 21

"How do you know?"

"Trust me, Jim. They're closing the doors June thirtieth. It's all over. Their lenders have passed the word they're not going to restructure them."

"You mean they'd really bankrupt them? In this economy?"

"Jim, you book them after June thirtieth—well, no one's gonna honor their paper! You're gonna be stuck with whatever you've got out."

The owner of a San Francisco area travel agency had been talking to a sales representative for one of Braniff's competitors, who had called this clear, blue March afternoon with an urgent warning.

The owner sat silently for a minute, listening to the buzz of conversations from his agents at their desks and computer terminals. Dirty tricks weren't unusual in this business, but if this guy was right, he'd better listen. If he had to refund $20,000 or $30,000 in tickets, he'd go under. In this age of deregulation and constant fare changes and cut rates, his agency business lived on the thin edge—too close to the margin to survive much of a disaster. They didn't write that much Braniff business, but he was always surprised at how much they had out in dollar amounts at any given time for some of the smaller carriers.

"Look, I know you guys, and I'm just concerned about my customers. I don't want Braniff to go under, but if they do, and the word is that they definitely will, I don't want to see my friends and customers pulled into bankruptcy along with them. Besides, I remember you sell some of their South American trips too, and those are big-buck tickets."

"June thirtieth, huh?"

"That's it. Just a friendly tip. Don't, for God's sake, tell my regional manager I told you this. He might think I was just bad-mouthing a competitor."

"I hope that's not what you're up to, because I don't like that sort of trash a bit."

"It isn't, Jim, really."

The new suspense date of July 1 sent a chill of apprehension into any travel agency owner who booked Braniff. The ink had scarcely dried on the debt payment deferral from March 1 before competing sales reps were making sure their client agencies knew what the new suspense date might mean: a shutdown. Thousands of people were holding tickets for flights on Braniff written on travel agency stock, for which money had been paid to the travel agencies, which in turn had been paid to Braniff and for which money would then have to be refunded to the travel agency's clients if no other airline would honor the ticket. If a shutdown did occur and another airline, such as American, were to honor a Braniff ticket, American could expect no repayment through the New York clearinghouse that handled the ticket accounts between airlines. Therefore, the tickets of a defunct carrier, even in the first hours after a shutdown, would probably be worthless for travel. Passengers who had paid their ticket money to the dead carrier would simply become unsecured creditors. People who had charged their tickets on credit cards would be better off, since they would have recourse against the credit card company. In most cases, if the product hadn't been delivered, the charge would have to be removed. Passengers with dishonored tickets bought at a travel agency, however, would look to the agency for refund. If the agency had too much business written in those tickets, they could be bankrupted themselves refunding money to their customers—money they had paid to the bankrupt airline and now couldn't recover. It was a legitimate concern for the travel agencies, but the pattern that began in the spring of 1981 to make sure none of them missed the point was of questionable legitimacy, not to mention legality.

The flash point at which the cycle of declining customer confidence becomes self-sustaining—the ethereal trip wire that Lawrence had worried about six months before, and which worry prompted him to proclaim that Braniff "is not a financially troubled airline" when the facts seemed to scream otherwise—would, if reached, be the beginning of a death spiral. Someone out there seemed to be orchestrating a whisper campaign to make sure that flash point *was* reached.

Braniff by 1978 had become the largest carrier at DFW in every possible way, dominating all aspects of the western half of the airport property and beginning the construction of a second, huge semicircular international terminal to adjoin the existing Braniff terminal to the south. Although the project had first to be delayed, then scrapped in midexcavation in 1979 when the thunderclouds of massive loss began to appear, Braniff's domination seemed secure.

American Airlines had decided in late 1978 to forsake New York as its headquarters and move to Grand Prairie, just south of its pilot and technical training base, the American Airlines Flight Academy, located just south of DFW by old Amon Carter Field. The move was perceived by locals as a bit of a Yankee invasion, but American had in fact been part of the Dallas-Fort Worth community as one of the major carriers for many decades and, as few people realized, was actually a native.

American had been founded in the 1930s with its headquarters in Fort Worth and had been part of the area long before Braniff moved its corporate headquarters to Dallas's Love Field from Oklahoma City in 1942. True, it had grown up and forsaken Texas to headquarter in the sophisticated towers of Manhattan, but it was historically not a "Yankee carrier." Braniff was perceived as the airline of Dallas, and with American's return and their subsequent increase in DFW service, a low-grade dynamic tension began building between the local carrier and the "Yankee renegade."

American had made a strategic decision to alter its route structure after deregulation became law. Traditionally a coast-to-coast airline that formerly flew European routes as well, American had decided in late 1978 to begin building the same sort of hub-and-spoke approach to route expansion that Delta and Braniff had pioneered. For their hub they targeted Dallas-Fort Worth's DFW airport. The original thinking was that American, with its superior and consistent quality of service, could carve out enough of a market share at DFW to grow side by side with Braniff.

Competition between the two was nothing new, but Braniff under Lawrence had beaten American soundly in the previous round, which took place in the late sixties and early seventies, when American was battling Braniff for dominance in the Dallas–New York market and when Braniff was overwhelming American's expensive jumbo 747's and DC-10's with the smaller 727's at twice the departure frequency. Since that period, American had kept its distance from most Braniff-dominated routes.

Then came deregulation, and by 1980 the smell of Braniff's blood in the winds of change. American's upper management began perceiving a weakness in Braniff—financially and in terms of service and customer loyalty—that indicated great opportunity. Perhaps American could carve more than an equal market share from the DFW pie. The route planners in the heavily beaureaucratic administration of American began searching for which of Braniff's routes were the most vulnerable and devising plans to move in with parallel service. Chief among those targeted routes was Dallas–Honolulu, which American had wanted for years. They had lost the battle for Dallas–London to Braniff's and Pan Am's politicking, but now with Braniff awash in red ink, there was new opportunity.

It wasn't as if Lawrence hadn't foreseen American's thrust into DFW. It was his correct assessment of what American would do under deregulation that provided the urgency of his firm belief that Braniff had to grow fast or die. In 1979, when American completed their headquarters move, American had 220 planes compared to Braniff's nearly 100. It wasn't United, after all, that Lawrence had feared, it was American.

By early 1981, with the realization that Braniff was living on borrowed time as well as borrowed money, and the fact that they were literally being kept alive past March 1 by the forbearance of the lenders in granting what amounted to 0 percent interest, American (under Chairman Albert Casey and their new president, the brilliant but profane Robert Crandall), began planning for a massive, near-doubling of the DFW route structure. They planned the initiation of service in June on such traditional Braniff routes as DFW–Amarillo, Austin, Corpus Christi, Midland/Odessa, and Lubbock. The Honolulu run had been started in December as Lawrence was leaving, and although below the break-even point, American's traffic was gaining at Braniff's expense. Now other such traditionally Braniff-dominated, moneymaking routes as Dallas–Seattle were planned. American could count the days to June 30 like anyone else, and with an increasing amount of intelligence from various sources on how much traffic Braniff was carrying, Crandall and his people guessed that Braniff had only a few months to live. If that were true, there would be a huge vacuum to fill at DFW, and American would be ready. If Braniff survived longer—and that was always likely, given the gigantic losses the lenders would face trying to sell repossessed airplanes in the lousy used-aircraft market of 1981— American would simply be establishing itself on the Braniff routes it wanted against the day when American would become the dominant carrier. In the final analysis, American's people knew of the problems Braniff was having with service quality and morale, and correctly figured that on the basis of service alone, American could achieve a sufficient market share and eventually make money.

As long as they didn't end up in a ruinous fare war with Braniff (which, they figured, Braniff could not afford to initiate), American could hold out. So the plans for service doubling at DFW moved ahead, targeted on June. After June 30, with or without Braniff, there would be a parallel choice for worried travel agents. American, though pinched like every other carrier by fuel costs and low traffic, had a large war chest of cash and could survive.

Meanwhile, in Atlanta, Delta too was eyeing the prospects of increased capacity at DFW. Having been firmly entrenched in the market anyway, though not with enough flights to consider it a hub, Delta began a similar, lower-grade assault of Braniff routes such as Dallas–Seattle and others. The start-up of that particular route was also timed for June 1981. Instead of one carrier and four flights a day between Dallas and Sea-Tac International Airport, overnight the new flights by American and Delta created a three-carrier market with eleven daily flights, and a total capacity of over sixteen hundred seats each way. There simply weren't that many people who wanted to make the trip originating out of the DFW airport or through that hub. The load factor for Braniff, and for Delta and American, was destined to be horrendously low, even in the high-traffic summertime.

There had been no hate-Braniff attitude at American before 1981, though there was still some residual anger about Lawrence's arrogant cancellation of interline pass privileges in 1978, which had blocked many of American's people from vacation trips to Braniff destinations in and out of the country—destinations that American didn't serve. But then, most of the industry had been infuriated at the move.

Suddenly, however, there appeared the first indications of intercompany hostility, noticed principally by those in the community who worked for Braniff and had neighbors or acquaintances who worked for American. On the job as well, the level of friendly cooperation between the passenger service and baggage service people of both companies began to decline just a bit.

Braniff's frantic moves to reduce the size and thus the costs of its operations led to a progressive but haphazard cancellation of service to many destinations. This in turn played havoc with the way the arrival and departure times of the remaining inbound flights into DFW dovetailed with other outbound Braniff flights. The purpose of a hub in a hub-and-spoke system is to provide the passenger with the greatest possible convenience in flying into the hub from anywhere on the system and having close, convenient connections at that one location to all of the other destinations the airline serves. Thus flights would be launched from many of Braniff's Texas cities to DFW early in the morning that would arrive in the Dallas-Fort Worth hub around 8:00 A.M. The passengers who came in on those flights could then have a quick and easy transfer to any of a volley of flights to all other Braniff destinations leaving about 8:30 to 9:30 A.M. There would be similar waves of coordinated inbounds and outbounds throughout the day, but when a city such as Lubbock, for instance, was cut back from six flights a day to four flights a day, the arrivals and departures no longer fit as well, and passenger connections become more difficult.

Then too, when the frequent business travelers who were the backbone of Braniff's business had come to depend on a certain schedule, constant changing of that schedule became vexatious and confusing. That lack of consistency can lose as much business as bad service, and with Braniff in panicked contraction, that was the case all over the system.

Even Braniff's reservations department had trouble keeping up with the changes. There were instances of flights departing several days in a row with virtually no one aboard but the crew because the new flight schedule had somehow never found its way into the reservations computer system. Not enough attention was being given to smoothing all the schedule problems, and each passenger lost to American as a result was another nail in Braniff's coffin. As 1981 progressed, schedules began changing so fast and so often that in several instances the latest general schedule of the airline appeared on the ticket counters showing flights and even destinations that already had been discontinued.

211

The battle of DFW would be won or lost on service considerations of personal contact and convenience. Increasingly, and on both counts, Braniff was trying to fight the battle unarmed. Bit by bit, through internal confusion as well as negligence, the company was abdicating its leadership position at DFW.

Other forces were moving against Braniff as well. Longtime creditors such as Marriott (who did the lion's share of Braniff's food service catering) had tried to help during the previous year with liberalized credit terms, but the shabby record Braniff had been compiling of slow payments on many millions of dollars of debts and the near-default of March 1 had scared Marriott and many other suppliers. They began contracting the credit terms and pushing for something closer to a cash-only basis. Now Casey ordered all the small creditors—anyone Braniff owed less than $5,000—paid in full, fearing that otherwise someone among them might get angry enough to try to bankrupt the company. The large creditors such as Marriott were simply put off.

The fuel companies held the trump cards. An airline obviously can't function without a continuous and uninterrupted supply of fuel, and following March 1, Braniff's principal suppliers began terminating Braniff's credit and demanding cash.[1]

Their caution was understandable, but the effect of their pressure was to be disastrous in the long run. Braniff's fuel usage amounted to approximately $8 million per week. The company had been working on thirty days' credit, allowing $32 million of float. To clear up the fuel credit accounts to a cash basis and then put Braniff on a one-week-at-a-time prepaid basis (which had occurred by June) meant a drain from the accounts of over $40 million at a time when an amount equal to that couldn't be raised to make the March 1 payment to the lenders. Somehow Braniff found the cash, but in doing so, the company's cash reserves were reduced to a super-critical level.

The pressure from the fuel companies seemed a bit too strong to be explained solely by panic over the near-default. Rumors, dark and vague, began to make their way through the grapevine of the industry that some other entity—perhaps a competitor—had been whispering about impending shutdowns in the collective ears of the

[1] Even Texaco, Braniff's principal supplier and with whom the company had been doing business for over fifty years, had the arrogance to demand cash in advance.

fuel suppliers. The fuel suppliers denied it, but the suspicions persisted.

Of course, the fuel companies themselves were going through a catharsis with a worldwide oil glut on the horizon and a massive recession deepening. The wheeler-dealer days of a mere three years before were giving way to more restraint and more financial troubles as many small suppliers saw an end to the wide-open horizons of the spot market in which Braniff had thrown so many millions to get the fuel for its limitless expansion.

Some of the deals from that period were about to come back to haunt both Braniff and some of the suppliers. A fellow named Jack Ward, who had been in charge of obtaining fuel in any manner and at any cost during the expansion period, had done too much unsupervised dealing. Within six months reports of some of his methods and allegations of kickbacks of the magnitude of $50 million to $60 million from fuel purchases in the Pacific would surface. With the infusion of new management, Ward would hastily resign under a substantial cloud and be criminally indicted a year and a half later, though for alleged theft of an amount under $1 million.

The press and electronic media, both local and national, contributed to the problem as well. Since there is no news value in headlines reading "EVERYTHING GOES OKAY WITH BRANIFF TODAY," in most cases the negative stories were simply the normal exercise of journalistic concentration on what does have news value: problems, troubles, and financial travails. Since stories about Braniff involved a major airline and a public corporation of significant size, it was automatically a target of interest. Since it was also the airline that Harding Lawrence had expanded in a manner many reporters viewed as arrogant and pretentious, the interest of the national business press, including publications such as *Business Week, Aviation Week,* and *The Wall Street Journal,* was keen in following every twist and turn of the descent into hell that Braniff's people were experiencing. Would the gamble of massive expansion finally kill the flashy Texas airline? Few if any of the stories could be called biased —in fact, there was much excellent and highly accurate reporting, despite the fact that the truth hurt in print. Some of the publications engaged in a bit of "I told you so," making certain that any earlier-expressed views of caution or alarm at Lawrence's expansion program were called to the reader's consciousness now that the program had been proven a failure. What was most damaging was simply the fact

213

that there was so much concentration on the story, with every new negative scrap of financial information, or any new labor disagreement, or any other problem associated with Braniff immediately placed before the public. All the bad publicity simply pushed Braniff closer to that flash point of self-sustaining decline of public confidence.

The darkest cloud of all over Braniff, however, was the inability of many of the thirty-nine lending institutions (now holding mortgages on Braniff's entire fleet) to agree on what form a restructure of the massive debt might take. Institutions such as Bankers Trust in New York and Bob Stewart's First National Bank in Dallas, along with smaller contributors like Seattle-First National Bank in Seattle and Bank of America in San Francisco had all supplied funds earning an interest rate at 1 percent over the prime. The prime had now soared to over 21 percent, which was one of the main reasons the payments had ballooned beyond all reason. One other major block of the lender group, however, were insurance companies, such as Prudential, which had come in originally with interest rates of 5 percent and later 9 percent. They were even more unhappy over what they perceived to be the banking institutions' plans for accepting a restructure that would leave each institution's interest realized proportionate to the original rates. And finally there were the work-out people, the unsmiling specialists who come into the picture when a major borrower gets into trouble. The majority of the lenders were beyond the point of compassion by the time they sent in their work-out people—they simply wanted their money "yesterday." There was a cadre of more friendly and helpful bankers and loan officers, some of whom were the officers who had originally made the loans, and they did much to persuade the less friendly among the diverse group to help Braniff get a little farther down the road. The work-out men, however, didn't give a damn about the people of Braniff or the health of Braniff. They had been sent in to extract the gold from the patient's teeth before burying the body!

With the events of early March 1981, the work-out people had begun to gather at sessions involving the lenders like vultures around a dying maverick.

In early 1981 a curious transfer took place. A fellow by the name of Robert R. Ferguson III, the same young lender from Bankers Trust who had all but demanded the resignation of Harding Lawrence on December 22, 1980, left that institution and joined Braniff International as vice president and treasurer below Ted Beckwith, who had recommended him to John Casey, who had promptly hired him. Some in the upper ranks wondered why Beckwith would bring in a man in his own field who might be a challenge to his own position later on, until they realized that Ted Beckwith was purposefully choosing his own successor, and assuming that once that was done, Casey would be free to elevate Beckwith to president. For his part Braniff's new treasurer professed to have left his former loyalties behind.

By mid-March, the practice of sending weekly communiqués to each of the lenders had commenced. The information was to keep them up to date on the status of the week's load factors, the yield figures, and any other information that would give them a feel for the pulse of the company, and hopefully let them see the positive changes taking place as Beckwith and Casey, with increasing friction, attempted in disorganized fashion to turn the operation around. The lenders, however, wanted to see a coherent plan for recovery. It was presumed that Casey would generate a plan within a month or two, both for debt restructure and revitalizing the operations of the airline. The first item would be forthcoming. The second never came. As March wore on, some of the younger, less gentlemanly among the work-out people began to lower their linguistic restraints. There were an increasing number of demands that before any restructure could be considered, more signs and gestures had to be seen that the enterprise was turning around.

Ted Beckwith was on the firing line daily, trying to cajole, reason, or just endure the conversations, and trying to forge some sort of agreement on how to turn a large portion of the hundreds of millions of dollars of principal and interest due in 1981 into equity through the issuance of stock.

Beckwith was not only battling the lenders, he was battling Casey as well. Neither could agree on any course of action, and their personalities were constantly clashing. Beckwith refused to be impressed or guided by Casey, regardless of Casey's position. In John Casey's view, Beckwith was incredibly devious—always keeping things to himself. Casey needed to know the financial details of Beckwith's proposals and negotiations with the lenders. Beckwith, however, avoided telling Casey much of anything.[2]

[2] Some of those details would remain a permanent mystery to Casey, though not as serious and worrisome as the murder mystery that would puzzle a sheriff in Sul-

Also in mid-March, after a particularly contentious meeting, John Casey made a characteristically impulsive decision: He fired Ted Beckwith one morning, despite his enthusiastic support of him to the Board just two months before. It was a terrible time to change the chief finance man, and Casey had to have a replacement immediately. He began courting a veteran airline finance man named Howard P. Swanson, a veteran of Trans World Airlines who had a substantial reputation in the financial community as a top-notch aviation finance executive. Ironically, it was the same Howard Swanson who, a decade earlier at TWA, had hired one Robert L. Crandall into the aviation business. Crandall (later destined to become president of American Airlines), in turn, would eventually be accused (in the popular press and by officials of Braniff) of orchestrating a sabotage campaign at American designed to bankrupt Braniff.[3]

For further explanation concerning the denials by American Airlines of this and other charges of impropriety, and for word about the outcome of CAB, FAA, and grand jury investigations, please refer to Chapter 36.

---

phur Springs, Texas, some eighteen months later: Who silenced Edson "Ted" Beckwith in an East Texas cornfield with a knife? And why?

[3] The incestuous nature of filling airline executive posts in the United States by raiding the executive suites of other airlines tends to create some ironic and fascinating changes in corporate loyalty. This is true at all managerial levels not under union protection, but it is especially true in the upper ranks. Ed Acker's background in aviation began with Braniff but has taken him to Air Florida and now to the chairmanship of Pan Am, where numerous other Braniff executives (many having come to Braniff from other carriers, including American) would eventually end up. There is no such lateral transferability in the union ranks, and especially not in the ranks of pilots and flight attendants. The end result is that the people who are wedded to a certain carrier (the contract employees principally) are subject to the managerial inadequacies of officers who can leave the smoking hulk of a corporate disaster, a disaster for which they may be responsible, and march directly to another carrier at a comfortable and substantial salary. The crew of the damaged or destroyed carrier has no such option; they go down with the ship.

This is not to impugn the integrity and professionalism of the large number of U.S. airline executives who maintain the highest levels of fiduciary responsibility. Rather it is to point out the inherent contradictions and opportunities for less-than-honorable conduct that can and do occur when the people at the top forget or ignore the impact of their actions on the human beings stuck in the holds of the corporate ship.

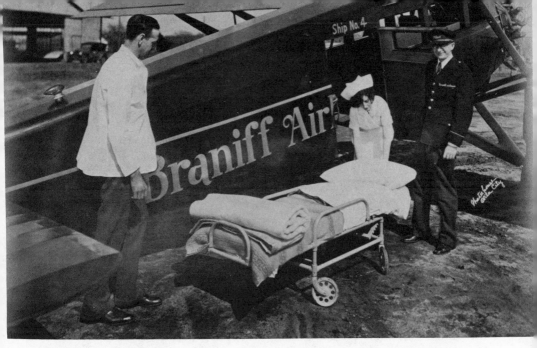

▲A 1929 promotional photo of Paul Braniff beside a Travel Air A-6000, demonstrating the company's air-ambulance capability. Note the word "pilot" on Braniff's cap.

▼A rare shot of (*left to right*) Bess Braniff, Tom Braniff, and daughter, Jeanne Braniff, unveiling one of the new Braniff DC-6 interiors designed by Jeanne.

▲Pioneer Braniff pilot (and later executive vice president) R. V. Carlton (*left*) with famed humorist Will Rogers in Oklahoma City in the early 1930s. The Braniff aircraft behind them is a Lockheed Vega similar to the "Winnie Mae," a modified Vega owned by pace-setting aviator Wiley Post. Rogers and Post would later meet their deaths in the crash of a Lockheed Orien at Point Barrow, Alaska, in 1935.

▲Braniff Executive Vice President Charles (Chuck) Beard relaxing with a cigar next to Bess Braniff at a company Christmas party circa 1949.

▶Braniff founder and president, Tom Braniff, playing Santa Claus at the annual Christmas party, a tradition he maintained for over a decade.

▶In late May of 1950, Tom Braniff flew to Buenos Aires aboard his airline's first regularly scheduled flight to Argentina. Received the following day by Argentine president Juan Perón and his charismatic wife, Braniff is pictured here on May 30 with Eva Perón at an official reception.

◀Tom Braniff (*second from left*) and his executive vice president Charles Beard (*second from right*) with two area businessmen during the celebration of Braniff Airways' twenty-fifth anniversary.

▲(*Left to right*): Harding Lawrence; his brother Eugene Lawrence; his mother, Mrs. Moncey Luther (Helen) Lawrence; his other brother Don Lawrence; and his eldest son, Jim Lawrence. The family members are pictured in front of the Lawrence Hotel in Gladewater, Texas, in the mid-sixties.

◄Harding Lawrence and Mary Wells Lawrence after their wedding in Paris, 1967.

Harding Lawrence with his wife, Mary Wells Lawrence, at a Braniff reception in 1972.

Harding and Mary Lawrence in Acapulco, Mexico, in 1977.

▲Braniff Chairman Harding Lawrence announcing the spring 1968 "Fast Buck" campaign, which was later involved in the crash of Captain John Phillip's Electra near Dawson, Texas.

▶Braniff President C. Edward Acker in the early 1970s.

The aftermath of disaster: the Braniff DFW terminal on the morning of May 13, 1982.

▲Braniff's pre-inaugural celebration of the new Dallas-London route be-
gan with the arrival of Braniff's first Boeing 747, Ship 601 (the original
"Great Pumpkin"), at London's Gatwick Airport, loaded with 250 guests.
Pictured (*left to right*) are Dallas Mayor Robert Folsom (who would later
join the Braniff Board of Directors), Flight Attendants Fran Claycomb and
Sandy Gravatt, and New Mexico Governor Jerry Apodaca.

▼Aerial view of Braniff World Headquarters complex at DFW Airport.

Harding Luther Lawrence, Chairman and Chief Executive Officer of Braniff International and Braniff Airways Corporations.

The Concorde supersonic jetliner in Braniff markings. This retouched publicity photo was issued to show how the new color scheme would appear on the left side of each Concorde used in the interchange service. The right sides were to retain either British Airways or Air France markings. The Braniff paint job was never actually applied.

Braniff staff photo provided courtesy of Tom Robertson

▲The "snake" on the number 3 engine cowling (the right-rear, side-mounted engine) of Braniff Ship 408, the Boeing 727 bearing the bicentennial Calder painting and referred to by the crews as "Sneaky Snake."

David Woo, *The Dallas Morning News*

◄Howard D. Putnam. Hired away from Southwest Airlines by Braniff Chairman John Casey at the specific direction of three senior Dallas bankers, Putnam became president of Braniff in late September 1981, and subsequently presided over its bankruptcy.

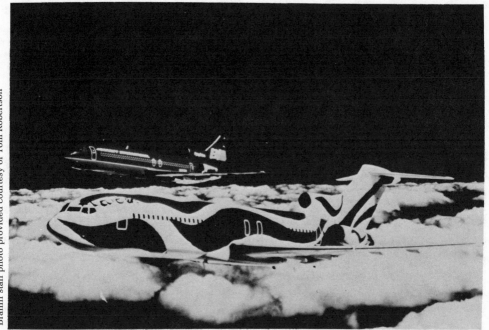

Braniff staff photo provided courtesy of Tom Robertson

▲The Calder 727 in flight. Braniff claimed that by 1979, more people had seen this flying work of art in person than any other painting in recorded history.

Wide World Photos

►Howard Putnam (*right*) and Pan Am Chairman Ed Acker (formerly president of Braniff, Transway, and Air Florida) announcing in New York the later-abrogated agreement under which Pan Am was to lease Braniff's South American route system.

Howard Putnam at the news conference held the morning after the shutdown and bankruptcy filing.

Howard Putnam and Philip Guthrie (*in background, left*). Putnam refused to come to Braniff without his Southwest Airlines financial Vice President Guthrie, even though Guthrie had a scant two years of airline experience. John Casey's total acquiescence to Putnam's demands led to the brutal dismissal of highly experienced financial Vice President Howard Swanson after less than six months on the job.

▼Braniff Vice President John J. Casey (*far right*) with Braniff junior managers on an orientation visit to Dallas Headquarters in 1972. Bill McCutcheon, who would write the so-called Jericho Memos in 1980 as DFW Manager of Passenger Services, is on the far left.

A Loose Cannon
on a Rolling Deck

CHAPTER **22** John Casey had a near-revolt on his hands. The Board, which thought it had bound him to the promise that he would work closely with the Executive Committee and stay, in effect, on a short leash, had been presented with a sudden *fait accompli:* Beckwith's dismissal. Casey hadn't consulted with the Board members before doing the deed.

The outside directors were alarmed at the independence of the action and perturbed that Casey, who had been so much in support of Beckwith in January, could fire him two months later. On top of that, Casey's announcement that he wanted to hire Howard Swanson, but would need a three-year employment contract and a position on the Board to get him, did not set well. The outside directors were not the sort of people who enjoyed being forced into a vote, but Casey had boxed himself and the Board in a corner. Braniff had to have a new financial officer immediately, but the directors had not been prepared to give Casey a contract, nor were they happy with the idea of pledging Braniff's dwindling resources to a multi-year contract for a new man. If Braniff should fail, Swanson would be protected by the proposed golden parachute provision for the next three years. The Board didn't object to Howard Swanson; they objected to the way Casey was attempting to force approval of Swanson's contract.

There was the problem of unanimity, however. The dangers of open disagreement or even the impression of it among the Board members and what that would do to the lenders' cooperation grew greater with each day. The initial response from the outside directors was "No, John, you go find someone good who will come in without a contract, or get Swanson without a contract." Casey maintained that it couldn't be done. With the lenders breathing down his neck, he told them he needed Swanson immediately.

Once again Bob Stewart made the decision and began implementing it. Talking by phone to one of the East Coast directors, Stewart revealed the latest twist in the saga.

"Look, I know you don't like voting under the gun like this, but John says if he doesn't get Swanson—which he says he can't do without the contract—he's going to quit. I hope you'll see your way clear to go along with this. I don't really care for it either, but we can't let John walk out."

"Bob, I don't like it—I don't like it at all—but if that's what has to be, I'll reluctantly go along with it."

Casey's independent action with Beckwith and his one-man nomination of Swanson was just one of a series of acts that had the other Board members upset. In another sudden move, Casey fired Braniff's longtime investment firm, Goldman/Sachs, and hired the firm of Lazard Frères, again without telling anyone on the Board. None of the directors were used to that sort of treatment, and the irritation grew.

Harding Lawrence, for all his concentration of power, had never failed to keep his Board informed. Between sending them voluminous amounts of information, Lawrence made a point of always calling each of his directors and discussing a proposed action that might require Board approval before the action was completed. Never were his fellow Board members confronted with an irreversible deed on a decision of great import. Of course, there was no way for the directors to know whether the facts and figures constantly supplied by Lawrence were correct, but they had no reason to believe otherwise. Lawrence was the expert, and as long as it all looked correct, it probably was.[1]

John Casey, on the other hand, despite his agreed restrictions of authority, was making a habit of using his Board like a rubber stamp. Since the directors were personally liable for certain aspects of the decisions the Board made, the position Casey was putting

[1] In the words of one of the directors, Sloan McCrea, "Harding would say, 'Now, Sloan, I've got this fellow I'd like to propose for Board membership,' or 'I've got this proposal for the company, and I'd like to talk it over with you.' . . . and we'd talk, and I'd usually say, 'That sounds fine to me, Harding.' I don't know what he would have said if I'd said 'no,' but the fact was that most of the time his ideas were good."

them in was very uncomfortable. In the interest of presenting a unanimous, solid front to the rest of the world, however, they backed him one more time and approved the Swanson contract. Howard P. Swanson took over as executive vice president for finance and the company's chief financial officer.

Casey's request for Swanson's membership on the Board was another thing. That was delayed because the head of the Nominating Committee refused to be used like a rubber stamp and would not formally submit Swanson's name.

There was a growing feeling among outside directors that Casey was uncontrollable and that putting him in the chairman's position had been a drastic mistake. It was just a feeling—nothing that could be acted on at that late a date—but an unsettling gnawing in the pits of several directorial stomachs that what they had created in John Casey was a loose cannon on a rolling deck. The possibility existed that in flailing around with impulsive decisions that should have had prior Board consideration, he could bring them all to ruin.

Casey's success with the Teamsters had instilled a new self-confidence in his abilities to marshal rank-and-file support. The positive press treatment he was getting and the flow of letters from the employees (many of them asking for help with managerial problems) demonstrated that he had actually changed the way many of the people perceived Braniff management. For the first time they trusted someone in Braniff's management, and he was determined not to let them down. Even Teamster Business Manager Marvin Schlinke had gained trust and respect for Casey—something he had never felt for any other Braniff leader.

Casey began to spend quite a bit of time reading and listening to employee complaints, making sure they were handled personally, as he had promised. His open-door policy was a refreshing change to the rank and file, and they responded with a flood of communications, including many excellent suggestions and revelations of where the "leaky faucets" were located. (Unfortunately, the age-old Braniff problem of loose security and employee theft on the ramp and elsewhere continued unabated—Braniff had never appropriated the money to attempt better enforcement.) Casey's commitment to solving the problems in passenger service and improving the quality of lower management gave some of the younger, junior managers further support in bringing in new training courses and new techniques. At DFW, Billy McCutcheon and his vice president,

Doug MacArthur, brought in a Dale Carnegie course to teach public-contact managers and lead agents how to handle angry passengers and turn such incidents into opportunities for selling Braniff. It was the first formalized course in a decade, though it too was only a one-shot assault on the problem. Although the effect was very positive, the lack of time and money to follow it up with reinforcement and further training limited its overall impact.

As the managers at DFW and elsewhere attempted to weed out the long-entrenched bad apples in the union and lower-management ranks, Casey's desk was being crossed by an increasing number of complaints that had their roots in that very cleanup. A man with a long-standing record of trouble would be dismissed for cause or disciplined, only to have the case end up on Casey's desk as a complaint against unjustified management harassment. Casey was very concerned about keeping faith with the rank and file now that he seemed to have gained it. He wanted no diminution of confidence. Therefore his methods of solving such conflicts between his rank and file and his managers was to err on the side of the rank and file and order a course reversal for the managers. This trend increased as the union people found how immediate and effective a complaint to Casey could be. Of course, in many cases the complaints were justified—Braniff still was plagued with an over-abundance of incompetent lower-level managers whose abilities to manage their people were marginal at best. In just as many cases, however, Chairman Casey's actions, while reassuring to the ranks, undermined the efforts of his front-line management, who as of late March were still grossly underpaid and leaving in substantial numbers.

On March 25 Casey released a statement to the company and the press that Braniff would recall from furlough forty-nine pilots and an undetermined number of flight attendants on May 1, with more to come back June 1. The reason was a summer increase in scheduled service by 10 percent. It was encouraging to the employees—it even sounded as if there might be some light at the end of the tunnel. Unfortunately, it was a shock for both the lenders—who wondered where the money was going to come from for expansion—and once again for the Board, most of whom read about it first in *The Wall Street Journal*.

Casey was enjoying the good comments from his people. In fact, he was positively basking in the glow of the affection when a singular act in early April threatened to scuttle his newfound acceptance. Casey raised the salaries of Braniff's nonofficer managers by an average of 11.4 percent.

It was a much-needed raise to be sure, and one that had been promised to many managers to try to keep them in the company as they attempted to manage contract people making much more than their salaries. The 10 percent pay cut still came out of their newly raised total, but all the contract people could see was the timing: Braniff union's give 10 percent, Casey gives it to management.

The press picked up the cry as well, aided by a flurry of angry calls from union leaders who claimed that Casey, contrary to his statements, had never informed them that such a raise was in the works. As *The Wall Street Journal* reported on April 13:

BRANIFF BOOSTS SALARIES FOR CERTAIN NON-UNION EMPLOYEES

Dallas— Braniff Airways boosted salaries an average 11.4% for about 775 management employees, retroactive to April first. Early last month the airline's union employees accepted a 10% pay cut to help bail out their beleaguered employer. Directors of Braniff International Corporation, Braniff Airways' holding company, approved the pay increase last week.

A Braniff spokesman said the pay boost covers primarily lower and middle managers, as well as secretaries. Braniff's officers, vice presidents and up, weren't given a pay increase, the spokesman said.

He said the pay was boosted to "correct inequities" in the salary scales between union and nonunion employees and to prevent the further exodus of management employees who recently have left for better-paying jobs.

". . . some managers haven't had a raise in two years while contract people they supervise" have had cost-of-living and other contractually stipulated pay increases, the spokesman said. As a result, he said, "some managers are earning less than the people they supervise."

The Braniff spokesman said that union officials were told about the management pay increases last month when they agreed to accept a pay cut . . . with the understanding that certain nonunion employees would receive a pay increase later "to remove salary discrepancies."

The spokesman said he believes most union employees "understand" the need for the management pay increase. "I don't expect any hard feelings," he said.

But the International Association of Machinists, which represent 1,900 Braniff employees, said Braniff officials never mentioned a pay raise for management employees during last month's negotiations on an across-the-board 10% pay cut.

"We weren't told a thing about it," said Jerry Emmel, a spokesman for the machinists. He predicted that the management pay boost "won't sit very well" with his members.

He added: "The timing of this thing is terrible. If Braniff had done this a few months from now, our membership would have understood it. But to ask the union to take a 10% pay cut and then turn around one month later and give management an 11.4% pay increase is a tough thing to swallow."

Indeed, among the ranks Casey's new reputation was damaged, if not in ruins in some hard-line quarters. Those who railed against the raise reflected the ostrichlike attitude that the only problems in the company were those created by management, that all the talk of impending doom was simply a scare tactic, and that now this pay raise confirmed it. The 10 percent cut, they said, had been merely a method of raising the funds to pay the managers. The stupidity of that argument in even simple economic terms was lost on such proponents. It was a chance to say "I told you so!" to those in their midst who had had the naiveté to trust Casey and management in the first place.

Casey's timing had been awful, but in at least this instance, he had consulted his Board first. Now with rumbles of discontent from below filling his ears, he dove into the task of mending the fences once again, starting with a memo to all the employees confirming the statements made to the press about the pay inequities and the "exodus of management personnel," and ending with a plea for support and unity: "Your company needs the continuing support of all employees if we are to survive. We have had excellent spirit and effort and I pray that everyone will continue to support your company in these very difficult times."

To further recement the relationship, Casey accepted an invitation from the owner of a new country-and-western nightclub in Fort Worth called Billy Bob's Texas (patterned after Gilly's in the Houston area of *Urban Cowboy* fame) for a "Braniff Night." Circulars calling up to six thousand Braniff people to the shindig from anywhere in the mainland United States Braniff system (with fee-waived employee passes, and western wear authorized on the flights) were distributed throughout Dallas-Fort Worth and the system. The circular, which began: "To All Braniff Employees (Mainland USA). You and Your Spouse Are Invited For a Thank You To Braniff Employees From John J. Casey," went on to describe the affair in detail. The owner of Billy Bob's was providing the event, but Casey was going to take credit.

Within roughly two weeks, the ruffled feathers of the flock had been significantly smoothed, and Casey had been unofficially forgiven. The employees, especially those who were helping to organize the ground swell of self-help sales campaigns, had an eager source of cooperation in Chairman Casey, and that was more important than holding a grudge over the salary raise. After all, many of the same union people who had yelled the loudest when the 11.4 percent pay hike was announced had expended much effort in the past yelling about how poorly trained and underpaid were the managers their people were forced to work under. It was best to let this issue drop and avoid the obvious hypocrisy.

The self-help sales campaigns had brought in a growing force of Braniff people from many areas of the company, including many pilots and flight attendants in Braniff cities throughout the system, all of whom began teaming up with Braniff sales representatives and going as volunteer teams to call on travel agents in their communities to seek bookings and support despite the bad financial publicity. The flight crews usually went in uniform, and the program did seem to help reassure the agents that, whatever else was happening to the company, Braniff's people were fighting hard to survive. Despite the ingrained problems, the presence of a traditional Braniff pride and dedication seemed to be evident in even the most callous and disillusioned employees. The amount of energy and off-duty time that went into the campaigns began at a high level and increased through the following year. A photocopied handbook was

235

put together for the volunteers, and coordinators began popping up in various regions, also on a volunteer basis.[2]

There was a growing enthusiasm in the ranks that Braniff's people could pick up the pieces and remake the airline into a success, whatever the odds. After all, Braniff was people, so a rejuvenated commitment to service and teamwork by the people, and a united front in asking the public for support, were bound to work. Although these did have positive effects, there were more storm clouds looming on Braniff's horizon than volunteer sales programs and enthusiasm could possibly overcome, and more ammunition for the competitors who had smelled the red ink—the lifeblood of the company as it drained away from the bottom line—competitors who were closing for the kill.

A New Round of Fear

CHAPTER **23** On March 30, John Casey put his initials at the bottom of the final draft of the "Chairman's Statement," a one-page letter to shareholders that was about to be typeset and printed in the Braniff 1980 annual report. His opening sentence was a studied understatement: "The year 1980 will probably be remembered as the most difficult for the airline industry. Certainly it was for Braniff."

---

[2] A similar program was begun later the same year by United Airlines, utilizing pilots still on the payroll but without flying assignments to augment their sales departments. It was a revealing and typical contrast between the managerial styles of the two carriers: Braniff's was an *ad hoc* effort of dedicated, concerned, hardworking volunteer employees who received no significant training, no significant coordination—and no pay. United, on the other hand, created and ran a special training course for their program.

The fifteen hundred Braniff people (including the pilots) put in vastly greater effort in the "sell Braniff" volunteer campaign, but the effectiveness of their efforts was hampered by the lack of the type of company commitment United had made. As an isolated instance, it would have been understandable in the crisis atmosphere of Braniff's management structure. It was, however, sadly typical.

Casey knew that the report, which would reach the public on April 15, would be another bombshell. The reported total loss for 1980 (adjusted since the initial report of 1980 results) was $131,436,000, but that had already been announced. The bomb Casey could hear ticking away concerned the report of Braniff's independent certified public accounting firm, Deloitte, Haskins, & Sells, which would appear on page nineteen. Buried in the boilerplate corporate language of the third paragraph sat the incendiary sentence, waiting for the wide-eyed and shocked discovery of the press: ". . . there are conditions which indicate that the Company may be unable to continue as a going concern."

From the initial uneasiness of 1979 to the summer panic of 1980 through the vociferous denials of difficulties by Lawrence in the fall of 1980, the speculation in the press that Braniff might have an uncertain future had accelerated on an almost linear basis, increasing in intensity through Casey's takeover, the 10 percent pay cut, and the debt payment deferral. The word "bankruptcy" had never been spoken officially by the company, and despite the obviously perilous situation, there had been no hard-core confirmation that Braniff might, in fact, cease to exist as the ultimate result of all its travails.

On April 15, however, the one-line warning of the CPA's ripped away the taboos for the company and the press alike. There it was in black-and-white (Casey had wisely ordered the report printed in black-and-white instead of the usual flashy four colors to save money and promote the image of frugality). Even Braniff's CPA's were telling the public, in effect: "Hey folks, be careful. This firm is on the very brink of extinction!"

Casey, the Board, and the senior officers expected another firestorm of reaction. Casey, bowing to the need to acknowledge that he and his team were fully aware of the implications, wrote on page three under "Management's Discussion and Analysis of Financial Condition and Results of Operations":

Commencing in 1980 the Corporation and the Airline experienced a severe shortage of cash. Effective March 2, 1981, the Corporation and its principal subsidiaries, Braniff Airways Incorporated and Braniff Realty Company, arranged with their private debtholders for the deferral until July 1, 1981 of the principal and interest payments due during the

237

period February 10, 1981, through June 30, 1981. These companies are commencing negotiations with these lenders to restructure their outstanding debt. The ability of the Corporation and its subsidiaries to continue as a going concern and to meet their obligations as they come due will, in the short term, be dependent upon a restructuring of their outstanding debt, the ability to successfully complete the cash sale of surplus aircraft, and ultimately upon a return to successful operations.

As expected, the significance of all this was not lost on the press:

April 16, 1981 (*Dallas Morning News*):
AUDITORS: BRANIFF SURVIVAL IN DOUBT . . . BRANIFF TRADING HALTED FOR REPORT ON FINANCIAL STATUS

April 16, 1981 (*The Wall Street Journal*):
DOUBTS ON BRANIFF'S CONTINUED VIABILITY ARE RAISED BY AUDITORS IN ANNUAL REPORT

A new round of fear swept through the travel agencies and through the stomachs of Braniff's employees. Travel agency people who had resisted the whisper campaign began to rethink their exposure. The Braniff people who had tried to ignore the possibilities had to face now the new round of open doomsday discussions with either a realistic acceptance of what might happen, or a denial that the press and the industry knew what they were talking about. Amazingly enough, a significant percentage chose the latter. An airline as big as Braniff, they reasoned, simply couldn't go out of business, or shut down, or cease to exist. A smaller number of these folks even managed to convince themselves that the questionable survival talk was another company plot—designed to separate them from their raises and benefits.

The self-help employee sales campaigns took on a new note of urgency, and a significant number of very concerned Braniff people from a wide variety of departments joined the effort, going on sales calls, buttonholing local companies for support and the purchase of Braniff tickets, and phoning leads into an employee hotline set up for that purpose by Jeff Krida, vice president for sales.

Casey, awash in a tidal wave of employee concern that had

238

flooded through the doorway of his office the minute the report hit the papers, turned his attention to rallying the troops, using in part the news of the tiny operating profit which had just been tabulated for the first quarter of 1981:

ALLOFBN

DFWGPBN 21153 ODR

TO ALL EMPLOYEES/PLEASE POST ON ALL BULLETIN BOARDS

LAST WEEK WE HAD SOME UNPLEASANT PUBLICITY, SOME OF WHICH RELATED TO OUR AUDITOR'S REPORT CONCERNING THE 1980 FINANCIAL STATEMENT.

I THINK IT WOULD BE HELPFUL IF I GAVE YOU THE CONTENTS OF A MAILGRAM SENT TO 17000 TRAVEL AGENTS LAST WEEK CONCERNING THIS MATTER.

DEAR TRAVEL AGENT

SOME CONCERN HAS BEEN EXPRESSED AMONG THE TRADE REGARDING PRESS REPORTS ON OUR AUDITOR'S COMMENTS IN THE 1980 ANNUAL REPORT CONCERNING BRANIFF'S STATUS AS A GOING CONCERN.

I WISH TO EMPHASIZE TO YOU THAT DURING THE FIRST QUARTER OF 1981 BRANIFF'S NEW MANAGEMENT HAS TAKEN A NUMBER OF STEPS TO CORRECT OUR FINANCIAL PROBLEMS. WE HAVE TODAY REPORTED A FIRST QUARTER OPERATING PROFIT OF USD 454,000 AGAINST AN OPERATING LOSS OF USD 22,523,000 IN THE FIRST QUARTER OF 1980. THIS IS A SUBSTANTIAL IMPROVEMENT FROM THE FOURTH QUARTER AS WELL.

OUR NET LOSS IS USD 24.6 MILLION VERSUS A LOSS OF USD 21.9 MILLION LAST YEAR ALTHOUGH LAST YEAR WE HAD CREDITS AND CAPITAL GAINS OF MORE THAN USD 18 MILLION.

WE HAVE ELIMINATED UNPROFITABLE TRANSATLANTIC AND TRANSPACIFIC OPERATIONS RETAINING OUR SUCCESSFUL OPERATIONS FROM DALLAS-FORT WORTH TO LONDON AND HONOLULU. WE HAVE REDUCED THE NUMBER OF U.S. CITIES WE SERVE AND HAVE REDEPLOYED OUR ASSETS TO ROUTES WHICH CAN GENERATE THE MOST REVENUE PARTICULARLY THOSE SERVING BUSINESS TRAVELERS. WE ARE INCREASING OUR FLIGHT SCHEDULES APRIL 26 AND JUNE 1 RECALLING EMPLOYEES AND ADDING 747 SERVICE IN SOUTH AMERICA. WE HAVE SUBSTANTIALLY REDUCED OUR COSTS INCLUDING A 10 PERCENT SALARY REDUCTION FOR

ALL EMPLOYEES AND A DEFERRAL OF OUR PRINCIPAL AND INTER-
EST PAYMENTS DUE TO OUR INSTITUTIONAL LENDERS.

WITH ALL OF THESE ACTIONS YOUR CONTINUED SUPPORT AND THE
DEDICATION OF OUR 11,500 EMPLOYEES WE ARE MAKING PROG-
RESS.

WE ARE WORKING HARD TO BE YOUR AIRLINE AND YOUR CUS-
TOMERS' AIRLINE. WE APPRECIATE YOUR CONTINUING SUPPORT.

JOHN J. CASEY

CHAIRMAN AND PRESIDENT

BRANIFF INTERNATIONAL

KEEP YOUR SPIRITS UP. BELIEVE IN YOUR COMPANY. WE ARE
STILL MOVING FORWARD.

It would be unfair to say that Casey's Mailgram to the travel agents had no effect—there were some who were moved to loyalty towards Braniff as to any noble underdog fighting a desperate battle. However, the travel industry tends by nature to be realistic, if not cynical. The fact that June 30 was approaching and Braniff still had not achieved a debt restructure meant that nothing had changed in the risk equation for the travel agencies. Summer traffic had to be booked, and they had to decide whether booking people on Braniff was worth the risk.

The teletype's effect on the employees was mixed as well, but it added still one more bit of evidence to support the conclusion that the threat was real.

On Thursday, May 7, in the auditorium at the world headquarters, the 1981 annual stockholders' meeting was scheduled to be held. As was usual, the directors had their morning Board meeting before the 10:00 A.M. stockholders' affair was to get under way. The Board met in Lawrence's custom-designed boardroom, which contained a large, square table covered entirely with black leather, and which featured a panoramic view of the world headquarters campus through the large north windows. The veteran directors had to remind themselves that Harding wasn't going to walk through the double doors from his apartment to join them. The king had been deposed largely by their hand, and now they were having to deal with the results.

In accordance with normal procedure, most of the agenda had been tacitly agreed to in advance through numerous telephone calls crisscrossing the country. There was, however, one additional item decided at the meeting: The Board authorized Chairman Casey to threaten the lenders with bankruptcy if they decided to drag their feet on a debt restructure—bankruptcy under Chapter 11 of the United States Bankruptcy Code.

Casey was aghast at the idea. He was sure that no airline, including Braniff, could operate under Chapter 11, even though one supplemental cargo airline (Airlift International) had already been doing so. Several of the outside directors had been pressing for more than that. One member in particular wanted an immediate Chapter 11 filing and then a business-as-usual operation based on the realization of what was about to happen to the cash position of the company if the fuel suppliers succeeded (as they were close to doing) in forcing Braniff into a one-week-at-a-time prepaid position for fuel. "Why not file now while we've got the cash and the assets to operate on a cash basis? Why wait until our backs are to the wall and there's not enough cash to continue?" he had pressed, admitting that perhaps the public apprehension over the safety implications of an airline operating in bankruptcy might make such a move impossible. Bob Stewart, Troy Post, Perry Bass, and Herman Lay, among others, were afraid of the plan. Their attitude was that even though you'd preserve your cash and assets and probably get enough suppliers to continue serving your needs in catering and fuel and other support services, the flying public would believe that maintenance had been eliminated, and fear-of-flying jitters would take care of the rest.

In compromise, the Board authorized Casey to threaten. As it would turn out, he was too frightened of Chapter 11 to do even that.

Other emergency steps had already been tried by Troy Post, who had approached Jay Pritzker, one of the very wealthy owners of the highly respected Hyatt Corporation. Would Pritzker be interested, Post asked, in buying a slightly encumbered airline? The answer had been a polite no, couched in lukewarm interest. (Jay Pritzker's eye, however, would remain on Braniff, though it would take two years to spur him to action.) Casey wasn't at all enthusiastic about the possibility of a sale to Hyatt. Despite the depth of the financial crisis, he really thought he was on a roll and could save it single-handedly.

At 10:00 A.M. what was traditionally a sparsely attended, gentlemanly exercise for Braniff got under way in a hostile atmosphere with an auditorium full of upset stockholders, many employees, and a scattering of reporters. John Casey gaveled the meeting to order and nervously realized how upset and angry many of the people appeared to be. He read his prepared statement, a slightly breezy rundown on the status of the company, and drew loud applause when he mentioned that the company's contract with Harding Lawrence had been terminated by Lawrence. The mention of the attempts to sell the Acapulco residence and the sale of Lawrence's limousine also brought applause and a few cheers. Casey felt a bit better, and playing to the anti-Lawrence atmosphere, he continued:

> The causes [of our financial problems], which have continued into 1981, aren't mysterious. They are industry-wide, and not unique to Braniff . . . [however] as if those weren't enough, we contributed one more problem of our own . . . poor judgment, particularly as it relates to over-zealous expenditures for expansion.

The press would read "Lawrence" for "we" and "our" into that statement, which was as Casey intended.

Casey looked up, wondering why that line had received such little applause. Behind him, several of the directors were inwardly wincing at the reference. Most of them had been Board members during that period. Of course, for that matter, so had John Casey. The irony, lost on Casey, was a bit embarrassing.

He continued:

> Where our company has been may not be the end of the world, but, as someone said, you could sure see it from there. So we know we have faced the worst of our problems . . . and, with the aid of our lenders, survived. We know Braniff is on the comeback trail and we can prove it!

Some chuckles from the audience wafted toward the front.

> We still face a continuing perilous period, yet we have taken a big step away from the bottom . . . away and up.

The reaction had not been too bad. John Casey was feeling as if the meeting might turn out all right after all as he opened the floor to comments before the reelection of the directors, which was in effect already over, since the existing Board held 73 percent of the proxies for reelection. A group of stockholding employees had tried to nominate and elect their own slate of directors, and many of them were present and angry that their bid hadn't had a chance.

"Mr. Chairman?"

"Yes, sir . . . in the third row there."

Bob Bagley, a senior account executive from an investment banking firm in Dallas, was on his feet, looking Casey coldly in the eye: "Mr. Casey, there's a point I feel needs to be made. Many of the ladies and gentlemen on this Board have very little stock in Braniff . . . to sit on this Board, I would think, would dictate an obligation to have more of a stake in this company. I'd like to see some people on the Board who have a more substantial stake . . . who have money on the line!"

Applause drowned Casey's reply, forcing him to start over.

"Well, Mr., uh . . ."

"Bagley . . . Bob Bagley."

"Mr. Bagley, regardless of their stake in the company in terms of stockholdings, every one of our directors has invested great time and effort . . . every bit as much as if they held much more stock. I'm sure there isn't one of our directors who would have given more or done anything differently were they in a greater ownership position. . . . I'm very proud of our Board."

"Well, I'm not very proud of our Board, Mr. Casey. As a share-holder, I'm not proud at all. I think they've done a miserable job!"

More applause.

The meeting went downhill from there. One of the employee candidates, Patricia Patterson-D'Argenio, a supervisor from the Chicago station, got to her feet during the next few minutes and with barely restrained emotion began assailing the past record of the Board under Lawrence.

"We're here today to put some people on this Board who have a stake in this company . . . whose . . . uh . . . careers are on the line. We want honest representation on the Board!"

As the comments continued, Sloan McCrea, the banker from Miami who had been elected to the Board in 1972, got to his feet and motioned for quiet.

"Folks, I know there are some strong feelings here today, and I . . . I don't know what you think of us, but I want you to know what we on the Board think of you, the employees of Braniff."

The employees in the auditorium quieted a bit, listening for what McCrea meant. The banker, a distinguished man with rounded features and a moustache, fixed the group with a friendly gaze and continued in a sonorous voice reminiscent of actor Walter Pidgeon:

"You people are the most dedicated, loyal group of professionals I've ever seen, and I've lived for many years among airline people in Miami. I want you to know that regardless of how you regard us, we're proud to be on your Board."

Sloan McCrea sat down to moderate clapping from the group.

As the double doors of the auditorium (just down the hall from the world headquarters' cafeteria) opened just after 11:00 A.M., a small group of Braniff's South American flight attendants were sitting down with coffee at one of the tables, discussing their recurrent training class in animated Spanish as John Casey walked by in equally animated conversation with Bob Stewart and two other male members of the newly reelected Board. One of the girls looked up as the chairman passed. *"¿Es Señor Casey, no?"* she asked one of the others.

"¡Sí . . . el jefe de nuestra aerolineas enfermas!" (Yes, the chief of our sick airline.)

Though John Casey would later claim that he was "proud of that meeting," in fact the affair had been a disaster, as *The Wall Street Journal* chronicled the following day with the headlines "BRANIFF'S DIRECTORS CALLED 'YES' MEN AT ANNUAL MEETING" . . . "HOLDERS SAY BOARD DID LITTLE TO CHALLENGE JUDGMENT OF FORMER CHAIRMAN." In addition, Casey's performance at the meeting did little to calm the worries of the Board. Casey realized he had irritated many of his fellow directors in the previous months, but in his view, there was too much to do to permit careful "stroking" of them. Unfortunately, he seemed unaware of the depth of the misgivings the others were having about his leadership.

In mid-May, Bob Stewart submitted his resignation. Among the other worries that prompted his action was the growing uneasiness over the potential conflict in his dual position: a Braniff lender in his capacity as chairman of the Executive Committee of First International Bancshares Corporation, to whom Braniff owed millions, and a Braniff Board member at the same time. With discussions of Chapter 11 and restructuring, Stewart had been strongly advised by his attorneys to get off the Braniff Board to avoid the conflict and the possibility of creating legal "preferences" that could impair the bank's secured loans in a bankruptcy. He did so, and with him went one of the more powerful voices of the Executive Committee (though he continued to stay involved from outside).

As the June 30 deadline approached, John Casey's schedule was becoming reminiscent of Lawrence's workaholic calendar as Casey attempted to function as chairman, president, chief executive officer, and chief employee-liaison man all at the same time. To Casey, the employee trust and morale he had built in the preceding months was critical to the company's recovery, and he devoted an increasing amount of each day to employee problems, complaints, and suggestions. The remaining bulk of the critical, ongoing problems overwhelmed the rest of his time. The need for a comprehensive recovery plan as well as a reorganization plan increased daily. John Casey, however, was facing the rising tide of troubles and red ink like the proverbial Dutch boy, with barely enough time to plug the holes in the dike—let alone repair them.

Search for the Master Plan

CHAPTER **24** One day in the late spring of 1981, a Braniff charter flight returning to Dallas was making a shallow left bank onto the final approach for a visual landing on DFW's Runway 17-Right—Braniff's western half of the airport. At the controls in the left seat of the DC-8-62, the captain and his crew ran the before-landing checklist, and bouncing slightly through the heat-created convection currents of a Texas late summer day, stabilized at ten knots above approach speed for the last few miles of the approach, nearing the familiar dam at the eastern end of Grapevine Lake.

The flight had been cleared to land and was now number one on final following an American Airlines 727, which had landed just seconds before, was rolling out on the runway, and now was almost down to taxi speed.

"American, I've got a Braniff on short final—first high-speed on your left, please—contact ground when off." The tower instructions were for American to leave the runway by means of a shallow-angled taxiway (resembling a freeway off-ramp) called a high-speed taxiway, which, as the name implies, permits jetliners to clear a runway at a higher speed than the traditional right-angle taxiways.

"Hey, look at him—he's going right past it!" The first officer of the charter watched with consternation as the American 727 passed the midfield turnoff, still taxiing slowly down the runway.

The tower had noticed as well: "American, I told you the first high-speed, sir. Please take the next one and expedite. Braniff DC-8 crossing the dam."

The pilot reduced the power a bit as the four-engine intercontinental jet passed abeam of the Grapevine dam and called for Flaps 50 (landing flaps), letting the airspeed diminish to Vref (pronounced "Vee-Ref," standing for the charted minimum approach speed with landing flaps). All three pilots craned forward a bit, watching as the American 727 approached the next high-speed turnoff.

"American, you copy regional tower?"

No reply.

"American, regional tower; if you copy, expedite departing the runway at first available."

Still no reply. The captain and his crew calculated that if the 727 missed the next one, there would be no time left for another try. Braniff would have to go around, which would cost nearly $1,000 of fuel and operating time before the DC-8 could climb back into the pattern, be resequenced by approach control, reconfigured, and land. There was no way such a jet could be legally or safely landed on a runway with another aircraft still on it. As the pilots in the American cockpit knew—as all airline crews knew—too much time spent rolling out from landing at a busy airport like DFW would probably cause someone behind them to go around. Most crews, regardless of their airline, were very sensitive to the problem and very anxious to help each other and the tower.

The Braniff charter had another half mile and fifteen seconds to go before reaching the decision point. Still, the 727 continued taxiing. Even though the DC-8 was traveling over 130 miles per hour at that point, less than a half mile from the end of the runway, time and distance seemed to the crew to crawl by in slow motion.

"Braniff, stand by for a go-around—I can't raise him."

"Roger," the first officer replied into the microphone. Go-arounds, while practiced in training constantly, were rare in actual operation.

The 727 was practically abeam the next high-speed taxiway now, and finally—slowly—it began turning off the runway. "That clown knows we're back here—I'll bet anything!" The second officer had his side-facing seat swiveled forward for landing, watching the drama, ready with the checklist and the cabin pressurization controls if the go-around became necessary. Finally—leisurely—the American jet cleared the runway, simultaneously coming up on tower frequency.

"Uh, you hear us now, tower? American, clearing the runway. Sorry about the Braniff. Had a, ah, radio problem."

The tower controller pressed his mike button and said as rapidly as he could: "Braniff charter cleared to land. American, contact ground, and thanks for the 'help.' You were instructed to take the first high-speed." The controller's voice was acidic.

The captain pulled the power off and flared the four-engine jetliner to a moderately firm touchdown. All three of them were convinced the 727's delay had been purposeful. But why? Professional airline pilots simply don't play such games. Maybe, they wondered, the conclusion was incorrect. Maybe there had been a radio problem.

With two weeks left before the deadline for payment of the previously deferred $37.5 million, Executive Vice President for Finance Howard Swanson, the new finance man Casey had brought in at such personal and financial cost, had managed to wrest a tentative agreement from the majority of the lenders. All of them appeared to be willing on a grudging basis to slip the debt repayments once more to give time for negotiating a restructure agreement and to give Casey time to show a consistent profit. The first-quarter operating profit had helped, but the actions that Casey had taken to trim the operation and gain the cooperation of the personnel had been positive factors in the minds of the lenders as well.

The majority of the lenders were by that time far beyond the sentimental stage. Their worries were limited to the question of whether Braniff under Casey could produce the expense cutting and the increase in revenue that would portend an eventual return to profit. The lenders wanted their money; they had lent it to Braniff in good faith and (as some of them kept saying) on the strength of questionable profit projections. It was no secret in the industry, however, that the resale market for used jetliners was all but dead. That made the idea of forcing Braniff into a default and a shutdown a sure disaster, whereas riding with them a bit farther held some possibilities of greater monetary recovery. The deal for another payment delay still wasn't sealed, but Swanson was getting close.[1]

Casey had been digging up some new carrots for the employees in addition to spending hours a day dealing with letters from the ranks—letters that seemed to keep his in-basket filled to the brim. He and the Board had approved an employee stock ownership program, known by the acronym "ESOP," which was designed to foster employee stock ownership by using payroll deductions over a two-year period for the purchase of up to 5 percent of the company's common stock. The fund would provide more cash for Braniff and was destined to meet with enthusiastic approval of the rank and file. There had been a longtime irritation (especially among the pilots) at being refused any formal, company-sponsored stock program, however limited. Whether Harding Lawrence actually said it or not, it was widely believed that he had once made the statement "If my employees want Braniff stock, they can go find a stockbroker and buy Braniff stock."[2] Casey's reversal of that perceived policy further bolstered his stock with the employees. It was one more thing they perceived that Casey was changing for the better.

There was another employee-oriented program in the formative stage as well, this one a sort of companywide pep rally that Casey was getting ready to launch. He had achieved gratifying success in speaking to the employees and showing his concern for them through the meetings and the attention he was giving to their letters and phone calls. He was actually whipping up a "we'll beat these troubles!" spirit. Now he had decided a formalized program with an

[1] Boeing and United Technologies, suppliers of most of Braniff's aircraft and engines, respectively, were also Braniff lenders, having financed some of the purchases and even lent Braniff cash. The respective chairmen of both companies, T. A. Wilson of Boeing and Harry Gray of United Technologies, went far beyond the bounds of customary courtesy in trying to help Braniff. Both men buttonholed the Braniff lenders with whom they did business to press for more cooperation.

[2] In 1971, when LTV had just agreed to divest themselves of Braniff's stock, Lawrence told his pilots that if they would accept greater flight hours and several other rather significant concessions, Braniff would buy controlling interest in its own stock from LTV and give it to the pilots, thus making it the only pilot-owned major carrier in the nation. The concessions he asked for were too severe for the pilot's union leadership, however, and they turned it down.

248

appropriate catchphrase was needed. Casey now felt sure of himself on the stump, and he figured a little "rah-rah" to engender more emotional support would not only help wrest a few more sacrifices of time and effort from the people but also show the lenders a façade of profound change as well. The program was to be called the "Braniff Bandwagon," and Casey tentatively scheduled its kickoff for July 1. By then it would either be on the heels of another companywide sigh of relief at the news of a further debt payment delay, or superfluous on the heels of a financial Armageddon.

There was a chilling possibility that the hoped-for debt delay might be anticlimactic. The date of June 22, 1981, held a major threat, this one totally—maddeningly—out of John Casey's control. PATCO, the Professional Air Traffic Controllers Organization, which had become a virulent labor union entwined throughout the FAA's air traffic control system, was threatening to go on strike in an attempt to shut down all air traffic in the nation. Although the FAA had been polishing contingency plans to keep the system going without PATCO employees, it was no secret to any of the carriers that the disruption and flight cancellations that would inevitably result from such a strike would be horrendous. For a cash-squeezed airline such as Braniff, that meant a death threat. Cut off from any significant part of the already-reduced flow of revenue as the result of a cutback in the flight schedules, Braniff could last only for a matter of weeks—if that long.

President Reagan's Secretary of Transportation, Drew Lewis, and FAA Chief J. Lynn Helms had been negotiating with the PATCO group and PATCO's president, Robert Poli, but PATCO's demands were so extreme that it looked very grim for a settlement. In addition, they were approaching President Ronald Reagan as if they expected a Jimmy Carter-style cave-in at the first sign of resistance. PATCO had been one of the few labor unions to endorse Reagan's candidacy, and Poli naïvely believed he could use that fact as a trump card in forcing the President to accept the gigantic pay raises and other wish lists contained in the contract PATCO was demanding. It was apparent to everyone but PATCO that they were trying to bully the wrong President.

The deadline and the threatened shutdown was 8:00 A.M., Monday, June 22. The controllers, if they walked out, would be committing a federal crime, a felony, but the agitation of the membership was at such a fever pitch that anything seemed possible. PATCO had

249

convinced their members that the criminal aspect of a strike would be forgotten, and that erroneous assumption led many otherwise professional and responsible controllers to join the hysterical demands for huge raises or a strike. Casey and his senior officers had discussed the dark implications of such a shutdown, and everyone had been shaken.

The ranks were not shaken, however, since the full implications of a strike—the full realization of what a long shutdown might do to Braniff's critically squeezed cash flow—was obscured by the growing feeling among the Braniff people that Braniff could pull itself up by its own bootstraps, come what may. Then too, there were many employees, especially contract employees throughout the company, who insulated themselves against the daily hand-wringing by submerging in their jobs. That was to be expected. It wasn't the responsibility of the mechanics or the aircraft cleaning crews or the gate guards of Braniff to lead the company out of the woods. What was surprising, though, was the number of middle-level management people who also insulated themselves, and often to the same degree. Corporate managers at whatever level must remind themselves that the fact the company's building still stands, the fact that the receptionist and the secretaries are there every morning and the coffee is hot does not guarantee that nothing could happen to alter their status quo drastically. There were too many in the middle administrative and executive ranks of Braniff who mistook the reassuring daily familiarity of their particular office as evidence of guaranteed corporate continuity—a belief that "it is, therefore so shall it always be." For these people there was still an insufficient sense of urgency in their efforts to cut costs and take on their share of the responsibilities for recovery.

John Casey was trying ideas out again, this time on one of his fellow directors by long distance. "I think what I'm going to do is go to an all-coach configuration and sell the South American system."

"John, you know how much money South America is worth in cash flow, in revenue. That just isn't reasonable."

"It's not making money, though; it's losing money."

Casey was leaning back in his chair in his world headquarters office, toying with a ballpoint pen as he waited for the response. No one else had liked the ideas either. The reply crackled over the line after a short, somewhat consternated delay.

"You, John, of all people, should know why. Look at the accounting techniques! Stop dumping all the domestic allocations in there and it'll make money. And the idea of all coach—have you studied the first class yields?"

"Yeah, of course I have, but they're not consistent enough, and we could probably do better with the extra seats."

"Well, I'm not in favor of either idea, and I'm not at all sure any of the others will be either. Take out first class and you're just another Southwest, but without the low-cost expenses."

The search for some sort of comprehensive master plan for the company was still a confused flurry of ideas, few of which had been subjected to extensive scrutiny. The market share that Braniff had already lost to American and Delta at DFW was frightening (American by late summer of 1981 was close to surpassing Braniff as the dominant carrier at DFW), and the implications for the next few months were clear: If traffic continued to forsake Braniff for its competitors because of shutdown jitters, service problems, or whatever other reasons, decreasing revenue alone would convince the lenders that a restructure of the $540 million private debt was futile. The lenders were becoming more clamorous in their demands for some clear indication that Braniff had touched bottom and was climbing out of the hole. The airline had to be breaking even on an operational basis soon or there would be no further concessions from Bankers Trust, Marine Midland, First National, Prudential, and the thirty-five others.

Casey and the senior officers of the company—especially Neal Robinson—had been worrying constantly over the central problem of how to make Braniff sufficiently different to steal back the traffic American and Delta had taken. The central argument to the lenders had been ineffective so far: We can't improve the revenues and get to break-even load factors until we have the confidence of the travel agencies, and we can't get the confidence of the travel agencies until we have a restructure of the debt. The lenders' reply was the last part of the "Catch-22": We won't restructure the debt until you get the confidence of the travel agents and the public and improve the revenues!

Something new and innovative had to be devised rapidly. An all-coach airline was one way to improve the yields by increasing the available seats, but Braniff's mainstay was the business traveler, and the loss of first class service would send still another horde of businesspeople to the competition, in this case the type who were not about to fly coach.

Lower fares were another double-edged sword. They might attract a few more passengers before the competition lowered their fares to match, but the dollar yields for each passenger carried would drop as well. The trick was forecasting the trade-off on any idea and deciding whether the loss of revenue per seat resulting from lower fares would be equaled or exceeded by the revenue from the increased number of seats sold. As June 30 approached, Braniff was prompting its frequent-traveler discount program, by which passengers earned "points" on each flight, which were redeemable for free flights when enough were amassed. But each of the major carriers had a similar program, and it had done little to stem the exodus of reservations from Braniff at the hands of the jittery travel agents.

Just after 5:00 A.M. on June 22, PATCO's previously intransigent leaders announced in Washington that they had agreed to a contract with the FAA that they would submit to their membership. The airline industry breathed a collective sigh of relief, not realizing that nothing had, in fact, been settled. PATCO had apparently accepted the contract because the PATCO membership around the country had voted only 75 percent in favor of going ahead with the illegal strike, and 75 percent was not enough solidarity. Rather than show his weakened hand when he got the news at the bargaining table, Poli accepted the Department of Transportation's offer. Within days he would preside over PATCO's strong recommendation to its membership that the contract be flatly rejected by the rank and file—a recommendation that would shock the Department of Transportation negotiators, who were left with the impression that Poli had not intended to support the settlement when he had accepted it. In fact, as the tensions of July increased, Poli seemed determined to get all his demands, and intent on orchestrating a strike to demonstrate his union's strength.

The news of the PATCO settlement was a relief for Braniff, but the cost of dumped reservations in anticipation of a walkout had been very damaging.

As American prepared to initiate another round of increased service at DFW, on Tuesday, June 30, the final lender gave in to the redeferment. Swanson's hard-won agreement with the lenders deferred the debt payment of $37.5 million due on Wednesday, July 1, and the $83 million which would become due in the following seven months, to February 1, 1982—charging no interest in the meantime. Braniff had another reprieve. Despite the fact that still another deadline had been announced—a deadline that would give the competition more ammunition against Braniff and that would give the travel agents more cause for worry—Braniff apparently would be around through the end of the year. Several miles south of DFW, at American's headquarters, there was general amazement bordering on apprehension. A risky expansion of service in the midst of a recession had just been undertaken by American, based in part on the theory that Braniff wouldn't be kept alive by its lenders, some of whom were American's lenders too. Now that they had given Braniff 0 percent interest rates on the half-billion-dollar portfolio of private loans, American was going to have to battle a subsidized cripple.

On July 1, freshly aglow with the new deferral and what he felt was an indication of the lenders' commitment to eventual debt restructure, John Casey left the world headquarters for a short ride to the Braniff hangar on the western side of DFW.

A freshly painted Braniff 727, sporting the new color scheme Lawrence had commissioned in 1978, had been towed to the front of the hangar, with a truck-mounted set of airstairs placed at the front door. Well over a thousand Braniff employees, most off-duty, had been invited from all over the system to come stand in the late-morning summer heat in uniform and witness the kickoff of Casey's "Braniff Bandwagon."

After shaking hands all through the crowd and talking to some of the photographers and newsmen on hand, Casey climbed the steps to the door of the 727, where a microphone had been set up. When the crowd quieted down, he began his speech.

"There is," he said, "a new spirit and a new enthusiasm in Braniff, and with the tremendous support of all of our people, we are going to bring our airline back to stability and profitability. This is what we're here for today, to dedicate ourselves to increased support and service for our customers with a symbol of that renewed spirit—for all of us to climb aboard the new Braniff Bandwagon and make this airline the best in every way!"

As Casey talked, using his pauses effectively and professionally while a slight breeze whipped his thinning hair, the majority of the employees were listening with rapt attention. When he finished, after being interrupted numerous times by applause, the photographers moved in as a large number of balloons were released and a local band played. With the photographers taking over and asking for various poses, Casey was reveling in the enthusiastic attitude and the near-adoration of the crowd. He had grown really to enjoy this sort of public gathering, and since the essence of this rally was, in effect, to sign up to follow him, John Casey, the personal gratification of it all was substantial. After all the hoopla on the ramp, the entire group filed into the hangar to several tables to sign a long sheet pledging: "We're aboard the Braniff Bandwagon, John!" There were bumper stickers and buttons and banners and enthusiasm along with not a few tears.

Those who didn't attend the festivities of July 1 were confronted with pictures and banners and bumper stickers just the same. The campaign, a huge success with those at the kickoff, was a bit of a puzzlement for many of the Braniff family, who weren't exactly sure what getting on the Braniff Bandwagon was supposed to mean in relation to their jobs. As had been the tradition at Braniff, there was no follow-up—no sustained blitz of training programs to instill a fresh approach to customer service. Not that there wasn't an effort to build a fresh approach. Many Braniff public-contact people as well as pilots and flight attendants and salespeople simply used their own ideas of what the "new" Braniff was supposed to be, and their efforts did have an effect throughout the system. Unfortunately, the seeds of discontent with Braniff's service and inconsistency had been sown for so many years among Braniff's customers at DFW that only an equally long-term period of superlative service could reverse the prejudice. Far too many Braniff passengers had long since given up being Braniff passengers when they had a choice, and now with American and Delta busily adding flights, they did have a choice. The traffic continued to slip.

The PATCO near-strike of June 22 had also hurt. Braniff and the entire industry had watched helplessly as tens of thousands of worried would-be travelers changed or canceled their vacation flight reservations, fearing a lengthy shutdown. Even without the strike, Braniff had been damaged.

Casey was holding more employee meetings all over the system, selling the Bandwagon and whipping up support. Most Braniff people had never had a chairman come to talk to, and with, them before. Such contacts had not been Lawrence's style. The employees were enjoying it, and so was Casey. Even some of his most hard-ened critics among the pilot group were reassessing their view-points. It wasn't exactly a ground swell of love, but it was a better relationship between chief executive and front-line employee than Braniff had had in a decade.

The enthusiasm extended to the world headquarters as well. On July 6, a broiling hot Texas Monday afternoon, with Casey due in from New York with one of the investment advisers of Lazard Frères, Braniff Vice Presidents Neal Robinson and Jeff Krida decided that the Bandwagon theme that Casey had kicked off the previous week demanded more than a quiet return to the office. The Braniff sales department had been helping nearby Duncanville High School's band raise money for a trip they wanted to take to a band contest in London. Jeff Krida picked up his phone at about 11:00 A.M. and called the band's director:

"Look, I tell you what. We'll give you a couple of tickets to Lon-don for you to raffle off to raise some more money for the band if you'll round up as many of your band members as you can find in about three hours."

"Okay, Mr. Krida . . . what do they have to do?" he asked, chuckling.

"We'd like 'em to be out here at our headquarters building to play a little oom-pah music for our chairman, John Casey, when he comes in from New York this afternoon. Can you do that?"

"I think I can track down enough of 'em. About two o'clock you want them out there?"

"That'll be great!"

Krida coordinated the welcome with Casey's secretary as to ex-actly when Casey would be into DFW and on the way to the world headquarters. With about thirteen of Duncanville High School's band on hand by the fountain in the middle of a circular diveway in front of the entrance to the building, Krida's secretary began calling every department head's secretary in the complex until the building had been virtually emptied.

As Casey and the investment banker rounded the corner of the entryway to the fountain area, the thirteen band members began puffing away on a noisy rendition of "For He's a Jolly Good Fellow" as the large crowd began cheering. Casey, finally realizing what was going on, parked the car and got out waving, with the banker (who at first tried to hide behind the car) following cautiously behind. The banker had a very worried expression on his face—as if he had inadvertently walked through a door expecting to find a boardroom and found himself instead on a sound stage in the middle of a Hollywood production complete with the proverbial "cast of thousands."

John Casey made a short, impromptu speech to the assemblage, introduced the Lazard Frères man, and then said to him, "You know, you're not going to believe this, but they really don't do this every time I come back!"

The banker managed a smile but still looked somewhat worried about the rather odd group he seemed to have fallen in with. The crowd roared with laughter and the band started up once again. John Casey was enormously pleased.

In the late morning of Friday, July 31, 1981, in a large meeting room at Denver's Stapleton International Airport, John Casey once again stood before a group of his employees, smiling, and nodding to a couple of pilots he recognized as the group applauded. A large cross section of Braniff's Denver personnel had come in for the meeting, which was another of a long series Casey had been putting on around the country.

"If I may have your attention, I would like to say hello and tell you how happy I am to be up here in Denver with you this morning. I have been having a lot of fun since the first of this year. Of course, we are fifty-three years old this month and I like to think we have a new Braniff going that is just seven months old. And the things that are happening and we are doing is clearly indicative of the wonderful people we have and what a really fine airline we have.

"I think your ten percent contribution was most important in helping us reach the point where we are today. As you know, we have been working with our lenders . . . we've got them to agree to what I like to call "accrued interest at zero percent."

Casey chuckled as laughter swept through the group.

"It's called divide and conquer!"

More laughter.

"We are working very hard at moving forth and restructuring this debt on a long-term basis. Once we get that . . . they can stop saying 'financially troubled Braniff' . . . you know, that's our name, 'Financially Troubled Braniff.'

"And—and if we can get that worked out on a long-term basis it will be good—take that worry off the travel agents. The travel agents have been concerned because the other carriers have been saying Braniff won't be around after July first. As a result of that, a lot of the bookings for July and August that we should have had we did not get.

"I feel good about Braniff . . . that's why we have the Bandwagon. The Bandwagon is really a symbol. A piece of metal"— Casey looked down at his lapel and touched the metal emblem of a bandwagon for emphasis— "or a bumper sticker isn't important in itself. The Bandwagon as a coined word is meaningful, I think, in that it is a word of action. Each one of us has committed ourselves to the success of our company. That's what this means and I want to keep this in moving form through probably the end of October. At that time we may come up with another program, but at the moment I think that the Bandwagon is important. The travel agents are very impressed with the whole idea of it and I will be talking to them and business accounts today [in Denver].

"Two little pieces of news. One is that we finally got rid of the house in Acapulco!"

The group roared, as Casey knew they would. That punch line was as surefire as the best of Henny Youngman's lines. The feeling that Lawrence was to blame for all that ailed the company was one Casey had learned to exploit. It formed a rallying point of agreement for any group of Braniff people—a bonding process of pointing out that everyone, including Casey, had been victimized by Braniff under Lawrence. Whatever the truth might be in reality didn't bother Casey. Like any good leader or good performer, he had learned to use what tools he could muster.

"So—that's a good piece of information."

"[The second item] is . . . that we had our Board of Directors make available a stock purchase plan and that we are going to the SEC and come out with a prospectus for all of us in August."

Casey figured he had come to the end of the group's attention span. "I am glad to be here. Denver is one of my favorite cities."

Casey asked for questions from the group and spent the next twenty minutes amiably fielding various friendly inquiries. All in all, he felt, the meeting had been another success. John Casey was in fine form in front of his people, and he was having a ball.

Too Late to Mend Fences

25 The same damaging, costly countdown was beginning again. PATCO's people had voted down the June 22 contract settlement their leaders had accepted, and were now threatening a strike once more. Braniff reservations agents were receiving waves of cancellations each time a newscast carried another report on the impending walkout. More revenue was slipping forever from Braniff's grasp.

Casey was facing another type of slippage—an exodus of sorts from his Board. New York philanthropist Mary Lasker and Dallas banker Bob Stewart had left the Board in May, but now Sloan McCrea, Anne Armstrong, and Noel Gayler had all made their excuses and informed Casey they were leaving in August. All three directors cited pressing outside commitments as the reason for their respective resignations, and certainly all three did have many other business and foundation memberships and responsibilities. Casey realized, however, that it was the underlying irritation with his performance as well as legal apprehension over his independence that had cost him their confidence. It was too late to mend fences.

The remaining members (who, of course included the most influential outside directors, Troy Post, Herman Lay, and Perry Bass) were going to stick it out, but they also weren't exactly overjoyed by the way Casey had used the Board, and they were quite upset over the resignations of their longtime fellow members. The subject of replacement began to come up in various conversations among the Dallas-Fort Worth area directors. Replacement not of the departing directors, but of Casey.

It was obvious that Casey couldn't be ousted from the company altogether, due to the volatile attitudes that existed among the lenders. Even though Howard Swanson was doing most of the liaison work with the banks and insurance companies and had gained substantial trust among the disparate group, Casey's accomplishments in stabilizing the attitude of the Braniff rank and file, and his acceptance among them as a rallying point of sorts, were factors that must not be disrupted. The fact that Casey held three titles (chairman, president, and chief operating officer) and obviously couldn't handle all three of them opened the way to a solution. Stewart and Post and the others, responding in part to some pointed suggestions from the lenders that Casey's performance was disappointing, began thinking about finding a new occupant for the office of president.

The same drawbacks over bringing in an outsider that were valid in January were valid now, but back in January no one had realized how independent Casey was going to be.

In honoring the rest of the deal with Howard Swanson, the Board had voted him into membership as a director during the meeting of July 27, which was held at the world headquarters. Anne Armstrong, chairman of the nominating committee, had never dropped her opposition to the method in which the deal had been forced on the board by Casey. She felt very strongly about having her hand forced and yet knew how critical was the appearance of Board unanimity. She solved the dilemma by an abstention—she stayed away from the meeting. Herman Lay entered the nomination in her place.

Casey had been too busy with the Bandwagon promotion to spend much time formulating a new master plan for the company. His suggestions about selling the South American routes and converting the domestic 727 fleet to all-coach had been greeted with dismay by his senior officers, but a plan to go to a split-fleet system was gaining some acceptance if for no other reason than recognition of the pressing need to do something substantial and do it fast. The proposal involved a system in which some flights would use Boeing 727's featuring the current mixture of coach and first class seats, and others would be 727's that would be refitted to eliminate first class cabins, leaving an all-coach arrangement. (The single-class, all-coach service would be put on the shorter legs and high-density traffic runs where Braniff faced the discount fares of Southwest and Texas International.) Executive Vice President for Marketing Neal Robinson and his people had been deeply involved in the brainstorming of those ideas—all with the awareness that time was running out. Braniff had to differentiate its product or lose its revenue passengers to the competition. As the PATCO countdown to the second strike date continued, Casey finally focused on the problem.

He had a difficult time making strategic decisions that might be of major import, and this was no exception. He had agonized over what would happen if he were wrong while losing sight of the fact that doing nothing to revamp Braniff's product was a sure death sentence. Finally, with great uncertainty, he approved a campaign called "Braniff Strikes Back," featuring the split-fleet system and a coordinated campaign of fares and advertising, all set to hit in early September.

PATCO, however, hit first.

In the early hours of August 3, Robert Poli once again walked out of the all-night negotiations with the Department of Transportation, this time with the knowledge that his people had voted overwhelmingly in favor of the strike he, Poli, had seemed determined to initiate. By 7:00 A.M. Eastern Daylight Time, controllers had begun abandoning their posts or failing to report for their morning shifts in air route traffic control centers and control towers all across the Eastern Seaboard. By evening, more than twelve thousand controllers had decided to participate—each of them simultaneously committing a federal felony and, under the law, simultaneously firing himself.

Casey and the entire staff initiated what amounted to a crisis-management posture, watching and controlling the almost hourly changes in the situation from the world headquarters. Among Braniff's OCC (Operations Control Center, the nerve center of flight operations located at Dallas's Love Field in the Braniff maintenance building), pilot and flight attendant scheduling departments, ship routing department, maintenance control, and all the other vital elements of the airline's "neurological" system, Casey and all his department heads began putting approximately 30 percent of the domestic flights on the ground (no international-flight cutbacks proved necessary). At first it appeared that about fifteen hundred Braniff employees would need to be furloughed immediately. Union leaders were asked in for rapid planning sessions, and with the pressure of the unfolding situation the level of cooperation was incredible. Agreements were hammered out verbally in minutes that would normally have taken weeks. Some advance preparation had been done, but the smooth precision with which Braniff handled the dislocations of flights, the decisions on personnel, and the massive rerouting of crews and support personnel was a worthy accomplishment.

Everyone realized that if the strike continued for some time and the FAA couldn't maintain the system at above 60 percent, Braniff might be doomed. Casey made the point as clearly as he could. Incredibly, however, within two days of the start of the criminal walkout, the FAA appeared to be exceeding their original estimates of how many flights could be handled.

When President Reagan gave the strikers a deadline of forty-eight hours there had been widespread hope that PATCO would call off the strike, or that the majority of the controllers would accept the President's amnesty offer and return to their positions.[1]

By the deadline on Wednesday, however, it was obvious that the strike was going to continue and that PATCO was going to win or commit professional suicide trying. It was equally obvious that the FAA, using supervisors, computers, and military controllers borrowed from the Air Force and the Navy, was going to be able to operate up to 75 percent of normal commercial traffic. That meant a possible reprieve for Braniff. With the international routes all but untouched and domestic at no more than a 25 percent cutback, the company could squeak through, damaged but alive. One important factor was the quick agreement of Braniff's unions that in general, people would be paid only for the hours worked, and that depended on how many flights could be operated. This was especially important in relation to the flight crews and saved the company from ruinous expenses. It seemed that in times of great peril, the unions and the company could pull together. It was going to be a while, however, before the "Braniff Strikes Back" campaign could be launched with any force and effect.

As the various control centers of the Braniff operation continued

---

[1] President Reagan really didn't possess the legal authority to offer amnesty, since in strict legal terms the strikers dismissed themselves the very instant they began participating in the strike, by the operation of a federal statute that the President does not have the legal authority to waive or ignore. The only coloration of legality, interestingly enough, was in the argument that the President does have the authority to make the determination of exactly when a particular action becomes an illegal job action or strike. In this case alone, if he decided that it was illegal only after forty-eight hours, could the amnesty offer (which less than a thousand accepted) be valid. Otherwise the FAA was reemploying unconvicted felons, which, according to Civil Service regulations, couldn't be done in any case for two years.

The nation's press, including the networks employing legal correspondents who were licensed attorneys, missed or ignored this point entirely. The public was being given the impression that the President could suspend any civil or criminal statute at will—a totally preposterous and cynical assumption.

an hour-by-hour liaison with the FAA's control center, Braniff pilots were discovering something rather shocking: The air traffic control system of the United States under PATCO had been screwed up beyond belief!

"Denver center, Braniff 182 with you, level, flight level 350—requesting 390."

Braniff's late-afternoon DFW–Seattle flight was crossing into Denver air route traffic control center's airspace as it flew past the Texas–New Mexico border near Clayton, New Mexico, less than one hour into the flight. It was just over one week into the controllers' strike, and the crew of Flight 182 (like the crews of most domestic airliners) were amazed at the smoothness of the system and the level of cooperation.

"Good evening, Braniff 182, and welcome to Denver. We've got radar contact, and give me just a minute, sir, I'll see what we can do about flight level 390. You folks having a rough ride at 350?"

The captain took the microphone—it was the copilot's leg (in common practice whoever isn't flying works the radio).

"A little light chop at 350, center—that's why we'd like to try higher. Sorry to bother you with it."

"No problem, 182, glad to help."

The copilot looked over at the captain. "That's the Denver center? Are you sure we're on the right frequency?"

"Amazing, isn't it!" the captain replied, holding the microphone at mouth level and thinking the situation over as the autopilot kept the three-engine jet boring straight and level on a magnetic heading of 290 degrees.

None of the three pilots had ever heard such a friendly voice coming from the Denver center—let alone a cooperative attitude. This was their first flight since the strike had begun. All three had been hearing stories about how, suddenly, the controllers who were manning the various positions were friendly and helpful as well as precise and professional and that the only significant problems were delays in getting a departure slot, but that once on your way, flying hadn't been as easy and as pleasant for a decade.

The captain pressed the button again. "Denver, 182—uh, how are you fellows holding out down there?"

The friendly male voice with a hint of a southern accent replied, "Just fine, Braniff. We're working long shifts, but everyone's cooperating here for a change, and the traffic isn't as bad with flow control in effect."

"Well, hang in there—we're with you!"

"Thanks, 182—we appreciate that. By the way, you fellows can climb on up to 390 [39,000 feet] now . . . and contact the Denver center on 125.8. Y'all have a good flight."

"Roger Denver, Braniff 182 cleared to flight level 390 . . . contact you on 125.8. Have a good day—and thanks."

The captain switched frequencies, shaking his head in disbelief and wondering if the next controller would be as friendly. He was. In fact, all over the United States the nation's airline pilots were realizing that what they were experiencing was not only the complete opposite of the scare-tactic tales that PATCO was feeding the eager press about unsafe skies, but also that never in the past ten years had there been such a level of cooperation and efficiency— and by no means was it due only to the diminished air traffic.

As the weeks wore on, it would become quite clear that the contentious infighting and harassment that had been festering in the nation's air traffic control facilities for the past eleven years between PATCO and non-PATCO people, and between PATCO people and their managers, had created an atmosphere of tension and occasionally outright hatred between the controllers and the pilots. Apparently there was no need to refuse consistently the request for altitude changes near Denver, for instance (which had been a common practice under the old group). Apparently it wasn't necessarily part of the controller's job to get sharp and sarcastic when a flight crew requested anything else out of the ordinary.[2]

---

[2] PATCO had been making quite a few very legitimate complaints over the years. The technology, and the human relations and management structure of the FAA's administration of the air traffic control system were antiquated. Ironically, in much the same fashion as Braniff had abdicated control to the unions at certain lower-level management positions and had permitted the Teamsters to run things, so too had the FAA permitted PATCO to move into the management void it had refused to address. Once in control, PATCO's abuse of its ability to threaten and control and intimidate the FAA became a form of self-congratulatory arrogance, created in part by the collective influence of too many men who were essentially products of the anti-establishment culture of the 1960s and the Viet Nam era and who were not about to take orders from anyone. (That attitude, which seemed far more prevalent among those who passed their twenty-first birthday in the last few years of the 1960s, had been a factor as well among those who joined the ranks of the Braniff Teamsters during the same period through negligent and indiscriminate hiring.) The airline pilots these air controllers dealt with constantly were on the receiving end of much of the hatred this created. The pilots made more money, had better hours, and had more public respect than the controllers, and PATCO wanted the controllers in an equal position on all counts—despite the fact that the pilots had, to a man, many more years of training and qualification for their position, and de-

Even with the financial damage it was causing their respective companies, the vast majority of U.S. airline pilots (and virtually all of Braniff's) totally supported President Reagan's stance on the issue and the firing of the outlaw controllers. This was especially true when PATCO pulled out all the stops in an effort to convince the flying public that airline pilots were flying in a horribly dangerous environment. Not only was the charge demonstrably false, but also the insulting implication that any airline could force its pilots to fly in an obviously dangerous environment was infuriating. Most airline captains of major airlines are fiercely independent when it comes to retaining the right to make the final decision on whether a flight is safe to proceed. PATCO had counted on the support of ALPA and the pilots; PATCO received almost no support from them, although John J. O'Donnell, president of ALPA (which is affiliated with the AFL-CIO), tried to play a balancing act during the strike to avoid angering AFL-CIO President Lane Kirkland.[3]

In addition, the role of the nation's press was pivotal and tawdry. Local, cable, and network news programs provided PATCO with a perfect medium for making the false claim that the air traffic control system their membership had attempted to shut down was unsafe. The press pandered to PATCO, printing, reporting, and telecasting every word or proclamation—and playing down the principal fact that every one of the strikers had committed a federal felony. It was a shameful period of hysterical, unprofessional, and largely inaccurate reporting of which the vast majority of the media—especially radio and TV—were guilty.

By the third week of the strike, Braniff had finally stabilized op-

spite the fact that regardless of the controllers' responsibilities, it was the pilots who actually flew the aircraft. (PATCO issued bumper stickers in the mid-1970s saying: "PATCO members tell pilots where to go!") Thus, airline pilots became their enemies, and the relationship of overall cooperation and goodwill that had originally been standard in the sixties deteriorated to contentiousness and hatred.

One of the greatest tragedies in the ruination of over eleven thousand careers created by PATCO's suicide was that the many legitimate complaints, some of which raised serious questions about the safety of the system, were submerged and all but destroyed by PATCO's lemminglike drive to extinction.

[3] Lane Kirkland joined Poli in the silly circus surrounding PATCO's "safety" claims. O'Donnell was later censured by Delta's branch of ALPA and roundly denounced by the majority of his union. He would be defeated for reelection the following year by Delta Captain Henry Duffy, due in no small measure to O'Donnell's unrepresentative performance during the strike.

erations at nearly 90 percent, and it looked as if the slightly increased load factors had lessened the impact even more.

As Casey and most of the senior officers grappled with the PATCO strike, Casey had been forced to turn his attention away from the constant stream of employee complaints for a change, thus giving some of the junior managers a bit of relief.

John Casey had become so zealous of his good relations with the rank and file that he had come to adopt a self-created maxim: Whatever an employee said in a letter was true. The conclusion, once reached, caused him increasingly to undermine his lower-management people in disciplinary matters whenever the subject employee knew enough to complain directly to the chairman.

Casey had appeared one afternoon in the doorway of Jeff Krida's office at the world headquarters. "Jeff, about this problem in reservations"—he came in and laid a paper on Krida's desk with a reservations manager's name on it—"we're going to have to get rid of him. I can't excuse the kind of sex-discrimination attitude the man displayed."

"John, that was two years ago." Krida was familiar with the case.

"I don't care . . . just get rid of him."

"John, pardon me, but what we really need to do is get this fellow's side of the story. All we have is the young lady's side of it . . . we don't know what happened."

"Look, Jeff, I've promised these people [the union steward] I'd take care of this. . . . I don't have time to listen to the man's excuses . . . the union people are all over me to get rid of him, and we need to keep their confidence. Besides, I'm sure what she described here is what happened."

"But how can we be sure?"

"Just get rid of him, please."

As long as they could get through to Casey, they could accomplish just about anything. A manager who got crossways with a union employee didn't have much of a chance in that atmosphere, and it had damaged a lot of feelings and stifled a lot of renewed initiative. Many of the lower-level managers had come to be more worried about what their people thought of them than how their people were doing the job. They didn't feel that they had much support from the top. Apparently, went the grumbling, the Braniff Bandwagon was for contract people only.

Finally, on September 1, Braniff launched what would have to serve as the new master plan, the "Braniff Strikes Back" campaign, featuring what proved to be a confusing split between "Premier Service," with standard first class and coach configurations and full meal service, as always, and "Express Service," designed to rival the Southwest Airlines style with all-coach and very reduced snack service coupled with deeply discounted fares.

The promotion also featured a new "short-form" ticket and a "ten-second check-in," neither of which were ever made fully operational.

In explaining the new approach to the press, Casey was quoted as saying: "We've been feeling the squeeze between the major trunks on top and the nonunion regionals on the bottom. We feel the best way to compete against that squeeze is to strike back at both—so we're calling our plan, 'Braniff Strikes Back.'"

While the press, the public, and the competition mulled over the new promotion, Braniff maintenance worked overtime to convert the designated 727's to all-coach, and Braniff's first class passengers began mistakenly showing up for "Express Service" flights only to end up stuck in an unwanted coach seat and flying all the way to Tulsa or Washington or Chicago in a foul mood and with an angry conviction to avoid Braniff in the future. There were a growing number of Braniff passengers who simply didn't understand the new system and didn't have the time or the energy to learn. They went to the competition—and so, for that matter, did the Braniff Board. John Casey had finally gone too far.

Dr. Putnam to the Rescue

26 Jojo's in Dallas is one of those coffee shop chains that have grown to include plush decor heavily laced with plants and greenery, rugs, comfortably upholstered booths, and a rather lengthy menu.

At 7:00 A.M. on Monday, September 14, 1981, Southwest Airlines President Howard Putnam, forty-four years of age—balding, given to wire-rimmed glasses, expensive monogrammed shirts, and well-tailored, conservative suits—walked through the front doorway of the Jojo's near Carrollton on Belt Line Road in North Dallas looking for the other airline executive he was there to meet. Putnam, a trim Midwesterner from Ohio with a disarmingly open and unpretentious manner, had been an ambitious, rising executive with United Airlines when he was hired away in 1978 to take over Southwest Airlines in Dallas—after one of Southwest's founders, the flamboyant Lamar Muse, lost a power-play contest with Southwest's Board. Now Putnam was standing in the entry to a North Dallas restaurant on a muggy North Texas morning, not quite sure why he was there.

Within a few seconds Putnam spotted the man he was looking for—the chief executive of another Dallas-based airline who had called the previous Friday to invite him to this meeting for reasons yet unknown, John J. Casey of Braniff. Apparently Casey had arrived early—he was sitting at one of the booths working with a yellow legal pad when Putnam walked in.

John Casey met him halfway. The two men exchanged greetings, then went back to Casey's booth. After a few pleasantries and their breakfast orders, John Casey motioned to his yellow pad and dropped a small bomb on Putnam.

"Howard, I'd like you to join us at Braniff—as president."

Putnam looked shocked. "Now, why would I want to leave the world's greatest airline president's job for—for—*that*?"

As the plates of eggs and bacon were set down in front of them, Casey began outlining the organizational chart he had been sketching on the legal pad and explaining what he had in mind, going over the present status of the company to the extent he could legally.

"But—I just don't know why I should leave Southwest. I mean, from what you say, John, I'm not all that sure it can be turned around."

Casey pressed harder, enthusiastically describing the challenge.

"John—no. I'm just not interested. I'm very flattered, but I just don't think I want to consider this."

Casey leaned over the table slightly, the palm of his right hand held up to Putnam in a stop gesture. "Don't say no. You think about it—you think about it, but don't say no right now—you go back and think about it." Casey seemed anxious; he obviously didn't want the door slammed on the proposal. His eagerness puzzled Putnam.

"Well, I can tell you the answer will still be no. But I'll think it over."

"The only thing, Howard, if we do it, we have to do it fast. We've got to get a new team in place quickly."

"I'll call you by Wednesday—okay?"

"That's fine."

The previous week John Casey had met First International Bancshares Executive Committee Chairman Bob Stewart and two of his senior officers, Dewey Presley and Elvis Mason, for a 7:00 A.M. breakfast in downtown Dallas. Presley had been assigned full-time to the task of helping Braniff and had taken a lead position with the remainder of the banks that held Braniff's senior debts. Stewart had left the Braniff Board several months before, but he was doing everything possible to help save the airline. First International (corporate holding company of First National Bank in Dallas) was, of course, a major Braniff lender as well as its principal banker. The meetings weren't unusual, but the agenda this particular morning was.

"John, have you given any thought to getting somebody in to help you [as President]?"

Casey had been trying to avoid doing so; he was happy running the show, but he sensed the others were impatient with his failure to formulate a good recovery plan. He had toyed around with a few names, but mainly so he could say he had done so—which was his response now. "Yeah, I've got a list I've been looking at."

"Well, John, we've got a list, too."

"What do you mean, you've got a list?"

The bankers pulled out some papers with a number of names of corporate executives on them. On the top of the list was the name of Howard Putnam of Southwest Airlines. The group was insistent that Putnam should be approached to become Braniff's president under Casey. Dewey Presley looked at Casey. "We'll call him for you, John."

"No, you won't. I'll call him."

"Okay. Let us hear."

Casey went back to the world headquarters and by Friday had phoned Putnam, asking for a Monday morning meeting.

Casey figured that if he brought in this Putnam fellow, who was reputed to be an excellent marketing man in the forefront of deregulated commercial aviation, he could split up the executive duties with him and retain the overall authority as Chairman. Casey would retain the direct authority for such functions as legal, security, and personnel, but overall the day-to-day business of running the airline and the new "Braniff Strikes Back" campaign would be the responsibility of the new man—under Casey's supervision as chairman of the Board. Casey was unsure of the idea but liked some of the possibilities. It would give him time to concentrate on the strategic planning that always bothered and worried him so much. Nevertheless, he wasn't happy about having to share the limelight. He had done much to turn this airline around, and if it all turned out okay, he didn't want his share of the credit diluted.

He had to admit the move made sense (and he would later take credit publicly for it, claiming to have thought up the idea of hiring Putnam). The lenders were all over them to remake the airline into a profitable entity, and Braniff simply no longer had the capability to beat American and Delta at their own game—that of a major trunk airline. The "Braniff Strikes Back" move had been an attempt to retain the character of a trunk carrier while fielding the direct competition of the Southwests of the world. If they had to emulate Southwest, what better way was there to build a surrogate Southwest than by stealing its chief executive?

If Casey suspected the real reason that his most powerful directors were urging Howard Putnam on him, he kept it to himself. Apparently he believed such an arrangement could work, and in that John Casey displayed a naïveté that should have been surprising for a man of his experience—but that had become too characteristic of his handling of the more subtle elements of the chairman's job. He couldn't see the power play going on in the background, or hear the phone calls crisscrossing Dallas and Fort Worth. The older members of the Board, such as Post and Lay and Bass, had come to the end of their patience. They didn't engage the new Board members such as Howard Swanson in the discussions—the shadowy but urgent moves were all in the background, designed not to show up in the minutes of the Board meetings. The discussions involved the Dallas bankers and a select couple of the out-of-state lenders as well. The decision in its most simple form was that Casey had to be removed from power without being removed from the premises or the office and without the most uncooperative among the lenders, or the public, sensing the revolt.

It was obvious that Putnam would be a fool to come over without a tremendous monetary incentive—and he might be a fool to come over at any price. Casey knew there were some terribly frightening aspects of the current state of the company that he couldn't legally discuss with Putnam unless Putnam joined the team—and Casey had no idea whether he could be persuaded.

Putnam was astounded, but, amazingly, by midweek he was actually considering it. The whole idea had sounded ridiculous at first, but no one had ever turned around a monster such as Braniff before, although Ed Acker was now attempting to do the same thing in New York with Pan Am. Southwest was a comfortable haven, though, and the thought of leaving such a compatible environment to jump into a hurricane of problems was exciting as well as a bit frightening.

Putnam and his wife, Krista, talked it over numerous times, and by midweek, Putnam had thrown some additional—hypothetical—questions at Casey, as to the exact terms of the contract they were offering. He said nothing to Chairman Herb Kelleher or anyone else at Southwest. Putnam still had no intention of taking it.

Still, with a big enough option of Braniff stock, which was then trading at about $3 per share, if he took the job and succeeded in bringing Braniff out of the woods—and raising the stock to, say, $20 or $30 per share—he could earn a small fortune, not that the proposed salary and benefits weren't substantial as well. Casey's offer was for $250,000 per year, guaranteed for three years in the event some corporate consolidation or collapse threw him out of office (this was the "golden parachute"). In addition, he would get a company car, an insurance policy for $750,000, the stock options for 300,000 shares, a country club membership, and paid investment counseling—along with an upfront $50,000, payable on signing. It was quite an offer!

As Howard Putnam agonized over the choice, he also worried about the exact extent of his real authority under Casey's chairmanship. The organizational chart Casey had drawn would give Putnam most of the direct operating power, even though Casey would retain the titles of chief executive officer and chairman. Putnam would be president and chief operating officer. But who, wondered Putnam, would really be the final authority? He had heard rumors about Casey's impulsive style and that his Board had been leaving en masse.

The answer came late in the week. In phone calls from Bob Stewart and Elvis Mason, off-the-record communications from the people who had forced Casey to pursue Putnam in the first place, Howard Putnam was assured of what the real organizational order would be: Putnam would have the confidence and backing of the Board and would be expected to lead in fact, if not totally in title. He would be expected to remake Braniff into a low-cost, operationally profitable carrier very, very rapidly—using whatever reasonable methods might be necessary to get the costs down to achieve the goal, including the drastic reduction of union contract wages and all other operational expenses. Finally, he had to put on a sufficiently good show to convince the lenders to restructure the debt, and he must understand that effectively he would be working to please the lenders—who could call it quits at almost any time.

The surprise was the part about Casey. John Casey, they indicated, was essentially superfluous but had to be retained due to the sensitivity of the situation. What's more, Casey did not know and was not to know, unless he could figure it out for himself. Regardless of title, Putnam was to be completely in charge.

That put a slightly different light on it. Being in total control, he'd have a better chance of remaking the airline into a low-cost, no-frills carrier that could turn a profit, thus convincing the lenders to accept their losses and restructure. If Putnam could pull off such a rescue, his personal stock in the industry would be astronomical. That would put him right up there with Ed Acker—make him a legend. If he failed—well, he could always say that the patient was dead before Dr. Putnam arrived to save it. Professionally, he could survive a Braniff corporate failure. It was to be the first of many flawed assumptions.

Putnam realized that he was probably getting just a bit bored, deep inside, at Southwest. Things had gone well there since he had become president. No monstrous challenges had faced him, although he had kept the airline operating through a strike by the IAM, improved the personnel relations (though many people at Southwest would be very glad to see him leave), and had presided over the tripling of the airline's size and its enormous profitability. The majority of the changes at Southwest, however, had been pre-ordained in a master plan constructed by Chairman Herb Kelleher just before Putnam was hired from United. Putnam's most impressive contribution to the company had been employee communications and stabilizing upper-management functions. There had been little innovation as such by Putnam, though at times he appeared to take individual credit for tripling the size of the company. He hadn't done badly at Southwest, but that was a county stock car race compared to the International Grand Prix of financial headaches now approaching the checkered flag out at Braniff. Did he really need such a challenge? Could he handle such a challenge?

Putnam figured by the end of the week that if he didn't take the job—and especially if Braniff ultimately went under—he'd wonder all his life whether he could have made a difference.

Howard Putnam by Friday also knew that his bargaining power was massive. He in effect held all the cards, since the powers behind the throne wanted him as president. He did not, however, want to go to Braniff alone. One thing he had learned from his days at United was always to take a friendly team-player when you joined an enemy camp (much the same as Lawrence had brought in Acker in 1965). The challenge he would face at Braniff was a financial challenge as well as a marketing nightmare, and he would need a finance man he knew and trusted—someone with whom he could work from the first day.

Putnam was a marketing executive, the same area of expertise that Russ Thayer claimed. It was quite normal for an airline chief executive to be something of a neophyte at corporate finance, and Howard Putnam was no exception. (He once asked a startled Southwest pilot for a quick explanation of how corporate debt-to-equity ratios were figured moments before going in to address a meeting of his employees on company financial matters.) In Putnam's view, since he had needed a strong finance man at stable, profitable Southwest, taking on the granddaddy of all airline financial headaches at Braniff without the same help would be ridiculous if not professionally suicidal.

M. Phillip Guthrie, vice president for finance and chief financial officer of Southwest, was the man who had provided that help in the past, so Putnam decided he had enough chips on his side of the table to tell Braniff and Casey flatly: You'll have to hire Guthrie along with me, or I won't come.

Guthrie was a sharp, young finance man of thirty-six, but he had never played in the Braniff-class big leagues before. Putnam, however, figured his friend could handle it. Putnam took Guthrie aside, filled him in, got his permission, and relayed the demand to Casey.

Casey and the Board huddled over the new development. Bringing in Guthrie as vice president for finance would mean that Swanson, hired just six months before, would have to be moved aside as chief financial officer. Putnam was not interested in working with anyone else—even temporarily. Swanson would be in good shape regardless of what happened, thanks to his three-year golden parachute at $145,000 per year, but it was going to be embarrassing. Nevertheless, the pressure on Casey was massive: Putnam must be brought in at all costs, regardless of what they did with Swanson. (Guthrie was also given a generous employment contract for three years at a base salary of $130,000 per year with a stock option on 100,000 shares of Braniff stock.) The Board approved and Putnam accepted.

On Tuesday, September 22, at 7:30 A.M., Howard Swanson arrived at his office in the world headquarters and walked a few yards down the corridor toward Lawrence's old outer office to report to John Casey on the labor negotiations with the pilots that had been in progress over the weekend. Casey had left word with Swanson's secretary to see him as soon as he came in, so Swanson figured Casey was eager for the report.

"Good morning, John." Swanson came through the doorway of Casey's office and headed for one of the chairs on the other side of the desk. Casey was standing behind his desk, looking rather glum.

"Hello, Howard."

"Well, we're going good on the talks." Swanson had sat down and now looked up to see something else was bothering Casey.

"Uh, Howard, there's going to be a staff meeting this morning—in about thirty minutes."

"Oh? What's up?"

Casey avoided Swanson's eyes and looked out the window, his head down somewhat. "Well—uh—there have been some changes—over the weekend."

"What changes?"

"Well, I've been wearing all three of these hats—you know—and I figured we ought to get someone in here with me as president. . . ."

"Well, that's good, John, I agree. You've been carrying a hell of a lot by yourself. Have you picked the man?"

"Yes—Howard—we, uh, are bringing on Howard Putnam—Southwest Airlines' president. That's what I'm going to announce in a little while."

"Hey, that's great. You'll still be CEO and chairman then, won't you?"

Casey paused again, looking at his desk, one hand in his pocket, the other absently moving things around his blotter.

"Yeah. Yeah, I will."

"Well, that's good."

"No—uh, Howard—that's not so good. Putnam wants to bring in his own man—in finance, y'know."

"Okay. That's fine. Anybody I know?"

"He's bringing in Phillip Guthrie, who was his vice president for finance at Southwest."

Swanson hadn't understood, and Casey was hating every second of this.

"How are you going to set up the titles, then?"

"What?"

Casey finally looked at Swanson—momentarily, then looked away—still with the pained expression on his face.

"The titles, John. What's Guthrie going to function as?"

Casey sighed and glanced at the single painting in the room—a Calder, of course. That's all Lawrence allowed in the executive offices, and this one was hanging behind Swanson. John Casey looked over Swanson's head to focus on it—then back at his desk—and finally looked Swanson in the eye.

"Howard—he's going to be vice president for finance here too."

Swanson tried to absorb the words. There couldn't be two vice presidents for finance—so that meant . . .

"I hate to tell you this, Howard—I really do—but we had no choice. We had to have Putnam, and he insisted on bringing Guthrie."

Swanson studied Casey's face, a sinking feeling in the pit of his stomach. "Where does that leave me, John?"

"Out. I'm afraid he's—we're—you'll have to go."

Howard Swanson's face dropped in shock. He sat back a bit in the chair. Casey was telling him that after six months of furious, dedicated, and mostly successful effort to save this damned airline, they were going to boot him out? Incredible! Impossible! Where was the nondescript title and the face-saving job that were standard protocol in the industry in such cases? They'd have to pay him for two and a half more years. Did they really want nothing for that money? People wouldn't understand—this would damage his career. A hundred thoughts, few of them happy, flashed through Swanson's mind: ". . . must phone my wife . . . stop the sale of our house . . . should fly home . . . haven't checked my calendar this morning . . . don't *need* to check it now . . . has he told my secretary? . . ."

"Howard, I'm really sorry, I mean, you've done a wonderful job—top-notch in every way—and this certainly in no way reflects on you professionally or personally—it's just that Putnam demanded—wanted—to bring Guthrie along, or he wouldn't come—and we had to have him."

"Just like that? I could stay and work with him. I mean, for Christ's sake, John, look what I've been able to do with the lenders group. I've got the trust of a lot of them now. Are you going to throw that away? This is stupid!"

Casey resumed pushing objects around his desk pad. "Howard, I need to get you out. When can you be off the premises?"

Swanson looked dumbfounded. "What?"

"When can you be off the premises? We need to clear everything for Putnam and Guthrie—office space, y'know, is a factor too—and I need you out as fast as possible."

"Well—I need some time."

"How much?"

Through the pain and the shock, a hard edge was creeping into Swanson's voice. He'd never been so insulted. Off the premises? He was being treated like a thief!

Swanson fixed Casey with a hard stare. "Well, I don't know. One doesn't plan how much time one needs to leave a premises—I haven't thought about it."

"Well, I need you off the premises as soon as possible."

"Certainly within a week."

"Well, that's good, because I don't want you to be around here too long."

Swanson walked in a daze back to his office. He had less than ten minutes to get ready for the staff meeting at which the whole shameful thing would be announced. He hadn't even been given the courtesy of a day to absorb the impact.

Swanson called his wife in New York to tell her what had happened and that he was going to fly home that afternoon. He didn't want to be alone. The thing that kept kicking him in the gut was Casey's statement "I need you off the premises as soon as possible."

The staff meeting was held in the boardroom. Swanson, trying hard to keep an even expression, took his seat as Casey announced that Putnam and Guthrie would be joining the team and Swanson would be leaving. He praised Swanson's performance and said he was sorry the move was unavoidable but that Putnam had an abiding confidence in Guthrie and insisted on bringing him in. The senior management of Braniff International was somewhat stunned, too. When Swanson got up to leave, they gave him a standing ovation. Swanson left fighting back tears. He had really fought hard for this damned airline—for what?

Following a twelve-o'clock news conference with Casey, Putnam, and Guthrie, the announcement of the Putnam defection to Braniff rolled through the industry like a thunderclap, picking up sage interpretations as it echoed from analyst to lender to rival executive. Most analysts saw the surprise development as an indicator that all was not hopeless at Braniff after all. Surely, the argument went, someone as secure and successful as Howard Putnam wouldn't leave a comfortable position to step on the listing deck of a burning ship unless he knew it really wasn't sinking. The resident airline analyst for Lehman Brothers Kuhn Loeb in New York, Robert Joedicke (the one analyst Dennis Fulton, the *Dallas Morning News* business writer quoted constantly), told *The Wall Street Journal* the next day, ". . . he [Putnam] must have had enough exposure to Braniff's financial [books] to believe Braniff can be turned around. It's an encouraging announcement."

For most members of the Braniff family, the announcement that clattered off the teletypes this time held a bit of hope—as well as a new fear, which was to gather momentum in the rumor mill: Oh, my God! What was he brought here to do?

DFWGPBN

PLEASE POST ON ALL BULLETIN BOARDS AND PILOT AND FLIGHT ATTENDANT BRIEFING BOOKS FOR THE INFORMATION OF ALL EM-PLOYEES

WHEN I WAS ELECTED AS CHIEF EXECUTIVE OFFICER OF BRANIFF IN EARLY 1981, I WAS GIVEN THE MANDATE OF REBUILDING A NEW BRANIFF. OVER THE PAST NINE MONTHS WE HAVE MOVED RAPIDLY AND SUCCESSFULLY TOWARD THAT DIRECTION. MY MOST RECENT ANNOUNCEMENT REGARDING THE TWO-TIER AIRLINE THAT WE ARE NOW FLYING REQUIRES THAT WE CONTINUE TO BUILD UPON MANAGEMENT STRENGTH OF BRANIFF. IN MY OPIN-ION NO ONE IN THE AIRLINE INDUSTRY HAS A MORE UNIQUE BACKGROUND EXPERIENCE THAN DOES MR. HOWARD PUTNAM, PRESIDENT AND CHIEF EXECUTIVE OFFICER OF SOUTHWEST AIR-LINES. MR. PUTNAM'S PAST AND PROVEN EXPERIENCE AS THE HEAD OF A HIGHLY SUCCESSFUL REGIONAL AIRLINE AND HIS MANY POSITIONS WITH A MAJOR TRUNK AIRLINE—UNITED— MAKE HIM UNIQUELY QUALIFIED FOR THE PRESIDENCY OF BRAN-IFF. . . .

WE HAVE ALSO MADE ANOTHER ANNOUNCEMENT IN THAT WE HAVE BROUGHT ONBOARD MR. PHIL GUTHRIE WHO IS A MOST RESPECTED CHIEF FINANCIAL OFFICER WITHIN THE AIRLINE IN-DUSTRY. THIS PERHAPS WAS THE MOST DIFFICULT DECISION WE HAD TO MAKE IN THAT HE WILL REPLACE HOWARD SWANSON WHOSE PERFORMANCE HAS BEEN OUTSTANDING. HOWEVER, HOWARD PUTNAM HAS ENORMOUS CONFIDENCE IN GUTHRIE AND FELT THAT THEIR COMBINED CONTRIBUTIONS WOULD BEST SERVE BRANIFF AND THAT THE EXPERIENCE AND SUCCESS THEY HAVE HAD TOGETHER IS SOMETHING THEY WANT TO CONTINUE.

MR. PUTNAM ALSO WAS ELECTED A DIRECTOR OF BRANIFF INTER-NATIONAL AND BRANIFF AIRWAYS INC.

Howard Putnam and Phil Guthrie picked Saturday, September 26 to drive out to Braniff's world headquarters with several boxes of personal items for their new offices. Swanson and his wife had been in earlier in the week, had cleaned out his office, and had left for New York.

It was a windy, pleasant day as Putnam turned his Olds into the circular drive at the entrance to the headquarters complex and got out. A bell-like clanging filled the air around the fountain, and Putnam looked up to see the twenty-eight flagpoles—now empty—that Lawrence had installed to fly the flag of every nation Braniff served. It was their drawropes slapping the hollow metal poles that was making the cacophonous ringing. "My God," he thought, "they look just like the masts of a sunken ship!" The nautical metaphor used so much by the press over the past week to describe Braniff's plight and Putnam's coming flickered across his mind.

John Casey met the two and showed Guthrie to his office. When Putnam walked into his new office, the first thing he noticed was the single Calder painting on the wall.

"John, why only Calders? That's all I see around here. No diplomas—no airplane pictures—just Calders?"

"Aw—that's the rule around here. You're only allowed one painting on the wall, and that's got to be one of the Calders."

Putnam looked at Casey's face. He was serious. Incredibly, he was serious! Here was the chairman of the Board, and he was still—automatically—bowing to a rule set up by a predecessor who had been gone nine months.

"Well, John, I just changed the rule, 'cause I'm not going to look at a Calder." Putnam smiled at Casey as he said that, and Casey just shrugged. Putnam continued, "When I look at a Calder, all it does is remind me of the past."

Later that afternoon, while Guthrie adorned his walls with his favorite certificates and pictures and filled his credenza (a standard one of lightly stained oak was behind each desk) with personal bric-a-brac and more pictures, Putnam did the same thing in his office—hanging up his Southwest Airlines Boeing 737 picture first. Another Lawrencian rule forbade bric-a-brac on the credenza. If you could find room in the single desk drawer, fine. But no personal items were allowed on the credenza. The significance of the contempt Putnam and Guthrie were displaying for the old regime—which included John Casey—wouldn't hit Casey for months.

A week had passed since the announcement as the company's officers assembled on Tuesday, September 29, for what would be Putnam's first staff meeting. The question on most everyone's mind was: Who's actually going to be in charge? Rumors had ricocheted throughout the company in the past week, but no one seemed to know the answer. Casey was acting as if he had thought up the entire idea and was still to be in charge, as his title indicated. But what kind of mandate did Putnam have tucked in his pocket? The events of mid-September with the bankers had been top secret—no one in the executive suite knew.

Chairman Casey called the meeting to order and then began a short introduction of the new president and chief operating officer, who was standing behind him along the wall.

"So with great pleasure that we got him, I'd like to formally introduce you to Howard Swanson!" With that Casey gestured toward Howard Putnam with a warm smile.

The room was very quiet. It was obvious to all present that John Casey did not realize he had committed the double faux pas of substituting the brutally ousted Swanson's surname for Putnam's. Several dropped their eyes, others just watched—stiffly—as Casey sat down, still smiling—and Putnam, who had been standing behind Casey, moved forward a couple of feet to the small dais at the head of the table.

Only a few seconds had passed, but they seemed like years. Those who really liked Casey personally were awash in a wave of embarrassment, all the more acute for his failure to recognize what he had said. Those who didn't care for him were embarrassed and disgusted—Casey couldn't even get this right. They had all heard the details of Swanson's unceremonious treatment.

Howard Putnam was somewhat used to being introduced by the wrong name. He had been introduced once by United's Dick Ferris as "Fred" Putnam, and another time by Southwest's chairman as "Harold Putman." Putnam figured this time it was a joke.

Without missing a beat, Putnam stepped up behind the dais, hesitating long enough to make eye contact around the room in a quick, sweeping movement of his head. Putnam then looked down at John Casey, seated on his left, put his left hand on Casey's shoulder, looked up at the group again, and said simply:

"Thank you—Harding!"

The room virtually exploded in laughter, several of the executives laughing so hard they were having trouble staying in their chairs. Casey looked puzzled at first, then finally made the connection and joined in the laughter. Putnam's adroit wit had spoken volumes. Suddenly it was very, very clear who was going to be in charge.

A Double-edged Sword

CHAPTER 27 PLEASE POST ON COMPANY BULLETIN BOARDS AND IN PILOT AND FLIGHT ATTENDANT BRIEFING BOOKS FOR THE INFORMATION OF ALL EMPLOYEES

TODAY IS THE FIRST DAY ON THE JOB AT BRANIFF FOR PHIL GUTHRIE EXECUTIVE VICE PRESIDENT—FINANCE AND MYSELF. WE ARE DEDICATED TO WORKING WITH ALL OF YOU AS A TEAM TO GET BRANIFF BACK TO FINANCIAL STABILITY. THIS IS GOING TO BE THE MOST DIFFICULT TASK I HAVE EVER BEEN ASSOCIATED WITH. I CANNOT DO IT MYSELF. IF ALL OF YOU ARE WILLING, I THINK WE HAVE A CHANCE BUT TIME IS SHORT AND WE ARE GOING TO HAVE TO TAKE SOME ACTIONS QUICKLY, SOME OF WHICH MAY NOT BE RECEIVED WITH GREAT ENTHUSIASM.

MY PRIORITIES START WITH HAVING PHIL GUTHRIE IMMEDI-ATELY WORK WITH THE KEY BANKS AND LENDERS TO COME UP WITH A FINANCIAL RESTRUCTURING OF OUR LONG TERM DEBT. THE LENDERS HAVE FORGIVEN US INTEREST PAYMENTS UNTIL FEBRUARY 1, 1982, BUT PRIOR TO THAT WE MUST HAVE A VIA-BLE AND CREATIVE PLAN IN PLACE.

WE MUST EVALUATE WHAT BRANIFF'S MARKETING "NICHE" IS. WE HAVE TO FLY THOSE ROUTES THAT CAN BE PROFITABLE IN THE LONG RUN AND ADDRESS THOSE SPECIFIC CUSTOMERS THAT WE ARE CAPABLE OF SERVICING BETTER THAN ANYONE ELSE.

WE ARE GOING TO IMMEDIATELY LOOK AT THE PRODUCTIVITY OF ALL OF OUR PEOPLE, OUR AIRCRAFT, OUR FACILITIES, AND THE

WAY WE UTILIZE OUR CASH FLOW. IT IS MANDATORY THAT THE
PRODUCTIVITY IN EVERY AREA BE INCREASED IMMEDIATELY. THE
PAYCUTS WHICH YOU ALL TOOK EARLIER THIS YEAR WILL PROBA-
BLY HAVE TO STAY IN PLACE THROUGH THE END OF 1983. I DO
NOT ANTICIPATE FURTHER PAY REDUCTIONS, HOWEVER, THE AIR-
LINE MAY HAVE TO GET SMALLER IN SIZE IN THE SHORT RUN IF
WE HOPE TO EVER GROW IN SIZE AND HAVE A FUTURE.

WE WILL LOOK IMMEDIATELY AT OUR MANAGEMENT STRUC-
TURE FROM THE TOP DOWN TO BE CERTAIN IT IS LEAN AND EFFEC-
TIVE.

I LOOK FORWARD TO THIS OPPORTUNITY TO WORK WITH
JOHN CASEY AND ALL OF YOU IN SHAPING A NEW BRANIFF AND TO
MEETING YOU AS I TRAVEL ACROSS THE SYSTEM.

HOWARD D. PUTNAM
PRESIDENT AND CHIEF OPERATING OFFICER

"What do you suppose he means, 'shaping a new Braniff'?" One
of the Minneapolis flight attendants was holding a copy of the message as she stood in the western end of their crew room at Minneapolis-St. Paul International Airport, talking with a senior flight
attendant.

"What he means, honey, is that we're in a lot of trouble. Mr.
Putnam is going to try to make this airline into a copy of Southwest
Airlines. Braniff, as we know it, is dead!"

Braniff's new vice president for finance had walked in with a
stack of papers to Howard Putnam's office, pulled a chair from the
small, circular marble table on the other side of Putnam's desk, and
sat down heavily. He had spent the first week on the job getting a
feel of the financial apparatus Howard Swanson had set up after
Swanson had restructured the Byzantine system Beckwith had
used. Both Putnam and Guthrie had expected things to be grim, but
what Guthrie had found was a deep shock. Braniff International
Corporation and its subsidiary, Braniff Airways, Incorporated, was
in one hell of a bad position. It had far more debts and far less
revenue and traffic then Putnam had figured. The cash level was
hovering between $40 million and $50 million, which Guthrie interpreted as "ten days of cash"—or enough to run the company and
make the payroll for ten days without another cent coming in. It

had been lower at times in the past, but Putnam seized on that line, and the cry of "when we got here Braniff only had ten days of cash" was to be heard internally at Braniff (and later in the press) as Putnam and Guthrie attempted to administer the necessary shock treatment to the rank and file to get their quick cooperation.

There were certainly no outside sources of dollars available—by this point the idea that anyone would lend Braniff any significant amount of cash was laughable. In addition, cash that might have been realized from the continuing frantic sale of spare aircraft and equipment couldn't be kept. The lenders, especially the insurance company work-out people, wanted every dollar applied to the debt.[1]

If the company continued to lose money—money that would come from that small cash cushion—the day would finally come when Braniff wouldn't have the cash to pay the new bills it incurred every day for fuel and catering and payroll and a thousand other things. They had to prepay the fuel a week at a time. The day they couldn't write a covered check for the fuel—well, the house of cards would collapse. The February 1 repayment deadline meant little— Braniff wouldn't be able to spare cash for repaying principal or interest for years. A total restructuring of the debt in which the lenders would take newly issued stock—equity in the company—in place of dollars for much of the $668 million debt, and defer payments on the remainder for three to five years, was the only way.

Guthrie would have to work a miracle or two. He had to get to know the lenders and gain their respect and confidence practically overnight. Unfortunately, thanks to Putnam's insistence on a clean

---

[1] These work-out people, especially the younger ones in their late twenties and early thirties, were finance specialists in the area of extracting dollars from a recalcitrant or financially ill client. They knew little of airlines and most couldn't have cared less. Some were shrill, ungentlemanly people who by late December were pointing fingers across tables and yelling obscenities in meetings with Braniff executives with a ferocity they seemed to enjoy. As Bill Huskins would say in early 1982, "You'd be amazed what some of these young men in their three-piece suits can say to an airline chairman almost twice their age!" The tragedy was that in their drive to intimidate and squeeze cash from Braniff, they refused to face the fact that if allowed to retain some of the funds from sold equipment, Braniff might survive to pay back all or a greater percentage of the loans. Their collective attitude was a flippant dismissal of the problem: An airline was a cash machine, therefore Braniff would find a way if pushed hard enough. The lenders themselves were a major contributor to the problem—they just didn't want to listen.

slate, Howard Swanson wasn't around to do the introductions or ease the transition.[2]

As he and Putnam agreed, a restructure was desperately needed before Christmas. Otherwise the Christmas traffic would fall victim to the same travel agency dithering that had already brought Braniff to the brink.

The two men were awed by the enormity of the task and the condition of the company. Putnam's distaste for anything that reminded him of Lawrence deepened as he learned where so many of the dollars were going: Leases and commitments from the 1978–79 expansion frenzy were continuing to drain the treasury. Just the lease at Atlanta's new terminal, where Braniff had committed to several very expensive gates—now almost unused except for a little contract work for Ozark Air Lines—was draining $60,000 from the accounts monthly.

Putnam was appalled at the business-as-usual attitude he had already encountered in several lower-level management people who didn't seem to understand that the castle was surrounded by the enemy and the moat was dry. He was also appalled at the many different layers of management. Braniff had over forty officers, a legacy of Lawrence's willingness to bring in new blood but reluctance to fire the deadwood. It was a number Putnam was determined to reduce rapidly.

Howard Putnam was known for his straightforward management style. He tried to reduce a management structure to its simplest possible form and attack problems in the same manner. The style reflected enlightened modern managerial methods, but to many in the industry it was simplistic. This criticism would surface time and again in the industry assessments of Putnam's approach.

Guthrie lifted himself out of the decorator chair and headed out the doorway to plan the first meeting with the principal lender banks in New York, who were curious (and apprehensive) about the new finance kid at Braniff.

M. Phillip Guthrie was approaching his thirty-seventh birthday with a good reputation in finance, but he was regarded as inexperienced for the enormity of the Braniff challenge by many holding the loan papers. He had graduated from Louisiana Tech and the University of Michigan Graduate School of Business, and by the

[2] Casey, when later asked why Swanson wasn't retained for a transition period to work with Guthrie, said, "That's an interesting idea! I did think of using him in legal—you know, he's a lawyer—but it just didn't work out."

time he joined Southwest at Putnam's invitation he was a CPA in both Texas and Louisiana. Guthrie had begun his career as a financial consultant to Price, Waterhouse in Houston, but in 1972 he moved to Dallas to become vice president for finance for a small pharmaceutical firm called Vicra—which manufactured medical equipment in Dallas. When Vicra was acquired by Baxter-Travenoll Corporation, Guthrie was transferred to Chicago. He wasn't interested in Chicago, so he began looking around Dallas for another position. A mutual friend sent Putnam one of Guthrie's résumés, which led to the start of a most unique working relationship.

On February 20, 1979—2½ years before his move with Putnam to Braniff—Guthrie came on board at Southwest as vice president for finance and chief financial officer under Putnam. It was Guthrie's first exposure to the airline business, and that's exactly the sort of virgin financier Putnam had been looking for. Putnam wanted a fresh approach. What he got was an insecure younger man from Monroe, Louisiana, with extensive talents in finance—a man whose personal tastes differed from Putnam's but with whom Putnam could work in great harmony. Putnam and Guthrie always seemed to know what the other was thinking. (They would later develop the slightly unnerving habit of finishing each other's sentences in interviews.) The two men formed a team that worked as smoothly as a system of finely meshed gears, and that team approach developed into a dependency, making the idea of Braniff without Guthrie unacceptable to Putnam.

The close teamwork with which Putnam and Guthrie were able to attack their massive task in the first few weeks on the job was a double-edged sword: It permitted an efficient coordination of their efforts, but it also made it apparent to the rest of the upper management at Braniff that it was a two-man show. From the Southwest 737 pictures on their walls to the new-entry airline philosophies they were getting ready to impose on the patient, Howard Putnam and Phil Guthrie had obviously arrived on a rescue mission—but had not joined Braniff. They simply didn't have time. The situation was too critical. Instead of Putnam and Guthrie joining Braniff management, Braniff management had joined Putnam and Guthrie and had yet to prove themselves worthy of being retained. If there had been any doubts as to Casey's true position before, the events of October would erase them.

Putnam had to decide rapidly which of the existing Braniff officers could be brought into his circle and trusted, and for this task he turned to an industrial psychologist he had used in more leisurely times at Southwest—Dr. John Mauer.

Mauer's specialty included drawing up profiles of the different members of a management team, and deciding on the basis of interviews and involved psychological test results who would be compatible with the management style of the person running the organization. There is much to be said for the technique, which is on the cutting edge of modern managerial theory, but its most significant defect involves speed—it is difficult to do the job well in a hurry. When Mauer had used the same technique at Southwest, there were no crises—no army of angry creditors beating down the door. The resulting realignment of senior personnel at Southwest had been handled with at least some care and concern for the people involved.

At Braniff, Mauer had to work fast. Since many of the executives he was interviewing and testing were working at a frantic pace trying to contribute to the salvage of their company, Mauer's efforts seemed somewhat trivial at best, an infuriating insult at worst.

The personnel changes started before Mauer had begun his work. Neal Robinson, for one, finally accepted an offer from a new long-distance phone company based in Dallas, U.S. Tel, which had been trying to separate him from Braniff for a year. Robinson recognized the fact that only one man would be making the marketing decisions for Braniff, and that man was Howard Putnam. A separate, strong-willed marketing officer would be incompatible.

Harding Lawrence's son, Jim Lawrence, turned in his resignation in early October as well. With the shutdown of the Pacific routes the year before, he had taken over the job of vice president for domestic and international affairs. Now Sam Coats, the lawyer who had handled the divorce of Jim's parents fourteen years before, was brought in from his position as director of the Texas Research League in Austin to fill the post. Coats, who had in the interim served as general counsel of Texas International (which had undergone a metamorphosis from a regional carrier to a low-cost, low-fare competitor to Southwest), had wanted to leave law practice behind. The Braniff job was an exciting chance to do just that.

John Casey had been an effective communicator in the previous year but had been caught up in the aura of the acceptability his direct contact with the rank and file had produced, and in the end he had become captive to it—enjoying the spotlight and worried about losing it. Now with Putnam on center stage, Casey's public appearances began to lose their meaning—for him as well as the employees.

Putnam believed in employee communication as a cornerstone of his corporate organization. Similar in style to Miami chief pilot Ken Mase, Putnam didn't believe in cloaking the operations or the strategic planning of the company in secrecy and hiding it from the people who made up the organization (although Putnam's conclusions regarding what Braniff would have to become were not fully revealed). An informed employee would be less likely to impede needed changes and less likely to feign ignorance of the financial plight while hiding behind the potboiler rhetoric of a union spokesman. Putnam just as firmly believed in keeping the management layers thin. He wanted the top people—himself included—close enough to the employees to be able to hear plainly the complaints, suggestions, problems, and the overall heartbeat of the operation. It was a refreshing attitude—Braniff had never been managed that way.

Putnam was no pushover, however. Although he tended to err on the side of sensitivity to employee complaints, he demanded his people honestly investigate and fairly deal with the problems the ranks might bring to his attention. Braniff under Putnam would not be whipsawed by the union in the manner Casey had permitted, although some of his managers still felt a lack of support and believed that Putnam as well was more concerned about what the employees thought of them than what they, the managers, thought of the employees.

Then again, he didn't have time to be concerned about feelings—the castle was on fire! For all the positive aspects of his open approach to employee relations, Putnam's failure (or refusal) to attempt to understand certain issues of historical concern and great importance to the various labor groups led him to act insensitively—a mistake that would damage his ability to dissolve the old distrust of management.

For instance, while Putnam technically understood the role of seniority in the ranks of pilots, flight attendants, mechanics, and the rest of the contract force, he had little respect for it. He saw too many prime examples of incompetent people attaining higher positions solely because of seniority. Although he was correct in concluding that the system had serious problems, he was thoroughly unmoved by the emotional and professional attachment his contract people had to the system.[3]

Among the many employee meetings Howard Putnam organized in the first month at the world headquarters was one for the chief pilots, who had come in from Braniff's outstation pilot bases to meet Putnam and Guthrie and hear the details of the new order. The meeting was held in the entry-area conference room at the world headquarters.

Howard Putnam had greeted everyone individually before beginning his formal presentation.

"Folks, I first want to thank you for giving up a night at home to come in and get together with us. Guthrie and I have been trying to meet everyone and get the message out. The basic message, I guess, would be the fact that there is change in the air. Are we going to adjust, and live to grow again, or are we going to be internally rigid, and go the way of the dinosaur?"

Putnam's style of delivery was very conversational, and his timing—especially for quips, or one-liners—was good. He discussed his background with the group—the fact that he was a pilot only to the extent of three-hundred hours in his father's Piper J-3 Cub and that his wife was a former stewardess—before turning to the more serious subjects.

"I came here because of the challenge. It's an opportunity to do something no one has ever done before. Acker is going to try it at Pan Am, but we have a better chance here. What we have to do by Christmas Eve, December twenty-fourth—we have to, one: come up with and submit and get approved a new, creative financial restructure plan for the lenders; two: we have to decide, Who is Bran-

---

[3] The seniority system is at its worst when no valid, independent system of qualification exists to control the quality of those promoted. The systems controlling the qualification of pilots are governed by the Federal Air Regulations (administered by the FAA), and therefore, despite the use of an airline's own people as check pilots, there is enough FAA supervision to prevent unqualified people from advancing to captain or copilot just because they have the seniority to bid for the position. In the ranks of the Teamsters, the IAM, and most other unions, however, the advancement-quality screening process—or qualification—was governed by a series of tests for which the answers were too readily available, and that did little to test for some of the most important talents and personality traits needed in the job. The testing system was all but useless; therefore, the only thing that governed advancement in the Teamster ranks was politics (who gave you the answers, who scored your test, etc.) and seniority numbers.

iff? What routes should we keep? and three: we have to get some productivity back into this company and create credibility and trust in management. You know our people, our employees, really believe that they can't trust management at Braniff. We've got to change that."

Putnam had the rapt attention of everyone in the room and was making constant eye contact—pressing home the importance of what he was saying.

"Now, the bottom line: I'm not going to the bankers unless and until we have substantial changes—I'd lose all credibility. So we've got to get those in place immediately, because we must have this restructuring done by Christmas. Also, we can't afford to let our ground equipment look like it is. This is another thing we've got to get changed—right now. The uniforms are shabby on too many people—DFW people at the gates and counters, for instance, and some of our pilots, I notice, aren't wearing the uniform right. We need to get uniforms for our ground people, and we're going to spend the money to do this, because as we're cutting back, if passengers look out and see shabby equipment and shabby clothes, they're going to lose confidence in us—figure the airline's maintenance must be shot to hell and we don't care—so we're going to change that.

"We've also got to get out of here—the world headquarters."

Putnam looked around the ceiling as he gestured to the room around them.

"I mean, it's a fabulous place, but it's much too big for Braniff now, and it's costing nearly eight hundred thousand dollars a month! I don't know where we'll relocate yet, but we've got to get out from under this expense, and we're looking for a company to lease this place."

Putnam motioned to Phil Guthrie, who was seated next to him.

"I'm going to ask Phil to tell you what we've found so far. It's not pretty, but we can overcome it."

Guthrie stood up, consulted his notes, and began. He was uncomfortable as a speaker, but he could get his message across.

"We've been here now thirteen days, and in that time we've found the company has a negative stockholder equity—more debt than assets—negative working capital—adequate capital for the short term, fortunately, but one of the major problems is the lenders' exaction of immediate improvements—they don't even want to talk about restructure until they're convinced we can show a profit."

Guthrie let that sink in before proceeding.

"Our debt, as of today, is six hundred sixty-eight million dollars, and that does not include four undelivered 747's at Boeing."

Guthrie looked around the group; most were hastily scribbling notes on the figures he was revealing.

"What are we doing about all this? Well—we're working with our attorneys and our accountants to come up with a good restructure plan so that we can get this—these deferment deadlines—off our back and get back some of the travel agencies, which is necessary for us to emerge healthy and prosperous down the road. I do want to make it clear that right now, there is no deal—no deal whatsoever with the lenders—and any deal we may get will be totally contingent on improvement in the company."

Putnam paused and then began again, slowly, emphasizing what he was saying. "I can't stress this enough—we must have long-term changes, not short-term—the lenders will disregard short-term stuff. We must have immediate change if we're going to survive—I mean if we're going to have an airline and jobs at all. It's that serious and that urgent. There is no more capital from outside—forget that, it's impossible. We have to do it from within!"

The members of the group left the next morning to return to their bases, all of them shaken.

Braniff First Officer Rod Williams was just getting ready to leave the Miami crewroom after arriving from a South American trip when the phone rang. It was 2:00 A.M. on a tropical October night, but the pilot on the other end of the line was calling from the West Coast, where it was three hours earlier. He had just heard a rumor about Putnam's intentions—that the airline was going to be dropping some South American routes—and wanted to find a fellow pilot or someone still around one of the crewrooms who could, he hoped, confirm that no such thing had been announced. Williams didn't have the best attitude toward the company—he, like so many others, had been buffeted by all the worries and cutbacks and base and seat changes so much lately, he really didn't care much anymore. Anyway, he thought he had Putnam figured out, and if this fellow pilot wanted an opinion, he'd give him one.

"I tell you what they're going to do, guy. Putnam's going to get rid of South America and London and Hawaii, start a Southwest-style airline with one class and low fares, eliminate all the bases except Dallas and maybe Houston, sell all but fifty-two of the 727's, and if you want to work for forty or fifty percent of what you're getting now, okay—otherwise get lost, we don't need you. He'll try to do it without a shutdown, but if everyone doesn't cave in, he'll file bankruptcy and restart it without the unions in a week or two. Braniff as we know it, chum, was dead the second they hired him. He's here to preside over the death of the Braniff we've been working for."

There was silence on the other end for a minute, then, "Rod, what've you been drinking? That's the most ridiculous thing I've ever heard. You're not serious?"

"Just wait, fella! Just wait!"

The Path of Despair
and Disgust

CHAPTER **28** Robert Crandall was stunned—not too stunned to be muttering some overt, salty descriptions through clenched teeth, but stunned nevertheless. In front of him on his desk sat a listing of what Braniff's new fare structure would be on November 24, 1981—twenty days away. It was devastating! That goddamn Putnam was trying to play Southwest Airlines with a dying trunk carrier. Crandall was sure Braniff was dead—now, with these ridiculous fares, they were going to try to take American along with them to financial ruin!

On November 5, six weeks after taking over, Howard Putnam announced the new market assault that the industry had been expecting. Braniff, in an ironic twist of phraseology sure to produce sophisticated snickering on the East Coast, launched "Texas class" service. It was a drastic contradiction of Braniff's traditional image sure to be seen as reverse snobbery.

After countless meetings and planning sessions that obscured the degree to which he had already made up his mind, Putnam announced the decision he had been hired to implement: Braniff would become a one-class, high-frequency, reduced-meal-service carrier with a cut-rate, simplified fare structure in imitation of so-called new-entry airlines such as Southwest, PSA, and New York Air. The key element, of course, was to get the costs down so they could charge whatever fares they wanted, but in the process Braniff was abdicating as a trunk carrier, as Putnam had felt it had to all along.

It was that reduced fare structure, however, that raised eyebrows and inflamed tempers in the corporate headquarters of American and Delta—who would have to match them or watch traffic stampede to "Texas class." Braniff was dropping the traditional mix of regular and special fares that numbered in the hundreds and substituting a list of only fifteen domestic fares—each of them representing an average drop of 40 percent from normal coach.

Putnam maintained that Braniff wouldn't be giving up 40 percent in revenue. The old system—the one which would be thrown out November 24—had so many discounted excursion fares in it that Braniff's average income from a coach seat was as much as 28 percent lower than the regular coach fares. If Texas class didn't increase the load factor (the average number of seats actually sold vs. the seats available on the aircraft), Braniff's already shrinking revenues would drop only another 11 to 13 percent. If enough additional passengers were attracted to Braniff flights because of Texas class, the higher resulting load factors might put enough extra dollars in the till to cancel out the loss, and with luck might exceed the loss and leave a profit. Of course, the low-cost side of the equation had not yet been achieved, so an immediate profit was unlikely.

The service itself was a contradiction of everything Braniff had ever tried to be. From the days of the free Braniff limousine (which would pick up a passenger at his home for a Braniff flight) through the El Dorado Silver Service in the fifties to the continental cuisine and splashy designer image under Lawrence in the late sixties and the image of elegance and somewhat snobbish affluence in the late seventies, Braniff had tried, with whatever degree of success, to personify in image the traditional meaning of the word "class." First class on a Braniff flight was usually an experience few international carriers could match. To take out the first class seats (except on the London, Honolulu, and South American runs, which would keep first class), cancel the sumptuous cuisine and in its place serve barbecue sandwiches or, too often, nothing at all—then on top of it to embrace the "Texas chic" back-to-basics movement of the urban cowboy by calling this plebeian exercise in airborne bus transportation for the masses "Texas class"—grated on the refined sensibilities of Texans who considered themselves cosmopolitan (and who wore boots only on weekends) like a fingernail on a blackboard.

The new Texas class image was true to Braniff tradition in only one respect: It was one hell of a gamble!

On October 26, Braniff had released the results for the third quarter of 1981: a net loss of $19.3 million and an operating loss of $13.9 million. As the analysts pointed out, the losses were smaller, but they were still losses, and those dollars had diminished the cash cushion. With a few more quarters like that, the cash well would run dry.

The load factors were below the break-even point and dropping. Something new and innovative had to be done, but the other factor in the equation was the high-traffic Christmas season. Braniff needed all the revenue it could get from Christmas. Should it launch the new, low-fare, low-yield service before Christmas and lose 13 percent of the revenue while hoping for greater load factors? Or should it hold on through Christmas with the existing high fares?

The travel agents were worried about a Braniff collapse during Christmas. If such a collapse occurred, a lot of trusting agencies might go down the drain, too. The agencies were going to protect themselves no matter how many goodwill visits they had from Casey, Braniff sales representatives, or concerned employees. It was a matter of survival. Consequently they began "plating away" from Braniff in increasing numbers, diverting cash much needed by Braniff to other carriers.[1]

---

[1] "Plating away" is a travel industry term that refers to the identification plates agencies use for particular carriers when they stamp a ticket. If an agency wants to write a ticket on Braniff but have American collect the cash, they use their in-house ticket stock and their American plate to stamp the ticket, and then they send the money collected to American. If the passenger actually uses the ticket on Braniff, the ticket is then presented by Braniff through the New York ticket clearinghouse against American's account, and American pays the money it originally collected

Something had to be done to get passengers either to bypass the agencies and buy their tickets directly from Braniff, or order their travel agents to book them on Braniff specifically. Launching Texas class in late November looked like the best solution when viewed from the bunker.

There was little doubt at the world headquarters that American and Delta would match the fares almost immediately (which is exactly what they did, while grumbling in public about Braniff's irresponsibility—presumably the irresponsibility of refusing to die without a fight). There was also great hope that the new jingles and promotion, the simplified fare structure, and the all-out effort of Braniff's remaining salespeople would generate a public ground swell of support for Texas class that would overwhelm the agencies' self-protective instincts.[2]

With Texas class, Braniff couldn't plan to get the customers on

---

on the ticket to Braniff. If Braniff should go under before the ticket can be used and the passenger subsequently demands a refund from the agency, the agency can make the refund from their own accounts, knowing that American in turn will refund the agency with the money they, American, had been holding from the original sale. The practice was widely denied—and just as widely used. Since nearly 60 percent of Braniff's business came through travel agencies, this meant that more and more ticket dollars were going to someone else for weeks or months until the ticket was used. Braniff's cash-flow problems were partially the result of the impact of this practice, but there was nothing Braniff could do. As the agencies lost faith in Braniff's ability to survive, their self-protective instinct took over.

[2] On top of the travel agencies' jitters over financial failure, Texas class presented them with lower aggregate commissions (same percentage but lower ticket price). It also embodied an implied philosophy that eventually an airline such as Braniff was trying to become would have no need for travel agency bookings. The travel agencies were losing sleep over this growing philosophy and losing faith in Putnam's ability to see the long-term damage he was doing to their relationship with Braniff.

Putnam did not enjoy a good reputation among the travel agents. While at Southwest, he had begun an innovative marketing technique called "Ticket-Net," which gave travel agencies a substantial discount on Southwest tickets only if they purchased them by cash in advance in large blocks. Southwest had survived largely without travel agencies because it was all short-haul, high-density, and had been built without dependency on the agencies. If Braniff had possessed a large enough war chest of cash, it might have achieved the same thing in the long run. In the short run, however, a large percentage of Braniff's existing business depended on travel agent bookings, and there was no margin in the cash drawer for losing any of that revenue while changing character. The travel agency employees might find Braniff's simplified fares easier to work with, but their employers were looking at a view of long-term survival—*their* long-term survival—and it was increasingly clear that Braniff had no place in that picture.

the basis of inflight amenities—there weren't many compared to the previous level of Braniff inflight service. They had to get them with fares. The Texas class message was: "Look here, America—good old Braniff is the only carrier that cares enough about giving you a good deal that they're willing to forgo the annual Christmas fare-gouge and give you an honest bargain! Are you going to reward that kind of public-spirited move by paying the same fare to the competition—who match Braniff's reductions only on routes they share with Braniff?"

The effectiveness of the message would depend on the depth and professionalism of the advertising campaign that would carry it, and Putnam hadn't been impressed with the ad agency at Braniff when he came in. (Wells Rich Greene was long gone, having been dismissed by Casey in early 1981.)

Putnam had a finance man he felt comfortable with; now he needed an ad agency he knew and trusted. At Southwest Airlines, he had developed a fast friendship and good working relationship with Tony Wainwright, chairman of The Bloom Agency in Dallas. Wainwright's people had done an excellent job for Southwest, and Putnam wished he had Bloom at Braniff. There was one way to accomplish that: He asked Wainwright to take the hefty risk of switching. The Bloom Agency thought it over and decided to gamble, too. They resigned Southwest and signed with Braniff, promptly getting to work on designing the Texas class promotion, which would include some of the best jingles Braniff had had in fifteen years.

Tony Wainwright, a rather diminutive man in physical stature in his late forties who ever so slightly resembles a smiling Irish leprechaun, had achieved substantial success and respect in the advertising business. He attacked the Braniff account challenge with Lawrencian dedication. An early riser, Wainwright took over an office at the world headquarters, arriving at seven each morning and heading back to his Dallas office at Bloom just after noon, where he'd work until dark. Wainwright was to keep up that pace for the next six months, participating in Braniff staff meetings and helping with the myriad of decisions as if he were an executive vice president (he was never on the Braniff payroll).

By the time Texas class was announced, Bloom had constructed the campaign around the slogan, "Braniff, the Airline with Texas Class." As Putnam told the press, "We want to show our Texas heritage and demonstrate to the public that Braniff is one of the things that makes Texas great. We're proud to be a Texas airline, and we want everyone to be proud of Braniff.''

Just south of the world headquarters, at American Airlines' corporate offices, a state of war had been declared. Braniff's new fares had been matched within a day, but American was already bleeding at the bottom line themselves. As Braniff had brought costs down with employee pay cuts and reduced ranks, American had been making a profit doing things the old way. Its fleet of jets was among the oldest of the trunk carriers, its pay scales were among the highest, and the fuel inefficiency of the four-engine Boeing 707's that American still used extensively was costing the company millions of dollars in extra fuel expense. American, facing the same recession that was beating the rest of the industry to death, now had to face a loss of the same 11 to 13 percent of revenues on routes it was trying to wrest from Braniff. American had enough cash to last through quite a few quarters of red ink, but the losses that Crandall and his people saw as inevitable because of the Texas class fares were staggering.

Meetings, formal and informal, went on for several days as Crandall tried to formulate strategy. The atmosphere was one of deep concern. Crandall and his senior staff decided on several steps, one of which was to go to American's people and ask for a 5 percent pay cut similar to Braniff's—a move that within the month would be resoundingly, angrily rejected. Another was to let the American employees know exactly how hard things were going to get if American had to face Braniff at these fare levels indefinitely. If there was a plan beyond this administered from the executive suite—a plan for directing the hate-Braniff rage that resulted from whipping up employee discontent and blaming all on Braniff's new fares and its stubborn refusal to go out of business—American's leaders tried to hide it. Within months, however, the question would arise publicly of whether such actions were maverick—or whether they were part of a grand, desperate plan. The question would also arise as to whether American intended to use its Sabre reservations computer system as a weapon, or whether the growing list of complaints and reports of anti-Braniff activities related to Sabre were somehow coincidental or inherent to the normal programming. The motive for almost any action American might take could be found in their general alarm reaction to the Texas class fare structure. It was a monkey Crandall was frantic to get off his back.

Braniff Flight 501, DFW to Honolulu, departed daily from Gate 12 at 1:15 P.M. In the first two weeks of the Texas class fares, and with the Christmas season building up steam, the advance reservations had been good. On this particular day, however, the *Great Pumpkin* 747 had only about a hundred passengers booked out of over three hundred seats available. Within two hours of departure American had called Braniff reservations and asked to block another one hundred seats. Their competing flight—a 747 also—had a mechanical at the gate, and they were going to send their passengers on Braniff. A hundred more meals were ordered by Braniff at the usual, considerable expense, but by 12:45 P.M., none of American's people had shown up at the gate. At 1:05 P.M. the word came in through the computer: American had fixed their problem; they didn't need the hundred seats. Of course, it was too late to turn back the hundreds of dollars' worth of extra meals Braniff had ordered.

Two days later a Braniff agent was talking to a friend who worked for American and usually worked their Honolulu flight. He had been on duty the same day American's supposedly cancelled jumbo went out on time. He was puzzled by his Braniff friend's statement—there had been no mechanical as far as he knew. Neither man could figure it out.

DFW Customer Service Manager Billy McCutcheon sat back in his chair—disgusted. He had just spent the past thirty minutes of a cold December Friday evening trying to convince one of his lead agents why all of them ought to try the new idea for outside agents, that of greeting passengers instead of dropping the 727 rear stairway. It had been all but useless. The agent was one of the union representatives for the Teamster group and one of the best of the customer-service people. But in his representation, he was one of the people McCutcheon considered a hothead. Instead of suggesting to and guiding the people he represented, he simply reacted to their opinions and passed them on. The agents who had been talking to him were some of the hard-core dissidents. They wanted no part of management-sponsored tests of new ideas. The company was only lying to them—plotting to take away more of their jobs. The customers could get along without someone in the jetway.

As McCutcheon knew, this agent himself had tried the idea and

296

really liked it. But he refused to impress that on the others. After over a year of fighting this battle, which Regional Vice President for DFW Doug MacArthur had handed him in the first place, he was still miles from the goal. The Dale Carnegie course they had brought in in the previous spring had done wonders in changing the public-contact persona of many of the agents, but when it came to listening to anyone in management, regardless of the worth of the recommendation, nothing had changed. Braniff still had no one to meet deplaning passengers.

There was a genuine anger rippling through the pilot ranks. Their contract negotiations had stalled, and binding arbitration was the next step. The ALPA bargaining representatives had opened in August with a change from tradition. Instead of the usual "Christmas tree" opener asking for everything but pay for no work, they opened with a rescue package: no pay increase, substantial increases in productivity, and what they felt was a massive package of professional restraint and sacrifice for Braniff. The company negotiators, however, simply accepted the pilots' proposal and promptly demanded much more. Putnam had then arrived, and after being briefed that the pilots were so scared they would agree to anything, he began demanding an immediate end to such sacred cows as duty rigs and single layover rooms.[3]

---

[3] Pilot pay calculations are somewhat complicated and are based on what are called duty rigs. At Braniff, a pilot was paid the greatest of three calculated numbers. For example, if he had flown five hours and been on duty for ten hours and been away from base for thirty-five hours on a particular flight, the calculations were as follows: Five hours of flight (on a 1 for 1 basis) equaled five hours of pay. Ten hours of on-duty time (on a 1 for 2 basis) meant one hour of pay for every two hours on-duty, a total of five hours of pay. Thirty-five hours away from home base (on a 1 for 3½ basis) meant ten hours of pay. Taking the greatest number, such a pilot would receive ten hours of pay for that flight sequence.

Substantial productivity increases can be realized by an airline when it minimizes the time the pilots spend away without flying—and minimizes the time on duty between flights. This is where efficient, enlightened, but humanistic scheduling can save or lose millions for an airline. The duty rigs are to protect pilots from being left on duty or in the system for long periods without being paid for their time. Thus carefully written duty rigs provide as much an incentive for an airline to schedule its pilots efficiently as they provide a protective shield for the aircrews against callous mishandling. To try to loosen drastically or do away with duty rigs, which was Putnam's original demand, would mean a major realignment of lifestyle for the aircrews. With no duty rigs, a pilot could be kept away from home for thirty days and paid for only fifteen days of flying. This was one of the areas of great and historic pilot concern about which Howard Putnam was insensitive and that almost wrecked his new relationship with the pilots before it began.

The pilots were furious. As they were the only pilot group in the nation to agree regularly to a no-strike, binding-arbitration clause in each contract, they knew that at worst, if they had to go to binding arbitration, they'd end up with terms at least as good as the present contract. Putnam claimed that would be ruinous to Braniff. If they permitted a binding-arbitration award at the same contract rates, the lenders would never accept it and Braniff would die. He'd shut it down. Thus, warned Putnam, it all depended on them.

The response Putnam got was not what he had expected. Many of the group were indeed scared—they had nowhere to go but Braniff—but the essence of an airline pilot is usually self-assured independence, and the prevailing attitude was that no one was going to march in from Southwest Airlines or anywhere else and ruin their jobs without getting a fight. They didn't feel they were ignoring the peril the company faced—they had offered a landmark contract with unprecedented concessions and had been rebuffed. Putnam suddenly found himself facing a union of angry pilots in revolt. As many of the senior captains saw it, Putnam was demanding they give up in one stroke things that had taken decades to win. The ALPA negotiators tried the idea of agreeing to the current contract with a side letter of temporary relief. "No way," was Putnam's reply. "The lenders won't buy it. Labor expense reduction has to be real and permanent."

Neither Putnam nor his key people understood just how far the pilots (as many other groups within the company) had come down the path of despair and disgust. More than most, they (as well as their crew companions, the flight attendants) had been moved around the country with frightening frequency as bases opened and closed like doors in a carnival fun house, leaving captains as first officers while second officers found themselves furloughed or barely hanging on to junior positions. Salaries were cut by as much as half by the reductions in flying position, and every trip into a crewroom was a descent into hell—the hell of reading and hearing nothing but bad news, trip after trip after trip. They were, as a group, tired and disgusted with all of it. The battle cry—more of a dismissal—gathered steam in the first few days of December: "Tell Putnam either to accept the offer or fold the sonofabitch—I don't really care anymore." The deep weariness could be read on another scale as well, as the number of pilot sick leave days used throughout the force soared to unheard-of levels.

On December 6 the company gave in and accepted a modified form of what the ALPA negotiators had offered to begin with. Putnam was able to call it a mutual victory—the pay concessions would save Braniff millions in both the long and the short term. To many of the pilots, however, the contract (which was eventually signed on New Year's Eve) was anticlimactic, and Putnam had already been discredited.

Under Putnam's new regime, management changes were being made with increasing urgency, as he was determined to get rid of the many-layered managerial structure that had traditionally choked vertical communication in the company. With Dr. Mauer's help, Putnam had trimmed the ranks of management steadily up through Christmas. There wasn't time to worry about feelings. People had to be let go or moved.

One of those reassigned was taken from his position in the employee-relations disaster area known as Braniff reservations. This manager's methods of handling people were felt by many to be the principal cause of the atmosphere of hatred and distrust that fulminated through the ranks of the reservations agents. As one reservations employee of fifteen years put it, "Braniff [reservations] taught me to hate. I never knew how before." In his place, to try to clean up the incredible mess, Putnam brought in a man with years of experience in the reservations branch of another major carrier, American Airlines, though he too had to be replaced by early spring.

A second industrial psychologist, Dr. Don Beck, came on board in December. While John Mauer was working on senior management, Beck was to analyze the ranks and lower management and design an ideal organizational structure for the company to use in attacking the overall bad morale and the human problems in the public-contact positions. He was also to try to change the nearly pathological distrust of management that permeated the company. Beck seemed appalled at the state of things at DFW and throughout the company and was faced with the task of correcting it almost overnight.

As Christmas approached, it was apparent that Texas class was neither a flop nor a savior. The load factors were rising, but the bottom line was still red. The pilots had agreed to a concessionary contract, but the Teamsters and the IAM remained to be dealt with, and the leader of the mechanics' union—a fulminating individual by the name of L. T. Faircloth—had told Putnam point-blank that he'd see Braniff shut down and liquidated before he'd agree to concessions of any sort.

Now the February 1 restructure deadline would begin to haunt them. The before-Christmas restructure that Howard Putnam had confidently figured he could achieve had been a dream.

The Monkey on American's Back

It was a Monday morning in December when Tony Wainwright looked across the world headquarters conference table and threw out the idea. "Why don't we have a two-fer?"

The reaction was less than overwhelming. "What's a 'two-fer,' Tony?"

Every other Thursday had become a crisis at Braniff with a major payroll and more advance payments due to the fuel companies. Meetings like this had been held since Putnam's arrival to figure out ways to raise enough cash to meet the obligations of the upcoming Thursday and still maintain the cash cushion. Tony Wainwright's idea was one of many thrown out during such sessions.

The advertising executive explained the well-known gambit of bars and theaters and retailers: Buy one, get one free. A two-for-one, otherwise known as a cleverly packaged 50 percent discount.

"Naw—that's too expensive." Putnam went on to other subjects.

Over the next month, Wainwright spent some time lobbying the other senior officers for the "two-fer." By mid-January, faced with the realization that Texas class was still not pulling Braniff load factors up over the ledge and into the black, Howard Putnam decided to take another look. Wainwright was ready with the figures, which seemed to make sense. the sale would run for only six hours and would involve only the Dallas-Fort Worth area. Anyone buying a full-fare ticket at the Texas class rates to anywhere on the Braniff domestic system would receive a second identical ticket for $1. Putnam along with Phil Guthrie, Sam Coats, Tony Wainwright, and Ron Ridgeway (vice president for customer service) made the decision in the hall.

"Why not a three-for-the-price-of-two?" Ridgeway wanted to know as the meeting broke up with no decision yet. "It wouldn't cost as much."

Guthrie and Coats both shook their heads. Guthrie spoke up. "People don't travel in threes, Ron."

Sam Coats, whose speaking voice is in the range of a tenor reminiscent of Dennis Day, had a characteristic manner of cocking his head to one side with furrowed brow when he was concerned or skeptical about something. Putnam had started to tease him good-naturedly. "Uh-oh, Sam's got that worried look again!" He did indeed.

"Tony, do you suppose the travel agents can handle the rush if this thing really does go over big? I mean, we won't be letting them know till the last minute."

"They'll handle it."

"Okay, guys," Putnam concluded. "Let's do it. Get the planning started."

The traditional after-Christmas traffic slump had set in, but Braniff couldn't afford it. Now Wainwright's idea of a two-for-one sale provided a glimmer of renewed hope.

There were drawbacks to the idea. The press would see it as a desperate cash-grab by Braniff. The lenders would have to be told in advance, and their reaction might not be good. In addition, the tickets sold might be purchased in place of some of the full-fare tickets that people would buy anyway later in the spring, and many customers might cash in full-fare tickets already purchased to get the two-for-one offer. On the other hand, the plan held an important enticement: cash. If it worked, the resulting cash probably would see the company through the next two months by building back the cash reserve.

The project had to be kept top secret. The company began the planning with elaborate precautions. If American or Delta got word of it, they would find a way to destroy its effect. Braniff could pull it off only with complete surprise.

Braniff computer programmers were sworn to secrecy in preparing the programs, radio spots were produced in remote studios and the tapes kept under guard, and artwork was done piecemeal by people at Bloom so that only a handful knew what the final product actually said. The target date was tentatively set for February 5. All of them knew that American and Delta would match the deal instantly, but they wouldn't be able to match the momentum. Putnam expected a howl of protest from American and specifically Robert Crandall. Putnam had no way of knowing how loudly Crandall was already yelling behind closed doors about all other aspects of Braniff's Texas class, but Putnam was about to find out. Within a week, Crandall would make an intemperate and profane telephone call, a recording of which would eventually find its way to a federal criminal grand jury.

The press had been keeping a close and jaundiced eye on Braniff. The February 1 deadline set by Braniff's lenders was now mere days away, and everyone from *The Wall Street Journal* to the *Dallas Morning News* was watching for signs and signals. *The Wall Street Journal* weighed in on January 26 with a darkly optimistic article:

HOLDING PATTERN: DESPITE BLEAK OUTLOOK, BRANIFF IS EX-
PECTED TO KEEP ON FLYING.
. . . BANKS ARE LIKELY TO EXTEND LOAN-PAYMENT DEADLINE;
AIRLINE CUTS COSTS, FARES.
. . . CAJOLING AND ARM-TWISTING.

DALLAS—It sounds like the perils of Pauline. Will Braniff International, which has lost hundreds of millions of dollars in the last couple of years, be able to survive? Will the banks and insurance companies, which have allowed Braniff to continue flying without making payments on its loans grant another extension beyond February 1?

Even if Braniff is given another lease on life by its lenders, can it survive the pounding it is getting from its much bigger archrival, American Airlines? American is doing what it can to hasten Braniff's demise, including adding new American flights on Braniff routes. Sources say American has also been trying to persuade lenders to pull the plug on Braniff and let it go broke.

As bleak as Braniff's future appears, most analysts think the airline will keep flying. The lenders are expected to extend the Feb. 1 payments deadline. With this help, Braniff says, it can generate enough cash on its own to parry American's competitive thrusts.

"It's like defying the law of gravity," says one securities analyst. "Braniff, for all practical purposes, is broke, but they're still flying."

Braniff recently slashed its unrestricted coach fares 45%, a move that American had to match to stay competitive. That, says American, will cost it $7 million a month in lost revenues. "American is saying to its lenders, 'if you keep a failing carrier like Braniff going with those damned interest-free loans, you're going to drive American to the wall too,'" says one securities analyst. That could endanger loans that many of the same lenders have made to American.

The reason that the lenders are nevertheless expected to keep Braniff going is simple. If they forced the airline into bankruptcy Feb. 1 and operations halted, the lenders would wind up with the collateral backing their loans: dozens of 727 jets. But because the whole industry is suffering from the prolonged U.S. travel slump, there is practically no market for 727's now.

"What would we do with a bunch of 727's sitting in our parking lot?" asks an executive at one insurance company.

Braniff is under fire from other carriers. Smallish Southwest Airlines, which flies short-haul routes in Braniff territory, is planning to expand rapidly. The Southwest fleet is scheduled to grow from 25 jets in 1981 to 38 by 1983. And Delta Airlines, a big and powerful carrier like American, is increasingly invading Dallas. Recently, for example, it began service between Dallas and New York, a major Braniff route.

"We're being squeezed, both from the top by the likes of American and Delta and from the bottom by airlines such as Southwest," says Braniff's Chairman, Mr. Casey. The squeeze, Mr. Casey has estimated, cost Braniff over $100 million in revenues from June through December.

Soaring interest charges on its debt, coupled with its operating losses, have wiped out Braniff's equity. The carrier now has a negative net worth. "Braniff," says one securities analyst, "has bled to death."

Braniff Captain Ken Sundmark was sitting on a rather tattered couch near the coatracks on the south wall of DFW's pilot lounge, looking grim. He had been the leader of the ALPA negotiating team that had wrangled long and hard to conclude the new concession-laced contract now being hailed by Putnam as an example for the other unions to follow. Several fellow pilots had cornered him, asking about the true state of things, and one in particular had been pressing him about an item of personal interest that hadn't been corrected in the new contract. Sundmark was tired.

"Look, you simply have no idea what the situation was in there—the demands they were making and the figures they were showing us. We're down to just a couple of weeks of operating money."

"Ken, did you see that *Wall Street* article on the bulletin board?"

"Yeah."

"They think we're going to make it. Did Putnam indicate otherwise?"

Sundmark sighed and looked pained. He couldn't possibly give these fellows in ten minutes a true sense of what he had been through and the impending disaster he had sensed in the past few months . . . a disaster not only for the company, but even if it survived, a disaster for the Braniff they all knew. It was gone. How do you tell that to someone with so many years invested and nowhere else to go?

"The lenders will go along with another deferment—probably to October."

"And after that?"

Sundmark just looked at him.

"Ken?"

"I—I don't think we're going to make it. We may get through the summer, but after that . . ."

He could see the other pilots were stunned—in the midst of the intensive self-help programs (they were less than five feet from a volunteer desk in the crewroom), admitting that it was hopeless was heretical.

Putnam and Guthrie shared the news by phone first. The final lender had relented, figuratively kicking and screaming all the way, and the payment deadline had once again been extended—this time to October 31. Midland Marine and Prudential (among others) had let it be known, however, that this was it. Involuntary bankruptcy would await Tom Braniff's airline on November 1 if Braniff hadn't jumped through enough hoops in the interim to earn a restructure.

Howard Putnam had walked into Braniff General Counsel Jim Riley's office with an amazed look on his face and told him about the telephone message Irma Jensen (his secretary) had just handed him. It said to call Bob Crandall. Crandall was the president of American. When Putnam had come on board, he had been sternly warned by Braniff's lawyers that with the suspicions the company had about American's activities against Braniff, he must have no unprotected contact with the officers of American. The potential for civil and criminal antitrust law violations was just too great. Now Crandall waited a return call.

"You can't do it, Howard, unless you're protected," Riley told him flatly.

Riley pulled a tape recorder and a suction-cup telephone pickup device from his desk and connected them to his phone receiver. Putnam dialed the number of Crandall's office, and as Riley's tape machine recorded the call, began listening to Crandall's attempts to bait him.

Principally Crandall was upset about a new advertisement Braniff had been running proclaiming Braniff better than American in on-time performance. Robert Crandall was incensed.

"Don't you know we've always had an agreement that we wouldn't run that type of ad against each other?"

"No, Bob, I never heard of such an agreement. Besides, that sort of agreement would be illegal."

Crandall continued, lapsing into his usual vocabulary as he got on the general subject of the Texas class monkey Braniff had put on his back.

"I think it's dumb as hell for Christ's sake, all right, to sit here and pound the shit out of each other and neither one of us making a fucking dime."

As the recorder picked up the sounds, Putnam looked at his attorney. Neither he nor Riley could believe this call. Putnam began to answer—carefully. "Well . . ."

Crandall continued, "I mean, you know, goddamn, what the fuck is the point of it?"

Putnam took a deep breath and replied.

"Nobody asked American to serve Harlingen. Nobody asked American to serve Kansas City, and there were low fares in there, you know, before. So . . ."

"You better believe it, Howard. But, you, you, you know, the complex is here—ain't gonna change a goddamn thing, all right? We can, we can both live here and there ain't no room for Delta. But there's, ah, no reason that I can see, all right, to put both companies out of business."

"But if you're going to overlay every route of American's on top of over, on top of every route that Braniff has—I can't just sit here and allow you to bury us without giving our best effort."

"Oh, sure, but Eastern and Delta do the same thing in Atlanta [to Braniff] and have for years."

Putnam paused, glancing again at Riley. Crandall had spent the first half of the call trying to bait Putnam into a suggestion. Now he was being coy. "Do you have a suggestion for me?"

Crandall's voice came back loud and emphatic: "Yes. I have a suggestion for you. Raise your goddamn fares twenty percent. I'll raise mine the next morning."

"Robert, we . . ."

"You'll make more money and I will too!"

"We can't talk about pricing."

"Oh, bullshit, Howard. We can talk about any goddamn thing we want to talk about!"

When the conversation was over and the receiver was back on the hook, Putnam and Riley sat there for a minute, shaking their heads. Riley turned off the tape recorder, removed the suction-cup device from the phone receiver, and mulled over what to say as Howard Putnam mentally reviewed the call, wondering if he had handled the exchange correctly. Of one thing he was certain: Getting Riley's help had been the right thing to do. Obviously Crandall and American were so frantic to get rid of Braniff's fares, or Braniff, that not even legal constraints seemed to guide their actions—at least not in this case. Crandall's words on that tape, if ever heard by a federal investigator, would end up burning Robert Crandall and American. If nothing else, that sort of language in the Bible Belt was not what the Dallas business community expected from their corporate leaders—not that their corporate leaders didn't know how to hold their own with undeleted expletives. There was a time and a place. Crandall apparently had no feel for this truth.

What was more ominous was the way the obvious, enraged desperation Crandall displayed dovetailed with the things Braniff had been hearing officially and unofficially. Even *The Wall Street Journal* had reported on American's alleged meetings with mutual lenders—something Braniff had heard about shortly after those meetings were supposed to have taken place. It seemed incredible. There was a legal line of demarcation between fair competition and unfair actions in violation of the Sherman antitrust laws. You could take your company up to the line and peer over, but one toenail placed across that line could bring the U.S. Justice Department and the Securities and Exchange Commission, not to mention the Civil Aeronautics Board and a myriad of other federal agencies, storming in to punish the offending company. If American really had asked the creditors—any creditors—to pull the plug on Braniff's loans, at the very least an initial legal question would be raised as to whether that, in itself, constituted a violation. It was a dangerous move if it had actually been done.

There were many other strange occurrences, however, that people in the industry began reporting to Braniff (usually clandestinely) just after the first of the year. There were questions about Braniff's flight listings that Braniff paid American to list in the American Sabre system, American's reservations computer system, which a majority of the travel agents in the nation use in their offices. Suddenly, according to numerous reports that were at the time unconfirmed, Braniff's listings were more difficult to pull up—and the accuracy had become questionable. A Braniff flight would have a substantial number of available seats, but the Sabre computers would show it overbooked and unavailable for sale.

Jim Riley took charge of the tape recording and locked it away. For Crandall, it was a ticking incendiary bomb—and neither he nor American's legal people knew it existed.

By Friday, February 5, the target date for the two-for-one sale, all had been prepared. On Thursday, private messengers had delivered sealed tape cartridges of the radio commercials to fifteen Dallas radio stations, to be opened only by designated station authorities at the proper time the next day. The copy for full-page newspaper ads for the Friday afternoon edition were also delivered in secrecy. Everything cooperated but the weather. On Friday morning, an ice storm hit Dallas.

After some rapid consultation among Wainwright, Putnam, and Coats, the fear that the hazardous driving conditions would damage the sales prevailed: The order to cancel went out. At one radio station, the spot with the announcement of the sale was pulled from the cartridge machine ten seconds after the opening jingle had started. They almost blew it.

On Monday, February 8, the officers decided on a new target date of Wednesday, February 10, and this time they scheduled it to run for forty-eight hours, from Wednesday midnight to Friday midnight. Everyone was getting nervous. The copy had been circulating through too many hands. Would the secret hold?

Tuesday night a number of Braniff pilots and flight attendants who were constantly volunteering to help with anything to do with selling Braniff received calls from Ron Ridgeway: Could they come out the following morning for a secret assignment? Most accepted. As Wednesday morning passed the coffee-break hour, the pilots and a group of recruited flight attendants were on the phones, calling over six hundred Dallas-Fort Worth area travel agencies and the travel departments of large area companies to tell them that at noon Braniff would announce a major promotion that could overwhelm their offices. They were given a quick explanation of the sale. The agencies were puzzled but brought in extra help just in case. In the meantime, a number of the agencies who could not be counted among Braniff's best friends kept their receivers to their ear at the end of the Braniff call and immediately phoned American's sales department to tip them off.

The announcements hit the airwaves just before noon on fifteen area stations. They had been flashed to American and Delta by area travel agents, but radios were sought out and turned on all over the American offices to get the details of the promotion. Within two hours, American's vice president for sales, Robert Baker, had assembled a small emergency war council in his office—over fifty of American's top officers including attorneys, salespeople, and computer programmers, some of them unceremoniously sitting on the carpet, others leaning against walls. It took about an hour to design a matching program. American had possessed no contingency plan.

Delta's executives in Atlanta had received the first flash from their Dallas sales office just before noon. By late afternoon, the decision had been made not to match the offer, but the next morning, faced with long lines at travel agencies all over Dallas and Fort Worth, Delta had to join in as well.

In American's headquarters Crandall achieved a towering rage amply expressed with scathing linguistic descriptions of Putnam and Braniff and everything connected with it. This latest Braniff assault would take whatever revenues American was still collecting and slash them neatly in half!

The sale was an instant, overwhelming success, and Braniff began reaping the lion's share of the revenues despite American's and Delta's me-too entries. Just after midnight, when the sale began, incredibly long lines began to move in front of the extra-staffed DFW ticket counters. It seemed Wainwright had touched the precise nerve he wanted to reach in the public's late-winter/early-spring mentality, and psychologically the ice storm a week before had helped. People were ready to get away, and this gave them an excuse. Despite the fact that they had to spend the money on one full-fare ticket to get the second one, customers were reacting as if they had won a sweepstakes with the $1 coupon. It was a festive, holiday atmosphere wherever the tickets were sold, but not everyone was exhilarated. The travel agency owners, for example, were furious.

By Thursday noon, travel agencies all throughout the area were running low on help and ticket stock. The reservations switchboards of Braniff and American were jammed, and would-be ticket buyers were calling from all across the country to local travel agencies to get the two-for-one tickets. American, however, had jumped beyond the rules that Braniff had prescribed, and by Thursday was selling the two-for-one offer anywhere in the nation, although the trips had to begin or end at DFW. Braniff followed that move and opened the sale everywhere—though it was advertised only in the Dallas-Fort Worth area. The travel agents, however, were getting merely a dime on commission on the second ticket, which sold for $1, and they knew many of the full-fare tickets they had sold in the preceding weeks would be cashed in so people could take advantage of the new offer. Not only would they lose their normal 10 percent commission, all they would get in its place was a lousy dime. Late Wednesday afternoon Dee Yaran of "THE Travel Agency" in Dallas (one of the largest chains) and John Wile of Professional Travel asked for an emergency meeting with Putnam and Vice President for Sales Jeff Krida. Yaran and Wile were furious and were representing the fury of other agencies in the area. Krida and Putnam boosted the commission to 15 percent from the existing 10 percent but the agents still felt they were being victimized, and they complained loudly to the press in the following days. When the smoke had cleared Friday at midnight at the end of the sale, Braniff had poured millions in cold cash into the accounts—but at a high cost. The anger of the travel agencies at Braniff's insensitivity to their problems with the sale was visceral and damaging, and Braniff had robbed the late spring traffic to finance the short term.

As Jeff Krida hinted publicly that Braniff might spring another two-for-one somewhere in the country in the near future, and as newfound customers clutched their $1 tickets and dreamed of sun and surf and getaways, the level of desperation at American escalated another notch.

The Braniff world headquarters sits on the western flank of DFW, nearly a mile from the Braniff terminal itself. To get from the terminal to the complex (which includes the Braniff House Hotel and the crew training facilities as well as the company offices) Braniff ran a shuttle bus every half hour. On an early Monday morning in mid-February, Braniff Vice President Sam Coats sat with fourteen Braniff crew members as the shuttle headed to the bunker and the Braniff House Hotel. Suddenly he and the other employees realized that what they were looking at through the windows of the shuttle was out of the ordinary. They were rolling over the blacktop service road that skirted the end of the western runway (17R/35L). The runways on the western side and the eastern side were connected by taxiways that traversed bridges—one on the north, and one on the south end of the terminal complexes. The bridges permitted even the giant 747's to taxi serenely over the divided highway, which ran literally through the middle of DFW.

On this cool, clear morning, standing on the taxiways leading to the end of the Braniff-side runway and stacked in a long line all the way back over the north bridge like a traffic jam were sixteen American Airlines jetliners of various types waiting for takeoff.

Coats leaned forward, trying to get a better look through the window as one of the captains spoke: "Have they closed down the east runway?"

One of the first officers who normally transited DFW replied: "Naw, that's just started in the last few weeks. American's guys keep asking for the west runway—even if they're going to New York. Take a look at that jam-up. Any question what they're trying to do?"

The group watched the scene as the van headed past the runway

310

end, toward the hangars and the world headquarters. A growing number of departing Braniff flights were holding in various places by the Braniff terminal, waiting for ground control to sequence them in for takeoff between the American jets.

"You mean they're trying to delay us? Why on earth? They're delaying themselves, too!" The question went unanswered.

Self-inflicted Wounds

CHAPTER **30** The bombs began falling around the world headquarters on Friday, February 26. A couple of hurried and worried conferences among Putnam, Guthrie, Bob Ferguson, and others of the senior staff in early February had focused with dismay at the figures from the New York ticket clearinghouse. Because of Braniff's size, it usually had a surplus of between $3 million and $6 million at the end of each month. The January clearing had resulted in a deficit—a bill to Braniff of $4 million, which had to be paid immediately. It didn't make any sense, especially considering the number of plating-away ticket dollars that must be in the pockets of the other carriers. Those dollars alone should have given Braniff a positive balance when they hit the clearinghouse.

In late February it happened again—not as much this time, but Braniff got advance warning that it would owe several million more at the February clearing. There just wasn't enough elasticity in the accounts to absorb that easily and maintain the cash cushion Guthrie considered vital—even with the success of the two-for-one sale. The staff huddled again and decided to talk to union leaders about deferring half of the paychecks for the coming week. They could be told that the situation was desperate, but they weren't told why— Braniff had to retain enough money to restart the airline in case it had to go into bankruptcy.

On February 26, however, Braniff had to release its figures for

1981. Braniff International Incorporated had lost $160.1 million in 1981; $63.4 million of it was in the last quarter. The news swept through Wall Street and the financial press as a harbinger of an impending elegy.

On February 26, several Braniff officers met with several different union representatives to broach the subject of cash flow and the possible need for a one-week pay deferment of half of the upcoming March 5 paychecks. The reception was lukewarm, but they were told to think it over during the weekend. On Monday, March 1, Guthrie decided that the idea was past the asking stage. The unions were told it was 50 percent pay or nothing. If Braniff paid the full payroll, Guthrie said, it might not have enough money left to pay for the next week's fuel bill.

On Tuesday, March 2 (thanks to some early, angry tips to the local news media by disgruntled union employees), both the *Dallas News* and the *Dallas Times Herald* bannerlined the news of the pay cuts and predictably offered up analysts' and accountants' opinions that it was a "last resort" move and that survival was doubtful. Braniff's Guthrie denied in print the "last resort" angle, and he was truthful to a point. Without the paycuts Braniff would simply have been too close to Guthrie's and Ferguson's minimum acceptable cash figure—not out of cash. *The Wall Street Journal* picked it up as well on March 4, quoting one of Braniff's more dissident labor leaders, Lanny Rogers of the IAM:

> Although Braniff said it consulted with unions representing many company employees the day before the announcement, some union leaders were bitter about the short notice they were given. "We have bills to pay, you know," said Lanny Rogers, President of the Machinery and Aerospace Workers union local. "We're alienated by what we think is a ploy by the company to set the unions up to give more labor concessions."

All that was bad enough, but the shocks were just beginning. At Braniff's urging, the CAB was considering a plan to require certificated air carriers to honor the tickets of any carrier that ceased flying. Although the proposal wasn't named the "Braniff rescue provision," there was no doubt for whom it was intended. CAB

Chairman Dan McKinnon could see the dangerous precedent in what was happening to Braniff at the hands of the worried travel agencies and the worried public. Perhaps if there was a guarantee, the exodus would abate.[1]

In the midst of getting ready to leave for Washington to present Braniff's request for the ticket guarantee plan, Putnam was interrupted by a call from business writer Dennis Fulton of the *Dallas News*.

"In light of all that's gone on, Howard, we conducted a telephone survey down here of the travel agencies—about whether they're supporting you or not—and the results are pretty bad. Most of them are saying off the record that they're only booking you a week in advance—no more—and their customers are demanding not to be booked on Braniff for fear the tickets won't be honored. This story is not going to look good. Why don't I come on out and get an update? I think it would be best if you'd just lay your cards on the table and say, here's where we stand."

Putnam already had a full morning ahead.

"Dennis, I'm just getting ready to leave this afternoon for D.C. I've got to talk to the CAB about this ticket guarantee thing. I guess if you come right on out I could talk to you on the run."

"Okay, I'll come right out."

Putnam had dealt with Fulton many times before, and while his attention to Braniff's problems (which he had been covering since 1978) rankled everybody in the airline, basically he was a careful, professional reporter. This time, though, Putnam had unwittingly set up an interview that would lead to the most damaging article of all. What would transpire in the next twenty-four hours would forge one of the final links in the chain of destruction.

Fulton sat down across from Putnam's desk in a chair by the circular marble table. At age twenty-seven, Dennis Fulton looked a bit older. With a slender build and dark hair against a very midwestern face and a propensity for conservative suits, he could have

[1] The previous month, Tony Wainwright had come up with a brilliant idea to obtain a multimillion-dollar insurance policy from Lloyd's of London to protect any travel agency or passenger against a Braniff bankruptcy. Lloyd's told Braniff that such a policy would plow new ground—no such thing had ever been written, and without a way of knowing how many tickets were out there written on Braniff (and such specificity was impossible), the premium would be far more than Braniff could afford.

313

passed for any of the younger businessmen he was used to interviewing.

Phil Guthrie was already in the office, sitting by the window. Putnam seemed tired and somewhat distracted to Fulton as the Braniff president shuffled through some papers, trying to decide which ones to put in his briefcase. As Putnam sat down, Fulton pulled out his notebook and dove right into the central question.

"The travel agent community has no confidence in Braniff's future—that's apparent from what we've found. Can you, to satisfy them and to satisfy me and my article—can you *guarantee* that Braniff will be in existence a month from now?"

Howard Putnam, now sitting back in his chair, looked Fulton in the eye and chewed on a fingernail—resting his right elbow on the right arm of the chair. He quickly analyzed the question, running through in his mind all the possible answers. He wasn't going to get caught in the trap of guaranteeing something like that and then have it come back on him later on. He was already pretty sure what was coming, and he didn't want to end up under investigation by the SEC. If Fulton had only used another word.

"No, I can't."

Fulton was amazed. Did he mean that? Putnam had always been disarmingly candid, but that was quite an answer. He tried to pin it down. "Well, can you give a date and say, 'I guarantee we have cash up to this point'?"

Again Putnam looked Fulton in the eye.

"No, I can't."

Fulton was groping. These answers were indictments—surely Putnam would take a stand somewhere. Surely he wasn't ready to let the press go out the door thinking the end was hours away.

"Well, there's bound to be some point. Can you—can you tell me if Braniff's going to be here tomorrow?"

Putnam answered at the same pace.

"Yeah, I think we'll be here tomorrow."

Guthrie was very quiet—simply sitting with one arm resting on the marble table, quietly moving a pen around in his left hand.

Fulton worked the words around on his pad and let the silence fill the small office for a few seconds before he looked back up at Putnam. "Where is the point I'm looking for, Howard?"

Putnam sighed. "A woman called on the phone today, Dennis, and asked if her ticket to Honolulu would be good in May." He paused, looking down at the desk, then back at the young reporter. "I told her I didn't know. She probably went right out and traded the ticket in for one on another airline."

Putnam shifted forward slightly and stopped gnawing on his forefinger. "I can't tell how much cash is going to be coming in—we have just about gone off the cliff as far as traffic is concerned—traffic is looking awfully bad. We're trying a few things—we have a few more cards up our sleeves as Phil says, but we can't predict—I can't guarantee—what's going to happen."

Putnam and Guthrie exchanged glances, and Putnam gestured with both hands, palms up. "I can't just name a date and say I know we have enough cash to operate until then. It's not that easy."

Bankruptcy was still a repugnant concept to Putnam—he had said so when he came on board. It would be an admission of defeat. Nevertheless, just to be safe, he and Guthrie and Ferguson had the New York bankruptcy specialists in the law firm of Levin and Weintraub come down to Dallas and give them a course in bankruptcy law and procedure. "Bankruptcy 101," according to the prevailing humor. Putnam told them to prepare a contingency plan for a shutdown and filing under Chapter 11 of the United States Bankruptcy Code—just in case. It would be a last resort, but it would be a parachute of sorts that should be readied.

Only Howard Putnam, Phil Guthrie, and Bob Ferguson really knew the full extent of the preparations. None of them, however, realized the psychological significance to them or the eventual effect on their thinking of the subtle shift from "never" to "last resort."

Howard Putnam awoke Thursday morning in his Washington, D.C., hotel room to a phone call from Guthrie in Dallas. The two talked by phone constantly when one of them was out of town. This morning's call wasn't unusual until he realized what Guthrie was saying.

"God, Howard, you won't believe the front-page story in the *Dallas Morning News*—it's disastrous!"

Dennis Fulton had ruminated all evening about the interview and the story. If he wrote it the way he heard it, the effects could be very serious for Braniff—suffering as the airline was from a public no-confidence vote. Good Lord, he thought, I gave Putnam several chances to moderate his statement, and the guy just sits there and keeps saying it—"No, I can't." Even after Fulton had the article polished and shipped over to his editor in the newsroom computer, he worried about it. When the black ink hit the streets the next morning, the predictable shocked reactions began to echo around the community, and angry phone calls from infuriated Braniff employees began flooding the *Morning News* switchboard.

BRANIFF CHIEF UNCERTAIN FIRM CAN SURVIVE

"We certainly have no current plans to cease operations, but I can't guarantee we won't." Howard Putnam
Braniff employees wonder where it will all end? Page 1D

At 8:20 P.M. on Thursday evening, March 4, Braniff Flight 205 from Washington's National Airport nosed into its gate at DFW. The moderate load of passengers appeared at the top of the jetway, filing into the terminal and through an enormous crowd of Braniff employees, some of whom were holding signs and a huge banner: "We're behind you, Mr. Putnam!"

Several television camera crews were there, lights blazing, as the last passenger, Howard Putnam, walked into the terminal to thunderous cheers.

There were shouts of "Where's Dennis Fulton?" and "Put the *Morning News* out of business!" as Putnam, with no advance warning of the rally, tried to size up the situation.

The employees had prepared a very emotional letter of support for Putnam. When handed the gate area public-address microphone from behind the ticket podium, he read the message for everyone, with tears visible in his eyes. Putnam spoke for a few minutes on the situation and how the company had a better than fifty-fifty chance of making it if everyone would pull together.

"We're going to have more crises ahead of us, folks, but together—together we can make it."

Someone toward the back of the crowd yelled out: "Was the article true? Did you say those things?"

Putnam motioned for quiet and again punched the microphone's "on" button. "The quotes were correct—I did say those things—but they were taken out of context. They're saying the glass is half empty, and I'm trying to say it's half full!"

The crowd cheered, and Putnam, in the glare of television lights, wiped back a few more tears before working his way toward the Braniff VIP room, where several of the senior officers were waiting—along with one fellow who had remained near the back of the crowd, making certain he stayed anonymous. Dennis Fulton slipped into the room just before Putnam and caught his attention when the door was closed to the crowd.

"Howard—how can you say that? How can you say that was taken out of context when that was all we talked about in the interview?" Fulton was upset—all his print competition was there, and all of them had just been told that Dennis Fulton couldn't get his quotations in context.

Putnam shrugged. "I know it, Dennis, but you saw how they were." The Braniff president turned to talk to one of the vice presidents. The sound of the crowd outside was dying down.

Along with the story of Putnam's rally (which had been orchestrated by Sam Coats) and his tearful words to the employees, the papers of Friday, March 5, carried the news that the CAB had tentatively approved the ticket-guarantee plan, formally called the default protection plan. At the world headquarters there were great sighs of relief on the part of most of the senior staff. This perhaps, would turn it around.

One thing had already begun to change: A substantial number of Dallas businessmen began organizing support for Braniff as early as Friday, taking out a full-page ad in the *Morning News* on Sunday, saying, "In Support of Braniff: We applaud and support Braniff and its employees and hope for their full success in their valiant efforts to remain a viable airline. We will continue to support them in any possible way." It was signed by eleven of Dallas's most substantial citizens, with the postscript ". . . and almost everybody else."

More importantly, many of these men began organizing an *ad hoc* campaign to get Dallas companies, regardless of some who harbored long-standing prejudice against Braniff born of past service shortcomings, to switch for the short term all their company-paid flying to Braniff. It appeared that maybe Putnam's candor had helped instead of hurt.

On Monday, March 8, Putnam sent a teletype to everyone:

ALLOFBN ALLINBN DFWGQBN 081500DR PLEASE POST

THE EVENTS OF LAST WEEK DEMONSTRATED THE TRUE CHARAC-
TER OF BRANIFF'S PEOPLE. YOU ARE WINNERS . . . BUT EVEN
MORE THAN THAT YOU HAVE A HEART AND REALLY DO CARE. I

AM VERY FORTUNATE AND VERY PROUD TO BE ASSOCIATED WITH YOU.

BRANIFF WILL CONTINUE TO FACE MAJOR CHALLENGES IN THE DAYS AHEAD BECAUSE THESE ARE TROUBLED TIMES FOR OUR COMPANY AND OUR NATION. WE WILL HAVE TO MEET THESE CHALLENGES ONE BY ONE . . . AND DO SO TOGETHER. YOU WILL HEAR RUMORS. YOU WILL HEAR BAD NEWS. I CAN'T PREVENT EITHER. NO ONE CAN.

AS WE MOVE FORWARD WE WILL GAIN STRENGTH, CONFIDENCE, AND STABILITY. THESE QUALITIES WILL COME FROM WORKING TOGETHER TO SAVE AND BUILD A NEW BRANIFF . . . A BRANIFF THAT WILL BLEND THE TRADITIONAL WITH THE INNOVATIVE IN ORDER TO DO WHAT'S RIGHT FOR US . . . AND OUR FLYING PUBLIC. THE PUBLIC IS BEHIND US. THIS HAS BEEN DEMONSTRATED IN SO MANY DIFFERENT AND WONDERFUL WAYS. IF WE DO OUR JOBS WELL, ACCEPT OUR RESPONSIBILITIES AS PROFESSIONAL PEOPLE AND SHOW WE'RE FIGHTERS . . . REGARDLESS OF THE ODDS THE PUBLIC WILL CONTINUE TO RALLY BEHIND US. I KNOW THAT TOM BRANIFF WOULD BE PLEASED THAT THE AIRLINE CONTINUES TO WEAR HIS NAME.

WE HAVE WITNESSED THE REBIRTH OF THE TRUE SPIRIT OF BRAN-IFF.

THANK YOU FOR YOUR SUPPORT
HOWARD D. PUTNAM

Two of the reservationists were standing at the bulletin board at the maintenance base, reading Putnam's memo. One of them, a silver-haired lady who had been with Braniff since 1948, said softly: "You know . . . that's about the first time in seventeen years I've seen a Braniff president mention Mr. Braniff. It would break his heart to see us today."

The attention of the local press was firmly focused on the drama now. Every day had a new story.

March 9, 1982 (*Dallas Times Herald*): BRANIFF VOWS TO PAY 2ND HALF OF WAGES . . . PAYROLL DEFERRED LAST WEEK
March 9, 1982 (*Dallas Morning News*): BRANIFF OFFICIALS BUOYED BY BACKING . . . AIRLINE'S PRESIDENT TO MEET WITH DEBTHOLDERS IN NEW YORK

March 10, 1982 (*Dallas Times Herald*): BRANIFF BOOSTERS TO TAPE TV PROGRAM
March 10, 1982 (*Dallas Morning News*): [Dallas Mayor] EVANS DROPS PLAN TO HELP BRANIFF [due to vociferous protest from Robert Crandall of city favoritism]

And on March 11 there was a bomb burst over American's headquarters:

(*Dallas Morning News*):AIRLINE [American] ACCUSED OF DIRTY TRICKS
(*Dallas Times Herald*): THE TEXAS AIR WAR TURNS NASTY . . . AMERICAN'S CRANDALL WANTS BRANIFF TO FOLD. and: C.A.B. INVESTIGATING TICKET ALLEGATIONS . . . C.A.B. INVESTIGATES AMERICAN

Suddenly all eyes turned toward American. The CAB had begun an investigation into the problems Braniff had experienced with the New York clearinghouse accounts, and the articles openly inferred that American was suspected of having held back $7 million in tickets written on Braniff and dumped them on the clearinghouse at once to create a cash crisis, thereby forcing the one-half pay deferral for Braniff employees. American vehemently denied all, but now the allegations were before the public. Braniff disclaimed any responsibility for putting them there, and there were rumors that an area congressman had done it for them.

The day before it all broke against American, Robert Crandall, speaking to a roomful of airline analysts in New York, took careless verbal aim once again and shot himself and American in the foot: "I don't want those people [Braniff] to stay in business. I would much rather have them go out of business." The quotes, reported by the New York bureau of the *Dallas Times Herald*, were accompanied by a quote from Howard Putnam in reaction: "I can't believe he said that! God. Well, I think it says he has some fear of Braniff!"

Now the Dallas-Fort Worth community began to get incensed. Competition was one thing, but out-and-out venality and mean-spirited wishes for your corporate neighbor's catastrophic demise were not in the handbook of proper corporate behavior—at least not in public. The newspaper reports fanned a glowing ember of dislike for American.

Two days later, speaking to a Dallas civic group, Crandall did it again. Using a string of all-too-characteristic expletives, Crandall railed against Braniff and railed against Texas class fares, two-for-one sales, and inaccurate press reports. The newspapers had another field day. A joke began circulating that by the end of the week, American's public-relations department had bound and gagged Crandall and chained him to the boardroom table—and his staff was getting rabies shots.

As the repercussions from the revelation of a CAB probe widened against American, a Delta marketing officer, Bob Pope from Delta's Dallas office, was quoted in the local press as saying that apparently American's "dirty tricks" had been used on Delta as well.* On several occasions, he told reporters, Delta had detected American's Sabre system as showing Delta flights full when the airline had seats available for sale. "We've started calling what American does 'zeroing out availability.'"

March 13, 1981 (*Dallas Morning News*): U.S. WON'T GIVE FUNDS TO BRANIFF . . . BRANIFF WON'T GET FEDERAL AID

March 17, 1982 (*The Wall Street Journal*): BRANIFF CHAIRMAN CASEY RESIGNS, JOINS PAN AM

John Casey had finally figured it out in the late fall: He had no authority. His three friends from First International Bancshares had admitted that they had given up the scepter and the crown to Putnam without telling Casey, which had set the two up for the continual conflict that the senior staff had observed. Casey was told that Putnam couldn't have been lured away from Southwest otherwise, but all Casey could see was that his position at Braniff was intolerable. Finally, in the spring, he began talking with his old friend Ed Acker, chairman of Pan Am, which was flirting with bankruptcy itself. Putnam knew it was just a matter of time before Casey left. The Board had made Putnam chief executive officer at the January Board meeting.[2]

Just before the middle of March—with the papers full of articles on Braniff—another top-secret Braniff operation was nearing com-

---

* Although Delta subsequently withdrew the charge.

[2] Putnam tried briefly to work with Casey on some matters, but the two men were too dissimilar in style to work harmoniously. Putnam complained to one officer, ". . . Casey is too slow—he wants to consider everything and mull it over, so you know what I do? I just ignore him and go do what I want to do."

pletion. It was a potential deal between Braniff and Pan Am which, if consummated, would rip away one of the most valuable assets Braniff possessed. In the meantime, the negotiations had thrown John Casey and Ed Acker together once again, and Casey was looking for a way out.

On March 15, Casey told Putnam he was very close to signing an agreement with Acker. Casey would, he said, attend the March 16 Braniff Board meeting, submit his resignation at the beginning, then leave and head for New York over the following weekend to become Pan Am's executive vice president for operations. The announcement was made the next day. The employees for whom Casey had worked so hard the previous year—the ones whose adoration and trust had become a holy grail for Casey—were so preoccupied with the daily flurry of stories and changes, speculation, furloughs, and the growing ranks of vultures gathering in a macabre deathwatch on the industry's back fence that they hardly even noticed his departure.

March 18, 1982 (*Dallas Morning News*): BRANIFF WANTS PAN AM TO LEASE ROUTES

Suddenly Putnam's overtures to Pan Am, which had begun in secret four weeks earlier as the two-for-one sale drew to a close, culminated in an agreement. But for what? Braniff was proposing to lease its South American route system to Pan Am for four years. Pan Am was to pay Braniff $7 million on signing the agreement, $13 million when the deal was approved by the CAB, and $10 million starting in 1983. When the lease expired, if Braniff couldn't take the routes back, they would revert to Pan Am. The whole thing was dependent on CAB approval, which cast a wary eye on the proposition from the first due to monopolistic considerations—Pan Am was already the second largest U.S. carrier in South America.

From the moment he arrived at the world headquarters, Braniff veterans had been trying to tell Putnam how profitable the South American system really was and how it had carried the North American operations during several years in the seventies. Howard Putnam was planning a domestic low-cost operation. He knew nothing about South America and he didn't have time to learn. What's more, he was getting tired of everyone trying to get him interested in the South American system. Guthrie told him it appeared to be a loser, and that was good enough for Putnam. Besides, the long history of high kickbacks and commissions, shady dealings and intense competition was repugnant to Putnam's sense of managerial neatness. Then too, there was the matter of the DC-8-62's that were the backbone of Braniff's fleet in South America and that would be illegal to fly in the United States after December 1983 (due to tougher federal noise limits). Braniff couldn't afford to buy new aircraft, and it couldn't operate the deep southern routes with the 727's. Further, it had to go to the lenders with a recovery plan—a viable, believable, long-term recovery plan. There was no way they could look the lenders in the eye and recommend keeping South America in full operation without talking about replacement airplanes in the long term. There might be other possibilities, but Putnam didn't have the time, he felt, to look into them. Instead he asked George Aims of Lazard Frères to try to figure out how much the system was worth. Maybe Braniff could lease it.[3]

In fact, Putnam found he could lease it—a highly innovative move in which he took a certain amount of pride. The lease with Pan Am, however, had several basic problems, one of which concerned personnel. It totally forgot Braniff's flight crews.

Under the terms worked out by the two airlines, virtually all of Braniff's South American flight attendants would be fired. The ground people would all become Pan Am employees, but the pilots would lose over 175 positions. The pilots flying South America were mostly senior, so they would simply fall off to more junior assign-

[3] Panama Regional Vice President Camilo Fabrega was rumored to have a group of Panamanian investors ready to finance a new Braniff fleet for South American service, though Putnam claimed he never heard of such a plan. In addition, there were many Lockheed L-1011's available for lease during this period, but Putnam felt Braniff's best posture was to figure out what the lenders wanted to hear and give them exactly that. New aircraft for South America, whether begged, borrowed, bought, or stolen, was not what he felt they wanted to hear about. They had enough trouble understanding North American airline operations, let alone operations in South America. Of course, it was ironic that Casey had been toying with the same idea during the summer of 1981 and had dropped it in the face of opposition from the directors and his senior officers. John Casey, who had been intimately involved in South America even to the extent of legal entanglement in the off-the-books ticket scandal, should have known better than anyone else the great value of the system in terms of cash flow, and the long history of purposefully depressed earnings figures. It's unclear whether his mention of the idea of selling the system was a red herring, or a lapse of memory and understanding, but whereas Putnam's decision had no basis in personal historical knowledge and can be better understood, Casey's flirtation with the idea is incredible.

ments on the domestic system. The bottom 175 would be furloughed. Braniff's pilots' union felt betrayed, and it threatened to go to court to force Pan Am to take the pilots—with appropriate seniority—along with the routes.

Finally, the press and Braniff's people took notice of Casey's departure. It seemed too coincidental. What nefarious connection with the Pan Am lease did this have? There was none, in fact, but the events of the spring of 1982 were beginning to resemble a thriller by Agatha Christie, and anything was possible.

March 19, 1982 (*Dallas Morning News*): BRANIFF PASSENGER
TRAFFIC DROPS . . . AMERICAN, DELTA TRAFFIC UP
March 19, 1982 (*Dallas Times Herald*): BRANIFF MAY FACE
TROUBLE AT C.A.B. . . . ROUTE LEASE APPROVAL IN DOUBT

Eastern and Air Florida, both of whom had coveted the idea of deep penetration into South America, were trying to block Pan Am's Braniff route lease. The CAB was worrying in the press about the monopolistic overtones of the deal, while Putnam and Acker tried to get everyone to jump through their hoop: They wanted to start the Pan Am service on April 25 and had petitioned the CAB for approval by April 13. By the end of the first week, it was becoming apparent that the CAB was not going to be stampeded. Too many other airlines had protested, and the deal itself was so totally unprecedented that the CAB members wanted to be very cautious.

Having sensed that the cash from the Pan Am deal might allow Braniff to live even longer, American had rushed to Washington to apply for all the routes themselves. Clearly the application wasn't prompted by long-term yearning for a southern route system— Crandall was simply covering all bases. The ambulance must not reach the patient in time.

By effectively selling its Latin soul for thirty million pieces of silver, Braniff had instantly induced another crisis: Braniff traffic in South America began to erode as soon as the story was out that it was trying to leave. As Putnam himself told the *Dallas Times Herald* with usual self-damaging candor, "Who is going to buy a ticket to fly Braniff to South America after they've heard we want to stop serving there? If we don't get the CAB approval, we'll just have to quit operating in South America. We really have no choice."

Braniff had already received the first $7 million from Pan Am.

Now they needed that additional $13 million—fast. While sage airline observers chuckled knowingly over Putnam's bluff about shutting down South America, Putnam and Guthrie were watching the cash position in the South American Braniff accounts erode daily. They had ignited a flash point of diminishing ridership. The minute they had gone public with the South American lease proposal, there could be no turning back.

The domestic system load factors for March were holding below the break-even point, but they were holding. It appeared to the employees as they read the daily load figures on company bulletin boards that maybe the erosion had stopped. No one seemed to realize that the steady load factors didn't represent the real monetary yield—just the presence of the two-for-one $1 passengers on the airplanes where full-fare passengers were needed. The actual revenue yield was equivalent to a much lower load factor.

With a ground swell of public support in Texas, including gratis TV ads by such people as Tom Landry and Mickey Gilley asking people to fly Braniff and help them out of the hole, perhaps, Braniff officials hoped, the loads would now increase as summer approached. Maybe all was not lost. The furor and the intensity of the self-help volunteer sales campaigns increased, though many participated with hollow smiles and a burning, sinking feeling in the pit of their stomach. One day up, one day down, going to work for many was a descent into hell—having to read and listen to a merciless avalanche of bad press and rumors and the riptides of human emotion: First we will, then we won't make it—back and forth, day after day.

Guthrie and Putnam knew, of course. The figures showed the effect of Fulton's article and the aftermath. Despite the public support and the ticket guarantee plan, the business written by travel agents was dropping like a rock.[4]

In mid-March Putnam began circulating a chilling message to the ranks: Braniff would size itself down to about fifty airplanes and about six thousand people. The costs hadn't dropped fast enough. Three thousand Braniff employees would have to go.

---

[4] Practically the moment it was approved, the travel agents had attacked the new CAB Ticket Guarantee Plan as insufficient to reassure them. Jumping into the headlines as well, American had promptly sniffed that regardless of the CAB's mandate, it would refuse to honor any Braniff tickets if a Braniff shutdown occurred.

324

Like a fighter who with noble detemination refuses to quit, but who has taken so many punches he can barely see his opponent—the ringing in his ears and the pain in his head gradually numbing him to the searing pain of each gratuitous blow—Braniff's people, if not the entity Braniff itself, were benumbed. While Putnam, Guthrie, Coats, Ridgeway, and the rest of the senior officers kept their heads and continued trying everything they felt might work (including the South American lease), the human corpus of Braniff was reeling. The mood alternated between giddy determination and tearful fear: "What the hell will I do if it folds?" Men and women, husbands and wives, singles and divorcées, young and not so young, all with the common bond of having their picture on an identification card below the name Braniff, read the headlines of March and April and tried to avoid the panic that comes with not enough money for mortgage payments and investments, plans and savings accounts. The fact that the nation was in the grips of a job-destroying recession lent no comfort to those who looked beyond October 31 (the new deferment date) and wondered what kind of Christmas they would have.

There were many effective defense systems, the most common being the oft-repeated assurance that "airlines as big as Braniff just don't cease to exist." To minds that had long since accepted the theory that everyone in upper management was constantly involved in complicated plots and plans, the funereal speculation could be safely deflected with anger—anger at the company's presumed maneuvering to convince Braniff's workers falsely that the company was in danger of failing so as to gain greater labor concessions. A mentality of this kind could also point to such assumed Machiavellian maneuvers as evidence that corporate officers sufficiently clever to weave webs of intrigue like this would always have some other trick up their sleeve. "Don't worry," they would counsel. "Putnam knows what he's doing. He wants everyone to think it's critical, but he wouldn't have come aboard Braniff if there was any real danger. The press is just against Braniff."

The government defense was the saddest—the most uninformed.

"The government won't let us go out of business. Are you kidding? Braniff's too important."

That had been true once, back when the CAB would arrange a hasty marriage for a failing airline. Deregulation ripped away such thinking, pulling down the safety net beneath the confident performers on the high wire, leaving them with cold, hard concrete to embrace if the footing or the balance of their corporate maneuvers in the brave new world of deregulation should prove faulty. Now, they were saying, you have but one chance to do it right, and you have the right to fail. All the carriers were now children of the new age, without a road map, without the nets. Some would fall off the edge, as children are wont to do. To face the nightmare in the spring of 1982 as a Braniff employee was to scream deep within: "Oh, Lord, not us! The first one couldn't be Braniff!"

The truth—cruel and simple, direct and brutal—was glimpsed by too many in the ranks, though their vociferous denials might indicate otherwise. As Lawrence had said, "Braniff is alone."

A Ghost of a Chance

CHAPTER 31   There was a chance after all if the CAB approved the Pan Am deal on time. Ron Ridgeway's people were working with Tony Wainwright on a new type of sale to rival the two-for-one, and a tidal wave of Texas-based public support was keeping the loads and the ticket sales going. People were even sending in donations— hundreds of dollars of donations —and the personnel were volunteering their hearts out all over the system. If they made it to June, there was a chance. Of course, there had to be a summer for Braniff. There had to be the usual influx of heavy vacation travelers buying Braniff seats. As Putnam kept saying, if this was the year with no summer, it was all hopeless anyway.

For three months it had been up one day, down the next—good news, bad news, then good news again—alternating in the eyes of Braniff's people like an adaptation of the old vaudeville routine:

"Braniff's selling South America!"

"Oh, that's bad!"

"No, that's good—that means enough money to keep going!"

"Oh, well, that's good!"

"No, that's bad—the deal means we've got a lot of unhappy employees who're going to lose their jobs."

"Oh, well, that's bad!"

"No, that's good—cause now with fewer employees, we won't have as much payroll expense!"

Events were moving so fast now, it was hard to keep a good mental focus on the proverbial forest—the trees were whizzing by, demanding attention, just like the early-morning vista of the forest of downtown Dallas skyscrapers now visible through the small, round window in the Braniff 727's forward entry door by Howard Putnam's right shoulder. Putnam, wearing a monogrammed long-sleeve dress shirt and tie, stood next to the forward carry-on closet in the front aisle of the brown jetliner. He was visible to most of the passengers and had a PA microphone in his hand. It was a substantial load for Flight 79, the 7:55 A.M. DFW–Miami first flight of the day.

"Good morning, ladies and gentlemen, my name's Howard Putnam. I'm the president of Braniff. We have been going through a lot in our company in the last few weeks, and it's encouraging to stand up here and see all of you looking this way. We're going down to Miami to meet with all of our employees this morning—and talk about the South American joint venture that we've worked out with Pan American. Thanks a lot for flying with us!"

The passengers gave him a round of applause. Putnam went back to his seat, shaking a few hands on the way. He and Phil Guthrie were sitting together, accompanied on the flight by Ron Ridgeway and Bill Huskins.

They weren't in first class—there wasn't any. They were in Texas class, headed for a meeting Putnam dreaded.

The auditorium at Miami International Airport was filled with over 100 Braniff employees, many of them dressed casually in sports shirts, shorts, and T-shirts, having come in on their day off to hear Putnam's explanation. There were over 433 Braniff employees in the Miami base. When Pan Am took over, there would be 40. No one was in a good mood. Putnam was selling their jobs and their birthright (most spoke Spanish and served the South American traffic).

Putnam, flanked by Ridgeway on his left and the imposing hulk of Guthrie on his right, stepped behind a long, flat table that contained a small podium. Guthrie and Ridgeway sat down, and Putnam moved out to one side of the podium, studying the anger in the room—the clear body language of those who, with arms crossed and eyes narrowed, partially slumped in their chairs with heads cocked to one side, unwilling to believe anything he said. The flat, overhead fluorescent lights in the small auditorium contrasted against dark walls, making it very theatrical. Putnam wasn't feeling theatrical. Collected on the outside, he was shaking within.

"We know of—the emotional drain you are going through—the upsetting of personal lives—and I'm not sure I can change any of that—but I will try to tell you, as will Phil Guthrie and Ron—and Bill Huskins—why we're doing what we're doing and why it's a necessity."

In the midst of the session, after the others had given their reports, the questions began—civil, but hostile. Partway through, one of the lead agents stood up, carrying a tape recorder.

"You mean to tell me that an organization the size of Braniff with a countdown list of thirty days—that you can't give us actual figures on what's going to happen to Miami station—how many's going to be here?"

Putnam was sitting down now—leaning on one side of his chair, looking more tired than defensive. "Keep in mind it's a very . . ." He smacked the table with his right hand for emphasis—more a gesture of frustration with the inevitability of it all, then looked back up at the man, his voice neither hard-edged nor whining. ". . . it's a hard thing, but this company could have no jobs at all. We're trying to save *some* jobs, and whether you are a part of that sixty-five or sixty-eight hundred I'm talking about [who would be left in the "new" Braniff] I recognize makes a difference as to how you look at the end result."

A cargoman (baggage-buster in Braniff slang) spoke up from the back. "Why haven't you cared enough about the employees to try an' make out some kind of unique package to protect us with Pan Am's hiring—maybe?"

"Pan American agreed to take the ground employees—they did not agree to take flight attendants in South America, they did not agree to take pilots, and they did not agree to take any employees domestically, because they already have the employees and the staffing there. Our choice was—have no agreement at all—and end up liquidating South America, and put everyone on the street, or do what we could for some, and also infuse some cash in this company to try to keep part of it going. That was the alternative."

A few minutes later Putnam and the assemblage stood in the Braniff VIP lounge on the ticket-counter level of the airport, waiting for the return flight—182 to DFW. Putnam had a Coke in his hand. No fewer than five TV camera crews were waiting off to one side to interview him. As Guthrie had pointed out to a Dallas reporter, Putnam was tired and frazzled.

Putnam leaned against a ledge in the room, which contained some South American artifacts. "It certainly could have been worse —I was expecting the absolute worst." The meeting had lasted ninety minutes.

On the bus to the employee parking lot small groups of the Braniff people with numbered days talked and snarled angrily.

"The man says he gots to do it this-a-way—he's just trying to break the unions—that's the whole point of this."

"I tell you, he was brought in to bankrupt this company. That's what he's going to do!"

"He didn't fight to get us on with Pan Am. Damn! What am I gonna do now?"

Every time, it seemed, that Putnam got into deep discussions with the rank-and-file Teamsters or mechanics over the needed concessions, they would throw a tired and familiar subject in his face. "Well, you go get Mr. Lawrence to give us some concessions— cut his retirement pay and all—then come talk to us." Putnam was sick of it, and sitting in his office one afternoon after the Miami ordeal he decided to try just that. Howard Putnam, who had gone to obvious lengths to demonstrate his personal contempt for the administration of Braniff before January 1981, placed a call to Harding Lawrence in New York to "ask him to help us out."

Lawrence ignored what he thought Putnam was suggesting—a voluntary cut in his retirement pay—and instead waded into the issue of how he could help the company through direct intervention and advice. He told Putnam he would first need to see a long list of reports and studies, ". . . the ones you must have done prior to starting that Texas class concept, Howard, because I know you wouldn't have made a momentous decision like that without such detailed studies . . ." Then Lawrence demanded to talk with several different groups, including the bankers. "You do all that for me, Howard, and I'll be glad to help you out."

Putnam was nonplussed—this had not been his intention, drawing Harding Lawrence back into the camp. "Harding, you've got to understand I'm changing the entire scope and concept of this airline—it isn't going to be anything like it was before." his voice was only barely hiding the upset. Lawrence repeated his conditional offer, and Putnam ended the call.

Several days later Lawrence received a letter from General Counsel Jim Riley, who was an old friend. The letter was formal, thanking him for his time, but saying the call had been a mistake, and they wouldn't need his involvement after all. Putnam had come down the hall after his conversation with Lawrence and told Riley "I guess I made a mistake—I thought it would help, but now he wants to take over." Putnam could just see the resulting headlines: "HOWARD PUTNAM TURNS TO FORMER CHAIRMAN LAWRENCE FOR HELP." Besides, he didn't have any of those demanded studies— there had not been time.

Howard Putnam was getting tired, and he had good reason to be. He had spent the better part of a week with six-foot-four Ed Acker in Washington lobbying every congressman and senator they could find for support (five-foot-eight Putnam referred to himself and Acker as "The 'Mutt and Jeff' Show"). Putnam had left Sam Coats to finish the job and returned to Dallas to a twenty-four-hour-a-day schedule—which included approving the restructure plan Braniff would thrust at the lenders in a few days. As their Lazard Frères representative had said, there was something in there to offend everyone. It would be a bloody battle—getting that diverse group of angry special interests to sink a quarter of a billion dollars in debt into the uncertain metamorphosis of preferred stock, and that was a major part of the proposed restructure package.

April 1 (*Dallas Morning News*): BRANIFF RESTRUCTURE PLAN OFFERED
April 3 (*Dallas Morning News*): BRANIFF DEBTS EXCEED ASSETS
April 8 (*Dallas Morning News*): PUTNAM'S SALARY . . . 750 THOUSAND DOLLAR DEAL

The proxy statement for the May 7 stockholders' meeting had hit the stockholders—and the press—on April 8. The local papers pounced on the full disclosure of Putnam's salary as if they had uncovered a dastardly example of white-collar crime. Dennis Fulton wrote the lead article for the *Dallas Morning News*. They all had apparently forgotten what Putnam had said six months before: "I came on with two conditions—one, I bring Guthrie, and two, we both get paid well for our efforts." Obviously, both conditions had been met.

April 13 was a Tuesday. The CAB had dithered in the press for weeks about their antitrust worries over Pan Am. American Airlines had lobbied with a vengeance against the Pan Am deal, and Putnam had pounded home the point that without an approval, the routes would be abandoned as soon as the cash ran out down South. The State Department understood the consequences: Most of the South American governments would cancel the routes, keeping, of course, their national carriers' routes into the United States. A State Department letter had been sent to the CAB urging their quick action to save the routes in the national interest.

The CAB members were well aware of the dangers of rejection. There was enormous pressure on them, and on April 14, American tried to turn the screws some more.

April 14 (*Dallas Times Herald*): AMERICAN AIRLINES OFFERS TO PAY BRANIFF LOSSES TO GET HEARING

The filing was incredible—unprecedented—and even in the off-the-record word of one of the CAB members, "ludicrous!" American had filed, weeks after the closing date, a proposal to compensate Braniff for any losses in South America for however long it took the CAB to hold full hearings. The implication was that the CAB would act unfairly otherwise, so American needed to buy a fair hearing. The CAB was insulted.

Putnam sent Vice President for Regulatory Proceedings Bob Culp to the press: "The American proposal is a last gasp to try to overthrow the [Pan Am] agreement. Everything we have heard from Washington indicates the CAB will approve our application," Culp said. "The U.S. Department of Transportation has twice said it favors the proposal, and the U.S. Justice Department has said that it sees no antitrust problem in the case."

American trotted out another vice president to deny with wide-eyed innocence anything but a corporate interest in a fair hearing.

331

On Thursday, Braniff escalated the attack with a press release: "The American proposal is nothing more than a transparent effort to kill the Braniff-Pan Am plan." Phil Guthrie added, "There must be no misunderstanding about the misleading actions of American Airlines in this case. Their late filing has only one purpose. That is a last-gasp effort to kill the [agreement], and with it Braniff's major chance for survival."

Sam Coats also weighed in. "American has made it clear that it would be happy to see Braniff go out of business. It could then dominate the Dallas-Fort Worth hub and raise air fares at will. . . ."

American's Al Becker, an owlish-looking fellow, emerged in American's Grand Prairie corporate headquarters to retort: "Obviously Braniff misunderstands the nature and purpose of American's proposal."

Becker was wrong. Braniff understood it only too well. So did the CAB. American had shot themselves in the foot again.

On Thursday night the CAB finally adjourned late after wrangling over the issue for hours. They scheduled a Friday session. Chairman Dan McKinnon, fatigue showing on his face, told the press: "The general feeling of the Board is that we need some additional material. Our intent is to make as quick a decision as possible given the complexities involved." McKinnon also indicated the American proposal wasn't a significant factor in any part of the consideration. Privately he and the other Board members had some more descriptive words about that proposal, and the political pressure cascading through the deliberations like cosmic rays—invisible but effective.

On Thursday afternoon Braniff announced it was pulling out of Portland, Oregon; Fort Lauderdale, Florida; Nashville; and Philadelphia—all on May 1. Putnam and Guthrie and the rest of the team waited for the CAB decision and worried.

Howard Putnam and Phil Guthrie still hadn't really joined Braniff. They had accepted the stewardship—taken it to heart, in fact—but they still weren't Braniff. For that matter, the Putnam-Guthrie duo was a management unit in itself. The two were always conferring privately, always in touch by phone, always moving off in a corner to talk over strategy quietly before talking to the other officers. It gave the rest of senior management an eerie feeling sometimes—an uneasy recognition that whatever their titles, the other "Mutt and Jeff" team in the corner called all the shots. Now, as they waited, only Putnam and Guthrie were aware of just how fast the South American traffic was slipping.

Putnam had been in Hollywood, Florida, on Friday as the CAB met again to try for a solution. Putnam had gone on the road, this time to address a meeting of travel agents.

"Unfortunately, down in Texas we have a competitor called American Airlines. I have refrained from accusing them of anything because I had no proof and I don't like to operate that way. But American this week has very blatantly filed a sham, a transparent attempt to put Braniff out of business."

Called by the local press again, American's Al Becker was only too happy to provide a reply for Saturday's edition: "Of all the accusations made against American, not one single individual or group of individuals has yet had the intestinal fortitude to step forward and accuse American of anything."

Becker was about to be proven wrong. A certain tape recording with his master's voice had been safely stored away in Braniff's legal office, but it could be found by any federal investigator with a sufficiently broad subpoena for Braniff's records.

Braniff had just received such a subpoena.

Dan McKinnon stood at the podium in the pressroom at CAB headquarters in Washington, D.C. He was tired, but all this attention and national press play was not totally undesirable. Political ambitions or not, becoming a familiar face never hurt one's options. As the lights went on, McKinnon made his announcement:

"The CAB has today decided to deny interim approval of the proposed joint operating agreement between Braniff and Pan Am. The Board noted that the issue of the competitive impact of the U.S. South American market was so complex and contested that it could not now consider approving the proposal before completing an oral evidentiary hearing on the issue."

McKinnon promised a decision by the end of July. That might as well have been the next century as far as Braniff was concerned; according to their testimony, they couldn't last the next month.

American had won—not by what they had done so much as by whom they were battling. The CAB simply couldn't get past the presence of Pan Am as the suitor-carrier. Despite the positions of the Justice Department and Transportation Department, the CAB professed to be too worried about monopoly.

There was a curious bone thrown to Braniff, however. The board noted that Braniff, in the interim, was "invited" to find a more suitable partner. Putnam did not miss the innuendo.

Howard Putnam appeared on *The MacNeil-Lehrer Report* that Friday night. In Miami, sitting in front of his television watching the show, one of the few humans to gaze personally upon the far side of the moon started thinking about Eastern Air Lines and South America.

Putnam made the point as best he could. Braniff had no choice but to shut down South America as soon as it ran (as he called it) cash-negative. Somehow the CAB had refused to face this reality. As Putnam left the studio and headed for home, Dan McKinnon came on the second half of the PBS show to emphasize that the Board didn't object to the agreement, they objected to Pan Am as part of it. "Come back with another lease partner that doesn't present anticompetitive problems in South America," McKinnon told Putnam via the show, ". . . and the CAB will probably welcome the deal with open arms." Frank Borman, president of Eastern Air Lines, was not a man to miss such overtures.

Putnam was stunned—he and Acker and Guthrie and most of the people they felt were in the know had confidently expected the CAB to approve the agreement, at least in the interim. The Board had been boxed in, yet wiggled free under intense pressure from Braniff's competitors. Putnam sat in a large chair in his den the next morning talking to David Johnson, a Dallas area stockbroker and the host of a local educational TV show, who had been following the Braniff officers with TV camera crews since January—a project designed to tell the story of Putnam's save of Braniff. The story was to appear the next year on the PBS show *Enterprise*. Putnam, by now very used to having a $50,000 portable TV camera pointing at him, explained again how the minute the cash was gone down South, Braniff was gone down South. After Johnson and his camera crew had departed, Putnam's phone rang. It was just before noon in North Dallas.

"Howard, this is Frank Borman."

"Well, hello, Frank. How are you?"

"The question is, How are you? I saw *MacNeil-Lehrer* last night and listened to you and McKinnon. Are you serious now about what you said—about looking, uh, for another lease arrangement?"

Putnam stood at a small desk in his den, the phone in his right hand. "I sure am, Frank—I mean, we're bound to Pan Am, but the Board has effectively nullified the agreement."

"Okay, tell you what: Send someone down here next week and let's talk."

Braniff Flight 79 on Monday morning, April 19, had Bob Culp on board with a briefcase full of information and statistics—the same exhibits Braniff had used with Pan Am. Culp went directly to Eastern's headquarters and spent the day explaining why Braniff couldn't make a profit with DC-8's, but a carrier such as Eastern with jumbos and a little cash could. Culp also made it clear that Braniff had to have money in advance, and possibly a subsidy if a route transfer wasn't done by the end of April. While they conferred in Miami, Ed Acker had set up his next move in New York.

Pan Am President William Waltrip appeared at Braniff's world headquarters at DFW on Tuesday morning. Waltrip, Putnam, Guthrie, and Culp (just returned from Miami) held a series of strategy meetings, trying to decide how the deal could be remade and resubmitted to get past the CAB's objections. While they talked in one room, a call from Air Florida (Acker's former airline) came through in another office—followed closely by a call from Borman in Miami with more questions. "This is like Monty Hall's *Let's Make a Deal*" Putnam thought as he shuttled between offices. Air Florida was ready to talk—urgently—about becoming that other partner, and Eastern was getting more interested by the minute. Borman had long wanted a deep route system to South America. Now, perhaps, it could be within his grasp.

Contrary to Braniff's public stance and their testimony before the CAB, they had indicated to the three different airlines vying for the deal that as long as Braniff had some cash upfront (as with Pan Am's $7 million), Braniff could hang on until June. Now Guthrie hurried back down the hall on Thursday, April 22, to tell Putnam the latest shock. The self-sustaining cycle of distrust they had started in South America was spinning even faster than the worst estimates: Traffic was dropping alarmingly. Suddenly the initial testimony was entirely accurate. At this rate, Braniff had only a week before the cash would be gone. There was no longer enough revenue coming in down South to match the expenditures for fuel, leases, and support services.

Buried in the panic was the fact that prior to the announcement of the Pan Am deal, the system had been self-sustaining. The income equaled the outgo. Only the extraneous expense allocations from the North American system made the South American system a loser.[1]

By publicly announcing a withdrawal, however, Braniff had destroyed the South American structure. It had been an unnecessary but effective form of suicide.

Friday morning—one week after the CAB had punctured the Pan Am-Braniff balloon—Putnam phoned Pan Am, Eastern, and Air Florida, telling them that whatever happened must now happen by the middle of the following week. Braniff must have an agreement to take to the CAB by April 28. At that news, Air Florida, as Putnam would tell the Braniff Board a week later, "just kind of faded out of the picture." Putnam had spoken with Borman. "Howard, I've got a Board meeting next Tuesday and probably can't make an offer before then. But we want to be kept in on the deal."

"Okay, Frank, but I can't make any promises. Time is getting short."

At Pan Am headquarters, Waltrip took Putnam's call. "Okay, when do you expect the cash deficit in South America to occur?"

"Monday or Tuesday—Wednesday at the latest," Putnam replied. Guthrie was sitting across from him, listening and nodding.

On Friday afternoon Putnam talked by phone with Pan Am Chairman Ed Acker, who was in Houston delivering a speech to his employees. Acker had been pressing the White House for help in getting the CAB to change their minds about the Braniff-Pan Am deal and was worried about Putnam talking to other carriers.

"Now, Howard, within the hour that press release is going to come out of the White House. I know what that statement is going to be, and it's going to be a strong one in favor of our deal. Now, what we need is for you to go to the CAB on Monday and tell them how you're going to run out of money down there and shut it down by whenever—this, that, and the other—and they'll have to approve it."

Acker had been incensed that Putnam had been talking with other airlines. Pan Am had spent a considerable amount of time and

---

[1] Though Putnam disagrees with this conclusion, his own figures (from Braniff's 1981 annual report and SEC 10K filing) support the point. In 1981 the South American system earned $247,705,000 and lost a mere $7,539,000 or 3.044 percent. A minor shift in the allocations of nonoperating expenses would have changed the loss to a profit.

money on constructing the deal with Braniff, and Ed Acker wasn't at all interested in having Braniff make the deal elsewhere with all the prepaid legal work as an added attraction.

"Now, I gotta have your word on this, all right? If I don't get your word that you're going down there Monday and that you're going to stay hitched with our deal—say that you're going to stick with the deal you made—I'm gonna call a press conference right now and we're going to terminate this deal. I'm not going to sit here with an offer you can go out and trade with somebody else!"

Putnam tried to reassure him. "Okay, Ed, we're still committed to the deal—we just feel like we have to talk to anyone who wants to talk about the routes at this stage, but we'll see the CAB on Monday."

Putnam agreed to refile the petition with the CAB, emphasizing the terrible financial situation, and asking—or demanding—reconsideration immediately. The petition was filed by late Friday afternoon. The wire services picked it up almost immediately. As promised, the statement in support of reconsideration was released by the office of Mike Deaver, deputy chief of staff at the White House, within the hour. Acker flew home to Connecticut that night thinking everything was arranged and protected. By Tuesday, Pan Am and Braniff should have their deal approved. The CAB and Dan McKinnon would snarl and spit and be unhappy about the whole thing, but they'd have to approve it. They couldn't let the United States lose those routes.

The CAB, however, couldn't reconsider and then reapprove the Pan Am deal without losing face. There had to be another alternative, and the refiled emergency petition didn't propose one.

By late afternoon Friday, Borman's people had picked up the wire service reports of the refiled Pan Am-Braniff petition. Their Washington lawyers had reported the President's letter as well. Borman called Putnam, who was still at Braniff's world headquarters.

"Look, Howard, we're going to try to move earlier than Tuesday on the lease proposal. I've been in contact with many of my Board members. Why don't we get our people together and meet in New York Sunday afternoon or evening and see if we can put something together?"

"That's fine, Frank. Your offices okay?"

"You bet." (Eastern had offices in Manhattan as well, although the main corporate headquarters were in Miami.)

Shortly before 7:00 P.M., Eastern Daylight Saving Time on Sunday, April 25, a retinue of Braniff people including Putnam and Guthrie and two attorneys from Arnold and Porter in Washington walked into the Rockefeller Center offices of Eastern Air Lines in Manhattan.

Ed Acker was sitting out in the late-afternoon sunshine in his backyard in Connecticut when one of his executives called and pulled him back in the house.

"Ed? I hate to tell you, but it looks like Putnam is talking to Eastern again and they're trying to make a deal. It looks like they're getting ready to meet tonight here in New York to wrap it up."

Acker tried to phone Putnam in Dallas, and got his wife, Krista, instead—who confirmed he was headed for New York. "Have him call me at home as quick as possible, would you? Tell him it's urgent." Acker hung up the receiver, infuriated.

Just before midnight Putnam called Acker from Eastern's Manhattan offices.

"Ed? You called me, and I'm returning your call."

"What . . . are you doing, Howard?"

"We're here in New York talking to Eastern."

"What the hell for? Don't you remember what we discussed on Friday? You gave me your word you're still committed!"

Putnam told him not to worry, that they were just talking and nothing would probably come of it. "I don't think Borman even understands South America, Ed. Nothing's going to happen."

"Okay—fine—but don't forget your commitment."

Acker hung up with the distinct impression that a deal with Eastern wasn't too close—and Braniff would be in Washington the next day to appeal further to McKinnon's Board. It would prove to be an infuriatingly inaccurate assumption.

At the Eastern offices in New York midnight passed, then 1:00 A.M. and 2:00 A.M., and suddenly considerable progress had been made. What had looked like an impossibility of agreement just two hours previous was shaping into a deal—although a deal among very tired negotiators.

Eastern had agreed to a $30 million cash-out, with $11 million upfront—to lease, not to buy the routes. As Acker had feared, the legal structure constructed in part by Pan Am's money was the groundwork for Eastern's deal. In an improvement over the deal with Acker, however, Eastern was agreeing to take on the Braniff

South American flight attendants as well as the ground people, thus short-circuiting a clamorous round of governmental objections and veiled threats from many of the eleven Latin American countries that had accompanied Pan Am's refusal to hire the flight attendants—many of them daughters of high-ranking families and governmental ministers. Putnam tried (as hard as possible, he would later claim) to get Eastern to take the pilots. They wouldn't do it. Eastern, however, wanted the routes. If Putnam had made Eastern's hiring of the pilots a condition, what Eastern would have done is unclear. Putnam, however, tried no further, and that would prove to be a major mistake.

By 3:00 A.M., they had an agreement. The route structure pioneered by Tom Braniff and such early captains as R. V. Carleton, the system carved from an aviation wilderness by Braniff Airways and expanded with the proud Panagra and its history, was to be swept away on June 1—for $30 million. Technically it was a six-year lease, but only the employees would hold to the misconception that Braniff—if it survived—would ever fly the routes again.

Late Monday morning, April 26, 1982, Putnam and Guthrie and the attorneys reassembled at Eastern's offices, reread the documents to make sure what they had agreed to with bleary-eyed fatigue a few hours before was actually what they wanted, and signed the deal.

As Putnam and the retinue of airline executives headed for Washington on Eastern's shuttle to file the deal with the CAB, Ed Acker walked into his office high in the Pan Am Building (just north of Grand Central Station) and got another jolt over the phone. One of his people in Washington had just discovered what Eastern and Braniff had concluded.

"They're headed to Washington right now, Ed, and I understand they're going to file the agreement with the CAB by this afternoon."

Putnam and the Arnold and Porter lawyers had just completed the revised petition for the Board. One of the senior lawyers picked up the petition and looked at Putnam.

"They're still open over there [the docket section of the CAB], Howard. Do you want to file it today?"

"Why not? Let's go do it."

The deed was complete by 4:45 P.M. Washington time, and Putnam had spoken to Dan McKinnon, who had immediately called a meeting of the Board for that evening. McKinnon assured Putnam they wouldn't be making a final decision that night.

Putnam finally reached Acker by phone at about 6:00 P.M. Acker had made an emergency call to the head of Air Florida and had tentatively agreed to work out a joint application between Pan Am and Air Florida that would satisfy the CAB's monopoly objections. They understood that any such agreement would have to be concluded with lightning speed and taken to the CAB by 7:00 P.M. Monday.

"You don't need to do that, Ed," Putnam assured him. "McKinnon says they're not going to be deciding anything tonight, so you have until tomorrow. Anyway, we'd still rather do the deal with you."

"Okay, then, Howard, we'll get a filing down there tomorrow."

Acker was already infuriated. The next four hours would galvanize his fury.

The Civil Aeronautics Board of the United States met at 7:00 P.M. on Monday evening, April 26, 1982. Within two hours they had given full approval to the Eastern-Braniff route lease and "blown Pan Am out of the tub" (as Ed Acker would later characterize it).

Putnam got the news in his hotel room. He had prearranged with Guthrie months before that if either ever received a late-night phone call in a hotel and needed the other, they'd knock on the wall. Putnam started banging the daylights out of the hotel room wall as Guthrie raced around the corner into Putnam's room in a bathrobe.

"What's up?"

"The CAB's just approved the Eastern deal. What the hell do we do now?"

Acker had been right. The White House pressure and the plea of impending shutdown had worked—only for the wrong suitor. Acker and Putnam had a phone conversation the next morning—if it could be called a conversation. Acker was white-hot mad. "Don't think—Howard [he said the name with distaste]—that this will be forgotten."

Acker was in an acidic, towering rage, but characteristically, he expressed such rages with fulminating restraint. He informed Putnam that the Pan Am-Air Florida deal would be filed that day and he would push for reconsideration, to have it approved so that

340

Braniff could choose between either. He also reminded Putnam of Pan Am's $7 million—which Braniff had already spent—and the contract, which Putnam had treated as void. Ed Acker was infuriated at what he considered Putnam's treacherous duplicity.

On Tuesday afternoon, Pan Am and Air Florida filed. Two hours later, the CAB rejected the filing. For the usually glacial pace of the CAB to give way to such speed was unprecedented. Traditionally, they couldn't move that fast if their building was on fire.

Another arrival at DFW awaited Putnam at the end of the evening Washington–New York flight on Wednesday. The press had been alerted, and the cameras were there. "It's in the bag!" Putnam told the protruding microphones stuck in his face as he walked out of the jetway, grinning ear to ear. The $11 million would be wired to Braniff on Wednesday. Survival was at hand.

An Emotional Roller Coaster

CHAPTER 32   The relief supervisor on the Braniff reservations graveyard shift had heard the complaint once before since coming on duty. Now here was a second reservationist—still wearing her headset—standing over Joanne Miller's desk.

"Joanne, I've just pulled up a listing of today's last DFW-to-New York flight. The thing was booked full—but when it left the gate, it was nearly empty! I started looking back, and the reservation record in the computer is riddled with small-group no-shows—all of them put in by American reservations. Joanne, someone over there's playing sabotage games! You want me to run a hard copy?"

"Hang on—this is one too many." Joanne walked over to the night manager, and told him the problem and the suspicions and that several others had seen the same long lists on other Braniff flights. The cancellations were always for small groups of under ten. Any group over that number would need the approval of a Braniff manager, but under ten could be confirmed computer-to-computer—no one at Braniff would know. There were even individual names with some of the groups, but they all had one thing in common: When the flight left, the groups were no-shows.

The manager seemed uninterested. "Don't worry about it, Joanne, it's been happening for weeks. I don't think the company is trying to do anything about it."

"Good Lord, that's thousands of dollars of revenues they're stealing! If American reservations managers are told about this, I'm sure they can trace down who's doing it and fire them."

"Don't worry about it, Joanne. Our company doesn't have time."

Joanne went back to her position to tell the other woman. Someone at American—or American as a group—was invading Braniff's flights. Joanne walked over to a computer terminal, wondering how long this had been going on, and began punching up flight numbers of Braniff flights that had departed DFW during the previous day. The cancellations of small groups was endless. And the company didn't want to know.

Howard Putnam was standing in one of the headquarters conference rooms with Sam Coats and some of the staff. The layouts for the new, vitally important ticket sale promotion were spread around the room. Putnam, wearing his usual long-sleeve white shirt with an unbuttoned gray suit vest, stood just inside the closed door listening to Coats go over the details of the sale.

"We're ready to go. The ad will be called "The Great Escape," and when you buy two round-trip tickets for use between the fifteenth of May and the fifteenth of August, we give you a third round trip to anyplace on the mainland, for use after August fifteenth, for a dollar."

Putnam, hands in his pants pockets, rocked back on his feet a bit and asked Coats, "What's the focus of the copy?"

"The focus is escape and appreciation."

Putnam was frowning. "Does the word 'escape' bother anybody?"

He paused—looking around at everyone in turn, sampling their expressions. There was a muttered "no" from somewhere in the

342

room. "I'm not saying it bothers me, but does it give any implication of bankruptcy, or . . ."

Coats sat looking at the copy for a second, then turned to his left, looking up at Putnam and smiling. "You're overly sensitive these days!" The whole group laughed as Putnam jumped slightly in jest. Coats and Putnam often relieved the tension with such exchanges.[1]

When the laughter had subsided, Putnam turned serious again. "I don't know—I'd sit down, and I'd play around with this thing and play off of each other—'cause when you go out with this [next week], you've got one chance to do it right."

Tony Wainwright had warned them it wasn't going to work. It was too obscure and too late in the game. Braniff had staged other two-for-one sales in different cities since the first big Dallas area success in February, and the promotion had continued to work reasonably well (though bringing in less and less cash each time). The two-for-one was getting worn out, though, and they all agreed it wouldn't work again—especially in the Dallas area. But Braniff desperately needed the passengers and their revenue now to get through to summer. They needed something to jolt the passenger into risking his money on prepurchased Braniff tickets with the thought that whatever gamble he might be taking that Braniff would be around to honor the tickets, the deal was too good to pass up. Wainwright knew deep down that whatever that much-needed something was, it wasn't The Great Escape. Putnam and the staff were kidding themselves.

While Putnam and Guthrie had been frantically wrangling with the Pan Am and Eastern deals, the Dallas press had continued with the almost daily diet of good news/bad news concerning Braniff's perils. A federal grand jury had been impaneled by the Justice Department to investigate the sabotage reports against American, and

---

[1] Putnam and Coats were great fans of the hit movie *Airplane.* More than a few times in the tumultuous months of spring as he and Coats had walked away from a tough meeting, Putnam would shake his head and repeat one of Lloyd Bridges' lines from the movie: "Boy, I sure picked the wrong week to stop sniffing glue!" Unfortunately, the humor often seemed inappropriate, especially when joined by Bob Ferguson, who had caused not a few longtime Braniff people to wonder where his loyalties lay when he'd come up with a totally lighthearted joke at the height of a crisis. Whether such humor among Putnam, Guthrie, Ferguson, and Coats was simply a reflection of tension relief, or whether it portended something darker, was to become a more perplexing question as the events of spring tumbled toward summer.

the resulting subpoenas had launched a fishing expedition in Braniff's records, much to the delight of Putnam and General Counsel Jim Riley, who were only too happy to cooperate. That story had broken on Thursday, April 22—the same day Guthrie reported the imminent cash crisis in South America. That same Thursday afternoon, while the Dallas-Fort Worth area was reading the latest innuendos concerning American's behavior toward Braniff, Putnam was called to Fort Worth to spend two hours answering grand jury questions on the same subject. That story scalded American in the local press the following day.

Then, in the middle of the collective sigh of relief coming from Braniff's management team at the end of the South American cliffhanger, Braniff's pilots filed a federal lawsuit to stop the Eastern deal.[2]

Suddenly it was Saturday, May 1, and with the kickoff of "The Great Escape" sale three days away, the seismic tremors beneath Braniff's shaky foundation began again.

May 1, 1982 (*Dallas Morning News*): BRANIFF REPORTS LOSS OF 41.4 MILLION

The first-quarter report was hideous. Braniff had now lost $377 million since 1978. Putnam released some optimistic statements for press consumption about how costs were coming down and how much progress had been made, but it all sounded hollow.

On Monday, May 3, disc jockeys in fifteen Dallas-Fort Worth area stations began airing "The Great Escape" commercials. The sale was to start the following day. The spots began with a new tune—syncopated—sounding slightly like a circus, the announcer's

[2] The action was filed in U. S. District Court for the Southern District of New York, a district with a long history of high damage awards and sympathy for labor. The Braniff ALPA representatives, Captain Joe Baranowsky, chairman of the Master Executive Counsel, and Captain Phil Bradley, head of the pilots' Miami base ALPA council, were not at all interested in actually stopping the deal. They had 165 pilots scheduled for furlough because Putnam hadn't negotiated jobs for them with Eastern. The same problem had existed with the Pan Am deal, and in both cases it was a direct violation of the pilots' contract, which contained a so-called scope clause prohibiting the company from permitting any of the company routes to be flown by anyone other than Braniff pilots. Frustrated in getting Putnam to take their determination seriously, the Braniff ALPA group went to court to get his attention.

Putnam and Guthrie tried to explain to Baranowsky and Bradley that if they

voice starting simultaneously: "In honor of your loyal support, Braniff announces 'The Great Escape Sale'!"

The airline had done a better job with the travel agents this time, increasing the commission and giving them better advance notice while still keeping the secret. All over the Dallas-Fort Worth area, travel agents came in to work Tuesday expecting a repeat of the onslaught that had occurred in February.

By Thursday, May 6, the date of the annual stockholders' meeting, the agencies were still waiting. The onslaught hadn't come. As Wainwright had warned, "The Great Escape" was a dismal flop.

Putnam walked into the stockholders' meeting in the world headquarters auditorium to a standing ovation. It was like a pep rally. Those on the management team such as Bill Huskins and directors such as Troy Post who had been at the annual meeting the previous year were amazed at the contrast. It looked like the entire affair was going to be an upbeat, cheerleading exercise.

Putnam and Guthrie had gone over the figures the day before, then again by phone Wednesday evening—an all-too-familiar routine of constant consultation. There had been too many nights when Howard Putnam would walk into his house at nine or ten to be greeted by his wife, Krista, with a "plate of dinner" and a message to call Guthrie—whom he had just left twenty minutes before. Putnam would sit there, picking away at the food, discussing business with his compatriot, who often was doing the same thing at his house. Several times in the previous month they had sat on opposite ends of a telephone connection, fatigued and discouraged, saying: "Well, maybe we'd better go ahead and fold it—y'know." And the other of the two would say, "No, I've just found this [in the figures]—let's try it another week!" Like the rest of the company, Putnam and Guthrie had been on the same emotional roller coaster: up

---

won an injunction, Braniff would shut down everything and file bankruptcy. Baranowsky and Bradley kept trying to get Putnam to understand that all they wanted was for Putnam to reopen the issue with Frank Borman and his people and save those pilots' jobs. Neither side was listening to the other. Putnam had blatantly ignored the pilots' contract and had been surprised after the Eastern deal when his attorneys told him the pilots might in fact win. Of course, with the walls crumbling around them, Putnam couldn't understand why it mattered, and he characterized the lawsuit as "ridiculous!" Unfortunately, the pilots had no way of knowing how badly the walls had already crumbled, since Putnam could tell them only so much. It was a classic case of failure to communicate.

then down, hopeful then despondent—but they could keep each other fairly level emotionally through their constant communication and reinforcement. That was an advantage many of the other officers didn't have. Like so much of the information Guthrie and Putnam handled exclusively between themselves, they shared their shut-down discussions with no one else.

Now walking into this smiling, optimistic gathering at the stockholders' meeting, Putnam had a lead weight in the pit of his stomach. He and Guthrie alone knew how bad it looked—and it looked all but hopeless. "The Great Escape" had been the great hope, and it was gone. Their one chance to do it right had been blown to hell.

"Ladies and gentlemen, I'm Howard Putnam, and I'd like to thank you for being here today."

As Putnam talked, he noted that most of the people—especially the stockholding employees—weren't really interested in hearing the details. They were living on emotion—the comforting but irrational emotion that determination can conquer anything—a tradition in America, of course. Damn the torpedoes, full speed ahead. At that point only Howard Putnam and Phil Guthrie knew how misguided that belief was now. These poor people had no conception of the reality.

He reached the part he dreaded.

"There is always the possibility that, failing the anticipated infusion of cash from increasing public confidence, your company could be forced to seek protection under the provisions of Chapter Eleven of the federal Bankruptcy Act, but we are confident that such won't be necessary." Putnam looked around the room. They were applauding! It was amazing; either they hadn't heard him, or they were ignoring the words. He knew he had said them out loud—his mind wasn't playing tricks on him—but there was no ground swell of reaction, no sudden intake of breath at what he had just unveiled to them. It had been the first time Braniff ever had given public notification that such a course might be taken.

Even the press largely missed it, probably due to the positive emotional atmosphere of the meeting. The following day, only one paper even made reference to his warning.

The Board meeting, on the other hand, was no pep rally. The members, old and new, could see the figures Guthrie presented. It was sad to see the reaction of longtime directors such as Troy Post, Perry Bass, Herman Lay, and L. F. McCollum, Jr. Earlier, all of those men could have bought and sold Braniff with their personal fortunes. Now it was beyond their control. Either the cash would be there or it wouldn't, according to the black-and-white options Putnam laid out. Among the other resolutions authorized during the meeting was the one directing Putnam to call any other airlines he could find to seek an emergency merger of some sort.

On Friday morning the figures from "The Great Escape" still showed no upsurge of sales. Putnam called a morning meeting of just the senior staff, telling them there was still a chance all the preparations they were about to undertake were unnecessary, but in case the cash wasn't there in the next two weeks, they had better be ready. Only Putnam, Guthrie, Ferguson, and a handful of lawyers knew it, but the vast majority of "the plan" had already been completed months before. All Putnam had to do was trigger it—flip the switch, so to speak—and the lawyers would take over. He reserved the final decision, just as the President of the United States reserves the final decision on whether to launch Armageddon with a single command. This gun was loaded, however, and the hammer was cocked—the barrel pointing straight at the battered, staggering, and punch-drunk basket case known as Braniff.

It seemed no one really believed it was anything other than an exercise. Putnam was just getting panicky. Not to worry. Summer was three weeks away.

Putnam dispatched Bob Ferguson (vice president and treasurer) and Alan Stewart (one of Braniff's veteran lawyers under Jim Riley, and no relation to banker Bob Stewart) to New York to confer with Levin and Weintraub, the special bankruptcy law firm Braniff had quietly retained much earlier in the year—to get ready. Bill Huskins, executive vice president for operations (who was not aware of how far "the plan" had been developed), was directed to take a select team of his subordinates over the weekend, swear them to secrecy, and come up with two plans: one, how to scale down to a small, twenty-five-to-thirty-airplane airline overnight that can operate in Chapter 11. "And Bill," Putnam added, "just in case we can't operate in Eleven, you better start thinking about a shutdown plan, as to how we get all the airplanes home." Huskins wasn't aware of it, but part of his assignment was little more than window dressing. "The plan" had no provision for continuing a flying operation during a reorganization under Chapter 11.

The massive layoffs were scheduled for June 1, but even many of those who would be furloughed joined the rest of the company in feeling relieved that now, at least, with Eastern's cash, the airline would survive to grow again someday in the future. As such thoughts helped ease the jitters among the rank and file, a small group of Braniff's senior people were setting out on their contingency assignments to find out how to scuttle the ship.

On Friday evening Putnam attended an upbeat retirement celebration of the Braniff Silver Eagles—an association of Braniff pilots fifty-five years of age or over, most of them retired. The mood there was upbeat too, and Putnam was peppered with questions about the outlook and his planning to which he gave as many optimistic answers as possible. But Howard Putnam's smile was wearing thin. It was becoming a substantial effort to hide the foreboding he felt inside—especially while talking to such senior gentlemen who had helped build Braniff, men who had known the founder and flown the first routes to Peru, men such as Captain R. V. Carlton, who had gone from barnstorming pilot to senior vice president before his retirement—for whom the concept of the Braniff family had always been real. How does a forty-four-year-old president with the company a mere eight months look someone like that in the eye and say everything's going to work out fine, while knowing as he speaks that a team of executives he formed three hours earlier is working up a plan to end it all? The strain was getting to him.

Before coming over from the world headquarters, Guthrie had computed the day's load factor, which should have been at least 65 percent for a Friday; it was 48 percent. He and Putnam would later point to such deteriorating figures and express puzzlement over the decline. Some of the decline represented the continuing erosion of travel agent bookings, the exodus that was strangling the cash flow. The bulk of the decline from May 1 on, however, was quite understandable. The $1 coupon passengers from the two-for-one sales had to use their tickets before May 1. On that day, their numbers (which had swelled the load factors without swelling the revenue yield) disappeared from the load factor percentages. What was left was what had been there throughout late April.

The half-empty airliners were becoming obvious to Braniff's personnel. On Saturday, when load factors traditionally are the lowest, the systemwide figure sank to 30 percent. It was also the doldrums of early May, when few people travel for pleasure prior to the summer vacation rush. Outside the executive suite, however, no one could fathom how so many passengers could be diverted so suddenly by the actions of American—if that were the main cause—or the stampede of the travel agents. It didn't make sense, but it had to change.

Sunday followed at the same level. It was as if the public had suddenly been barred from Braniff flights. Where were they going? Where were the reservations? (The advance bookings were nearly nonexistent beyond a two-week period—thanks in no small measure to the panic produced by Putnam's refusal to guarantee the airline's continued existence.) The increasingly worried employees wondered whether the traffic would soon increase as Braniff's jets flew with a growing number of empty seats—hauling somewhat less than the same number of full-revenue passengers of late April. Sunday evening, with a profound feeling of gloom cloaking his energy, Howard Putnam put on a checkered red western shirt, a pair of blue jeans, and a straw western hat and headed for Billy Bob's Texas in Fort Worth. The club, which had given Casey's thank-you party a year before, was throwing another for Braniff's people, and several thousand employees from the Dallas-Fort Worth area would be there. Putnam had prepared a speech, but walking toward the door of his home, he couldn't take it with him—delivering a speech like that with what he already knew would be ridiculous. He probably shouldn't even go, but he couldn't stay away. His absence would be a foreboding, gaping hole in the evening. The employees would place all sorts of connotations on such an absence, none of them good, and with what he might have to do within a few days, the last thing he needed was for the rank and file to guess the impending truth and start reacting. "The plan" called for total secrecy.

Guthrie joined him at Billy Bob's, having come from the office in a gray sports coat with leather patches on the elbows and no better news—no last-minute turnarounds in the cash or the loads.

Guthrie took off his tie and left it in his car. Together they stood in a reception line and greeted the majority of the guests—every one of whom knew that "The Great Escape" had been a dismal, thudding flop, but most of whom would not and could not believe that the company wouldn't get through. Putnam shook hands and smiled and made small talk, but between the handshakes Guthrie could see the haunted look steal across the boss's face. This was worse than the Silver Eagles agony.

There were disturbing rumors rippling through the crowd about the load factors, like a complex pattern of interacting waves on an isolated, wind-whipped pond—some canceling, some reinforcing each other as the evening continued. There were just as many explanations: "It's just the end of the promotions, that's all. They'll pick up next week."

One of the country and western band members introduced Howard Putnam to loud applause, bowing full to the ground on his knees as Putnam came up onstage. Putnam, laughing, took off his hat and held it over his heart while the MC got up and handed him the microphone. Putnam didn't want to face the group, but he had no choice.

"Since this is a fun evening—and you all deserve a little bit of fun after what everybody has been through in the last few months, I'd just—simply like to say that—we really appreciate all the support you've given the management team, and the improvements are tremendous—the costs are coming down—Texas class is being accepted. We're gonna do it!" Putnam tried to make an enthusiastic gesture with his left hand sweeping triumphantly from left to right, like a knockout punch. All he could manage was a nervously clenched fist and a rather weak motion. Apparently no one had noticed. He left the stage to applause and cheers, but it was one of the most difficult evenings he had experienced. Here he was, trying to be happy in front of them, and he knew the loads were too low to sustain the cash in the absence of a successful sale. He knew what he was probably going to set in motion, and if it happened, these were the very people who would be hurt the worst. "The Great Escape" flop was bad enough, but having to face these people and smile was quite literally too much.

On Monday morning, May 10, Putnam got to the office earlier than usual, met with Guthrie to go over the latest figures on cash flow and load factors, and then sent for Sam Coats.

Coats came down the hall and into Putnam's office, sensing something was wrong.

"Sam, sit down, please." Coats sat down—that worried look on his face. Putnam stood, his hands behind him, resting on the edge of the desk, and shook his head.

"Sam, I think it's over. I think we're going to have to shut it down!"

Coats came out of his seat, his hands up in a stop gesture. "No! You can't—you can't—I can't accept that!" Sam Coats was looking alternately at Putnam and Guthrie for some glimmer of hope. There was none.

"Sam . . ."

"No, you can't—we came here to turn this thing around! We can't shut it down!"

Putnam just looked down and shook his head again.

"No, Sam, you don't understand. . . ."

"I just can't—I can't believe it—can't accept it, Howard. Isn't there something else we can do?"

Putnam fixed him with a tired gaze. "Sam, it's all been done, so get it through your head, this is probably what we're going to have to do."

Coats was stunned into silence. He had been so close to it, and yet no one penetrated the body of information that Putnam and Guthrie shared. They knew how bad it was; Coats hadn't sensed what was coming.

All three of them finally trudged down the hall to a larger conference room and joined the others.

Ferguson and Alan Stewart had returned the night before from their New York meeting with attorney Michael Crames of Levin and Weintraub. They related what they had learned.

Huskins reported on how Braniff could be run as a smaller carrier in Chapter 11 and what cash would be required, as well as how to go about shutting it all down. The mood was worse than somber. The participants in this inner circle simply couldn't believe it was really possible. Before ending the meeting, Putnam looked at the group and said: "I think it's obvious from what we've got here that if we end up without enough cash to run the airline, we won't have enough to run a small one, either. Unless a miracle happens to change things, I think we'd better focus on a possible shutdown later in the week." For a moment, no one said a thing. There had to be other options. Braniff always had another card up its sleeve.

Before Putnam left for New York, Ferguson's weekly letter to the lenders reporting on the company's condition was released for mailing. The management team led by a president who wouldn't take the chance of guaranteeing to a reporter that his company would be around in one month (which might have given Braniff more time) was sending a letter to the holders of $668 million in debt assuring them that Braniff had enough cash to last through the end of June.

If the statement was true, a host of other statements would be lies—
or vice versa. It was very puzzling.

At noon, Putnam drove over to the terminal side of DFW and got
on Braniff Flight 22 to New York's LaGuardia Airport. He had to
testify in the pilot lawsuit in U.S. District Court in Brooklyn the next
day, and he needed time to meet with the attorneys. Behind him at
the world headquarters a delegation from Northwest Orient Airlines
had arrived from Minneapolis in response to Putnam's weekend
call. Braniff wanted to talk about a quick marriage or joint agreement or something with cash behind it. Northwest's people were
only interested in the equipment. It seemed they were making notes
on what they might want to purchase at bargain prices from the
wreckage, if it came to that. With survival time down to hours,
Northwest Chairman Lapensky had carefully sent only executives
who had little or no negotiating authority. When Putnam heard
who was coming, he had no hesitation in leaving.

Putnam had called Dick Ferris of United and tried to get Dave
Garrett of Delta over the weekend but had no success with them or
any of the other fellow airline chiefs he approached. It was too
late—there simply wasn't enough time. A couple of outside investors were contacted as well, and some major oil companies—but the
same story emerged: The studies required would take too long, and
the debt was so tremendous, no one really wanted to get involved.

Now, on the way to New York, Putnam picked away at some
documents and spent an inordinate amount of time looking out the
window—wondering if there were any better options. "The plan"
appeared to be the only way out.

Putnam had a difficult time concentrating on the testimonial
preparations with the lawyers Monday night. He kept taking calls
from and making calls to Guthrie. The Monday loads had looked
like just as much of a disaster. They would be able to point to a load
factor of 30 percent as hopeless. Putnam and Guthrie ended the
evening with a midnight call, agreeing to touch base in the morning.
No irrevocable, final decision had been made yet in Putnam's mind
on when to pull that switch, but it was no longer a matter of if, just a
matter of when. Maybe something would turn up. In his thinking,
the ball was in the court of Fate, if not in the federal court in Brooklyn. Ever since that pilot suit had been filed, Putnam realized, he
had been so disgusted and disappointed that he was ready. He
wasn't searching for any last-minute, desperate solutions—there

weren't any, of that he was sure. Now, with the cash almost too low to continue, thoughts and efforts that might have gone into other frantic moves were focused more and more on one of two options: determine if there will be enough cash coming in to get through the week without dipping into the cash cushion, or trigger "the plan." All other options, however tenuous, had slipped to the back of his mind and were rapidly disappearing. It was all or nothing. Continue or kill it. The shades of gray had disappeared in the haze of disoriented fatigue—and now this "silly" lawsuit.

Tuesday, May 11 dawned fresh and crisp in New York City as Putnam and the attorneys motored to Brooklyn's Federal Courthouse. Putnam was worried that he would be asked for detailed financial figures by the ALPA lawyers while on the stand, or worse, asked if Braniff was contemplating filing bankruptcy. He couldn't reveal either without creating a firestorm and probably violating disclosure laws. His lawyers had worked out how he should sidestep such a question and how they would object.

One of the ALPA attorneys was examining the Braniff president on the stand. It was just before noon, New York time. "Mr. Putnam, you realize that the plaintiffs consider you to be in breach of contract. What would you think if the pilots went on strike?"

The ALPA lawyer was attempting to scare the Braniff president. The man had no way of knowing how far beyond that point Putnam was at that moment. Putnam hesitated a few seconds, fixing the young lawyer with an almost condescending gaze before answering. "If you want to end it all—that's the thing to do."

During the noon recess, Putnam headed for a row of phone booths in the echo-ridden, polished hallway just outside the courtroom, and using the company credit card number, called Guthrie. He knew what he was going to hear, but the call had to be made. Maybe there had been an upturn.

Phil Guthrie and Sam Coats were sitting in Guthrie's office around his round marble table when the call came through. There were several other officers in the room as well. They had all been going over the figures that Guthrie had put together and had just received the latest calculations of the day's load factors. Guthrie didn't use a speakerphone for the call. It was just between the two of them, as usual.

"What does it look like, Phil?"

"Howard, the load factor's running in the low thirties."

There was silence on Putnam's end.

"How's it going up there, Howard?"

"Not good. They tried to threaten us with a strike a bit ago. Do you believe that?"

The two men talked for nearly ten minutes, reviewing everything once again, and especially the fact that the lawsuit might just succeed. Finally there was no more left to say.

"You want to go ahead with it then, Howard?"

Putnam stood there in a public phone booth in a courthouse in Brooklyn, New York and flipped the switch. To the casual observer just another man using the phone—speaking the verbal orders to stop over nine thousand careers, ground seventy airplanes, throw into confusion thousands of travelers, impair $450 million in secured loans, and collapse an entity that had been in operation for fifty-four years.

"Okay, Phil, let's do it. Call the lawyers, have them fly in from up here in New York. I'll head back as soon as I can get out of court. Finish canceling South America—get those planes held up here and have everybody stay around this evening, and we'll meet when I get back."

Howard D. Putnam hung up the phone and stared at nothing in particular for a second. He was so numb, it just wouldn't sink in. Just another decision.

He got up and headed back to the courtroom. Only five people on the planet knew what had just happened.

All Hell Was
Breaking Loose

At 2:10 P.M. Miami time on Tuesday, May 11, 1982 (1:10 P.M. in Dallas), Braniff Flight 74 from DFW nosed into the gate at Miami International Airport. When the door opened into the jetway, Braniff Captain "Tiny" Mize, commuting in civilian clothes, picked up his battered brown suitcase and headed into the terminal, noticing almost immediately that his New York flight—976—was showing a "will advise" label. He was supposed to fly the DC-8 to New York's Kennedy International Airport Tuesday afternoon and right back to Miami that evening, where another crew would take it on to Lima, Peru.

Mize looked outside at the heat-soaked Miami ramp and noticed that his aircraft was on the ground, but no one seemed to be anywhere near it. That was exceedingly strange. There should have been all sorts of activity by that hour. Mize, puzzled and a little consternated that he might have made the trip for nothing, headed on down the slightly musty-smelling concourse to the escalator, through the two security doors, and into the Braniff office area and the crewroom. He picked up the phone and called Chester Hurt of crew scheduling.

"Hey, Chet, Tiny Mize in Miami. I've got a 'will advise' on my flight to Kennedy. What's up?"

Chester sounded distracted. Mize could hear a lot of voices in the background. "Tiny, just stand by down there, it's definitely a 'will advise' situation."

Mize replaced the receiver and walked back upstairs to the ticket counter, where now the screen was showing "canceled." He returned to the crewroom and called Chester once more.

"Now it's showing 'canceled,' Chet. What should I do? You want to send me down South?"

There was a pause on the line. "Why don't you just go on home, Tiny, and we'll see what happens."

This time when he put down the receiver, the words began to replay in his mind. "Why don't you go on home." Chester knew he had a commuter apartment in Miami but lived in Dallas. Why would he say "go on home"?

Dallas pilot crew scheduling was one of the most important nerve centers of the airline. You couldn't run an airline without pilots, and though few people outside the airline industry had any idea what a crew scheduler did, their skills could save or lose millions of company dollars.

Tom Irby had been watching Chester Hurt since Irby had arrived for his late-Tuesday shift, which began at 3:00 P.M. Hurt was one of the most senior of the Braniff pilot crew schedulers, and he had stayed over into the next shift to try to make some sense of the ever-increasing jumble of cancellations coming off the teletype machine from OCC (Operations Control Center) for the South American system. As Irby watched Chester's gyrations, Irby began to get a funny feeling—a premonition. Something wasn't right. For the moment, he wasn't entirely sure he wanted to know, so he kept on working on his job, matching up the domestic-system captains with their trips while Chester sweated over the reroutes of the crews down South, trying to bring twenty years of experience to bear on a rapidly deteriorating situation. The British-Argentine war in the Falklands was heating up, so it was possible, Irby thought, that the cancellations were related to that problem.

Howard Putnam had told one of the ALPA attorneys he needed to get away in time to catch the 3:15 P.M. LaGuardia flight to Dallas. The attorney told him he would probably miss it. He was right. At three-fifteen Putnam was still on the stand as the wheels turned in Dallas. That flight left without him.

Bill Huskins engaged the same small group of people he had kept busy over the weekend. Secrecy was vital, but his group had been so shaken by the glimpse into the inner sanctum of the figures and what was being planned that none of them had leaked a syllable to anyone. Now the circle was widening—more Braniff people had to know, but they still had to keep it to a minimum.

Huskins's task according to "the plan" was to keep any Braniff airplanes from leaving the country for foreign destinations and bring back to the States by tomorrow any planes that would normally remain in South America. At that moment, the man responsible for carrying out Huskins's orders was feeding the cancellations via telephone to OCC, and from there by teletype to crew sked, ship routing, and the rest of the airline. That way it would appear that OCC was responsible for all the cancellations, presumably for operational reasons. If people traced a series of cancellations to the world headquarters, someone might guess the truth. There was widespread consternation at having to interrupt a smoothly functioning operation without visible reason, but as yet there was no tangible suspicion.

Putnam finally got on Flight 5 to DFW at 5:30 P.M. He was calm and collected, simply making notes on the myriad of things that had to be done.

Marguerite Culhane, lead pilot scheduler on the night shift on Tuesday, had also been watching Chester Hurt. At first she had arrived at the same Argentine War conclusion that Irby had thought about, and it crossed her mind that if Braniff was sufficiently concerned about its crews to be canceling flights and paying so much attention to getting the fellows out of there, it was a real departure from the way things had been traditionally. Maybe Putnam was changing things—maybe the company had learned how to care about its people.

The group of senior executives planning the shutdown was waiting for Putnam when he arrived back at the world headquarters at about 8:30 P.M. Central Time. It was a somber gathering. Huskins ran down the list of international aircraft—where they were, when they would be back Stateside. Everyone was aware that the aircraft mustn't be out of the country when the filing took place—Braniff would never get them back. Only in the United States did the bankruptcy laws apply and protect assets.

The meeting lasted for hours, officers and staff coming and going on errands, bringing back figures and information. The word went out to the directors for an emergency Board meeting the following evening—Wednesday—without telling them why.

Michael Crames, the bankruptcy attorney from Levin and Weintraub in New York, had beaten Putnam to Dallas. Crames briefed the group on how the employees were to be handled in accordance with "the plan": Braniff would terminate all its contract people before the bankruptcy petition was filed to block claims for furlough pay and other benefits. For that matter, everyone else not on the essential list (some 225 people) should be terminated at the same time. The group listened to the words, but they didn't sink to an emotional level. How do you sit and calmly discuss "ter-

*minating" nearly ten thousand people? It was a ridiculous euphemism,
one of the assembled group thought—"firing" was more to the point.
"The plan" already had an expeditious and coldhearted answer. Legally,
it would work just fine. "It's easy, Howard. We just send them a Mailgram."*

*It was agreed that a Mailgram would be drawn up over Putnam's
signature, to go out the following night.*

In Miami, Ken Mase, chief pilot of the South American operation, was puzzled. No one in Dallas could explain why two flights
southbound had been canceled. He normally didn't get directly involved in the scheduling (except when his pilots did something
wrong—which was seldom), but there were some unsettling overtones in the lack of information. He made another trip to the teletype room before going home for the day, but he could find no solid
clues.

*The general shutdown strategy was laid out. It had to be kept secret. If
word leaked too soon, captains might refuse to fly aircraft back to Dallas;
small-creditors (including employees) might try to attach the aircraft; and
if the lenders got word of what was up, they might try God knows what.
None of the lenders must know anything. Acker's rage at the Eastern deal
would be a love call compared to the reaction they could expect from New
York in twenty-four hours. Putnam and Guthrie knew that better than
anyone in the room. They had almost achieved the lenders' trust; now they
were going to betray them.*

Chester Hurt chomped on his trademark cigar and contemplated
the mess in front of him. Every time he got a workable plan in his
head to move these crews around, something else was canceled and
threw the whole thing into confusion again. This was getting ridiculous. He wasn't overly concerned, since he knew Eastern was going
to take all the routes he was now trying to deal with. He figured that
over there in the puzzle palace—the bunker—Putnam had simply
decided to pull back or shut down South America early, and true to
Braniff tradition, hadn't bothered to tell anyone. Chester had been
on the OCC hotline a half-dozen times trying to wheedle some information out of the dispatchers on what was happening. They
wouldn't tell him anything.

Chester relit his cigar and poked a pencil at a crew listed in front
of him that he hadn't noticed before. He had to get them out of
Guayaquil, Ecuador. Damn!

There was another matter: security. Elaborate plans were laid out to get the employees off the property as quick as possible, lock them out, prevent a riot or whatever other theft or vandalism problems would be attempted when they discovered the truth. Despite the trend Putnam had initiated in the past nine months to be open and honest with the employees, now in the face of disaster, they would be told nothing and trusted only to riot and steal. That's what the lawyers had warned him to protect against, and they were experts in this sort of thing. Security guards were hired to protect Putnam's home and family and those of Coats, Huskins, and the other officers. Nondescript rental cars would be rented the next day, in case any employees might know what Putnam's or Coats' or Guthrie's personal autos looked like and be laying in wait for them. Orders on what to lock up, and when, went out regarding DFW, and shutdown messages were prepared for the managers of the outstations as well. Finally, an identification card machine was positioned. The old ID's were to be worthless as soon as it all started.

Tony Wainwright had received an afternoon call from Phil Guthrie. "Tony, it looks very bad. Howard would like you to come out in the morning for an early meeting, but in the meantime, you might start thinking about what exposure we have out there, what advertising contracts could be canceled, and how much money is owed to whom. It's not final yet, but it looks pretty bad."

Wainwright had called one of his employees at Bloom who handled the Braniff account. Now at 7:00 P.M. she was on the doorstep of his home, arms full of files and records and contract copies—her face full of worry. It might be a long evening.

OCC had called crew scheduling on the hotline. Flight 905, Miami–Bogotá, a 747, had been canceled. They needed a crew to ferry the airplane back to Dallas. Marguerite Culhane took the call. "Why?"

"Well, we've got some maintenance items, so we need to get her back tonight."

Marguerite punched up the current DFW flight board on her computer. "It can't be done—706 is our last flight to Miami tonight, and there's no way I can get a crew on board in the next ten minutes—which is when it leaves."

The controller at OCC hung up, and Marguerite sat there with a growing knot in her stomach. Why did they want that airplane back? Any maintenance work could be done in Miami just as easily, and that's where the plane was based, flying Miami–Bogotá. They were lying! What the heck was going on? She looked over at

Chester, who was biting the hell out of still another cigar and grumbling at the stack of yellow teletype sheets, and the knot got bigger. She wanted to run and hide, wanted to find a closet to scream in—the implications of what she was seeing were apocalyptic. Marguerite pulled herself up short, however, and decided she had to carry on, regardless of what was happening. Maybe it wasn't what it looked like.

By just after midnight, "the plan" had been explained to the necessary members of management, and the operational part of it was already under way. Putnam went home for some sleep and some clothes. He expected to be at the world headquarters for days. Behind him, the team worked on in his office.

In one of the rooms of the Braniff House Hotel, one of the pilots in for the night on a layover looked across the courtyard at the executive offices and noticed lights and people visible in almost every window. It was nearly 1:00 A.M. He sat down by the desk in front of the window, switched off the television, and wondered what the devil was going on. Like Marguerite Culhane, a knot began growing in the pit of his stomach as he eliminated all but one explanation. He'd noticed the empty airplanes, too.

Wednesday morning, May 12, 1982, dawned with a line of bad weather approaching Dallas-Fort Worth that was destined to provide perfect cover for the secret plan already in motion. By 11:30 A.M., dark clouds had developed into huge thunderstorms just west of the airport.

Jim Reynolds, one of the pilot crew schedulers, had come in on the day shift at 7:00 A.M. to find the long list of South American flight cancellations and flight crew reroutes. It seemed that nothing was going south. Reynolds tried to put it out of his mind, but it seemed pretty obvious that Braniff was getting out of South America three weeks early.

Several hundred feet from crew scheduling, in the executive suite of the world headquarters, a 7:30 A.M. meeting was about to get under way in the boardroom. Putnam, Guthrie, Ferguson, Coats, Harry Pizer (Braniff's head of security), Tony Wainwright (who had not been present in Tuesday's drama), and numerous others were waiting in the hallway as a giddiness prevailed. As Wainwright watched, thinking it a strange time for humor, Robert Ferguson was cracking a couple of jokes, a broad smile on his face, as several others engaged in a bit of kidding and some macabre humor. Ferguson almost seemed to be enjoying the excitement, but Wainwright marked it off as the reaction of people who had been under intense pressure for a long time—facing the end of the enterprise, but the end of the pressure as well.

When they all sat down, Putnam stood before the group, looking very tired.

"We don't have enough money to meet the payroll. We have to close it down to protect the company and its investments—we have to close it today, rather than phase it out and let people know. It's in the best interests of the company. We worked out most of the details last night. For those of you who weren't here, though, we'll go through it all again."

The lobby of the Crillon Hotel in Lima, Peru, was beginning to look like a Braniff crewroom. Pilots from a total of nine DC-8 crews were alternately milling around the lobby, ordering coffee or breakfast, and running back up to their rooms to call operations at the airport for some word, some guidance on what was going on. The rumors, which had begun last night, Tuesday, ranged from ridiculous to frightening—and this early Wednesday morning was no better. The gallows humor typically used by pilots trying to keep a steady hand on their emotions was wearing a bit thin in the uncertainty of the moment. One story had Baranowsky declaring a strike—they all knew that was ridiculous. Even if the ALPA leader tried it, few if any would go along. Joe would be booted out unceremoniously overnight. They all wanted their jobs protected, but almost no one still senior enough to fly South America was going to be in the furloughed group June 1, and none of them wanted to kill the company. The other rumor was a rerun of the old bankruptcy scare. Most of the pilots had heard it before, but always when operations were normal. Now, suddenly, Braniff was obviously shutting down South America—hopefully because of an early Eastern takeover, but no one knew for sure. The word from crew scheduling kept coming back down the teletypes as relayed by telephone from Lima operations: "Stay with your airplanes—we may need you to ferry—will advise. Chester."

Wednesday morning, 9:30 A.M. Central Time. Frank Borman was on the line. Rumors had been cascading into Eastern's head office all morning—something was up with Braniff. It looked like a South American pullback of some sort.

"Howard? Frank Borman. Howard, are you shutting down South America?"

Putnam took a deep breath. "Yes, Frank, we've gone cash-negative, and we don't have cash up here to take down there to make it."

Borman was calling from Washington, D.C., where he'd been lobby-

*ing intensively through embassy row in the past week, trying to smooth the
entry of Eastern to the eleven South American countries they would be
serving starting June 1. Borman paused after Putnam's confirmation.
"How much time have I got to put airplanes in the air? Weeks?"*

Putnam replied simply, "Nope."

"Days?"

"No."

There was another pause, and a pained sigh. "Hours?"

"Yeah, Frank. Hours."

*"Okay." Borman hung up and made preparations to fly back to
Miami immediately to get the operation started. Putnam couldn't tell him
that all of Braniff was about to screech to a halt. The stock exchange
hadn't been told yet. No one could be told before the exchange was told.*

The teletype had gone mad in crew scheduling. Craig Smith, one
of the managers, had been hiding in his office all morning. At about
ten, big Chester Hurt, cigar clamped between his teeth, appeared in
his doorway trailing reams of teletype paper bearing long lists of
cancellations and reroutes of crews all over South America.

"Craig—this is impossible! I can't do it! The whole damn thing
has come apart. Now, if you know what the hell is going on here,
and there's something I'm supposed to be doing that I can do, tell
me, damnit, 'cause this is impossible!"

Smith looked up wearily. He was too low in the management
chain to be told what was happening, but he had a sick suspicion.
"Just do the best you can, Chester. Just do the best you can."

One of Braniff's ticket agents at Sea-Tac International Airport
put the receiver back on the hook and experienced a feeling like the
room was caving in on her. Something was very, very wrong. Overnight, apparently the company had started shutting down South
America but hadn't announced it or admitted it to anyone. She
prayed that was all it was—just South America—but she had
worked the weekend, and the loads out of Sea-Tac had been almost
nonexistent, too. She had heard it was that way everywhere on the
system.

*Bill Huskins walked into Putnam's informal boardroom command
post a few minutes after eleven. "You know, we've got the London flight
scheduled to cancel around four P.M., Howard, but we ought to reconsider. The airplane's booked solid and oversold today, and if we wait until
four, we're going to create an awful lot of problems for people."*

"Can we do it without tipping our hand?"

"Yeah, I can make it a mechanical of some sort."

Everyone in the room seemed to be nodding. Putnam agreed: "Okay, Bill, kill it."

Braniff Flight 602, the pride of the international service, was a nonstop from DFW to London due out at 6:40 P.M. At 11:30 A.M., with the beautiful orange 747 sitting at the gate, operations cancelled the flight for maintenance reasons and directed maintenance to tow the bird to the hangar on the west side. No one in maintenance knew what was transpiring. As soon as the jet was parked on the western side, a puzzled group of mechanics began swarming all over it trying to figure out what could be wrong. All calls to maintenance control or operations drew noncommittal replies. By 1:00 P.M., a rumor had begun circulating that something was very fishy—something was wrong—but no one knew what. As yet, the fear had no name.

At noon one of the worst thunderstorms to lash DFW in years moved into the area, with frightening wind gusts, black clouds, and heavy sheets of rain. At two o'clock—after intermittent lulls that had permitted some flights to leave—the storm closed in again. At two o'clock as well, one of the worst rashes of flight cancellations in the airport's history began chewing into Braniff's flight listings on the television flight monitors, slowly at first, then accelerating— putting the word "canceled" and the phrase "will advise" after more and more flights.

The phones began ringing in brokerage houses on Wall Street around noon. The message was similar in each call, as the rumor mill picked up steam. "Something is happening with Braniff. They've shut down their South American operation. Eastern doesn't know what's happening, and Braniff management won't return anyone's calls."

By 3:00 P.M. New York time (2:00 P.M. in Dallas), the news of Flight 602's cancellation had been dumped into the mill. The worries had finally hit the floor of the New York Stock Exchange, and Braniff stock began trading frantically just before the bell.

As the list of cancellations began to lengthen on the television screens at DFW, Braniff customer-service employees were facing an ever-deepening wave of unhappy passengers as the storm outside lashed at the airport. Most told their customers that apparently the weather was causing the troubles. Some even believed it.

"WFAA Radio News."

"Hey, this is one of the baggage guys out at Braniff." The voice on the other end of the line sounded shaky—like the fellow was frightened. "Do you know what's going on out here?"

"No. What's going on?" The broadcast newsman grabbed a pencil as he cradled the phone on his left shoulder.

"I'm asking if you know. We've got flights canceling all over the place, and no one knows why!"

The newsman thought a second. Could there be a strike? The pilots had filed some sort of lawsuit. . . .

The scared Braniff employee started again. "I know the weather's bad, but the other airlines are still flying, and we're—it looks like—shutting everything down!"

"I don't know. We haven't heard a thing, unless it has something to do with your pilots' lawsuit."

"Naw, I'm sure it's not that. They're too many pilots out here now, and none of them knows what's happening either."

Braniff Flight 501 from DFW to Honolulu had held in the gate for over an hour because of the tremendous storm that hit around noon. Finally, at about 12:40 P.M., the huge 747 pushed back and started engines, only to be put on another one-hour hold on the taxiway. It was close to two o'clock before Captain Charlie Lamb pulled the nose of Braniff's original *Great Pumpkin* (Ship 601) off the runway and began the trip to Honolulu.

When they were established on climbout, Lamb's copilot—a ham operator in his spare time—began working with the on-board HF radio (high frequency, equivalent to what is popularly known as "shortwave"), trying to raise a friend in his hometown of Denver. He had stayed at the Braniff House Hotel the night before and was already suspicious. The fact that the lights had burned in Putnam's office almost all night had also caught his attention. Then, just before they pushed back, the word filtered through that the London flight had been canceled with a mechanical over six hours before departure. When they heard it had been oversold, that added to the mystery.

The clincher came as they got their departure clearance before takeoff. Braniff's "SP" (for special performance) 747 appeared on final approach and landed. Braniff no longer had a huge fleet of 747's, and since all three pilots flew nothing but the 747 in their current assignment, they were acutely aware of where each of the birds should be. That one—Ship 603—should have been in Miami!

At the boardroom command post, Bill Huskins initiated the security plan. With the mass cancellations beginning at DFW, the security guards were to begin taking their positions quietly.

All hell was breaking loose at DFW. By 3:30 P.M. it was becoming apparent that only a hurricane could explain all the cancellations. There was no word from the company, and no one seemed to know. The managers who could be found pleaded ignorance. Somewhere below, Billy McCutcheon had just received the sickening news, but he hadn't been able to summon his managers yet—they were all tied up answering questions from angry passengers and frightened employees. Someone floated the explanation that the pilots were going on strike. No one knew where it came from. Within minutes, the explanation had spread like a prairie fire through the half-mile-long terminal, whipped by the winds of a hundred frantic voices within the employee ranks. At Gate 15, one uniformed captain whose outbound flight had been canceled heard three different repetitions of the strike rumor and had had enough.

"Everybody—could I have your attention, please!"

The captain had picked up the PA microphone and was trying to get the attention of the startled passengers walking by.

"Your attention, please! There is a vicious rumor going around here that the pilots of Braniff International have gone on strike. This is an absolute lie! We are not, and would not, strike our company. We don't know what is going on, but we are not on strike!"

One of the passenger-service supervisors was standing nearby. Normally he would have ripped that mike out of the pilot's hand—he had no business intruding in the gate area like that. Today he didn't know what to do.

A secretary came in the boardroom and whispered to Huskins for a few seconds. As she left, he said to Putnam, "Howard, we've got the guards in place at our homes."

"Thanks, Bill."

The storm lashed DFW in alternating torrents of rain and lightning. Inside, the TV screens showed almost solid cancellation listings for Braniff. Confused people in Braniff uniforms, flight crews and agents alike, wandered around, some aimlessly, too numb to comprehend what was happening. Many still clung to the idea that the weather was the cause of it all. That took determination. It was obvious that American and Delta were still operating, their airplanes still taxiing out for takeoff between the storm cells.

"Dennis Fulton, please."

"This is he."

"Dennis?" The voice was one of the airline financial analysts in New York Fulton was constantly quoting in his articles about Braniff. "Dennis, what the hell's going on down there? Wall Street's running wild with rumors that Braniff's shutting down! Have you heard anything?"

"No, I haven't. I've been working on something else today."

"Well, you might want to check into it."

"I'll do that. Thanks."

Fulton punched up another line and called an inside number at the DFW airport authority's main office.

"Hello?"

"Yeah, hi. Dennis Fulton here, with the *Morning News*?"

"Oh, yeah. Hello, Dennis."

"Uh, I've just received a tip telling me that Braniff is shutting down. Do you know anything about it?"

"Gad—no, I don't—I haven't heard anything like that. The weather is beating the hell out of us, and some flights have canceled as a result. That's probably where the rumor started."

Fulton heard a phone ring in the background.

"Just a second, Dennis, let me get this other line."

He heard the phone clicked on hold. Thirty seconds later the man was back. "Oh, Lord, Dennis, your man was right. We just got the word. They're shutting down and going bankrupt!"

The line in front of Braniff ticket counter B-2 was growing longer by the minute. The ten-year veteran agent behind the counter, a woman, was getting punch-drunk trying to deal with all the reticketing—"patching" the tickets and making reservations for the people on other carriers. The weather must be unbelievable! Why, she kept wondering, was Braniff caving in to the weather while the other airlines were still operating? The commotion in the terminal around her was just background noise—she had been too busy to hear the rumors. Finally, though, she'd had enough. The next customer had just walked up to her. "Sir, excuse me a minute, I'm going to go find out what's going on here!"

The agent walked back in the back to try to find a manager. She must have searched for ten minutes before giving up. No one knew. There was talk of a shutdown, but it was obviously the weather. She returned to her position just as the phone rang.

"B-2 Ticketing."

There was a startled male voice on the other end. "What?"

"This is DFW ticket counter B-2."

"Well, we're all closed down and padlocked up here. What are you still doing there?"

She could have been listening to Swahili—the voice was making no sense. "What?"

"I said we're all closed down up here. Are you still open?"

"Well, of course we're still open—it's the middle of the day. Who is this?"

"This is Minneapolis-St. Paul ticket counter."

"Why are you closed?"

There was a long silence on the other end. "Honey, don't you know? We're bankrupt! This company's gone under."

She wasn't even aware of hanging up the phone, although somewhere in the opiate of a protective haze the shock had thrown around her brain she remembered telling the guy he was crazy. It must have been ten minutes later that it finally began to hit her. She decided to stay at the counter anyway and keep working. Maybe it was a bad joke.

One of Huskins' people had hurried into the room. "Bill, what do you want to do about 501?"

"What do you mean?"

"Well, she's about over Los Angeles. Shouldn't we have her come down in L.A.?"

"No need to. Honolulu's in the U.S. What do you think, Sam?"

Sam Coats turned to Huskins. "Hell, that's a leased airplane. Who cares? Let her go on."

The first officer on 501 had suspended his high-frequency conversation with his friend in Denver long enough to talk briefly to the Los Angeles center as their 747 flew over the city. Over the western side of Santa Catalina Island, his friend called again.

"Dick?"

"Yeah, I've got you four-by, go ahead."

The sound of static made the transmission difficult, but he could hear him all right. "Dick, I'm afraid I have some bad news for you."

The copilot sat up a bit straighter—he had just had a phone

patch to his wife, and everything was okay at home. "Go ahead."

"Dick, I've been monitoring the local newscasts to find out what was going on with Braniff. I'm sorry to be the one to tell you, but they're suspending operations, and it looks like they're going to file bankruptcy."

"What?" His contact repeated the message.

"Thank you. I'll—I'll call you later. We'll try and get some word up here."

"Charlie—Chic?"

The other two pilots leaned in his direction. "Yeah?"

"According to my friend in Denver—he heard a radio broadcast—we're, uh, bankrupt. They're shutting down."

For a moment, no one answered.

"Hell, you mean it?" Lamb asked.

"That's what he said."

"Let's get the ADF tuned in to L.A. and see if we can hear anything."

Lamb worked the knobs of the automatic direction finder, which could pick up AM radio broadcasts, until he heard the sounds of a radio news program. All three punched it up on their intercom panels. Within a few minutes, the story crackled through their headsets.

In Dallas this afternoon, Braniff Airlines has apparently gone bankrupt. The airline has been canceling flights and ordering its personnel to go home this afternoon, and although there has been no formal announcement, it is expected that the company will file bankruptcy papers this afternoon in Dallas. Several Braniff flights have been told to land in locations short of their destination, including Braniff's nonstop Dallas-to-Honolulu flight, which has diverted into Los Angeles International.

The three pilots looked at each other. "We have?"

Bill Huskins hung up the receiver. "Howard, only one problem so far. We've got a captain on the ground in Memphis who's refusing to bring the plane on to Dallas. They told him we've gone bankrupt and he apparently isn't going any farther."

In pilot crew scheduling, big Chester Hurt finally reached the end of his patience. The crews were totally out of control—they had "lost" the airline! Chester looked at the ashen faces of his coworkers and stood up, tossing a handful of computer sheets at the wall. "Holy shit, people, it's all coming down around our ears!"

Chic Smalley, flight engineer on Flight 501, raised Dallas operations (OCC) on the VHF ARINC (Aeronautical Radio, Inc.) frequency. "Are you going into L.A.?" asked OCC. Chic asked Charlie, "Are we?"

Lamb didn't hesitate. "Aw, hell. We've got perfect flying weather, three hundred people who've paid good money to go to Honolulu, and we've got enough fuel. Hell, no, we're not going into L.A."

"I get the impression he doesn't care," Smalley said. "He just asked, he didn't order us down."

"I don't care if he does order us down, we're going to Honolulu. If they don't like it—well, what can they do, fire me?"

All three laughed, and Smalley relayed the "no" to OCC, who put up no protest.

Captain Lamb rang for the chief flight attendant using the telephone-style handset. When she came on, he told her to come to the cockpit alone. He was going to tell her what had happened but order her not to tell anyone else. He would make an announcement when they got to Honolulu.

Betty Atheson knocked on the cockpit door within two minutes.

"Betty?" Lamb said, "Come here and sit down." He motioned her to the jump seat just behind the captain's seat.

Lamb swiveled around in his chair.

"Betty, I guess this is just about the hardest thing I've ever had to tell anyone in flight."

Betty Atheson stiffened. "What, Charlie?"

"Well, I've got some good news and some bad news. The good news is you're gonna get to go home tonight—we're not laying over. The bad news is, we're doing the rest of this trip free. The company's bankrupt—kaput. We're all out of a job."

Betty Atheson put her hand to her throat and closed her eyes and sighed, as if relieved. "Oh, is that all?"

"Wha-a-at?" Charlie looked taken aback.

"Charlie—damn you—I was afraid you were going to put this big sonofabitch in the water! I can always get another job."

By 5:00 P.M. Braniff's terminal at DFW was full of security guards. There had never been an official announcement, but gradually the word spread. Many employees worked on, regardless. Others wandered out. Still others sat or stood, unbelieving, numb, and unresponsive. Most of those who tried to go down to the crew lounges or lower levels were rudely blocked. Pilots couldn't get to flight bags, mechanics couldn't get personal possessions. Suddenly the cherished Braniff ID card was worthless. Hundreds of passengers milled around, as puzzled as the employees. Baggage had arrived on aircraft but no one was allowed below to unload them. Hundreds of passengers would arrive on one Braniff flight expecting to take a connecting flight—unaware as their crew of the disaster—only to be left in the terminal with no outbound flights, no guidance, and a ticket of dubious worth.

At the world headquarters, no employees without the new ID's were being admitted to the complex. The night shift, including Tom Irby and Marguerite Culhane, couldn't get in to crew scheduling.

At about four-thirty, Craig Smith had come out to the main control area and announced that the company was bankrupt, there was no payroll, and they could all go home. Chester bit through his cigar, glared at Smith, and thought about it. Smith, with a tear-stained face, sat down on a stool in the corner and just watched.

Chester Hurt finally got to his feet. "If the money's stopped, I'm leaving." He picked up his lunch box and disappeared out the doorway.

The last few schedulers had their hands full with the phones. Confused pilots were calling in from everywhere asking what to do. Teletype messages from all over the system were pleading for advice. The nine crews were still in Lima; there were Braniff pilots in Bogotá, Buenos Aires, Santiago, Panama, and a half-dozen other places outside the United States. Pilots were scattered all over the domestic system as well. Flight attendant crew scheduling had the same disaster. The word from the company—which hadn't come in until four-thirty—was simply to let them fend for themselves. It was all over.

The Last Pumpkin

CHAPTER **34** To the guards standing inside the lobby entrance to the world headquarters, the sheets of rain still cascading like a berserk waterfall in the circular driveway outside matched the mood of the men and women who had come in and out past their station all afternoon. One of the guards had a portable radio, and when the executives weren't around, he listened to the news reports on what was happening just across the field—out of sight. It struck him as strange that here he was in the middle of the disaster, and he was only a spectator. The young guard didn't realize how many other people around the building were feeling the same way.

The officers and senior staff members of Braniff were scattered throughout the executive offices. Small pockets of conversations would start up, then die down as one, then another managerial employee was told his career with Braniff was over and he could go home. Putnam, Guthrie, Coats, and the others of senior rank had monitored the progress of the shutdown minute by minute. Thanks to the violent storm, it had gone like clockwork with few exceptions. Putnam was especially thankful for the storm. "I guess the Lord was with us," he told Guthrie. "Apparently the rain and all kept the employees over there [at DFW] from wanting to do anything but go home. We've had no reports of wild crowds or damage."

One of the staff vice presidents—no longer employed as of midnight—overheard the comment. He had been with Braniff many years. "My God," he thought, "is that all he thinks of us? He expects our people to riot and loot?" He watched Putnam for a minute from the corner of the boardroom, the thought of that statement still running through his mind. "I thought for sure this was the first guy who really understood our people. My Lord, even the worst agent at DFW would have more dignity, more love of this company than that—even today."

At six forty-five, the outside Board members began arriving. By now they all knew from the constant radio and television reports what was going on. Putnam was in the boardroom talking with several others when Herman Lay came through the doorway, an incredulous expression on his face.

"Howard, how could you! How could you file for bankruptcy without Board approval? We hadn't authorized that—we—"

"Herman—Herman, please—sit down, relax, we haven't. Those are all rumors out there. We haven't filed anything yet!"

Lay glared at him, turned, and sat down. He felt horrid about the whole thing and had been very upset on the way to the meeting over what the press had treated as a *fait accompli:* the report that Braniff "had" filed for bankruptcy. The press had just naturally assumed that one meant the other.

One by one, ashen-faced, some of the longtime directors moved into the room: Mort Frayn, owner of a printing company in Seattle; Troy Post, the man whose hiring of Harding Lawrence transformed Braniff and thereby, some would say, condemned it to the ultimate fate they were there to seal; Perry Bass, an intensely private man, who walked in and sat down, shaking his head; oilman L. F. McCollum, Jr., from Houston; and former Dallas Mayor Robert Folsom, who had been on the Board barely eight months.

The attorneys were everywhere, it seemed: General Counsel Jim Riley; Braniff attorney Alan Stewart; Mitch Perkiel and Mel Garbo of Arnold and Porter; and Michael Crames, from Levin and Weintraub, along with a number of other officers and assistants. They were attending a funeral, and they knew it.

Someone had ordered sandwiches and Cokes from Marriott, and for some reason Marriott complied. Marriott would end up in the number one position on the list of unsecured creditors.

At just after 7:00 P.M., the meeting got under way in desultory fashion. Post and Lay and Frayn were studies in constrained grief. They couldn't believe it was happening.

Putnam spoke first. "Gentlemen, we all know why we're here." He went on to outline for the record what had been done over the weekend and the hopelessness of getting a "white knight" at the last minute. Guthrie explained the cash deterioration with charts.

They then proceeded to the steps to be taken, a resolution authorizing Chapter 11, and a "temporary" cessation of operations, along with the reasons for brutally dismissing the human corpus of Braniff. Some wondered what he meant by "temporary."

Crames passed around a copy of the Mailgram that was, at that moment, being transmitted to nearly ten thousand different addresses around the North and South American hemispheres as well as the United Kingdom.

And just as suddenly it was finished. Everyone got up, slowly, and began drifting here and there in groups. Unlike the usual response of busy millionaires and high-powered executives at the end of a Braniff Board meeting—dashing from the building to the next appointment—they just sort of hung around, with hands pushed deep in the pockets of expensive suits, voices as hushed as they would be in the presence of the corpse at the end of the services, and some, such as Troy Post (silently possessed by his own thoughts), occasionally wandering over to the window to look out through the rain-streaked glass at the sparkling complex Harding Lawrence had built, looking for the Braniff ramp a half-mile distant. It was a ramp now crowded with randomly parked Boeing jetliners in mockingly happy colors, besodden with the dampness of the storm and the tears of the employees who, taking a last look behind them as they left the parking lot in confusion and shock, could make out the forest of gaily painted tails in the macabre light of the lightning flashes—metallic structures bearing the stylized name of an Oklahoma insurance man long dead, visible for those few fractions of a second like some discarded sculpture of aerospace imagery crafted by Alexander Calder (now deceased as well), defiantly thrusting their magnesium skeletons into the gloom of the long night ahead.

A few minutes after 10:00 P.M., Putnam and Guthrie were sitting with Michael Crames and several of the officers crowded around the circular marble table in Putnam's office. Most of the aircraft were down now, though a few were still being ferried in from South America, and Ship 601 was on the ground in Honolulu. The principal task that remained was filing the petitions in the morning— one each for Braniff Airways, Braniff International, and Braniff Realty, another subsidiary.

One of them asked Crames, "Do you suppose there's any chance that a creditor could file involuntarily on us tomorrow morning in

New York before we could get to the judge here, and somebody like that put us into Chapter Seven [liquidation]?"

Crames shook his head. "It's never happened before with any bankruptcy this size." He thought about it a bit more. "I don't think it would happen."

Putnam leaned forward. "Can you tell us one hundred percent, Mike, that it will not happen?"

Crames answered with lawyerly restraint. "No, I can't. There's always a chance some little trade creditor just might do it."

Putnam tapped his desk lightly. "Well—no—we can't take that risk. We've got to go somewhere and get filed tonight!"

Crames had already made initial contact with the bankruptcy referee and knew that the filing would be made before Judge John Flowers in Fort Worth the following day. Someone found a residential phone book for Fort Worth, and Crames pawed through it until he located Judge Flowers's residence. He called him, and at first Crames and the judge agreed to meet at the courthouse. Flowers tried unsuccessfully to give Crames, a New Yorker, directions to downtown Fort Worth. "Tell you what, Mr. Crames, why don't you just take a cab on out to my house?"

Crames took down the address.

John Flowers put down the receiver. He had been reading in bed when Crames called. He and his wife both knew of Braniff's shutdown, and he told her the call wasn't a complete surprise and that the lawyer would be out in about an hour to file the papers. Mrs. Flowers got up to make some coffee.

Crames was down at the security desk by the front entrance when Putnam caught up to him. "How're you getting to Fort Worth?"

"I just ordered a cab."

"Gad, Mike, you can't take a cab all the way to Fort Worth. To start with, we can't afford it." Putnam tried to chuckle. "Come on, I'll drive you."

Putnam and Crames and Andy Kress, one of Crames's assistants, got in one of the Ford Fairlaines security had rented, and they set out for Fort Worth. The storm was still rumbling around the area, but the heavy rain had let up for a while.

Putnam found the Judge's address at about 11:45 P.M. They were greeted on the doorstep by Flowers, who had dressed in a pair of slacks and a sport shirt. The four men sat and talked about the unbelievable events of the day, and Flowers said he was sorry to see Braniff in such a predicament.

Since it was important in the lawyers' view that Braniff rid itself of employees a day before the filing, they waited until it was past midnight before handing the petitions to the judge.

John Flowers signed all the copies of the three petitions, wrote, "Filed—12:01 A.M." on each, and accepted the six $100 bills Crames had brought as the filing fee. He wrote a receipt for Crames on a legal pad.

With those few physical acts, Braniff was officially under the protection of Chapter 11 of the United States Bankruptcy Code—and a ward of the court.

John Flowers hesitated a moment at his door as he watched his three midnight visitors depart, their passage marked at intervals by the staccato flashes of lightning from a nearby thunderstorm cell. The judge's thoughts turned briefly to the summer ahead—a difficult and busy one, to be sure. The enormity of the disaster—the weight of the wreckage he would have to preside over—the odds against Braniff rising from its ashes (which would be calculated in no small measure by his actions), all of it was a bit hard to fathom, especially at 12:14 A.M.

Thirty-five hundred miles to the west, similar thoughts of an uncertain future were occupying the minds of the Braniff crew members gathered in the first class cabin of Braniff Flight 502, just then settling down at flight level 350, headed east over the dark Pacific.

At the exact moment that John Flowers had received the phone call from Michael Crames, Diamond Head's timeless form was drifting into view through the left-hand cabin windows of the original *Great Pumpkin*—Braniff Ship 601. The ponderously beautiful orange bird altered course slightly to pick up an assigned outbound heading of 080 degrees magnetic and began the climb out of nine thousand feet on her last, lonely journey as one of Tom Braniff's progeny. Braniff Flight 502 was airborne for the last time, and with it the last scheduled trip that Braniff Airways would operate. Behind Captain Gordon Winfield and crew on the flight deck the sunset was building to the grand finale of a spectacular show for the vacationers on Waikiki and elsewhere in the soft tropical air of Hawaii—red and orange hues of unbelievable depth playing against the edges of the few altocumulus clouds glowing cotton candy pink from the last direct rays of the distant fireball, promising another typically clear and balmy night under the splendid canopy of stars that seem to shine brighter in those latitudes than elsewhere in the world.

The beauty and the serenity were lost to the Braniff refugees on Flight 502 however, behind them now, relegated to yesterday's memories like their careers and an important chunk of their lives. Most of them sat, many crying softly through a shocked numbness, staring vacantly through the windows across the familiar expanse of Ship 601's First Class cabin to the deep purple visage beyond of gathering darkness and brooding uncertainty.

"Braniff 502, contact the Honolulu center now, 127.6. Goodbye, fellas—good trip," came the benediction from the departure controller at Honolulu International Airport as he watched the phosphorescent, computer-generated blip labeled BN502 crawl to the right edge of his scope and disappear. BN502 would appear no more on Honolulu's scopes. He had heard the news an hour before.

The controller realized he had a small lump in his throat.

The True Assets of Braniff

CHAPTER 35   The upper-deck first class lounge of a Boeing 747 is a unique and opulent place—vastly different from the color-coordinated, utilitarian passenger cabins some ten feet below. As Braniff had added more and more of the ponderous aircraft to the fleet during the late 1970s, such upper lounges had become semiprivate worlds of Onassis-like richness for Braniff employees as they shared the plush surroundings with full-fare first class passengers—flying in grand style to exotic destinations on $18 company passes (in Howard Putnam's estimation such employees were "freeloaders"). As the last Braniff flight—Flight 502 from Honolulu to Dallas—leveled off at cruise altitude in the early-morning darkness of May 13, 1982, the upper lounge of Ship 601 became a refuge from the harsh reality ahead for the now off-duty pilots and flight attendants who had flown the aircraft to Honolulu a few hours before. It seemed so comfortably familiar and eternal, as eternal as their airline and their jobs had been.

Like most of her fellow crew members, flight attendant Ginny Linder had merely picked at her dinner. Now she couldn't take the impersonal surroundings of the main first class cabin any longer. Leaving her seat, she walked the few steps to the circular stairway that transcended the distance between the public domain of the lower deck and the semiprivate environment of the upper lounge, and climbed the steps—experiencing again as so many times before that feeling of ascending through a warp in time and space into another world. Ginny felt an almost desperate need to escape, to be with her friends in a warmer surrounding, to hide in the familial feeling permeating the group of Braniff people who were holding what amounted to a wake.

The sound of the rarefied slipstream whispering past the orange skin of 601 at 80 percent of the speed of sound provided a sort of white noise as the background for the hushed and misty-eyed conversations among the group. They sat in various positions around the lounge, cigarettes held absently in one hand, drinks in the other, all seeking reassurance that something survivable would come of all this.

Captain Charlie Lamb, now off-duty and holding a drink, sat in one of the opulent swivel chairs in the lounge as Ginny Linder sat down on the carpeted floor by his feet, tears glistening in her eyes.

"How're you doin', girl?"

"Charlie, I just want to thank you, you know—for all the good years—it's been great, really. And thank you for not landing in L.A. It wouldn't have been the right way to end it."

Lamb patted her shoulder and studied the sidewall of the lounge.

"When did you join the company, Ginny?"

"In 1965. Harding and I have that in common. How about you, Charlie?"

"June the first, 1949."

She sat and looked at his face a minute, thinking how long that was—how much time and effort and love he must have invested in this company.

The numbness and the liquor combined with the cabin altitude

377

and the otherworldly atmosphere of the lounge eased the pain, and the conversations began to turn to remembrances of years before, of people and flights and airplanes—war stories, as they're known among crew members. Slowly but steadily they displaced the ether of reality with verbal pictures of happier trips and earlier times—tales of the first days as a new employee, the exciting changes in the company with Lawrence's arrival, the exhilaration of the international routes, and the opulence of beautiful evenings beneath reddish-golden sunsets in London or Amsterdam or Mainz, Germany, on the Rhine with a fun crew of Braniff companions on a layover. Any thoughts of unemployment, or financial crises, of wrenching personal decisions and relocations in a cold world without Braniff were put off, forced to fade into the future—a future that ended, for all practical purposes, ahead in Dallas. Far more words flowed than liquor, and they formed an insulating cocoon spun around their raw and ragged emotions.

The atmosphere began to turn from melancholy to the sort of wistful gaiety that an evening of camaraderie can sometimes engender, and smiles and laughter could be heard as the big jet left an unseen contrail over nighttime New Mexico and neared the descent point. The first glow of dawn was still a half hour over the horizon and just out of view to Captain Winfield and his copilot as they leaned forward, straining slightly in the subdued light of the cockpit to plan their way past the angry radar returns—echos of rain showers and turbulence from the problem weather still pummeling the DFW area, which was now coming up fast.

Suddenly the well-trained ears of the Braniff people in the lounge picked up the sound of the engines being throttled back to idle, the unmistakable prelude to descent into DFW and the maelstrom of reality they had been successfully holding at bay for hours. The realization of what lay ahead flooded in on the whine of the engines—through the walls and the tiny windows, which had shown only insular blackness for many hours—up the circular stairway, engulfing the anesthetized Braniff people in the upper lounge, renewing the tears and the stomach-churning feelings of panic and terror and uncertainty. Every foot of altitude they lost toward the North Texas terrain was another foot into hell. As they returned to the main cabin one by one, there was a near-desperation—a burning desire to cling to the security of the place, as if by staying there they could refuse to accept it, force the nightmare to go away.

As 601 appeared like a surrealistic apparition settling out of the

378

mist that hung over DFW, passing some fifty feet above the approach lights marking the northern boundary of the western runway, the Braniff people on board were confronted with a sickening visage through the first class windows: a veritable forest of Boeing 727 tails in a multitude of colors parked in haphazard fashion all around the terminal. It was real after all.

When the 747 had been parked and the passengers disgorged into a darkened terminal populated principally by television camera crews, the Braniff people filed out, carrying their flight bags and trying to avoid the bright TV lights—looking distraught and confused. Ginny Linder had left her car in the main parking lot on the inside of the semicircular terminal. She walked straight to it now, hardly noticing the rain, and began the drive home.

It still seemed so unreal. Perhaps what some of the pilots had said on the way back was right. Perhaps Putnam would get it back in the air again. Maybe this was only temporary. Confused thoughts darted in and out of her mind as she fought the rain and the high-water areas in her path and looked for a place to buy a newspaper. The overwhelming need to see something in print engulfed her. Maybe, just maybe, the reports would hold some new information and some new hope. Maybe she had accepted it all prematurely.

She maneuvered alongside a newspaper vending machine near the outside corner of a 7-11 store, close enough to reach the coin slot from the car. As she rolled down the window, Ginny turned her head to the left in one quick motion to look at the newsprint visible through the glass in the door of the machine and suddenly found herself staring into a nauseating vortex, a black hole of reality, the black ink of the headline on the *Dallas Morning News:*

BRANIFF HALTS FLIGHTS, SEEKS BANKRUPTCY

Ginny Linder felt herself go limp. Shaking, she put her forehead on the hard edge of the steering wheel and cried as she had never cried before.

As Flight 502 had begun the trip home from Honolulu, Howard Putnam and the two lawyers returned to the world headquarters, noting the irony of that name as they drove into the courtyard. The long faces of the Braniff people still milling around the offices made it look like the disaster it was—long faces on all except for two of the officers.

Vice President and Treasurer Robert Ferguson was "up." There was no better way to describe it. As several of the Braniff executives with more years invested in the company than Ferguson watched the young lender-turned-treasurer, he seemed to be on some sort of natural high—almost ecstatic with what had been accomplished. His inappropriate humor was well known around the building, but this was almost too much. Phil Guthrie also was wandering around with too much adrenaline apparent in his animated conversations and showing too much excitement—not as much as Ferguson, but incongruous for an evening that had witnessed the destruction of a fifty-four-year-old corporate institution and the slaughter of nearly nine thousand jobs. It was almost as if these two didn't realize the airline was dead. It was almost as if they knew something the rest of the group didn't. They were acting as if it were a beginning, not an end.

Howard Putnam, however, was in terrible spirits, as were most of the assemblage. Now that he had initiated "the plan," the enormity of the action gnawed at him. Putnam headed for his room in the Braniff House Hotel to get some sleep for the next ordeal. There would be a morning press conference.

It was the beginning of a nightmare for the Braniff people. There is no way to grasp fully the loss of a job of many years and (in the case of airline people) the loss of a way of life. To lose the entire airline as well—to be able no longer to dial a number in Dallas at any time of the day or night from anywhere on earth and hear a Braniff reservationist or crew controller answer at the other end—was beyond comprehension in the first few hours.

For those abandoned to their own devices in far-flung places, the first problem was repatriating themselves to home cities. Most (not all) of the other airlines, national and international, stepped forward almost instantly to help with sympathy and human kindness. As the doomed fleet was being assembled in accordance with "the plan" at DFW, Braniff people all over the nation were being ushered on flights of United, Delta, TWA, and even enemy American on the strength of a Braniff pass, or more often a heartfelt statement, "Just get on, you don't need a ticket today." Many of those who helped the Braniff refugees and watched them trudge on board with grim faces and distracted looks—people who had once applied to Braniff when they were entering the airline business—couldn't help but remember the familiar line, "There but for the grace of God go I."

In Lima, Peru, and Santiago, Chile—and in London, England, as

380

well—the level of sympathy was lower, but for the most part the confused and stranded Braniff crews got a helping hand to get home.

Braniff people on vacations suddenly awoke Thursday morning thousands of miles from home to the hollow loneliness of the news. Quite a few would have to pay their way home with money they would need for groceries in the months to come. There was no help from their company—they were no longer employed in the airline industry.

At noon the next day, Thursday, May 13, 1982, Howard Putnam walked into a crowded press conference at the world headquarters. The room was overflowing with television and print reporters, cameras, microphones, and lights. He walked in with a broad smile, but he lost it as soon as he stepped behind the podium.

"Last night, as you know, Braniff temporarily suspended operations." He went on to tell them that the company had filed for bankruptcy under Chapter 11 and would attempt a reorganization. He said that the shutdown had been an absolute necessity and that it ". . . was the only action we could take to preserve and protect our aircraft, the—assets. There was absolutely no need to keep on going another day or so, further jeopardizing what assets we have."

And then Putnam turned to the subject of the nearly nine thousand people he had fired in the previous hours, people who were just now beginning to receive the Mailgrams for which the company had been forced to present a cashier's check. "You've heard me compliment the Braniff employees before—they, uh, they've fought a very tough battle, they're a very dedicated group, they, ah, have gone through pay cuts and pay deferrals, they've supported us, they've worked as volunteers, and what we had to do last night was very difficult, not only for us but for them. It's a shock to them I know, and there is no payroll. They were taken off the payroll as of last night. The paychecks that are out there now will not go through, there is no cash to support them." Putnam was fighting for control during the statement as a few tears rolled down his face. He had cried on camera before, but he let the enormity of what he had done wash over him for a moment. He was sure it was the best decision, but as one of his people had said, none of them understood fully the human damage this action would cause.

During most of the news conference, however, Putnam exuded the confidence he was trying to maintain in "the plan." He tried as well to hide the hard edge of resentment he felt over the refusal of the Braniff unions to face reality and slash their contracts months before. They had helped make this inevitable. He might cry for the Braniff people while on camera, but damnit, they had contributed to their own demise by not forcing their unions' feet to the fire. They were partly responsible for destroying Howard Putnam's chance to be the man who saved Braniff.

As the newsmen left, Braniff people all over the country were ripping open Mailgram envelopes with shaking hands and finding the same message inside. As most unfolded the piece of paper, they expected to see some carefully phrased, heartfelt words of condolence, some passing comment to indicate that the author had at least some understanding of what he had done—what he was doing—in shutting down the airline. What they found instead were the utilitarian words of lawyers and young executives engaged in an exciting and exacting game in which lopping off the encumbrance of nine thousand people was merely another step in the sequence:

> EFFECTIVE AT 8:00 P.M., CDT, MAY 12, 1982, THERE WAS A TEMPORARY CESSATION OF WORK BECAUSE OF CIRCUMSTANCES BEYOND THE COMPANY'S CONTROL. IT HAS BEEN NECESSARY TO GROUND A SUBSTANTIAL NUMBER OF THE COMPANY'S AIRCRAFT.
>
> FOR THESE REASONS YOU ARE HEREBY NOTIFIED THAT THERE IS NO FURTHER WORK AUTHORIZED FOR YOUR POSITION AND THAT YOU ARE TERMINATED FROM EMPLOYMENT AS OF THE ABOVE TIME AND DATE. WE SERIOUSLY REGRET THE NECESSITY OF THIS ACTION. SINCERELY, HOWARD PUTNAM

In more than a few Braniff households the response was utter, paralytic amazement that Howard Putnam, the down-to-earth airline president who had been so persuasive in getting the trust of the Braniff people, could authorize such a coldhearted and cynical message over his name and ever again look at himself in a mirror. The gratuitous brutality and insensitivity of the Mailgram would burn in their memories.

In the following week the Dallas and Fort Worth communities rallied to help the Braniff people who had not had the fortune to be among the 225 still on the payroll at the world headquarters. The Texas Employment Commission began setting up special centers to help Braniff employees fill out unemployment forms, and newspapers offered free advertising space in the classifieds for job-hunting. Messages of condolence were printed in the same papers from various organizations, and rival airlines (such as Putnam's former employer Southwest) announced that they would honor Braniff tickets and employee passes, at least for a few weeks.

There was a dark side, however. Banks all over the area refused to honor Braniff Credit Union checks (which were perfectly good, since the credit union was independent and financially sound), and although some had received their paychecks before the filing, those who had deposited them on Wednesday were receiving dunning calls from their banks by Friday. The attitude of the bankers was hauntingly familiar: "It's not our problem. Pay up, or we sue." Some banks and mortgageholders bent over backward to be lenient, some slipping payments for several months. Others told Braniff families that there was nothing they could or would do to help. As one thirty-four-year-old Braniff homeowner was told by his mortgageholder, "The best thing you can do is get a loan, get a job, or go home to Mama. You don't make the payments, we take your house in a hundred twenty days."

Within the hearts and minds of the Braniff people there was a dogged feeling that it wasn't the end. Putnam himself had said they would be back, and in addition there was the historic cynicism of Braniff people that their management always worked from a secret plan. Since such a plan would never be revealed to the rank and file, the fact that Putnam acted as if it did not exist simply confirmed that it did exist. The entire exercise of shutdown and bankruptcy was merely a part of that sneaky plan, and it had obviously been implemented to break the unions.

In the meantime, the pressure of nearly two years spent in a deathwatch was over. The worst had finally occurred and need not be feared anymore. There were many parties and long June afternoons spent relaxing and unwinding and waiting for the recall.

But by early June, Howard Dean Putnam had to face a new, chilling lesson in reality. "The plan" that the employees suspected was there, the one Putnam had relied on with such absolute confidence wasn't working. Instead of the creditors rushing in to cooperate on a restructure, Putnam had been overwhelmed with waves of attorneys and apoplectic bankers and insurance company representatives, none of whom cared about reflying Braniff and all of whom wanted their money and secured assets. In addition, the backlash of the horrible public-relations disaster resulting from the shabby way the public and the employees had been treated in the shutdown was making it clear to everyone that Braniff had little chance to return to the skies under the name Braniff, at least in the near future. "The plan," however, had called for reflying it within four months—and Putnam had been confident he could do it within two months! There were possibilities, of course. In the first week of June Putnam had announced that Braniff was talking with Pan Am about flying as a subsidiary under Pan Am's colors, but that was a long shot.

In New York in the first few weeks of June, Acker's people began poring over the ideas presented by Putnam's people, and more important, began looking at the figures of what Braniff had in money and assets to bring into the deal—figures that wouldn't be filed with the bankruptcy court until July 26. The information was shocking. "Jesus Christ, did you see these figures?"

"Yeah."

"If they have this much to bring into a joint operation, that means they still had enough to operate!"

Putnam and Coats and Guthrie and most of the other senior executives had told the world that Braniff had simply run out of cash. It no longer had enough money to meet the payroll and pay for fuel. That was the cornerstone of justification. On July 26 documents were filed with the bankruptcy court in Fort Worth that showed the company was, indeed, down to critical levels in its banking accounts, with a little over $11 million in immediately available funds to draw on. The press moved in and examined the figures and accepted those now-familiar conclusions without further examination. Yes, in fact, they agreed, Braniff had run out of cash.

Buried in the figures, however, were two other important bits of information, the significance of which was missed. First, the prepaid fuel already "in the system" and available for use amounted to an additional $14 million, or enough to fly Braniff for two weeks. The second, though, was the ticking bomb. Braniff had indeed run out of cash, because the money it had earmarked for reflying a shutdown airline (in accordance with "the plan") was left safely on another part of the balance sheet.

Braniff had been taking in as much as $100 million per month in gross revenues as late as November 1981 (before Texas class was introduced), but by March and April 1982 this had dropped to $80 million in gross revenues per month. A healthy airline with such an income should have had no more than $90 million in receivables. A cash-strapped airline would have less than $80 million. Braniff (according to the sworn documents filed July 26, 1982) had a staggering $138.5 million! Braniff hadn't had enough cash in the accounts because it had failed to collect it.

Whether by design or incredible managerial negligence, the collection of Braniff's vital receivables had begun slowing down amid word of an impending shutdown (circulating among the employees of that department) as early as April 20, 1982. The result was the whopping nest egg of $129 million ($138.5 million less about $9 million for doubtful accounts). That was the location of the restart cash cushion.[1]

Perhaps there were no mortals who could have conquered and tamed the Hydra of a monster that Braniff's problems had become by September 1982, but in the glaring light of hindsight it seems very clear that Howard Putnam and Phillip Guthrie were not the men who should have been chosen to slash away at the beast.

It certainly wasn't their fault. Certainly Howard Putnam didn't seek out John Casey, the Braniff Board, or the Braniff bankers to lobby for the job. The bankers and the Board and Casey came out of the woodwork to convince Howard Putnam that he could handle it and should—and they came with hat and checkbook in hand. What is an ambitious man to think when such people gather on his doorstep and beg for his assistance? The thought had to have crossed the small-airline president's mind many times during that week of decision, "If they think I'm that capable, I guess I am."

John Casey thought he was being ordered to recruit one of the best marketing men in the business, and that was also the feeling of the bankers and Board members who forced the issue. Apparently they were unaware of how much of Southwest's expansion under Putnam had been preplanned and a group effort and thus how limited Putnam's experience in innovative command really was.

Howard Putnam, contrary to one line of popular belief, did not

[1] None of the $129 million figure reflects the potential value of the boxes and stacks of unprocessed tickets, returned items, overpaid accounts, and other interline documents that the people of the accounting areas were never given the help nor the time to process—items estimated by some to represent up to $50 million of potentially recoverable income to Braniff.

agree to become president of Braniff with a secret intention or a secret mission to destroy it by plunging it into bankruptcy. There is virtually no evidence to support such a conclusion. If any of the out-of-state lenders were expecting bankruptcy and liquidation to result from his selection as Braniff's new president, they were simply expecting him to fail—not do their bidding.

Howard Putnam, in fact, really thought he could save it, and with the limited information that Casey could legally give him in September 1981 regarding Braniff's condition, he felt it could be turned around by Christmas.

Unfortunately, the real world simply does not work that way. Neither the lenders nor the employees were ready to jump through hoops at his command, and the situation was worse than Casey could tell him.

In late January 1982 it all came crashing in on him. Putnam suddenly realized it was hopeless—he wasn't going to be able to save it. The naïveté of his confidence in a pre-Christmas turnaround and restructure seemed laughable in retrospect. Putnam didn't give up, but he shifted his thinking. Instead of turnarounds, he now needed lifeboats, both for himself and for the company.

The carefully planned use of Chapter 11 began to look like an option, and the New York bankruptcy specialist law firm of Levin and Weintraub was called in to brief the Braniff leadership on what it entailed and what it could accomplish. The moment that course of action became a viable option, it began to metastasize into a plan—and finally into "the plan"—for taking Braniff into bankruptcy, filing a reorganization plan, and reemerging as a flying entity free of the two major encumbrances that threatened to kill Braniff for all times and force it into liquidation: the huge senior debt and the costly union contracts.

"The plan" had begun to take on a life of its own by the date on which Dennis Fulton sat across from Putnam and Guthrie and fired off the fatal question: ". . . can you *guarantee* that Braniff will be in existence a month from now?"

Howard Putnam, in those few seconds of consideration of that question, knew he might well have to initiate the developing bankruptcy plan anytime in the next month. The idea was becoming less repugnant with every passing disaster. He also knew that to give Fulton such a guarantee, as Fulton had phrased it, would be to risk an investigation by the SEC as well as lawsuits by those who might make stock purchases supposedly in reliance on his guarantee if, indeed, bankruptcy was used. Such a risk, however minor, was unacceptable to the ordered mind of an accomplished upper-middle corporate manager, which had been his position at United. The swashbuckling willingness to face all challenges, take all risks, and lie all necessary lies to save his airline was not in him. Then too, it was not really his airline. Howard Putnam looked at Dennis Fulton and administered the coup de grâce to Braniff's chances for survival without bankruptcy: "No [Dennis], I can't."

In fact, there was no last-ditch, all-out, 100 percent effort made to collect enough cash to keep going. By May 10 it was an open question whether Putnam would have been responsible to keep operating any farther, but as long as the lifeboat was there—"the plan"—why try?

Of course, that means that the statement in those nine thousand Mailgrams was false. Whatever reasons might be cited for halting Braniff in its tracks, it was demonstrably not due to "circumstances beyond the company's control."

There were many things that could have been tried had "the plan" not been waiting in the wings as an alternative. The union leaders could have been cornered with an ultimatum, the receivables could have been factored, the fuel companies could have been approached, or Putnam could simply have tried to operate in Chapter 11 rather than dooming the airline with the flat statement that the public would not fly a bankrupt carrier.[2] Whether it would have worked was unimportant. He was not about to try. For "the plan" to work, the employees had to be left out in the cold world without their paychecks for a couple of months. Then, according to the scenario, they would sign anything to get back to work.

In these indications of elective shutdown lie the crux of the real reason Braniff entered bankruptcy the way it did. "The plan" had become a self-fulfilling prophecy, and it had been constructed by lawyers and a senior team who had developed into a synergistic entity, and who by reinforcing each other's views of the world as it should be rather than as it is, were able to convince themselves of

[2] This unsupported supposition would be proven wrong in the last quarter of 1983 when Continental Airlines began operating successfully in Chapter 11 even in the face of a bitter pilot strike. There were to be many differences between Continental's situation and Braniff's plight, but the fact remains that the passengers did not avoid a bankrupt airline.

things that were not true—specifically, that a company the size of Braniff could be shut down with no regard for the passengers or the employees and no dynamic plans for immediate restart, put into bankruptcy against thirty-nine major lending institutions and a thundering herd of self-interested unsecured creditors, and then manage to marshal assets and agreements from a galaxy of disparate interests to keep their material assets (the aircraft) and relaunch their aerial operations after two to four months of sitting on the ground! "The plan" was effectively an inadvertent fraud that Putnam, Guthrie, and Ferguson, along with the Levin and Weintraub law firm perpetrated on themselves (and ultimately on the people of Braniff).[3]

Of course, this all begs the question of the ultimate fate of Braniff if everything had been tried, and had failed. If the company had made it to summer, it might have limped through to September only to shut down with no restart cash cushion and a sure death sentence of liquidation. There is no doubt that the conditions of the company in spring of 1982 were as close to terminal as a corporation can get and still operate outside the courts. As *Fortune* magazine pointed out in a postmortem in June, "The amazing aspect of the Chapter Eleven filing was that it took so long to happen." Nevertheless, it was the gradual but inexorable movement toward acceptance of bankruptcy and ultimately "the plan" as a way out that predisposed the result. They didn't try harder because there was another way to do it, or so it seemed. They had the means (if not the instantly available cash) to continue operating. But as they saw things, it wasn't in the company's best interests to do so.

Could a dean of the industry such as Ed Acker have saved the company without involving Judge John Flowers' bankruptcy court?

---

[3] Unlike Continental Airlines, which would follow Braniff into bankruptcy in the fall of 1983, the Braniff "plan" never included a polished and coordinated restart program. Continental shut down smoothly with the announcement of exactly when it would be back in the air, and with minor deviations to the plan (and ignoring the cynical misuse of the bankruptcy laws to dump their unions), they succeeded. Braniff, however, planned only the shutdown, and that from a legal, instead of operational, point of view. Continental also had a solvent parent, Texas Air Corporation. Braniff, which had no solvent corporate parent, had further tied its hands by making its cash unavailable for any rapid restart. If Braniff had kept flying, or reflown the airline within days according to a carefully structured scenario, it could have succeeded. Doing it as Putnam did it, however, meant that Braniff didn't have a chance.

Acker and many senior airline executives say they would never have been lured into bankruptcy under the same conditions, and perhaps they're right. A sage manager such as Ed Acker (or Harding Lawrence) would never face a Dennis Fulton and refuse to guarantee his airline's continued existence, regardless of the legal dangers. In fact, Acker had taken just such risks within the same year in order to save Pan Am, a mission he apparently has accomplished with (at one point) one fourth of the cash Braniff had in its bank accounts on May 12th, 1982—and Pan Am is far larger than Braniff. Then too, someone such as Acker has sufficient long-standing contacts, acceptance, and trust within the banking and business community to pull it off. Ed Acker, however, wasn't available in September 1981, and whether his equivalent existed in the confused commercial aviation arena in the United States at that time is open to debate. For the Board of Braniff and the sage bankers of First International Bancshares in Dallas to turn to decent but inexperienced men such as Howard Putnam and Phil Guthrie and expect them to handle what probably constituted the worst financial mess in commercial aviation was an incredible act beyond comprehension or excuse, and an ultimate disservice to both the people of Braniff and to Putnam and Guthrie as well.

When the reality that the second part of "the plan" wasn't working imposed itself on Howard Putnam in June and July 1982, only the legions of lawyers were well off (with legal fees that will ultimately top $10 million). To his credit, however, Putnam fought on to protect the assets of the company from liquidation.

And that, in fact, touches the final irony. Under deregulation in 1982 the CAB routes were essentially worthless as assets of an airline, the FAA-imposed slots were similarly worthless as assets, and anyone with a few million dollars could get a certificate, lease gate space and airplanes, and start an airline. Howard Putnam shut down Braniff International to preserve the assets of the company. Unfortunately, there weren't any. By midnight on the evening of May 12, 1982, he had fired them all. However flawed, the true assets of Braniff were the people, and they were gone.

The Fight of a Phoenix

36 The agony of the Braniff people and their attempts to regain their financial and emotional balance in the summer of 1982 (as the hopes for a reflown Braniff remained alive) obscured one tragic aspect of their airline's death: They had never really had a chance to get it right.

Braniff's continuous growth and terrible internal failures in management since the early fifties had prevented the people, veterans and newcomers alike, from developing into a single organization—the sort of cohesive, involved, prideful operation it could have become.

The very essence of a labor-intensive, public-contact business is the body of people who make it work. Regardless of the size of the company or the personality of the principal officers, if this human truth is ignored and the people are regarded as production-line workers rather than as the airline itself, the airline will fail—especially under the acid test of deregulated competition.

For an established carrier to survive the gloves-off competitive nightmare that Congress has created with deregulation, every one of its people must focus on the most important element in the airline equation: the individual passenger. No single employee, whether he or she happens to be pushing a broom or running the Board of Directors, can afford the luxury of saying, literally or figuratively, "That's not my job" when it comes to luring and pampering and pleasing the individual passenger with nonstop service. In other words, neither union contracts nor union work rules can be allowed to eclipse the absolute necessity for each employee to accept eagerly the individual responsibility for the ultimate success or failure of the company. Only then can that group of humans operating within the legal structure called a "corporation" become a unified organization pulling in the same direction toward a common goal of profit and a stable paycheck.

To build such an organization requires a management team at the top and in the middle that never forgets its people on the front lines or anywhere else in the organization.[1]

This doesn't mean the airline's president has to "give away the farm" in terms of money and benefits, but it does mean that he and the people he chooses to be his senior management have a paramount responsibility to respect each human being who carries one of the company's ID cards and (regardless of the difficulty of doing so) to involve his people financially, whether through stock ownership or profit-sharing or whatever other methods might be available. The employee has to feel that his paycheck, and the stability of his job, is directly related to the success of the organization and that the success of the organization is, in turn, directly related to his own individual conduct as an employee. Equally important is the responsibility of the union people, shop stewards and members alike, to understand that their paycheck comes from the company, not the union.

Perhaps the most important aspect of this is communications, not just the traditional two-way communications taught in management seminars, but deep, constant, meaningful involvement of the people from top to bottom in daily figures and facts, the heart of the statistical pulse of the company's performance. Happy-talk company newspapers are necessary and fine, but they are never enough. It is equally important that the lowest-level employee *knows* that his ideas and comments (and gripes) are important and go right to the top level of management without being filtered through the sort of "cover your ass" barriers that characterized Braniff.

In addition, great emphasis must be placed on careful recruitment of the right people for the right jobs and on having the willingness quickly to move or terminate those people whose incompetence might threaten the enterprise and everyone's future.

---

[1] It is ironic that Herman Lay, one of the founders of Frito-Lay Corporation and a Braniff outside director for over a decade, would be cited repeatedly for creating in Frito-Lay one of the best-run corporations in the nation, principally because the organization literally lives to serve the route salesman, who is the front line of the company's continued marketing success. Herman Lay was still on the Braniff Board when he died of cancer in late 1982.

Finally, meeting the challenge means providing the proper preparation for a newly hired employee as well as the proper training for each position. New people must be hired to become part of the company and its history and traditions and pride first, then trained for a particular position. The role of the company personnel department should also include a vigorous program for constantly and professionally monitoring and evaluating the performance of line mechanic and senior vice president alike.

All this is a tall order, and though it seems idealistic, there are airlines (such as many new-entry carriers) that have successfully incorporated all of these methods and more. For the major air carriers, dealing with deregulation means fighting a war for survival, and getting the wholehearted participation of their people in every possible way is vital. Braniff, unfortunately, never stabilized on the way up or the way down long enough to change organizationally to these methods. Howard Putnam, to his great credit (and regardless of his having been mismatched in Braniff's battle for survival), was pulling Braniff in the right direction with the internal changes he was trying to make, but in that regard, he simply ran out of time. The fact that he couldn't completely overhaul the internal structure in a mere seven months didn't kill Braniff, however. Braniff simply came to the end of a long causal chain, of which Putnam's premature shutdown was simply the last link.

One of the saddest footnotes of all is the fact that Harding Lawrence came so close to success. Had just one of the major disasters of 1978–80 not occurred—had the fuel prices not gone into orbit, or the recession retarded the revenues, or the used-aircraft market not collapsed—Braniff probably would have survived even with Lawrence's massive expansion moves, and, with enough time to rectify the internal problems, he would have been able to retire in triumph from a world-class carrier.

As June drew to a close and legions of Braniff employees searched frantically for jobs, too many people simply waited at home for word that the nightmare was all over and Braniff would be returning to the skies. As one senior Braniff captain who would have retired in two years said conspiratorially one afternoon in late July, "Don't you think for a minute this isn't all going in accordance with Putnam's plan. We'll all be back at work by September, just making half as much." Indeed, that had been part of "the plan."

On July 18, 1982, former Braniff President Charles E. Beard died of heart failure. He had suffered a heart attack the night Braniff died, so great was his agitation over the collapse. A third coronary killed him two months later.

Then in mid-July Ed Acker announced from New York that the talks with Pan Am were off—there would be no Pan Am resurrection of Braniff. The announcement had a salutary effect: A huge number of Braniff people finally realized the long-shot nature of reflying the company and stopped waiting for it to happen.

The resiliency of the Braniff refugees began showing up in the form of new business ventures and new jobs all over Texas and the nation. The internal strength of the majority of the employees was far greater than many people had anticipated, and by midsummer thousands had picked themselves up, figuratively dusted themselves off, and gone on to something new, as painful as the process was.

As the various pension funds began landing in Judge Flowers's court, a "hate Lawrence, he's responsible" campaign began to surface—whipped into being by a highly inflammatory and sophomoric regional magazine article in July. By August it had been announced that Lawrence too had suffered a cut in his pension—down to $10,000 per month.

In October Ted Beckwith, fired by John Casey eighteen months before, failed to return from a business trip to East Texas. His car was found abandoned the next day. Beckwith had initially been scheduled to testify in a deposition relating to one of the many actions being pursued by a thundering herd of lawyers for various creditor committees and other interests. Speculation began immediately over whether his disappearance could be related somehow, especially since he had been the chief financial officer for Braniff during the period in which Braniff had granted a secured interest to the major lenders. Some looked toward New York and wondered.[2]

Then suddenly, on Monday, October 18, the announcement that so many of the overconfident unemployed and the rest of the Braniff people had been waiting for broke:

1,500 BRANIFF JOBS RESTORED IN PROPOSAL

The Dallas papers reported that Braniff and PSA, a pioneer intrastate airline in California that had grown beyond those borders, had

[2] On November 12, Ted Beckwith's partially decomposed body was found in an East Texas pasture. The fifty-one-year-old Beckwith had been stabbed nineteen times. As a Texas Ranger investigating the murder said later, "Someone was mad as hell at him." There are no suspects, and the case remains open and unsolved.

tentatively agreed to a plan to refly thirty Braniff jets in PSA colors as a contract division. The wave of relief through the Braniff families all over the country at the news that Braniff apparently would get back in the air—albeit under another name—was immediate, but it would be short-lived.

By mid-November most of the obstacles to the PSA deal had been cleared with the exception of the unions. PSA refused to incorporate the Braniff pilots, flight attendants, or mechanics into the PSA force on the basis of their Braniff seniority, and the wages offered in the contract proposal were mere fractions of what the Braniff people had been paid before the bankruptcy. What was worse (and even PSA's rank and file did not know this), the wages were a fraction of PSA's normal wage scale.

Although the wages would have been acceptable if disappointing, the loss of seniority was not. First the machinists, then the Braniff pilots refused to sacrifice their seniority lists. PSA demanded that even the most senior Braniff captains start as flight engineers with the new division and accept seniority numbers that would place them in junior positions to twenty-three-year-old PSA flight engineers then on furlough. The humiliating insult and the refusal even to consider bargaining over the terms was too much. The Braniff pilots turned it down and killed the entire deal.

Putnam would later say that he would never understand their refusal. Quite a few Braniff pilots shared his assessment of the end result, but Putnam's statement came from an inability to understand the fact that the pilots considered themselves engaged in a profession, and those who had risen to the top of that profession were not prepared to crawl and beg for crumbs—and be under the command of less experienced pilots. On the other hand, the PSA chairman (William Shimp, himself a former airline pilot) had promised his pilots he wouldn't budge on the seniority issue.

Once again the hopes of the Braniff people languished. On December 2 Judge Flowers threw out the machinists' contract and reinforced a growing legal precedent—that a corporation could rid itself of union contract obligations in bankruptcy if the unions refused to agree to a reasonable offer. The definition of what constituted a reasonable offer, of course, was subjective. On December 8, Putnam asked Judge Flowers to throw out the pilots' and flight attendants' contracts as well, and on December 9, the news broke that a new deal had been cut with PSA, this one not really involving Braniff as an operating entity.

This time, PSA planned to start a subsidiary division leasing Braniff airplanes and slots, and hiring mostly Braniff people—at their discretion. The plan made it over all the hurdles except one—the U.S. Fifth Circuit Court of Appeals in New Orleans, which on March 2, 1983 ruled that Judge Flowers could not order the return of the landing slots to the new entity, because it was not a true successor to Braniff.

Suddenly it was midspring and the second PSA deal was dead, Putnam was under increasing pressure to return the secured airplanes to the lenders, and no one seemed to be out there who wanted to help Braniff fly again. Howard Putnam was exhausted. As he told one Braniff pilot during that period, he was mentally and emotionally beaten. For Putnam it had also been a horrid series of good days and bad days. In February, for instance, the Justice Department had filed a civil antitrust action against Robert Crandall for his impertinent suggestion on price fixing made in that taped phone call to Putnam a year before, but the fact that Putnam had secretly taped the conversation (though on advice of counsel) rendered him persona non grata in the industry. Then, to his dismay, the accusations against American had begun to fall apart. No charges were brought against Robert Crandall in response to Braniff's report that he had orchestrated a "sabotage" campaign against the airline, though several agencies investigated. Even the allegation that American had somehow caused the "dumping" of Braniff tickets on the New York Clearing House came to nothing. The termination without charges of investigations by the CAB, FAA, and Justice Department appeared to support American's vociferous protests and documentation that they had done nothing wrong and had dumped no tickets. (American, in fact, had steadfastly denied throughout playing any "dirty tricks" on Braniff or doing anything illicit as a company.)[3]

It was in this period that Putnam, professing his complete exhaustion and disgust with the bankruptcy process (and with the legions of lawyers feeding on the financial corpse of Braniff), was contacted by Jay Pritzker, one of the wealthy owners of the highly successful Hyatt Corporation. Pritzker, who had turned down Troy Post's suggestion in the spring of 1981 that he buy Braniff, had been

[3] Later in 1983 the federal circuit suit against Crandall—the only action resulting from a lengthy federal grand jury probe into American's activities and Braniff's charges—ended in a dismissal, although the Justice Department attorneys subsequently appealed the dismissal, and the outcome of this appeal is still pending.

contacted in the early spring of 1983 by two retired Braniff captains, Jack Morton and Glen Shoop. Though Pritzker now was interested, Putnam was not.

Then the second PSA deal collapsed. Now, however, Putnam's attitude was that if he was going to pursue any other laborious attempts to refly the airline, he was certainly not going to take a backseat to a couple of "flaky do-gooder pilots" with some "off-the-wall proposal" (as he described them). Instead, Putnam set about designing a reorganization plan for Braniff as a pitiful little ground-services operator. At the same time he began looking for buyers for the remainder of the aircraft, which would get the secured lenders off his back at last but dash any hopes of flying again.

Pritzker and the two pilots were not ready to give up.

On April 6, word reached Pritzker that Putnam was about to receive an offer from Texas Air Corporation (Continental Airlines' parent company) to purchase all the remaining 727's. If the sale were approved by the court, it would all be over—Braniff would no longer have any aircraft to fly. Pritzker enlisted his Dallas Hyatt office in a marathon preparation of a final proposal, which Captains Morton and Shoop (along with a young Dallas lawyer) took to the world headquarters to present to Putnam on April 7.

The meeting was a disaster. The group, at Jay Pritzker's direction, had already set up a press conference, but Putnam refused to attend and warned them not to go public. Jay Pritzker, however, had emphasized that the proposal must be made public to tie Putnam's hands and forestall the sale of the remaining airplanes. Putnam blew up at the three men, railing at them that they were doing it all wrong. The Hyatt delegation attended their press conference alone.

The Hyatt proposal contained an offer to invest less than $10 million. Putnam had been yelled at and snarled at and ridiculed by the secured lenders and their lawyers before with far more lucrative proposals. He wasn't about to subject himself or the few remaining people around the ghostly world headquarters to that abuse again, and he was not about to be thrown off center stage by two pilots, of all people. With the lines clearly drawn, Putnam began a series of moves to wheedle more money out of Pritzker to satisfy the secured lenders. The actions Putnam took made it appear that he, Howard Putnam, the man who shut down Braniff and promised to resurrect it, in fact was now doing everything he could to sabotage the latest and most promising chance to do just that. (The Pritzker offer was even more exciting to the Braniff people, since he reportedly valued the Braniff name and wanted to refly the airline as Braniff.) Also at stake in all this was over $350 million of tax write-offs that Hyatt might be able to use in full if it acquired more than 80 percent of Braniff's stock.

On again, off again, hopes renewed, hopes dashed—it was becoming a way of life for the Braniff people who with or without jobs still dreamed of a resurrected airline. The cruelty of the incredible roller-coaster ride of ragged highs and lows since the bankruptcy took a terrible toll on the emotions, though by spring 1983 many were saying that they weren't interested in returning and that their forced weaning from Braniff had proven to be the best thing that had ever happened to them.

As April began, so did the same agony of daily headlines:

April 13, 1983 (*Dallas Times Herald*): CREDITORS TURN DOWN HYATT BID . . . PUTNAM SAYS TALKS CONTINUE

April 14, 1983 (*Dallas Morning News*): TEXAS AIR OFFERS TO BUY BRANIFF JETS, SOURCES SAY . . . WOULD PRECLUDE BRANIFF FROM FLYING AGAIN

April 15, 1983 (*Dallas Times Herald*): CREDITORS TO HEAR NEW PLAN . . . BRANIFF LENDERS, HYATT EXECUTIVES MEET

April 16, 1983 (*Dallas Times Herald*): HYATT TRIPLES OFFER, EX-PILOT SAYS

April 18, 1983 (UPI): HYATT'S BRANIFF OFFER IS FINAL

April 21, 1983 (*Dallas Times Herald*): HYATT SAYS BRANIFF BID IS DEAD . . . AIRLINE HAS OTHER OFFERS

May 13, 1983 (*Dallas Morning News*): BRANIFF, HYATT AGREE ON PLAN TO SAVE AIRLINE

This time Putnam and Guthrie attended the news conference. In fact, it was Putnam's smiling face that accompanied the article, as if he had been in the forefront throughout in driving the deal to a successful conclusion. That exposure resulted from something other than a casual decision on the part of the newspaper's editors—Putnam had developed a consummate skill during the previous year in dealing with the press and getting kid-glove, page-one treatment. He had become a favorite of the local media—always available, always willing to talk openly to them at almost any hour (he gave out his private unlisted home phone number to nearly every reporter in Dallas). To a press corps that had been very wary of him a mere ten months before ("I tell you, no one could be that open and honest—is he for real?"), Howard Putnam could do little wrong. Putnam for his part was proud of his claim that he had "never lied to the media." Of course, in retrospect it had been unnecessary, since he had become a master at forestalling deeper questioning by revealing selected truths in disarming fashion.

In the background, after having been publicly insulted, verbally assailed, and ultimately ignored by Putnam, the two retired pilots Morton and Shoop stood away from the limelight. It was interesting that few seemed to understand the altruistic nature of the two men's involvement; neither would be flying for the new Braniff.

June 7, 1983 (*Dallas Morning News*): PUTNAM, GUTHRIE TO RESIGN and BONDHOLDERS FIGHT HYATT PLAN
July 1, 1983 (AP): BRANIFF REPORTS LABOR ACCORD BY ALL UNIONS ON HYATT PLAN
And at long, bone-weary last:
July 16, 1983 (UPI): JUDGE APPROVES BRANIFF-HYATT DEAL . . .

On March 1, 1984, beneath blue skies, Braniff under Hyatt ownership launched its first scheduled flight in more than twenty-one months. (Putnam and Guthrie were pointedly absent.) Two thousand Braniff people had been hired in the first round. There were rumors of more to come. The strategy was to squeeze out a new Braniff market share with superior service from highly motivated people—and Braniff's people fit that description as did those of no other carrier. However flawed they had been before, the fact that the Braniff people did so much for so long with so little and with such poor management validates the existence of a vast, previously untapped reservoir of talent. Their new enthusiasm, forged in the fires of bankruptcy and the agony of unemployment, began propelling the new old carrier toward what promised to be a successful summer of '84, as American Airlines and others watched nervously from atop their war chests of cash. The flying public should agree that they deserve a chance—their first chance, really—to get it right.

APPENDIX 1

Braniff International Corporation Operating Revenues, Operating Profit or Loss, and Net Income by Year

Year	Operating Revenues	Operating Profit (or Loss)	Net Income (or Loss)
1965	$ 134,800,000	$ 13,763,000	$ 9,448,000
1966	194,588,000	24,423,000	17,816,000
1967	266,180,000	14,462,000	4,751,000
1968	301,068,000	25,369,000	10,416,000
1969	332,984,000	17,769,000	6,249,000
1970	331,206,000	8,174,000	(3,058,000)
1971	341,369,000	21,109,000	8,619,000
1972	383,898,000	29,320,000	17,151,000
1973	445,637,000	42,593,000	23,151,000
1974	552,396,000	55,751,000	26,137,000
1975	598,856,000	47,389,000	16,021,000*
1976	679,719,000	52,074,000	26,369,000
1977	791,157,000	69,028,000	36,629,000
1978	972,108,000	80,159,000	45,230,000
1979	1,346,275,000	(38,438,000)	(44,330,000)
1980	1,452,130,000	(107,493,000)	(128,511,000)
1981	1,188,975,000	(94,800,000)	(156,499,000)

( ) indicates a loss.
*This figure for 1975 was $20,388,000 before cumulative effect of an accounting change for vacation pay.

399

Braniff International Corporation Debt and New Aircraft Order Commitments by Year

Year	Current Debt	Long-term Debt	Total Debt	Aircraft on Order ($)
1965	0	$ 51,105,000	$ 51,105,000	$112,000,000
1966	0	204,753,000	204,753,000	130,000,000
1967	$ 44,535,000	199,000,000	243,535,000	20,966,000
1968	19,626,000	213,927,000	233,553,000	53,000,000
1969	20,596,000	200,773,000	221,369,000	58,200,000
1970	19,533,000	194,982,000	214,515,000	21,474,000
1971	8,114,000	180,823,000	188,937,000	63,126,000
1972	10,015,000	195,528,000	205,543,000	97,000,000
1973	19,800,000	234,463,000	254,263,000	31,000,000
1974	18,089,000	227,853,000	245,942,000	54,000,000
1975	19,486,000	234,913,000	254,399,000	68,864,000
1976	15,706,000	241,899,000	257,605,000	62,664,000
1977	14,534,000	272,619,000	287,153,000	186,512,000
1978	14,112,000	348,677,000	362,789,000	792,712,000
1979	23,393,000	578,198,000	601,591,000	748,000,000
1980	89,862,000	583,602,000	673,464,000	236,941,000
1981	148,388,000	591,012,000*	739,400,000*	180,000,000†

*This figure includes $71,782,000 in capital leases. This category was never included in the long-term debt or total debt listings before 1981, but was listed separately in the annual reports and SEC filings.

†This is an approximate figure representing the three remaining Boeing 747's that Braniff was unable to take delivery of or sell by December 31, 1981.

Braniff International Corporation Year-by-Year Comparison of Operating Factors and Employee Productivity

Year	Available Seat Miles (ASMs) (All Operations)	Revenue Passenger Miles (RPMs) (All Operations)	System Load Factor (Scheduled)	Break-even Load Factor (Scheduled)	Average Number of Employees	RPMs per Employee	Revenue per Employee
1965	3,364,467,000	1,818,701,000	54.0%	47.5%	5,728	317,511	$ 23,534
1966	5,150,072,000	3,059,574,000	56.1	48.5	7,203	424,764	27,015
1967	7,933,228,000	4,765,711,000	50.8	49.2	10,138	470,084	26,256
1968	9,310,065,000	5,597,847,000	51.1	47.6	11,153	501,914	26,994
1969	10,855,723,000	5,998,100,000	46.1	44.8	11,488	522,119	28,985
1970	10,582,908,000	5,336,616,000	44.7	45.2	10,255	520,392	32,297
1971	9,801,993,000	5,013,006,000	47.9	46.0	9,489	528,297	35,975

1972	10,565,450,000	5,455,820,000	49.4	46.0	9,675	563,909	39,679
1973	11,493,010,000	5,902,633,000	50.2	46.1	10,203	578,519	46,677
1974	12,684,500,000	6,464,144,000	49.9	46.0	10,740	601,876	51,431
1975	13,199,596,000	6,614,396,000	49.3	47.4	10,730	616,440	55,811
1976	13,881,440,000	7,170,135,000	51.1	47.9	10,538	680,408	64,502
1977	15,248,396,000	7,865,467,000	50.8	46.8	10,825	726,602	73,086
1978	18,330,385,000	9,999,987,000	53.8	50.2	11,995	833,680	81,043
1979	24,185,257,000	13,686,604,000	56.3	59.9	14,619	936,220	92,091
1980	20,497,529,000	11,998,311,000	58.4	64.5	15,200	789,362	95,535
1981	15,599,427,000	8,890,393,000	56.9	63.6	11,500	773,077	103,389

Braniff International Corporation Year-by-Year Comparison of Stockholders' Interests and Performance.

Year	Earnings: Net Income (or Loss) per Common Share	Cash Dividends	Common Shareholders' Equity (Adjusted)	Common Shares Outstanding	Long-term Debt	Return on Equity (Adjusted)	Long-term Debt-to-Equity (Unadjusted)
1965	$ .48	$ .017	$ 54,876,000	19,736,000	$ 51,105,000	17.22%	0.93:1
1966	.90	.083	71,219,000	19,736,000	204,753,000	25.02	2.88:1
1967	.24	.083	74,512,000	19,736,000	199,000,000	6.38	2.67:1
1968	.53	.375	83,804,000	19,818,000	213,927,000	12.43	2.55:1
1969	.32	.125	87,697,000	19,745,000	200,773,000	7.13	2.29:1
1970	(.15)	.165	81,364,000	19,745,000	194,982,000	(3.76)	2.40:1
1971	.43	.0	90,110,000	20,000,000	180,823,000	9.57	2.01:1
1972	.85	.0	108,402,000	20,202,000	195,528,000	15.82	1.80:1
1973	1.15	.0	131,905,000	20,125,000	234,463,000	17.55	1.78:1
1974	1.30	.15	155,066,000	20,033,000	227,853,000	16.86	1.47:1
1975	.78	.20	158,522,000	19,953,000	234,913,000	10.11	1.48:1
1976	1.31	.23	180,621,000	20,127,000	241,899,000	14.60	1.34:1
1977	1.83	.285	211,767,000	20,008,000	272,619,000	17.30	1.29:1
1978	2.26	.345	250,151,000	20,016,000	348,677,000	18.08	1.39:1
1979	(2.21)	.36	198,617,000	20,019,000	578,198,000	(22.28)	2.91:1
1980	(6.57)	.05	66,180,000	20,019,000	583,602,000	(194.18)	8.82:1
1981	(8.02)	.0	(94,431,000)	20,019,000	591,012,000	negative equity	negative equity

( ) indicates a loss.

Note: For comparison, 100 shares of Braniff Airways, Inc., common stock purchased in 1965 for $1,325 would have been subject to a two-for-one stock split in 1966, a one-for-three split in 1968, and a 3 percent stock dividend in 1971 and 1972, resulting in 636 shares by the end of 1973. On December 31, 1979, those shares would have been worth $7,339.52 (inclusive of dividends paid over the years) with the stock at $8.50 per share. By March 1982, those same shares would have dropped in value to $3,205, with the stock selling for $2 per share. The Common Shares Outstanding column above reflects the adjusted number of shares.

APPENDIX 2

"How did you find out about *that?*"

During the odyssey that has been the research phase of this book I have heard that question many times, and usually there has been no simple—or single—answer to give.

The body of nearly two hundred hours of interviews with over two hundred different individuals has provided the most dynamic and fascinating source of material. The majority of those interviews have been face-to-face meetings, sometimes of many hours' duration, most of them involving great hospitality and courtesy on the part of the interviewee, and most of them recorded and later laboriously transcripted for precision. Some have been by telephone; one was appropriately conducted in an airport concourse; another, incongruously enough, was on an Amtrak train bound for Austin, Texas.

No single individual stands alone as a source of any significant information affecting other people or important events—all the facts and data, impressions and attitudes, memories and quotations have been checked and rechecked against others, against written or tape-recorded record, or against the test of careful logical analysis in realistic and impartial terms. In addition, the interpretive assistance, analysis, and advice of numerous professionals in the fields of business management, aviation, finance, law, and government have helped greatly to shape and refine the presentation of the material and to identify what is and what is not significant.

The information gathered from interviews has been merged with and measured against a voluminous repository of written information ranging from Braniff corporate records and reports, SEC and CAB filings and proceedings, and internal Braniff letters and memos and teletypes, to newspapers, magazine, and wire service reports going back principally to 1965, but in several instances to 1928. The records of the United States Bankruptcy Court of Judge John Flowers in Fort Worth, Texas, have been a prime source of information on the periods 1981 through 1983, as have the personal records of many Braniff officers, only a few of whom have permitted the author to acknowledge publicly their indispensable assistance.

The descriptions of different locales are in almost every case from personal observation.

The dialogue in this book has been reconstituted, not paraphrased. Where recorded audio- or videotapes have been available, I have used them to provide a precise transcript of what was said. Where notes or unverified transcripts were available, I have checked their accuracy against the memories of those present. There were numerous cases in which the dialogue presented in these pages was spoken in my presence, and thus it is my recollection and notes that are utilized. In many instances, of course, only the memories of the participants or observers were available, and in such instances I have used a methodology of checking those remembered words and phrases with other participants or observers, or weighing the various recollections against the measure of reliability of each source, the normal speech patterns, and the surrounding circumstances. In the few instances that quotations attributed to a particular individual have been used based on the recollection of a single observer, the surrounding evidence supporting the accuracy of the quotation was overwhelming and the source considered unimpeachable. Where disagreements as to substance could not be resolved satisfactorily, I have either noted a difference, or in most cases refrained from using the conversation. Naturally, I cannot maintain that every quotation represents the precise words spoken at that place and time, but I do maintain that it represents the tenor, the spirit, and the essence of those conversations in accordance with the best recollection of the most reliable interviewees and that it is consistent with their personalities and linguistic styles.

There are no fabricated names. Where a character has been presented without a name, it is because he or she had requested anonymity, or because I felt the use of the name was not vital to the story, or both.

The descriptions of cockpits and details of aerial operations are drawn from many sources, including my own experience during almost 6½ years as a Braniff pilot, from December 5, 1975, to May 12, 1982. Though I had 7 years of credits as a radio and TV newsman and several more as a print journalist and writer by the time I joined Braniff, the love of aviation and a lifelong knowledge of and proximity to Braniff as a Dallas native lured me away from journalism, broadcasting, and legal practice to join the pilot force of Tom Braniff's airline (after 5 years as an Air Force pilot) just before the dawn of the age of deregulation. There have been many times during the tumultuous intervening years when I have found myself viewing events in far-flung places through a journalist's eye, though I was inextricably involved in the excitement or the despair of the moment. The preparation of this book, of course, has demanded a severe dedication to maintaining journalistic neutrality. What you have read in these pages reflects a strict, continuous, and I trust successful impartiality from a respectful point of view.

Because of the scope of this work in terms of time, participants, and impact of events, I have included below a more detailed listing (by chapter, part, or chapter groupings) of some of the source material available to everyone.

Chapters 1–5

The range of Braniff's postderegulatory expansion can be seen most graphically in the small-print details of the company's annual reports for the years 1977 through 1980, especially in the "Notes" to the financial data in each such report. The story is reflected as well in the company's 10K and 8K SEC (Securities and Exchange Commission) filings for the same period.

An extremely interesting account concerning LTV Corporation and James Ling in the heyday period of 1965 through 1970 (as well as the involvement of Greatamerica Corporation and Ed Acker) and the ousting of Jim Ling from his throne at LTV is available in the book *Ling: The Rise, Fall, and Return of a Texas Titan* by Stanley H. Brown (New York: Atheneum, 1972). Mr. Brown also authored an earlier look at Troy Post, entitled "The Golden Castles of Troy Post," for *Fortune* magazine's January 1965 edition.

Many of the details of Braniff's early years gathered from a multitude of interviews were further confirmed and placed in the proper sequence through information contained in the following sources: a privately published paperback, *Braniff: An Illustrated History* by George Walker Cearley, Jr. (Dallas: Robert Yaquinto Printing Company, 1980); Braniff in-house histories "Braniff's First Fifty Years" and "The Braniff Airways Story," both of which were authored in great degree by twenty-eight-year Braniff veteran and publicist Martha L. (Pat) Zahrt; a small publication of the Newcomen Society in 1955 of an address in New York by Braniff's then president, Charles Beard, "Thomas E. Braniff: Southwest Pioneer in Air Transportation"; voluminous articles from the *Dallas Daily Herald* (later the *Dallas Times Herald*) and the *Dallas Morning News* from 1945 through 1965 available on microfilm at Dallas area libraries; and the extensive collection of Braniff files contained in the History of Aviation Collection of the University of Texas at Dallas Library.

The hearings surrounding the passage of the Civil Aeronautics Act of 1938 and the text of the act itself can be found in the Library of Congress and is fascinating reading.

The details of the crash of January 10, 1954 that killed Tom Braniff were derived from a wide range of sources, including interviews and newspaper articles in the *Dallas Daily Herald,* the *Dallas Morning News,* and the *Shreveport Times* for January 11 and 12, 1954.

The portraits of Harding Lawrence's years at Continental Airlines and of Robert Six were aided by Robert Serling's excellent biography of Six, *Maverick* (Garden City, N.Y.: Doubleday, 1974).

The information regarding Mary Wells Lawrence and the formation of Wells Rich Greene, Inc. was drawn in part from a long list of magazine articles of the period 1965 through the 1970s, including: "On Lovable Madison Avenue with Mary, Dick, and Stew" (*Fortune,* August 1966); "The Wonderous World of WRG" (*Madison Avenue* magazine, July 1966); "The Wonderous World of WRG: Revisited" (*Madison Avenue* magazine, December 1967); "Mary Wells' Beautiful Wedding" (*Marketing/Communications,* January 1968); "As the World Turns on Madison Avenue" (*Fortune,* December 1968); "Leaders in Marketing" (*Journal of Marketing,* Vol. 36, January 1972); "Crystal Charity Ball" (*Gallery* magazine of the *Dallas Times Herald,* October 25, 1972); "The Crystal Charity Ball" (*The New York*

Times, December 3, 1972); "The All-Out Attractive Style of Mary Wells Lawrence" (*Vogue,* February 1978).

Chapters 6–8

The National Transportation Safety Board Accident Report (File No. 1-0003, accepted June 19, 1969) on the crash of Captain John Phillips' Flight 352 formed a basic element of factual control for the surrounding information regarding the sequence of the tragedy. Other important public sources include published reports in the *Dallas Morning News* and *Dallas Times Herald* of May 4 through 6, 1968, and my own notes and reports broadcast over WFAA radio and television news in Dallas (I was a staff newsman for the station during that period). The proceedings in several lawsuits brought against Lockheed Aircraft Corporation and Braniff in the following years have provided additional details.

The CAB deposition taken of Harding Lawrence and referred to on Page 61 of the text is taken from page 55 of the CAB transcript in the files of CAB Docket No. 26364, dated August 6, 1975.

The same deposition and all supporting documents, charges, pleadings, answers, and transcripts are in the same file under the same docket number, 26364, and are available to the public at the CAB's headquarters in Washington, D.C. The angry letters from Braniff employees and supporters contained in the same record make fascinating footnotes to the action. I have retained several hundred pages of copies from this record in my files.

Performance information on the DC-8-62 and the airport near La Paz, Bolivia, was extracted from the FAA-approved Braniff DC-8 flight manuals and the performance manual in use at the time.

Chapters 9–13

The testimony of Harding Lawrence before the U.S. Senate Committee on Commerce, Subcommittee on Aviation, along with the entire record of the hearing sequence conducted by Senator Howard

Cannon between April 6 and June 17, 1976, can be found at the Library of Congress under "U.S. 94th Congress, Hearings," J74.A23. This is a bound book and is an excellent source for reviewing the various positions, protests, and posturings of the politicians, the theoreticians, and the industry on the subject.

An excellent anthology of the battle for the London route and the subsequent start-up problems can be found in the numerous articles, notes, clips, and references on the subject in the issues of *Aviation Week & Space Technology* magazine between December 1977 and April 1978. This publication, which is a highly respected industry journal and news service, is published weekly, and the back issues for this period can be found at most major libraries. The CAB file for the case contained within their docket records is File No. 31100, dated July 8, 1977.

On the subject of the magnitude of the loss in the Pacific, an examination of the Braniff annual report for 1980, page 17, under Note 10, "International" and "Other," will reveal the combined loss of $85,913,000 for both the Atlantic and Pacific operations during 1979 and 1980. This was an operating loss, but what portion is attributable to the Pacific is the disputed question.

Chapters 14–16

The press reports referred to in Chapter 15, page 154, are principally those of the *Dallas Morning News,* the *Dallas Times Herald,* and the local electronic media, as well as the subsequent article "Bad Times at Braniff" (*D* magazine, February 1981).

There is an interesting, prophetic chronicle of Braniff's gathering peril contained in a fairly accurate article entitled "Braniff's Explosive Route Growth: Flying High or a Financial Crash?" published in the October 22, 1979 edition of *Dallas-Fort Worth Business.*

The facts surrounding the happenings of December 1980, and especially the lenders' showdown on December 22, 1980, have been among the most carefully researched sequences of this book due to the differences in the recollections of the participants. A surprising number of those interviewed cited the subsequent *Wall Street Journal* article of January 6, 1981 ("Clipped Wings: How Braniff's Lenders and Directors Forced Chairman to Resign") as being very close to the truth. Nevertheless, Harding Lawrence and several other former officers vociferously deny that he was "forced." In fact, and on balance, I feel that the version I have presented is highly precise, especially with regard to the various attitudes and goals of the participants. In many respects, there never was a meeting of the minds among the participants on that day. Their motivations for their various actions differed greatly. This can be seen in part in several of the depositions taken in relation to the unsecured creditors committee's attempts to desecure the principal lenders (the major secured creditors) by proving that they had seized illicit control of the corporation. Unfortunately, most of those depositions have not been filed in the public record.

Chapters 17–20

The murder of Ted Beckwith is still unsolved, but information related to the case may be obtained from—or given to—the Texas Rangers' office in Sulphur Springs, Texas.

Chapters 24–25

Excellent source material concerning PATCO's suicidal summer of 1981 can be found in *Aviation Week & Space Technology* issues of June 29, July 6, July 13, August 3, August 10, August 13, and August 24, 1981.

Chapters 26–28

A good reaction and summation of the Texas class announcement appeared in a *Wall Street Journal* article of November 5, 1981, on page 21.

Chapter 29

The quotations from Robert Crandall are contained in the complaint and the evidentiary record of *The United States of America* v. *American Airlines, Incorporated and Robert L. Crandall,* filed in the U.S. District Court for the Northern District of Texas, Case No. 3-83-0325-D, filed February 23, 1983. Surrounding circumstances and the activity at Braniff's world headquarters came from interviews.

Details of the reactions and excitement of the two-for-one ticket sale in February can be found in the articles of the *Dallas Times Herald* on February 11, 12, 13, and especially the summation article of February 18, 1982.

Chapters 30–31

From March 2, 1982 through the end of summer, the flow of articles in both the *Dallas Times Herald* and the *Dallas Morning News* is almost constant. For the serious researcher, a sequential examination of the microfilmed copies of each day's paper during that period, with emphasis on the front page and the business page of each edition, will be most rewarding.

The scene depicted on pages 327–29 of Chapter 31 can be seen in a videotape of the Public Broadcasting System's series *Enterprise* and their January 1982 production on Braniff entitled "Tailspin," produced by David Johnson of Dallas. The production, which was given only a thirty-minute time slot, is much too brief and simplistic in its presentation and conclusions but is nevertheless a well-produced visual re-creation of the last eight months of agony. When Howard Putnam agreed to the project to videotape the progress of his efforts to "save" the company, he still believed he could do it. It was to be the chronicle of how Braniff's new president pulled off a small miracle. Instead it became a visual elegy.

Chapter 32

The scene on pages 342 and 343 concerning the planning for the three-for-two sale is also available on the tape of the PBS program "Tailspin."

Chapters 33–36

The principal source of financial data within the Epilogue are from the voluminous court records of the United States Bankruptcy Court of Judge John Flowers in Forth Worth, Texas. The records, with the exception of one sealed deposition, are available to the public and may be examined either in the court office, or copies may be made commercially through a nearby quick-print firm. The court clerks may be contacted for help.

An excellent parting commentary on the real damage inflicted by the Airline Deregulation Act of 1978 is contained in a short article by attorney Thomas J. McGrew, "1978 Air Deregulation Act Yields Sorry Aftermath" (*Legal Times*, July 5, 1982, p. 11).

ACKNOWLEDGMENTS

The process of writing a book of this sort is one of capturing the living history in many minds and memories, structuring it against the written record, and transferring it onto paper (through the proper factual tests and balances). That can be accomplished only by talking to the people who have been intimately interwoven through the fabric of the story and those whose dynamic actions created its various segments. Even then, the process requires the voluntary co-operation of such people. In this case I have been accorded far more gracious and enthusiastic support from individuals all across this nation than I possibly could have expected.

To those gentlemen who gave me inordinate blocks of their valuable time and patiently fielded my never-ending questions and follow-up phone calls I am equally indebted—men such as Harding Lawrence, who provided me with three days of interview time in New York; Pan Am Chairman Ed Acker, who let me stretch a short interview into a long one; Pan Am Vice President John Casey, for the same courtesy; former Braniff President Howard Putnam, for his immediate assistance with interviews at the beginning of the research phase and later; retired Braniff Vice President for Regulatory Proceedings Tom Robertson, for his many hours of assistance; Southwest Airlines Vice President for External Affairs Sam Coats; former Braniff General Counsel Alan Stewart, whose friendly guarding of the palace gates made me dig even deeper; senior attorney Tom McGrew, a partner in the firm of Arnold and Porter in Washington, D.C.; former Braniff managers Joe Dean, Jerry Albers, Dick Flume, and Bill McCutcheon; former Braniff Staff Director Carolyn Corsey; former Braniff Vice Presidents Rex Brack, R. V. Carlton, Herman Rumsey, W. W. (Bill) Garbett, Terry Schrader, Jere Cox, Douglas MacArthur, Howard Swanson, Jeff Krida, Neil J.

Robinson, Jack Weinhart, Thom McCauley, Ron Ridgeway, Andy Hoffman, Tom Matthews, Wally Conrad, Buford Minter, Horace Bolding, and many, many more present and former officers and managers who gave me hours of their valuable time but did not give me permission to thank them publicly by name.

I am also profoundly appreciative of the many, many contributions of a long list of Braniff people from all parts of the company who spent hours talking to me by phone or in person, provided leads and phone numbers and introductions, and helped assure the accuracy of this work. I wish I could name them all, but there simply isn't space.

The contributions to this book (not to mention the hospitality, patience, encouragement, and friendship) of the following people were significant: Captain and Mrs. Harold "Tiny" Mize; Braniff crew Schedulers Marguerite Culhane, Tom Irby, Jim Reynolds, Bob Annear, Chester Hurt, and Lawrence Watson (now mayor of Alvord, Texas); longtime Braniff publicist Martha "Pat" Zhart; Vivian Daugherty (secretary to Charles Beard and Harding Lawrence); senior flight attendants Ginny Linder, Maria Sturgeon, Janet Dewey, and Betty Engle; and my Dallas research assistant, Clark Arnold, who never knew when I was going to call.

In Miami: Captain and Mrs. Ken Mase and Captain and Mrs. Joe Dean.

In Washington, D.C.: the Hon. Dan McKinnon, chairman of the CAB, and former Senator Howard Cannon of Nevada.

In Houston, Texas: Mr. and Mrs. Eugene Lawrence (Harding Lawrence's brother and sister-in-law) for their hospitality and assistance.

In Gladewater, Texas: Dr. Howard Lebus, Mrs. Gordon Mayer, Mr. and Mrs. L. L. Hickey, and Mr. Sam Moore.

In Seattle: Mr. Jim Huff, former Braniff regional sales manager.

In Austin: the Braniff alumni at Emerald Air, and my parents, Maj. Gen. and Mrs. Edmund Lynch.

The logistics support of hearth, home, pantry, and transportation above and beyond the call of family loyalty spur my heartfelt appreciation to my aunt and uncle, Ben and Martha Kanowsky of Dallas, and another aunt and uncle, Tom and Virginia MacCabe of Dobbs Ferry, New York (an NBC *Today* news writer).

Those who have proofread many hundreds of pages, offering enlightened comment and criticism and providing very valuable soundingboards, have made a corporeal contribution to this work, and their efforts are greatly appreciated:

Jim Nance (a cousin, and a first officer for Republic Airlines) and his wife, Jeanne, of Aurora, Colorado.

Tom Robertson of Dallas.

Dick and Robin Alm of Tacoma, Washington.

Neil and Marycarolyn Campbell of Lubbock, Texas.

Reverend Gerald A. Priest, pastor of St. Joseph's Catholic Church in Marshall, Texas.

Charles and Ruth Chapman of Jacksonville, Texas.

Margrette Lynch (the Peggy Zuleika of Texas poetry) of Austin, Texas.

Dennis Umstot, Ph.D., professor of management at the University of Puget Sound in Tacoma, Washington.

Pete and Christine Lancaster of Tacoma, Washington.

Richard A. Davenport, FAA air carrier inspector, Seattle, Washington.

Patricia A. Davenport, vice president of Emerald City Excursions of Seattle.

I owe a debt of appreciation in the first magnitude to my editor at William Morrow, Senior Editor Howard Cady, whose wisdom and encouragement have eased the process considerably, and to his assistant, Elizabeth Crosby.

A writer has only to deal with the material; his poor family has to deal with the writer. This book simply could not have been produced without the efforts of my wife and editor-of-first-resort, Bunny Nance, to whom this work is dedicated. She has plowed through hundreds of thousands of words, gone through a small stack of red felt-tips, and endured endless (and, I'm sure, mind-numbing) discussions of every aspect and facet of the story and the developing information, as well as listening to many of the hundreds of hours of interview tapes—and by her own admission somehow still loves me.

My oldest daughter, Dawn Michelle, has spent uncounted hours helping with the project when she could have been enjoying the summer, and my seven-year-old daughter, Bridgitte Cathleen, and two-year-old son, Christopher Sean, have worked mightily to "keep the noise down" and provide needed hugs.

Thanks are in order to the various executives of the following airlines who provided me with off-the-record assistance and fact confirmation: Southwest, Continental, Republic, American, Pan American, Eastern, Emerald Air, Muse Air, United, TWA, and Pacific East of Los Angeles.

I very much appreciate the help of the many employees and librarians, and the access to the materials contained in the collections of the UCLA Main Library in Los Angeles, New York Public Library, Dallas Public Library, SMU Fondren Library in Dallas, SMU Law Library in Dallas, the Library of the University of Puget Sound in Tacoma, the Tacoma Public Library, the Pierce County Library of Washington, and many more who responded to odd telephone inquiries from this writer working on a "Braniff book," and to the School of Business and Public Administration of the University of Puget Sound in Tacoma and its chairman, Dr. David Johnson, for their help.

I specifically want to call attention to the History of Aviation Collection in the Library of the University of Texas at Dallas, which is the repository for much of the deep historical files from Braniff's past and which provided many of the photographs in this book. The collection has lost its grant, and the future public access of the collection will be limited. For those who may be interested in preserving and perpetuating the Braniff historical materials, this is a worthy project, and I commend it to you.

Finally, and in many ways most importantly, I thank my literary agents, George and Olga Wieser and Bob Markel, who believed.

JOHN J. NANCE
Tacoma, Washington

Index

Acapulco party (1977), 108, 109
Acker, C. Edward (Ed), 20–21, 31, 32,
    39, 57, 60, 61, 63–65, 67–71,
    86, 87, 216*n*, 320, 321, 330,
    384, 388–89, 393
  lease of South American routes and,
    334–41
  resignation of, 80–81, 84–85
Advertising, 33, 47–49, 126, 141, 294,
    307–8, 324
  "The Great Escape," 342, 344–45
Aerolineas Argentinas, 160
Aims, George, 322
Aircraft, 33, 56–59, 322
  purchase of, 151, 153, 160, 162–63
  sale of surplus, 153–54, 160, 163,
    174
  See also individual models
Air Florida, 323, 335, 336, 340, 341
Air France, 124*n*
Airline Deregulation Act of 1978, 13,
    14, 26, 118
Air Line Pilots Association (ALPA),
    199–200, 264, 297–99, 344*n*,
    353, 356
Airmail routes, 24
Airplane (movie), 343*n*
Airports, 129*n*
  high-altitude, 73–79
Air traffic control system, 262–63
Albers, Jerry, 124–25
ALPA, *see* Air Line Pilots Association
Altitude
  density, 74

  See also High-altitude airports
American Airlines, 33, 65*n*, 99–101,
    148, 149, 153, 166*n*, 184–85,
    208–11, 251, 303, 305–11,
    319–20, 324*n*, 331
  Crandall-Putnam phone
    conversation and, 305–7
  sabotage by, 343
  Sabre Reservations system of, 295,
    307, 320, 341–42
  takeoff delays and, 310–11
  Texas class service and, 293, 295–
    96, 302, 305
  two-for-one sale and, 308–10
American National Insurance
    Company, 205
Andes mountain range, 73
Annear, Bob, 111–12
Armstrong, Mrs. Anne, 155*n*, 258, 259
Arnold and Porter (law firm), 13, 196,
    338
Atheson, Betty, 369
Aviation Consumer Action Project, 68–
    69
Aviation Corporation, 23
Aviation Daily, 13

BAC-111, 33, 34
Bagley, Bob, 243
Baker, Robert, 308
Bankruptcy, 172, 241, 315, 386
  See also Chapter 11 reorganization
Baranowsky, Joe, 344*n*–45*n*, 361

417

Bass, Perry, 155*n*, 156, 241, 258, 372
Beard, Charles E., 21–22, 24, 30, 31,
    40, 67, 392–93
Beck, Don, 299
Becker, Al, 332, 333
Beckwith, Edson (Ted), 85–86, 151–
    53, 159, 176, 200*n*, 202, 203,
    205, 214–16, 229, 393
Billy Bob's Texas, 349
Bishop, Gene, 117
Blevin, John, 167
Bloom Agency, The, 294–95
Board of Directors, 152, 154–57
    Casey and, 229–32, 258, 268–71
    members of, 155*n*
    offers of president's job to Putnam
        and, 268–71
    selection of successor to Harding
        Lawrence and, 173–78
    shutdown of operations and, 372–
        73
Boeing aircraft, 151, 153
Boeing 707-227, 33
Boeing 707-320, 57
Boeing 727, 57–59, 71, 160, 164, 303
Boeing 727-100, 43
Boeing 727-200, 59, 153, 154
Boeing 747, 58, 118–20, 133, 160,
    164–65, 174, 289, 376
Bond, Langhorne, 149–50, 196–97
Borman, Frank, 197–98, 361–62
    lease of South American routes and,
        334–38
Boston-Europe routes, 130, 148
Bowen Airlines, 24
Bradley, Phil, 344*n*–45*n*
Braniff, Jeanne, 28
Braniff, Paul, 23–25
Braniff, Thurman, 28
Braniff, Tom E., 21, 23–25, 27–30, 67
Braniff Airways
    Cargo Air Contract Division, 26
    early history of, 23–26
    international route system of, 22–23
    shutdown of operations, 350–85
    See also specific topics and individuals
Braniff Bandwagon program, 249,

    253–55, 257
Braniff Educations Systems, Inc.
    (BESI), 122*n*–23*n*
"Braniff family," 24, 28–30
"Braniff Strikes Back" campaign, 260,
    266, 269
Bribing of travel agents, 67, 68
British Airways, 114–15, 124*n*
British Caledonian Airways, 115
Brotherhood of Railway Clerks (BRC),
    61, 62
Burck, Bob, 64, 65
Business Week, 35, 147

Calder, Alexander, 79, 106, 278
Calder aircraft, 106–7
CAMFAB, 65, 68, 69
Cannon, Howard, 82
Cargo Air Contract Division, 26
Carlton, R.V., 22, 348
Carter, Jimmy (Carter Administration),
    13, 113, 115, 126
Casey, Albert (Al), 118, 119, 166*n*,
    181–82, 209
Casey, John J., 64, 65, 67–68, 86, 90,
    138, 139, 155*n*, 166*n*–67*n*,
    173–83, 195–205, 215, 229–
    45, 247, 267, 273–80, 303,
    322*n*, 385
    Beckwith fired by, 216, 229
    Board of Directors and, 229–32, 258,
        268–71
    Braniff Bandwagon program of, 249,
        253–55, 257
    employee relations, 200–201, 234–
        35, 248–49, 253–55, 259, 265,
        285–86
    mailgram sent to travel agents by,
        239–40
    merger talks and, 197–98
    1980 annual report and, 236–39
    1981 stockholders' meeting and,
        241–44
    as Pan American's executive vice
        president for operations, 321
    pay cut and, 195, 196, 199–204

personal characteristics of, 180–82
Putnam offered president's job by,
    267–72
resignation of, 320–21, 323
salaries of managers raised by, 233–
    35
selected to head Braniff, 175–78
Swanson's dismissal and, 273–76
Cessation of operations, 350–85
Chapter 11 reorganization, 241, 315,
    346, 347, 351, 373–75, 381,
    386, 387
Civil Aeronautics Act of 1938, 25
Civil Aeronautics Board (CAB), 13–15,
    22, 25, 63, 65, 80, 319
    fare regulation by, 82n–83n, 148
    investigation and enforcement action
        by (1974-1975), 69–71, 80, 81
    lease of South American routes and,
        321, 323, 326, 331–41
    London route and, 112–16
    new routes and, 120, 126, 129, 130
    ticket guarantee plan and, 312–13,
        317, 324
Clark, Bob, 95–96
Clearinghouse for tickets, 311, 319
Coats, Samuel D., 50, 285, 301, 310,
    317, 330, 342, 343, 350–51,
    353, 367, 371
Cole, Johnny, 133
Committee to Re-elect the President
    (CREEP), 63–64
Concorde, 124, 125
Conrad, Walter, 139
Continental Airlines, 19, 20, 33, 47,
    49, 387n, 388n
Corsey, Floyd, 141
Cox, Jere, 168–69
Crames, Michael, 351, 357, 372–75
Crandall, Robert L., 209, 216, 290,
    295, 296, 302, 305–9, 319–20,
    323, 395
Crashes, 54–57
Creditors, 212
    See also Lenders
Crossland, Don, 51
Culhane, Marguerite, 357, 359–60

Culp, Bob, 331, 335
Customer service, see Passenger service

Dallas-Fort Worth (DFW) airport,
    competition for leadership
    position at, 208–12
Dallas Morning News, 312, 331
    interview with Putnam in, 313–17
Dallas Times Herald, 198, 312, 318–19
Davis, Fred, 179
Dawson, crash near (1968), 56–57
DC-2, 25
DC-3, 25
DC-4, 26
DC-6, 26
DC-8-62, 74
DC-10, 58, 59
Dean, Joe, 179
Deaver, Mike, 337
Default protection plan (ticket
    guarantee plan), 312–13, 317,
    324
Delays, 89–91
    takeoff, 310–11
Deloitte, Haskins & Sells, 237
Delta Airlines, 66, 99–100, 130, 191,
    210, 251, 293, 303, 308, 320
Density altitude, 74
Denver routes, 112
Deregulation, 13–16, 81–84, 112, 117,
    163, 325–26, 389
    new routes and, 120–32
Dewey, Janet, 144
Disco music, 151n
Doyle Dane Bernbach, Inc., 47
Drinkard, Marion, 119, 150
Duffy, Henry, 264n

Eastern Airlines, 25n, 361
    lease of South American routes to,
        323, 334–35, 337–40, 344,
        345n
    merger talks with, 166, 172, 197–98
El Alto Airport (La Paz, Bolivia), 74–
    79

Electra aircraft, 54, 56, 57
Emmell, Jerry, 199, 234
Employees, *see* Personnel
Employee stock ownership program
    (ESOP), 248
European routes, 148, 158
   See also London routes

Fabrega, Camilo, 65, 68, 322*n*
Faircloth, L.T., 300
Fares, 160
  lower, 252
  regulation of, 82*n*–83*n*, 148
  Texas class, 290–96
  two-for-one, 300–302, 307–10,
    343, 348
  See also Off-the-books tickets
"Fast buck" campaign, 52–53, 57
Federal Air Regulations, 287*n*
Federal Aviation Administration
    (FAA), 122, 149–50, 196, 197,
    249, 261, 287*n*
Ferguson, Robert R. (Bob), III, 167,
    175, 214, 315, 343*n*, 347, 351,
    369, 379–80
Ferris, Dick, 118, 119, 279, 306, 352
Financial problems, 146–47
  auditor's report on (1980), 237–39
  Board of Directors and, 152, 154–57
  cash position, 151–53, 281–82
  Chapter 11 reorganization, 241, 315,
    346, 347, 351, 373–75, 381,
    386, 387
  debt payment deferral, 195, 204–7,
    214, 237, 253. *See also* Financial
    problems, restructuring of the
    debt
  depreciation and, 162
  fuel companies and, 212–13
  fuel prices and, 153, 159
  Guthrie as vice president for finance
    and, 280–84
  layoffs of personnel and, 158–59
  lease of South American routes and,
    321–24, 326–29, 331–41
  lenders and, 152, 166–68, 175, 195,
    202–5, 214–15, 247–48, 251–

    53, 282–83, 302–4, 330, 351
  management and, 167–68
  master plan for dealing with, 251–
    52, 259–60
  the media and, 213–14
  merger discussions with Eastern
    Airlines and, 166, 172, 197–98
  news conference on (1980), 161–63
  1980 annual report on, 236–39
  1981 annual stockholders' meeting
    and, 240–44
  Operation Turnaround and, 164
  pay cut and, 195, 196, 199–204
  purchase of aircraft and, 151, 153,
    160, 162–63
  restructuring of the debt, 282–83.
    See also Financial problems, debt
    payment deferral
  sale of surplus aircraft and, 153–54,
    160, 163, 174
  selection of successor to Harding
    Lawrence and, 173–78
  Texas class service and, 290–95
  unions and, 195, 199–204
First class service, 103–4
First International Bancshares, 155*n*,
    268
Fitts, Grant, 20, 31, 59–60
Flight attendants, 120–24, 136–37,
    141–46, 158, 308, 339
Flight 502 (last flight), 375–79
Flowers, John, 374, 375, 394, 395
Folsom, Robert, 372
Fortune (magazine), 388
Foster, John, 51, 53, 55
Frankfurt airport, 129*n*
Frayn, Mort, 372
Frayn, R. Mort, Sr., 155*n*
Fuel companies, 212–13
Fuel prices, 70–71, 148, 153, 159
Fulton, Dennis, 161, 169, 276–77,
    313–17, 331, 366, 386–87
Furloughs, 66, 197–98

Gann, Ernest, 57
Garbett, Bill, 125
Garbo, Mel, 372

Garrett, Dave, 352
Gate agents, 89, 92–93
    See also Outside agents
Gatwick Airport, 115, 116
Gayler, Noel, 155*n*, 174, 258
Geneen, Harold, 87
Gilley, Mickey, 324
Girard, Alexander, 33–35
Goldman/Sachs investment firm, 230
Grace, W.R., & Company, 41
Gray, Harry, 248*n*
Greatamerica Corporation, 19, 20, 22,
    31, 32*n*, 40, 41, 50*n*, 85
"Great Escape, The" sale promotion,
    342–47
Greene, Stew, 48
Guthrie, M. Phillip, 273–78, 280–84,
    287–89, 301, 304, 311, 312,
    314, 315, 321–22, 324, 327,
    328, 332, 334, 335, 338, 339,
    343–54, 371–73, 380, 397, 398

Halston, 108
Hare, David, 194
Harriman, Mrs. Pamela, 155*n*, 176
Hawaii routes, 118–20, 126, 209, 292
Hayes, Willard, 132
Headquarters complex, 109–10, 140,
    288, 310
Heathrow Airport, 115
Helms, J. Lynn, 249
High-altitude airports, 73–79
Hoffman, Andy, 151*n*
Honolulu routes, 209, 292
Hostesses, 25
"Hub-and-spoke" concept of airline
    route systems, 130–31, 208, 211
Huddleston, Buddy, 27–28
Huff, Jim, 39*n*
Hurt, Chester, 355–58, 362, 368–70
Huskins, William (Bill), 176, 177,
    282*n*, 327, 328, 347, 356–57,
    362–63, 365, 367, 368
Hyatt Corporation, 241, 395–98

IAM, *see* International Association of
    Machinists

IATA, *see* International Aviation Traffic
    Association
Image, 32–36, 48, 80
Interior design of aircraft, 33–34, 108
Interline pass privileges, 138–39
International Association of Machinists
    (IAM), 195, 199, 203, 204, 234,
    299–300
International Aviation Traffic
    Association (IATA), 67, 68
International Brotherhood of
    Teamsters, *see* Teamsters
Irby, Tom, 356

Jensen, Irma, 305
Joedicke, Robert, 276–77
Johnson, David, 334
Johnson, Lyndon B., 18
Jones & Laughlin Steel, 60
Jumbo jets, 58

Kahn, Alfred, 82, 83*n*
Kelleher, Herb, 272
Kennedy, Edward M., 81–82
Kennedy-Cannon airline deregulation
    bill, 81–82
Kirkland, Lane, 264
Koch, Ed, 149
Korean Air Lines, 127*n*
Kress, Andy, 374
Krida, Jeff, 181*n*, 238, 255, 265, 309,
    310

Lamb, Charlie, 364, 368, 369, 377
Landry, Tom, 324
La Paz, Bolivia, 73, 74
Lapensky (chairman of Northwest
    Orient Airlines), 352
Lasker, Mary, 155*n*, 258
Lawrence, Deborah, 47
Lawrence, Don, 45
Lawrence, Eugene, 45
Lawrence, Harding, 13–21, 31–52,
    57–66, 79–88, 104–7, 109–22,

Lawrence, Harding (*cont.*)
    200, 201, 202*n*, 248, 257, 278,
    329–30, 392
  Acker's resignation and, 80, 81, 84–
    85
  breakdown in communication with,
    150*n*–51*n*
  deregulation and, 82–84, 117, 127–
    28
  early life of, 45–47
  financial problems and, 152–69
  first formal meeting under, 31–33
  image campaign and, 32–36
  lower and middle management and,
    31, 38–40, 61–62
  management style of, 86–88
  marriage to Mary Wells, 50–51
  news conference held by (1980),
    161–63
  Nixon administration and, 63–65,
    68
  personal characteristics and style of,
    38–39, 44–45, 79–80, 142–43
  reduction of interline pass privileges
    and, 138, 139
  relations with employees, 142–46
  resignation of, 167–69
  retirement of, 163, 171
  selection of a successor to, 173–78
  work habits of, 36–38
Lawrence, Helen, 45
Lawrence, James, 47
Lawrence, Jim, 132–34, 285
Lawrence, Mary Wells, 33–36, 41, 47–
    51, 79–80
Lawrence, Mrs. Jimmie, 41–42, 50
Lawrence, Moncey, 45, 46
Lawrence, State Rights, 47
Lay, Herman, 154–56, 241, 258, 372,
    391*n*
Layoffs, *see* Furloughs
Lazard Frères, 230, 330
Lenders, 152, 166–68, 175, 202–5,
    214–15, 247–48, 251–53, 282–
    83, 302–4, 330, 351
Levin and Weintraub (law firm), 315,
    347, 351, 357, 386, 388

Levine, Mike, 126
Lewis, Drew, 249
Life magazine, 35
Linder, Ginny, 111, 377, 379
Ling, James J., 19, 50*n*, 59–60, 66,
    168
Lloyd's of London, 313*n*
Lockheed 1011, 58, 59
Lockheed Vega, 24
London routes, 112–17, 292
Long, W.F., 46
LTV Corporation, 50*n*, 58–61, 85,
    248*n*

MacArthur, Doug, 191, 232, 297
McCann-Erickson, Inc., 33, 47
McCollum, L.F., Jr., 155*n*, 372
McCrea, W. Sloan, 155*n*, 230*n*, 243–
    44, 258
McCutcheon, Billy, 183–84, 186–89,
    191, 192, 231–32, 296–97, 365
McGrew, Tom, 13–14
McKinnon, Dan, 313, 332–34, 337
MacNeil-Lehrer Report, The, 334
Maintenance violations, 149–50, 196–
    97
Management, 137, 150*n*–51*n*
  Casey's plan for restructuring, 175–
    77
  financial problems and, 167–68
  lower and middle, 31, 38–40, 61–
    62, 80, 102–3, 250
  under Putnam, 299
Management training, 40
Marketing, 176
  See also Sales promotions
Marriott, 212, 372
Mase, Ken, 178–80, 286, 358
Mason, Elvis, 268, 271
Mauer, John, 285, 299
Maxwell, Jim, 170–71
Media, the
  financial problems and, 213–14
  PATCO strike and, 264
Merger talks, Eastern-Braniff, 166,
    172, 197–98

Military Airlift Command (MAC), 57, 126
Miller, Joanne, 42–44, 341
Mize, Brenda, 102–4
Mize, "Tiny," 355–56
Morton, Jack, 395, 396, 398
Muse, Lamar, 117, 267

Nader, Ralph, 68–69
National Transportation Safety Board, 57n
Newsweek, 35
New York ticket clearinghouse, 311, 319
Nixon, Richard (Nixon Administration), 63–65, 68, 70
Northwest Orient Airlines, 352

O'Donnell, John J., 264
Off-the-books tickets, 68, 80
Okonite, 60
"Open skies" policy, 126–27
Operating expenses, 72
Operation Turnaround, 164
Outside agents, 191–92, 296–97
    See also Gate agents

Pacific routes, 126–29, 131–32, 158
    See also Hawaii routes
Panagra (Pan American Grace Airways), 41, 67
Pan American (Pan Am), 41, 113, 114, 130, 320, 384, 389, 393
    lease of South American routes to, 321–24, 326–29, 331–41, 344n–45n
Passenger service, 98–105, 123–24, 141–42, 183–94, 231–32, 296–97
    Teamsters and, 190–93
    See also Delays; Reservations
Pass privileges, 138
PATCO (Professional Air Traffic Controllers Organization), 249, 252, 254, 258–65
Paternalistic management style, 24, 28–30
Patterson-D'Argenio, Patricia, 243
Paychecks, deferment of (1982), 311–12, 319
Pay cut, 164, 195, 196, 199–204
Perkiel, Mitch, 372
Personnel (employees), 28–31, 38–39, 66, 89–97, 108–12, 129n, 135–43, 389–92
    Casey's relations with, 200–201, 234–35, 248–49, 253–55, 259, 265, 285–86
    financial problems and, 248–50
    furloughs of, 158–59, 197–98
    new routes and, 120–32
    passenger service, 98–105
    pass privileges for, 138
    pay cut and, 164, 195, 196, 199–204
    PSA deal and, 393–95
    self-help sales campaigns and, 235–36, 238
    shutdown of operations and, 357–61, 380–83
    training of, 99–100, 109
    See also Flight attendants; Gate agents; Management; Outside agents; Passenger service; Pilots; Teamsters; Unions
Phillips, Captain John R., 51–57
Pilots, 29, 130, 136, 149n–50n, 287–89, 297–99, 304, 308, 348
    furloughs of, 158
    lease of South American routes and, 322–23, 339, 344, 352, 353
    seniority system and, 158n–59n
    training of, 122
    work hours of, 120–22
    See also Air Line Pilots Association (ALPA)
Pizer, Harry, 360
Plating away, 292
Poli, Robert, 249, 252, 260
Pope, Bob, 320

Post, Troy V., 19, 20, 50*n*, 60, 155*n*,
      156, 241, 258, 372, 373
Presley, Dewey, 268, 269
Press, the, *see* Media, the
Pritzker, Jay, 241, 395, 396, 398
Professional Air Traffic Controllers
      Organization (PATCO), 249,
      252, 254, 258–65
Profits, 36, 128
  from South American operations,
      72–73
Profit sharing/salary reduction
      program, 196, 201–3
PSA, 393–96
Pucci, Emilio, 34–35
Putnam, Howard, 117, 267–91, 304,
      309, 313–54, 392
  Casey's departure from Braniff and,
      320, 321
  Crandall's phone conversation with,
      305–6
  employee relations, 286–87, 316–18
  first message to employees, 280–81
  first staff meeting of, 279–80
  "The Great Escape" promotion and,
      342–47
  Guthrie's working relationship with,
      284
  interview with Dennis Fulton, 313–
      17, 386–87
  Lawrence and, 329–30
  lease of South American routes and,
      321–24, 326–29, 331–41
  offer of president's job to, 267–72
  as persona non grata in the industry,
      395
  pilots and, 287–89, 297–99
  Pritzker offer and, 395–97
  PSA deal and, 394–96
  shutdown of operations and, 350–
      54, 356–62, 371–73, 379–84
  Texas class service and, 290–96
  two-for-one sale and, 300–302, 309
Putnam, Krista, 270, 338, 345

Reagan, Ronald (Reagan
      Administration), 197, 249, 261

Reservationists, 138–39
Reservations, 211, 299
  Sabre computer system for, 295,
      307, 320, 341–42
Revenue passenger mile (RPM), 21
Reynolds, Jim, 360
Rich, Dick, 48
Ridgeway, Ron, 301, 308, 326–28
Riley, Jim, 305–7, 330, 344, 372
Robertson, Tom, 13, 15–18, 21, 39,
      125–26
Robinson, Neal, 159, 176–77, 251,
      255, 259, 285
Rogers, Lanny, 312
Rossel, Willy, 39
Rotation, high altitude and, 75–77
Route(s), 108*n*
  American Airlines, 208–9
  Boston-Europe, 130
  Delta Airlines, 210
  Denver, 112
  deregulation and, 82–84
  dormant, 118–22
  elimination of, 157–58
  "hub-and-spoke" approach to, 130–
      31, 208, 211
  London-Dallas, 112–17
  new, 120–32, 136
  Pacific, 126–29, 131–32
  Seattle/Portland to Hawaii, 118–20
  South American, *see* South American
      routes
RPM (revenue passenger mile), 21
Rustad, Herb, 89, 90, 92, 93, 96

Sabre reservations system, 295, 307,
      320, 341–42
Safety record, on South American
      routes, 73, 79
Sales campaigns, self-help, 235–36,
      238
Sales promotions
  "The Great Escape," 342–47
  two-for-one, 300–302, 307–10,
      343, 348
Sallee, Jack, 133, 134
Schlinke, Marvin, 192, 204, 231

Schrader, Terry, 164*n*
Seattle routes, 118–20, 209
Seawell, William T., 114
Securities and Exchange Commission, 60
Self-help sales campaigns, 235–36, 238, 324
Senate Commerce Committee, Aviation Subcommittee of, 81–83
Seniority system, 286–87
Serling, Robert, 181
Service, *see* Passenger service
Service pins, 110
Shimp, William, 394
Shone, Pam, 178
Shoop, Glen, 395, 396, 398
Shutdown of operations, 350–85
Silver Eagles, 348
Singapore route, 147
Six, Bob, 19, 20, 37, 38
Smalley, Chic, 369
Smith, Craig, 362, 370
Sneaky Snake (Ship 408), 106–7
South, Charles, 64–65, 67–68
South American routes, 22, 26, 40–41, 66–69, 71–79, 131, 148, 250, 289–90, 292
    lease of, 321–24, 326–29, 331–41
    profits from, 72–73
    shutdown of, 358–63
South Korea, 126, 127*n*, 128
Southwest Airlines, 266, 303
Staff meetings, weekly, 31, 150
Stans, Maurice, 63–65
State Department, 331
Stewart, Alan, 177*n*, 347, 351, 372
Stewart, Robert H. (Bob), III, 50*n*, 59–60, 155, 156, 163, 169, 171, 173, 177, 230, 241, 244–45, 258, 268, 271
Stockholders' meeting (1981), 240–44
Stock issue (1979), 147
Stock issue (1980), 151
Stock ownership program for employees, 248
Strauss, Bob, 113
Strike (1953), 29

Sun, Wen Ann, 143
Sundmark, Ken, 303–4
Swanson, Howard P., 216, 229–31, 247, 248, 252, 258–59, 273–76, 279, 281, 283

Teamsters, 61–62, 66, 164, 183, 188–93, 195–96, 199, 201–4, 231, 287*n*, 299–300, 329
Texas Air Corporation, 388*n*, 396
Texas class service, 290–96, 299–300
Texas International Airlines, 160
Thayer, Russell, 13, 86, 151*n*, 155*n*, 160–61, 163–65, 173–74, 177
Thomas, W. Tack, 205
Thompson, Dee, 90–94
Ticket guarantee plan, 312–13, 317, 324
Tinker, Jack, 33
Tinker, Jack, and Associates, 47, 48
Tobin, Edgar, 27
Todd, Jerry, 183–86, 193–94
Tokyo route, 131–32
Training, personnel, 99, 109
Trans World Airways (TWA), 126
Travel agents, 206–7, 314, 348
    bribing of, 67, 68
    "The Great Escape" promotion and, 345
    mailgram to (1981), 239–40
    Texas class service and, 292–93
    two-for-one sale and, 308–10
Trippe, Juan, 41
Truman, Harry S, 22
Turbovitch, Sharon, 143
Two-for-one sale, 300–302, 307–10, 343, 348

Uniforms, 34, 49, 108, 288
Unions, 29, 31, 61–62, 233–34, 286–87, 329, 382
    financial problems and, 195, 199–204
    paycheck deferment and, 311–12, 319
    See also Air Line Pilots Association;

Unions (*cont.*)
    International Association of
    Machinists; Teamsters
United Airlines, 13, 117, 118
Universal Airlines System, 23

Velocity 1 (V1), 74–75
Velocity of rotation (VR), 75
Volcker, Paul, 147

Wainwright, Tony, 294, 300–301, 309,
    313*n*, 326, 343, 359–61
Wall Street Journal, The, 162*n*, 179,
    233–34, 244, 302–4, 307, 312
Waltrip, William, 335
Ward, Jack, 213
Warrants, stock, 151
Wells, Katy, 47

Wells, Mary, 33, 34, 35, 36, 41, 47–
    51, 79–80
Wells, Pam, 47
Wells Rich Greene, Inc. (WRG), 36,
    49–50, 52, 61*n*, 141*n*, 294
Wile, John, 309
Williams, Rod, 289–90
Wilson, T.A., 248*n*
Wind shear, 74
Winfield, Gordon, 375, 379
Woolman, C.E., 28
World headquarters complex, 109–10,
    140, 288, 310

Yaran, Dee, 309

Zang, Clem, 93

426